The
REAL
MEAT
Cookbook

FRANCES BISSELL

The REAL MEAT *Cookbook*

Chatto & Windus
LONDON

FOR MY PARENTS

Published in 1992 by
Chatto & Windus Ltd
20 Vauxhall Bridge Road
London SW1V 2SA

A CIP catalogue record for this book is available from the British
Library.

ISBN 0 7011 3645 6

Silhouettes and meat maps by Philip Hood.
Step-by-step diagrams by Ray Burrows.
Designed by David Fordham.
Typeset by SX Composing, Rayleigh, Essex.
Printed in Great Britain by Butler & Tanner Ltd,
Frome, Somerset.

Contents

Introduction

'If a chicken has been killed,
and it is not cooked properly, that
chicken has died in vain.'

LIN YUTANG

I BEGAN TO WRITE this book as a celebration of meat and meat cookery. It was to be about the pleasures to be had from cooking – and sharing with friends – a cassoulet on a winter evening, a joint of beef for the Sunday lunch table or a new recipe for liver learned when I last visited friends in Italy. But it is not about persuading you to eat more meat. Quite the opposite, in fact. It is about cooking and eating good quality meat, from animals raised in a humane fashion which respects their natural habitat, their feeding, breeding and nurturing habits. It takes time and money to produce such meat. It was an unwillingness to pay the real price of raising real meat in the past, based on an expectation that food should be cheap, which led to the intensification of farming, both of crops and livestock. If we want cheap meat, only intensive farming can supply it. In the following pages, I have examined aspects of intensive farming and some of the alternatives, and looked at some of the arguments put forward in the meat debate.

The seeds for the book were sown in 1987 when I was asked if I would like to write a series on meat cookery for *À la carte*. I did not like the idea at first. Fish, pasta and vegetables were the things I most liked cooking. We did not eat meat very often at home, and I could not remember the last time I cooked roast beef. Indeed, I began to doubt whether I *could* roast a traditional Sunday joint with all the trimmings. But I accepted the commission and began my research by visiting farmers, butchers and markets. I then moved on to the cooking and enjoyed myself so much with the roasts that it was this classic area of meat cookery I concentrated on in the *À la carte* series. All the while, I knew that there was so much more to meat cookery. This book is the result.

I am very grateful to all those at Chatto & Windus and Random Century who helped bring it about, particularly Rowena Skelton-Wallace, Julian Shuckburgh and, above all, Carmen Callil, who has supported me from the moment I went to her with the idea for the book, with enthusiasm, kindness, insight, patience, valuable criticism – everything one could ask for from a publisher but seldom gets. Vicky Hayward has been the most supportive, creative and encouraging editor one could hope for, and I feel very lucky to have had the benefit of her excellent judgment and thoroughness.

The book has changed in the writing. I realised very early on that it could not simply be a cookery book. In the recipes and their explanatory notes I was writing about meat, the ingredient. But it soon became evident that I should write about meat as a product; where it comes from, how it is reared and gets to our table, why some of us eat it and others do not.

Gradually a cast of thousands revealed themselves, all of whom have a part to play and an argument to pursue: farmers, supermarket owners, legislators, consumers, environmentalists, butchers, not only as individuals but also as interest groups and lobbies. And the roles overlap. The consumer might also be a supermarket share-owner, the environmentalist a farmer, the supermarket-owner a consumer. Add to this rich mixture a handful of food scares related to agriculture in general and meat in particular, plus a pinch of indifference and later defensiveness on the part of the industry and government, stir with a few investigative journalists, deeply concerned scientists and even more horrified consumers, and you soon reach a point where you feel tempted simply to concentrate on the recipes and how to carve a joint.

But as a cook, cookery writer and, above all, as a consumer, I want and need to know where my food comes from. I am privileged enough to have the opportunities to do so. In Italy I visit pasta factories, in California the plants where prunes and raisins are processed, in Ireland dairy farms producing cheese, in France the olive groves and *huileries*, in Spain the shellfish beds of Galicia. In Norway I have waited for the small fishing boats bringing in their daily catch to the town dock in Trondheim.

And in the same way, when I was writing the *À la carte* series, I wanted to know about meat – all of it, from the cheapest, few weeks' old supermarket chicken to the prime Scotch beef from a sturdy two-year-old animal.

This curiosity took me first to Easthill Farm, near Bath, where Gillian Metherell and Richard Guy farmed pigs and chickens. The thing that struck me first was the pleasant warm farmyard smell, without a trace of the pungent and offensive odours so often associated with pig farms. I saw chickens running around on Salisbury Plain and pigs, some with their piglets in wooden straw-strewn shelters, some in the fields approaching us with lively curiosity; they grunted contentedly, or so it seemed to me. Richard's and Gillian's company, the Real Meat Company, of which they are co-founders, was in its early days, supplying consumers who were prepared to pay more for meat that came from animals raised under a system which promoted their welfare up to, and including, the time of slaughter. I kept in touch with them as their activities developed. A late autumn telephone conversation with Gillian stands out clearly in my memory; she described the turkeys flying in to land over the garden wall.

Once I had decided to include more than recipes and cookery techniques in this book, and to expand it to explain the difference between cheap, or mass-produced meat, and meat of high quality produced to high standards of welfare and purity, I consulted Richard Guy in his role as a farmer who sets high standards for the meat he produces and who distributes meat for other farmers who follow his company's rigorous code of practice. I am very grateful for the detailed information he provided on animal husbandry, which has enabled me to include a section on this topic relevant to each type of meat covered in the book. His enthusiasm, and that of his wife Gillian, for my book has been very encouraging, and their observations on the meat debate enlightening. They provided me with a list of their suppliers, farmers all over the country, so that I could talk to them or visit them to find out more. I talked to and visited other farmers who rear livestock organically and are registered with the Soil Association who have their own code of practice (see p. 28). I met farmers and suppliers who adhere to the standards of the Guild of Conservation Farmers, with yet another code of practice (see p. 29). But I also met farmers who do things in their own way, some of whom who would undoubtedly be eligible for the various symbols and trade marks if they chose to apply, others who describe themselves as semi-intensive. I am grateful to them all for the time they spent helping me, particularly the following: Will Best, Jonathan Blackburn, Simon Gourlay, Joan Horn, Tim and Robin Mills, Sam Olive and Anne Petch.

Butchers, too, have been of great help to me, and I am particularly grateful to David Lidgate of the Q Guild of Butchers, Richard Garrett of Allens Butchers and John Doolin of Hampstead Butchers.

The Meat and Livestock Commission, the U.S. Meat Export Federation and SOPEXA, the French food and wine export organisation, were kind enough to provide documents and graphics which helped in the design of the meat maps in the book.

The Soil Association and Guild of Conservation Food Producers have been very helpful in answering my questions.

Gillian Riley provided me with much food for thought when she introduced me to Vilhjalmur Stefansson's all-meat diet, on which he existed in the Arctic Circle for more than five years in the early years of this century, and I am grateful to her for this and for her enthusiasm for my book.

I am immensely grateful to my friend Alice Waters for giving me a copy of *American Food, American Farms*, which helped to crystallise my thoughts about why I was writing this book. She also gave me copies of the detailed and lovingly compiled reports produced by her foragers, who hunt out the best food for Chez Panisse, Alice's restaurant in Berkeley, California. They visit farms, smallholdings and gardens all over the West Coast, looking for food, including real meat that has been produced by humane animal husbandry methods and sustainable systems of agriculture. Perhaps one day these principles and values will be so generally shared that there will be no need for the term 'real meat'.

I feel optimistic about this by analogy with the 'real ale' campaign; like that issue, this one is winnable. We shall finally see sense and return to the old ways of living in harmony with our land and our animals. Until that time we do need to distinguish between 'real meat' and the rest.

THE MEAT DEBATE

THE INDUSTRY

*A*CCORDING TO A RECENT SURVEY, the percentage of household food expenditure on meat has declined from 28.2% in 1979 to 23% in 1990, with a further decline to less than 21% forecast for 1996.

This decision, made by the consumer, affects everyone concerned with the production, supply and consumption of meat: other consumers, farmers, butchers, supermarkets and those involved in the meat-processing industry, which is important in terms of both employment and turnover. A labour force of some 100,000 and a £6 billion turnover represents about 20% of the meat-processing industry in the European Community. (Business Forecasts for the U.K. Food Market, Nankivell & Morrell, 1991)

Naturally, the meat industry is worried about this decline in expenditure. As part of their thoughts on giving meat a 'new image' at the beginning of 1990, the British Meat Information Service (the public relations arm of the meat industry) stated that the

> 'positive elements of meat being high in protein, sustaining, convenient and traditional must be presented to the opinion-formers. These are articulate ABC 1 men and women who talk about eating less meat and who may be "promoting" a negative feeling towards the eating of meat. A balanced diet, which includes the eating of meat, is as important today as it ever was. We must address the negative arguments that eating meat is somehow out of date, high in cholesterol and is closely associated with some form of loss of personal integrity before this image becomes firmly entrenched amongst these opinion-formers.'

At the same time the Meat and Livestock Commission has been constantly looking for ways to sell more meat. New value-added products and ready meals have been developed with the help of their home economists – for example, beef roulade, beef kebabs, beef olives, individual beef Wellingtons, ready-marinated meat, *goujons* of beef and savoury beef rolls. Yet at the same time, in May 1990, a Gallup survey of 526 men and women over the age of 16, published in the *Sunday Telegraph*, indicated that 40% said they were eating less beef, were considering cutting down or had stopped eating beef altogether.

There are many reasons for this decline in meat eating, as the report quoted above points out. It does not mention the worries that consumers have about contamination of meat and poultry with salmonella and other toxic organisms, and BSE (Bovine Spongiform Encephalopathy), which has been found in dairy herds.

NUTRITION

WE DO NEED PROTEIN TO SURVIVE. We do not need meat, nor indeed any other animal product, to obtain sufficient protein for survival. We can obtain the eight essential amino-acids, of which protein is the source, by eating meals containing grains and pulses which will provide protein of high biological value, such as that found in meat, fish and other animal protein and is also a good way of increasing our intake of fibre and complex carbohydrates, which, in the Western diet at least, we need to consume in larger quantities than we do.

The meat industry's attempts to reinforce the message it wishes to put over about the importance of meat in the diet do not seem to take this nutritional aspect, now widely known, into account. It produced *Your Seven Day Guide to Healthy Eating*, a week's menus with meat served twice a day and three times on Saturday and Sunday, since bacon was also recommended for breakfast. What a dull diet! It allowed for no cheese, hardly an egg except in a quiche, and pasta and rice only as accompaniments to meat rather than dishes in their own right or with a garnish of meat, and no fish at all. Vegetables played only a subordinate role. This was followed a year later by a vigorous campaign in the broadsheets to persuade us that we need meat to live. Eating meat two or three times a day one derives little pleasure from it. We are lucky enough to be able to enjoy a really wide variety of fresh natural products and thus we can eat food that we both enjoy and which suits our dietary needs.

Recent reports from the World Health Organisation (WHO) and from the Committee on the Medical Aspects of Food (COMA) have advised us to cut our intake of fat so that it provides no more than 30% of our energy intake, and preferably less, down to a lower limit of 15%. As an indicator, current consumption of fat in the UK gives us 42% of our energy (calories). The fat in all meat is made up of all three types of fatty acids; saturated, polyunsaturated and monounsaturated. Thus, not all the fat in meat is 'bad' for us. Saturated fat, which raises blood cholesterol and increases the risk of heart disease for those prone to it, should form no more than 10% of our energy intake and ideally less since saturated fatty acids are not essential nutrients. The essential fatty acids are to be found in polyunsaturated fat, of which linoleic acid is particularly important, for it helps to break down fatty deposits and cholesterol as well as helping to prevent blood cells clustering. Monounsaturated fatty acids hold a neutral position.

Since meat and meat products are the second largest contributor of total fat in the diet after fats and oils, one way to cut down on the fat intake is to cut down on the amount of fat consumed with meat. You can do this in several ways.

The large-scale meat industry, both in Britain and America, with the active participation of the supermarkets, rather than suggesting you eat meat less frequently, have developed, through specific breeding and feeding programmes, new ranges of lean meat, particularly pork and beef. The standard food tables used in Britain, McCance and Widdowson's *The Composition of Foods*, published in 1978, indicate that lean raw pork meat contained 7.1g of fat per 100g. In the intervening years breeding and feeding practices have resulted in a much lower fat content. According to a chemical analysis carried out by Ministry of Agriculture, Fisheries and Food/the Meat Livestock Commission (MAFF/MLC) in 1990, leg of pork contains 1.7g fat per 100g, loin 3.9g per 100g, and belly 4.9g per 100g. However, this meat on the whole comes from animals intensively reared in order to meet the large-scale demands of supermarkets.

If you eat 'real meat' just occasionally, you will automatically cut down the amount of fat you take in with meat. You can reduce that amount further by trimming off excess fat and removing skin from poultry before cooking, or by pouring or skimming off excess fat after cooking and removing poultry skin rather than eating it. There are those who argue that fat in meat does *not* contribute to its flavour or its tenderness but a loin chop of pork trimmed of all its fat can be dry and rather dull; a shoulder or spare rib chop with the intramuscular fat to baste it is much juicier. And I would never dream of roasting a chicken without its skin. On the other hand, poached chicken, poached lamb and *boeuf à la ficelle* are dishes in which little fat is left with the meat. But what happens to the fat which is trimmed from those lean chops and steaks in the butchers' or supermarkets' display counters? For however sleek and slender the pig or the beef animal, there will still be a layer of fat under the skin of the carcase which is bought from the farmer or meat market. The butcher or supermarket has paid for the fat, the customer who wants lean cuts of meat will not pay for it. Actually, the customer will pay for some of it, in a premium attached to the lean range. The rest goes into mince, into burgers, into pies, the so-called 'value added' products, which again can be sold at a premium. The fat also goes into further processed foods such as instant soups and other prepared dishes.

You see how complicated the meat question becomes. These last comments hardly refer to nutrition but to questions of economics, for both consumer and retailer.

SUPERMARKETS

As I WRITE THIS, I am trying to make sense of two press releases which crossed my desk within a week of each other, both from the same high-street supermarket press office. One announced price reductions over a Bank Holiday weekend, offering a frozen British 'Grade A' chicken for 39p per lb, a 32% reduction on the previous price of 58p per lb. This price-cut was made possible, we are told, as a direct result of the skill of their highly trained buyers in finding the right quality product at the right price, and passing the benefits straight to the customer. The second release announced the arrival of the supermarket's own-label 'traditional free-range' chicken, reared in accordance with the new EC regulations (see p. 194) and selling for about £1.40 per lb.

I was invited, as I frequently am, to visit one of the farms supplying these free-range chickens. I said I would be delighted to do so, and that I would also like to visit one of the farms supplying the 39p per lb bird. That request was refused.

The importance of the role of supermarkets in the meat chain cannot be too highly emphasised. Although meat is treated as a commodity, a product – like a box of soap powder, a book, or a pound of apples – meat retailing is certainly not a sideline for the supermarket. From a 55% share of the meat-retailing market in the early eighties, in-dependent butchers now account for less than 40%, with the supermarkets taking an in-creased share. (One supermarket is now said to be the country's largest butcher.) This gives supermarkets a great deal of power when it comes to buying produce, and thus controlling prices.

The supermarkets have taken due note of consumers' reaction to factory farming and the growing demand for real meat. They have responded, as they do to all consumer demands, thus making profits for their shareholders by giving the customers what they want. If customers want cheap chickens for the Bank Holiday, they shall have them; if the customer wants vegetarian food, the supermarkets will sell it; if the customer wants convenience food, the supermarkets will prepare and package it. And now that the customer wants real meat, the supermarkets have responded by introducing premium ranges of meat described as 'traditionally reared', 'naturally produced', 'organic' and 'free-range'. These meats are vigorously promoted with signs, leaflets and evidence of endorsement by the media. They are sold at higher prices than their standard ranges, to take account of the higher production costs. In the adjoining cabinet you will still find the standard range of pork, chicken, beef etc., the 39p per lb chicken next to the £1.40 per lb bird. The low-priced bird can only have been produced under the most intensive system. I question what importance the supermarkets really attach to the 'very highest standards of animal welfare'.

Some retailers see the demand for real meat as no more than a niche market, while others see it as a rapidly growing market in which demand already outstrips supply. Some supermarkets are working with the various organisations which promote humane and sustainable farming methods, stocking meat produced under their various codes of practice (see p. 30 for details). But as long as the consumer wants a chicken for 39p a lb and does not care how it was produced, then the supermarkets will continue to meet demand. In the same way, they will continue to sell meats with such labels as 'traditional', 'farm-fresh', 'additive free' or 'natural' – or other descriptions which are re-assuring to those who are just beginning to question what happens in our farms, but quite meaningless in that there is no independent published specification. They may conjure up images of animals that have been reared and slaughtered humanely, fed a chemical-free and appropriate diet (that is appropriate to the animal, not to the company's accountants' calculations) and managed under a system of agriculture that does the least possible harm to the environment. But the reality may be quite different.

Between them, the supermarkets have a dozen different, yet similar-sounding clasifications, very few of which are accompanied by published standards and specifications readily accessible to the consumer. Certainly, as yet, there are no legal definitions of 'natural', 'traditional' and so forth.

The supermarkets' response if you voice such criticisms is likely to be along the lines of, 'Well, you would not understand the technical terminology about feed ratios and stocking density.' Perhaps not, but some of us care enough about what we eat and what is done in our name to try to understand.

THE BUTCHER

*B*UTCHERS HAVE BEEN PART OF our traditional meat-eating culture for hundreds of years. This culture is reflected in place-names such as The Shambles, the name by which the slaughterhouse was once known. It is reflected even more strikingly in our family names: Slaughter, Butcher, Fletcher, Fowler, Tanner, Shepherd. In the same way that the Chinese word for 'rice' encompasses the meaning 'food', so do we in English use 'meat' to denote food, as in 'one man's meat is another man's poison'. We talk of 'meat and drink', of 'bakemeats' and 'sweetmeats'. Perhaps it will not be long before the family names are all we have left to remind us of this ancient and honourable craft. I hope not.

A number of butchers to whom I have spoken suggest that the future is likely to bring a polarisation in the meat supply. The supermarkets will continue to increase their share of the meat market while small independent butchers who provide a high quality product, coupled with expert and personal service, will flourish. What will gradually disappear will be those high-street butchers who aim to compete with the supermarkets by keeping the prices low.

These are the butchers who pile their meat high and sell it cheaply, with little indication of origin or quality. Very often the meat is already cut into chops, fillets and slices, and packaged in plastic-wrapped trays. There is little need for discussion between butcher and customer about the meat and, indeed, one often feels discouraged from doing so. Standards of hygiene, judging by smell and external appearance, do not seem to have a high priority. If these were the only places one could buy meat, I would soon stop eating it. One can see the problem. They are forced, very often by their location and catchment area, to compete with supermarkets. They feel that their customers would not pay the high prices attached to real meat and the butchers are not convinced of its merits. I think the future looks bleak for them.

The better independents will survive, I believe. They are run by professionals, people (usually men, although I know of at least a couple of woman butchers) well-trained in their craft, proud of their skills, dedicated to quality and often carrying on a family business. Of course they are business-people first; they have recognised that if the quality is right, then the appropriate price can be charged and the customer will not only not baulk but will come back again.

Butchers do not put animal welfare first; they put quality first. The butcher is not against real meat, but will not stock it if he cannot get a supply which satisfies his taste. The feeling amongst many butchers I spoke to was that the organic and real meat movement had encouraged into farming too many amateurs who proclaimed only all that they did *not* do to their livestock. But the butchers would like to hear what they have done for the animal in terms of breeding, feeding and management, and then at slaughter, post-slaughter and butchering to produce high quality meat. In fact, I believe that many of the producers of real meat do meet those quality requirements, but they are using different outlets and operate in different parts of the country.

One of the most encouraging developments I heard of from David Lidgate, of the Q Guild of Butchers (see p. 29), is that small groups of butchers in particular regions have started to work with local farmers to produce high-quality meat. This will also cover animal welfare, including feed and keeping conditions, since the butcher recognises that quality meat comes from an animal which has been allowed to follow its natural behaviour patterns to feed, exercise and forage as appropriate, and that this is only achieved through extensive rather than intensive farming.

It is vital to preserve this link between the consumer, the retailer and the farmer. It is precisely this that is in danger of being broken as the supermarkets take on a greater share of meat retailing because the farmer sees the supermarket as the consumer, while the consumer regards the supermarket as the producer. The butcher should be an important link between farmer and consumer. I know of butchers who can tell their customers which field the animal grazed in.

THE FARMER

*T*HE INTRODUCTION OF MODERN FARMING METHODS to produce large quantities of cheap meat as quickly as possible, in order to give the farmer a fast return on his investment, is just one very recent development in a long history of domestication. That history begins when man turns from being a hunter-gatherer to being a farmer-cultivator. Keeping a reliable food supply grazing in the field or on common land next to the settlement was much more attractive than having to organise a hunting party in order to survive. Our ancestors did not forget, however, how much they had enjoyed the thrill and yield of the hunt; thus hunting, and by extension, poaching became established in the fabric of society, but proceeded along quite separate lines from farming.

The early farmer and then his successors had to learn about animal behaviour patterns and how to exploit them in order to domesticate animals successfully. Cows, sheep and goats, which require large amounts of vegetation and pasture, were tended in flocks or herds in open country and then later in fields. Chickens and pigs, it was soon realised, were omnivores and could be kept in the yard or a shed by the back door where they could be fed on kitchen scraps, leftover grain or vegetables. This pattern remained very much the same until the beginning of the twentieth century and, indeed, images of lambs in the fields, pigs in a straw-strewn sty and chickens pecking in the farmyard live on in children's story books. And also in glossy promotional literature for rich food companies.

That is not to say that intensive animal husbandry was not practised long ago. We need look no further than *The Compleat Cook*, published in 1655, which gives a 'recipe' to fatten chicken in four or five days.

'Take a pint of French Wheat, and a pint of wheat-flour, half a pound of sugar. Make it up into a stiff paste, and rowl it into little rowls, wet them in warm ruth and so cram them [force them down the chicken's gullet], and they will be fat in four or five dayes, if you please you may sow them up behind one or two of the last days.'

16

Farming changed with the Industrial Revolution, its attendant increase of population in the towns and the need for a ready source of inexpensive food. Much of this could be, and was, supplied by large-scale extensive production in distant parts of the world while transport remained cheap. For a colonial power like Britain, there were few worries that supplies would be cut off by political upheavals.

But by the end of the Second World War it was evident that the population could never again rely on a food supply coming from the other side of the world. Rationing and food shortages had an ineradicable and perfectly understandable effect on a whole generation in Britain, giving rise to consumer demand for a secure and plentiful supply of cheap meat. It had to be cheap because it was often eaten twice a day, seven days a week.

It was at this time, in the post-war years, that livestock farming began to move indoors. Poultry for eggs and the table, pigs and, to some extent, cattle were reared in specially built 'factory' farms. Unnatural keeping conditions resulted from reducing the main overhead costs of food, labour and space. The animals' liberty was traded in for the saving of space. Thus, little or no straw was needed, creating more savings. Automated feeding and dung collection systems were devised, making savings on labour costs. Because the animals were housed in closely confined spaces, they did not use up energy on exercise and so required less food and of a lower quality; yet more savings accrued. With such automated, labour saving systems, large numbers of animals housed in ever larger buildings could be looked after by very few people. Just like a production line in fact. I do not think factory farming is a misnomer.

Since livestock does not take naturally to intensification, problems developed. Tail-biting, feather-pecking and even cannibalism meant that methods such as tail-docking of piglets and debeaking of birds had to be devised to combat this irrational fighting. Epidemic illness increased as the animals were kept in close quarters. Obvious when you think about it; if a child in a dormitory catches chicken-pox, the chances are that most of the children will catch it unless they're immune. The animals became depressed and listless, they failed to thrive. Just as we would in similar conditions.

For intensively reared animals pre-emptive drugs, that is drugs added to their feed on a permanent basis, were the answer to stop them getting ill and thus encourage growth. By 1970 there were over a hundred branded pre-emptive and curative drugs available. By 1990 there were thirty-three different growth-promoting drugs designed to improve the efficiency with which the animal converts its food into muscle or meat, commonly known as feed-conversion. None of these drugs improve the animal's well-being.

Other drugs have been developed too: colourants which, when fed to laying chickens, will make egg yolks a more appealing and consistent yellow. This, say the supermarkets and egg producers, is what the customer wants. Likewise, the chemical companies have provided the drugs to make chickens lay more eggs and cows produce more milk. Skin-colourant to make the skin and fat of intensively reared chickens turn yellow has been developed so that they can be marketed as corn-fed to consumers trying to avoid the standard broiler chicken. (Of course, they will have received some corn in their diet, too.) On the other hand, one butcher I know has difficulty selling real corn-fed chickens from a local farmer because one week the fat and flesh might be quite yellow, and another week it might be quite pale, depending entirely on the way the chicken has foraged for, and digested, everything else it has eaten as well as the corn.

Animal feed, too, has not escaped the advances of technology. After the Second World War animal feed in Britain was subject to many of the same constraints as the human diet. It was rationed until the mid-fifties and thereafter there was a great fluctuation in availability and pricing of the traditional commodities – barley, fish meal and soya meal – that made up animal feed. New sources of food had to be found. Just as our own diet now embraces what once would have been considered exotic foreign food, the modern animal is also fed a diet made up of an extraordinary range of ingredients, which might include shea nut meal, olive pulp, molasses, manioc, locust beans, kapok and pulp from apples and citrus fruits, all by-products of the human food industry, as well as the maize, sorghum and other foodstuffs which are human staples in many parts of the world. Less appetising ingredients include meat and bone meal, spent mushroom compost, old newspapers, rice bran, 'wood flour' (more familiar to us as sawdust), straw processed with caustic soda and cherco, which is coffee bean husks. Computers are used to calculate livestock feed formulations based on the cost and nutritional information of the various commodities, the dietary requirement of the particular animal and the most acceptable cost to the farmer, and by extension, the retailer. This is what we are responsible for in our quest for cheap meat.

Not all farmers respond to those particular demands. One of the most encouraging things for me in the writing of this book has been to meet farmers and to realise that there are many who are committed to rearing and producing real meat. What is striking, too, is that they have not set out to farm according to the Real Meat Company code, or the Soil Association Symbol or the Conservation Grade. Time and again I have heard, 'We've always farmed that way', or 'the farm suits the system, we haven't tailored our farming to suit it', or 'I wouldn't think of farming any other way.'

Richard Guy, whose father was a farmer, began rearing livestock in 1976, starting with one pig. He had decided to seek out an alternative to intensive livestock production once he had begun to investigate and discover what this represented. In 1984 he met Gillian Metherell, a pig farmer, and, by now married, together they set up the Real Meat Company, with a published code of welfare and purity that is followed on their own farm and by other farmers who sell their meat through the company. What they sought to do was to define their view of a proper way of rearing animals which would reflect how a caring consumer would keep animals if they were rearing their own livestock. The codes were drawn up after consultation with Compassion in World Farming and with advice from Professor John Webster of Bristol University Veterinary School (students from the Veterinary School perform the inspection of the Real Meat Company suppliers).

Another committed farmer, Anne Petch of Heal Farm in North Devon, was regarded as a crank when twenty years ago she started employing methods which were a return not just to pre-war standards but to pre-First World War methods. She is dedicated to genetic conservation and the survival of rare breeds. For her, quality meat comes from original breeds, or the original breed with a first-cross, not the 'mathematically' obtained hybrids designed to grow fast with minimum input. Her cows are Red Devon beef, slow-growing animals which are slaughtered at twenty-six months. (Intensively reared beef is slaughtered at eleven to twelve months, Real Meat Company beef from fourteen to twenty-eight months, depending on the breed.) The extra ten months or so are costly in terms of feed and management. Add to that the fact that the carcases are butchered by hand and very well trimmed with a great deal of waste, and the cost of the meat to the consumer is explained. Heal Farm pigs, too, are 'unimproved' breeds, that is, not modern slim-line porkers. Their feed is expensive, because it is made up to a specific recipe developed by Anne Petch, and it is more expensive again because it is produced without additives. One might think it would be cheaper without additives, but that costs extra, as I was told on several occasions by farmers, all of whom worked under different codes of practice, but all of whom wanted additive-free feed. The pigs are fed, scrubbed down and mucked out by stockmen, not by machines. This, too, is expensive; there are two stockmen for thirty sows, whereas in an intensive system one stockman can 'look after' a thousand animals. At Heal Farm the stockman takes the pigs to the slaughter-house in a trailer that they have seen around the farm and are familiar with, thus minimising the stress as far as possible. As with so many farmers I spoke to, Anne Petch is very fond of her pigs; she has one pet called August who is almost fifteen years old, still fit and well after many litters.

Robin Mills, who farms crops, cattle and 'gorse and rabbits' in Dorset, likes his cows, a herd of cross-breed cows, first cross between a dairy cow, either Friesian × Hereford or Friesian × Angus, crossed with a Simenthal bull, which makes for relatively fast-growing offspring. They live out on the downlands from spring and calve in April. The calves are suckled and remain with their mother for seven to eight months and then overwinter indoors in a large airy barn. Although the animals are looked at every day they rarely need anything doing to them; the cows are never wormed and the calves only at weaning, for example. They do not need it because of the transferred immunity. When I spoke to Robin he could remember having only three cows treated for specific ailments in the previous year. Imagine the overkill if a systemic antibiotic had been used. He told me that the Real Meat Company suits him quite well. 'It's not that I produce to their standards; I produce the cattle the way I like to. They like the way I do it and they're happy to pay me a little bit of a premium. The system fits the farm.'

Sam Olive prefers to use no antibiotics on his animals, even though he is permitted to under the code of Conservation Grade farming. Sam is part of one of the most perfect food chains I have come across. We went to meet him one morning after dining the night before at a favourite restaurant, the Old Manor House in Romsey. Mauro Bregoli, the chef-patron, is dedicated to the pursuit and preparation of the finest raw materials. We ate excellent *salami* with our aperitifs and enquired of its origins. This year was the first that Mauro, whose origins are in Emilia Romagna, the heart of Italy's *salami* country, had successfully made *salami* in Britain from a British pig. He was immensely enthusiastic about these animals and arranged for us to visit the farm.

What animals! The first we saw were Lech and Batori, two tense and suspicious English bred wild boars of Polish stock. Swift, sharp movements brought them close enough for us to admire them. Tamburlaine, Ghengis Khan and the rest ignored us, but beyond them were their offspring, the source of the excellent salami, called Wild Blue after their parents, a wild boar and a Blue Gilt sow. Mauro has helped Sam develop feeding and rearing techniques based on his own experience of pigs in Italy, and most of the meat is sold through the Pure Meat Company, although some is sold locally. Sam describes how his next-door neighbours were practically vegetarian when they arrived in the village from London, but they are now his local retailers, making up not only joints of boned and rolled Wild Blue, but also excellent sausages. While we were there Mauro did a deal to buy the unwanted pork rind which he could use in his prize-winning *cotechino*.

Sam's father started outdoor pig farming in the mid-fifties, but by the early eighties Sam decided that it was all getting out of hand. As he pointed out to me, in July 1991 pork prices dropped by one-third for the pig farmers; on July 1st they were getting £60 for a pig, and only £40 by the end of the month. He said to me, 'I don't mind working hard, I don't mind not making much money, but if I'm going to be bored and then go bust, I'm going to do it interestingly. And these chaps are fascinating and it works,' as he waved his hand towards the Wild Blue youngsters. He sold the second Wild Blue offspring to Mauro after following his suggestions for feeding, and when Mauro was satisfied he knew he'd got the right product, 'If you can please Mauro you can please anyone.'

The farm he likens more to a New Zealand ranch. It is farming without any subsidies, but it makes money. His animals range free and are slow-growing. This produces an animal with toned up muscles, which in turn yields a meat which cooks well, holds together and slices easily. The minimal water content means that it does not collapse when cooked. They are fed on Conservation-grade feed with no added antibiotics or growth promoters.

Sam believes that rearing pigs in this way removes from them the stress which lowers immunity and causes disease. These pigs have impressive immunity. They are slow-growing and take nine months to reach the size that intensively reared pigs reach in less than six months, but he doesn't rush them despite the extra feeding costs involved. When we went on the feed round with Sam, riding on the back of the trailer, we could hear the young pigs in the field across the road. We'd been talking so long that the round had been delayed. Not only were the pigs clamouring, but brightly plumed pheasants were also hanging around. Once the feed was down, birds and pigs ate together.

No such clamour awaits the visitor to Joan Horn and her small flock of pedigree Poll Dorsets, on the edge of the New Forest, next to a working water mill. Some of her lambs go to the Real Meat Company, some she sells for breeding at the important and ancient fair held in Dorchester every May, a market specifically for this pedigree breed and the Dorset Horn breed. Three of the lambs that we saw will be brought back for the Horns' own use. They like to eat year-old lamb or hoggett, an excellent meat full of flavour. This lowland native breed produces small fleshy sheep, which are unusual in that the ewes will come into season and lamb all year round, allowing the producer to wait for the highest prices in the winter and very early spring. She has supplied to the Real Meat Company for two years after a friend introduced her to them.

Once again, the farming methods she has chosen suit the Real Meat Company, but she hasn't set out deliberately to produce for them. When she has been inspected by the Bristol University Vet School they have approved the feed she uses, a coarse mix of crushed grains that Tom said 'looks like what you serve me for breakfast'. The hay she buys from a farmer she knows who keeps a natural, largely untreated downland pasture. And just as important, he makes it into the small familiar bales which one person can handle, not the giant wheels we're now familiar with, lying in newly mown fields, which require special machinery to produce them and special machinery to handle them in the farmyard. Joan tends her small flock herself. It started as a hobby ten years ago with two orphan lambs and she now looks after about seventy. She is convinced that the size of the flock affects the animals' welfare and their survival rate during lambing. Her lambs all get personal attention. The notion that a million lambs die every year at birth, or shortly after, bothers her. The large light airy barn, built by her husband, is where lambing takes place. It is divided into three pens, the first for those lambing, the second for those who have already lambed and the third for those not yet ready. The end wall is made up of bales of straw and hay. As the lambs grow bigger they automatically get more space since the straw is used up for bedding and the hay as fodder for the ewes. Joan changes the bedding every day and disinfects each pen between lambings. In cases of illness she treats them herself or calls in the vet. As with other organisations and individuals concerned with producing meat in a humane, non-intensive way, responsible use of therapeutic drugs is the key.

THE CONSUMER

*I*F VEGETARIANISM WAS the only alternative to eating the product of intensive farming, I would embrace it almost without hesitation.

The arguments are powerful indeed. The average meat eater in Britain, according to the Vegetarian Society, eats more than his or her own weight every year in meat and meat products, and in a lifetime each one of us will consume more than 750 poultry birds, thirty-six pigs, thirty-six sheep and up to eight cattle. Meat in such quantities can only be provided by intensive farming methods. Other arguments centre around world consumption of grain for cattle-feed and thus the areas needed for cultivation. These, too, are powerful; 60% of grain imported by the European Community comes from Third World countries, and while ten acres of land will grow enough grain to support two people on a diet of cattle meat, the same area will feed ten people on a diet of maize, two dozen on a diet of wheat and sixty-one on a diet of soya beans. Raising animals for food drains the planet's resources in other ways too, whether it is in the Brazilian rain-forests or the farmlands of the American mid-west. Flooding and soil erosion is caused when land is cleared for cattle-rearing; water is used on a vast scale – farm animals consume 80% of the world's available water supplies; and there is wide-scale pollution. Pesticides, chemical residues and animal waste are the major cause of water pollution in Britain. In deciding to eat meat the consumer is taking on a great responsibility.

In fact, a conscious decision to eat meat is rarely made. For the most part, those of the human race who eat meat do so because they always have. We eat meat now not so much from a strict dietary necessity, but because we enjoy it, an enjoyment derived from a familiarity acquired as part of a cultural background established over thousands of years.

The conscious decision usually made, by people prepared to break that patterning, is not to eat meat in order to avoid causing the death of another living creature. For them it is too great a responsibility to accept that animals, like ourselves a part of nature's cycle, must die to provide us with food.

I do not believe that killing animals for food is wrong and therefore I choose not to be a vegetarian. Cooking and eating meat is something I enjoy doing, and I am prepared to take the responsibility for it: if I roast a chicken or grill a pork chop, I know that I am as directly responsible for that animal's death as if I had killed it myself. What I do not enjoy, in fact find quite unacceptable, is the way in which so much of our livestock is reared and slaughtered for food. Thus I choose to buy, cook and eat meat that comes from animals bred, reared, managed and slaughtered in a caring way.

As an American bumper sticker of the 1980s proclaimed: 'if you eat, you're involved in agriculture'. Man chose to domesticate animals for his use thousands of years ago. Collectively we have a responsibility to make the most of what we have, to nurture our land and our animals so that we can hand them on to future generations. We don't own the land or animals; we just live here for a while. It is up to us to ask when we are shopping where the beef or pork has come from, what it has been fed on and how the turkeys and veal calves have been managed, and to reject the meat if we are not satisfied that it meets the standards every one of us would surely adopt if we were personally responsible for raising and slaughtering the pig or the turkey. If we put that individual power together, then the consumer, in the collective sense, has great power indeed. This is why I believe that the consumer has a third choice between becoming a vegetarian and supporting intensive farming practices, and that in the exercising of that choice by choosing to eat real meat, but not often, we can collectively influence what happens on our farms and in our shops.

For who is going to break the circle if not the consumer? Possibly a farmer might make a stand, and very many do, deciding not to practice intensive farming but to raise animals in a dignified, humane fashion. But this will be very expensive, and the farmer needs the support of the consumer to purchase this high-quality, high-cost meat. If we reduce our consumption of cheap factory-farmed livestock, there will be less incentive for its over-production and, in turn, less need to import feed grain from abroad. I do not feel that paying more for humanely reared meat and eating it less often entails any sacrifice, either to cook or eater. I would much rather buy a good piece of real beef once every week or two than eat much more often the lean, mass-produced inexpensive meat on offer. To eat better quality meat less frequently is much more of a treat.

I do not accept that this is a solution only for the more affluent. Of course, to eat meat of this kind would be expensive if you did it every day. But there is *no* reason to eat meat *every* day. Indeed, there are many reasons not to. We in the West are very lucky that we enjoy one of the greatest privileges of all: choice. Just as we do not have to eat Dover sole and turbot to include fish in our diet, but can choose equally (if not more) nutritious fish such as inexpensive herring and mackerel, so the switch from intensively reared to real meat need not add to the cost of the budget. Real meat encompasses the normal range of cuts, as I describe in the following chapters. Beef fillet is very expensive indeed, skirt steak and shin is not, and the dishes these produce can be absolutely wonderful. Likewise, a saddle of lamb is considerably more expensive than lamb shanks, but lamb shanks make up into very good dishes.

I do not think the supermarkets will break the circle. As long as there are consumers who want cheap meat and who are prepared to accept the responsibility for, or not to think about, what goes on in intensive farming systems, then the supermarkets will continue to supply them. To take a parallel case, a senior official in the European egg industry is said to have commented that battery eggs could very soon be phased out. If the supermarkets labelled their standard range of battery eggs as readily as they label their free-range eggs, then perhaps, indeed, no one would buy them because the consumer is now more aware of what a battery hen system represents. But they are not labelled and so continue selling.

Buying our meat ready-jointed in polystyrene trays, as neatly packed as the packets of dried pasta, bottles of mineral water and fancy lettuces on nearby shelves, reinforces our isolation not only from the producer but from the product itself. We know from childhood memories, perhaps, or scenes from a train window that food comes from farms, but in reality our consciousness stops at those little neat packages in the super-markets. We begin to shy away from butchers' shops whose carcases hanging on hooks above the sawdust floor reminds us that our Sunday joint was once a two-year-old steer and that our favourite stew was once a lamb born on the Welsh hillsides, and whose dis-plays of game birds in full, vivid plumage show that these creatures once inhabited our moorland and wild places. If we are going to eat them we need to be reminded of this, not just from time to time, but every time we cook and eat meat. Not to make us feel guilty, but to make us conscious of what we are eating, to make us eat responsibly, to be aware that we are consuming part of our planet's natural resources.

Preparing meat gives me pleasure in that it is a challenge to my skills, my senses and, I suppose, to my sensibilities. The first times I cleaned a chicken and skinned a rabbit were occasions that I still remember vividly. I felt I had to do it and was glad I did, although it was messy at the time. Like most people I do not enjoy dealing with the mysterious, the bloody and the slippery. But I enjoy it much more if I know I am dealing with meat from an animal that has been reared in a manner which is sympathetic to its natural habits, and which has been fed a natural diet.

Do I still clean chickens and skin rabbits? No, I ask my butcher to do this, for the same reasons that I do not pluck game. I did it once or twice in my small kitchen, but it is not practical and I prefer to have it done by an expert. That may be a rationalisation for not dealing with the less tidy and agreeable aspects of meat preparation, but I do not think so. It is very satisfying to be able to joint a chicken or bone a duck, not only in the skill which is exercised but in the fact that you then have far more options open to you as to how to cook the meat.

Let me give you an example. One of my favourite pieces of meat preparation is to take a large loin of pork – I once bought a 10 lb joint in Springfield, Missouri and pre-pared it for a large group of friends who had 'commissioned' me to cook us all a lengthy dinner – and to bone it. I remove all the skin with a sharp knife and put it aside, so that I can use it to cover and baste the stuffed joint as it cooks. Most of the fat is taken off, with a thin covering left on to add succulence to the meat as it cooks. Then, working with a sharp and not too flexible knife, I work down the length of the chine bone, that thick square of half back bone to which the ribs are attached, and scrape the meat away from the bone, cutting into the flesh as little as possible. The task gets easier as you reach the ribs, and you can work swiftly to detach the meat in one large neat cushion from the bones. I then make two horizontal slits in the meat, without cutting it through, and fill these pockets with a flavoursome stuffing before rolling and tying the meat at intervals into a long rolled joint ready to be braised or roasted. The bones are not wasted but chopped and browned and used for stock; or I rest the meat on the chopped bones, splash on a little water or wine and let them add extra flavour to the roasting juices.

This preparation, which I find satisfyingly complete working with good quality meat, becomes quite unpleasant to me when working with intensively reared pork because of its offensive smell. As described on p. 119, the animal lives in close contact with its own waste right up to the time of its death. That waste is made particularly noxious by the additives, such as copper sulphate that are fed to the animal. Since an animal's skin is, like our own, porous, it seems to me that it absorbs into its flesh these odours which are still present in the raw meat.

We are in great danger of losing forever the real pleasures involved in selecting prime foodstuffs, handling them and assessing how best to use them, preparing them in the most appropriate way to show off texture, flavour, aroma and appearance, and finally, and just as important, in sitting down to eat the food, sharing it with others in a spirit of enjoyment and community.

That is, for me, what *The Real Meat Cookbook* is about. I hope that the recipes will encourage and help to preserve those pleasures. In putting the recipes together I wanted to reflect several things, the main element of which is the universality of meat as a foodstuff. It is an immensely versatile ingredient, suitable for any climate, for every and any season, for any time of the day, for high days and holidays, as well as for Mondays. It includes a wide variety of cuts and joints, some expensive, some not. Meat can be the main focus of the meal, or it can garnish or season a dish of rice or pasta. It is a part of the diet of almost every racial, religious or cultural group and is eaten in every country. Above all, I wanted the recipes to reflect this diversity. I have been lucky enough to experience this rich diversity in my travels, which have been the source of many of the recipes collected here. Some I have left out. In Bogota we were served bull's penis soup in a small *cocina popular* in the huge *corabastos* or wholesale produce market. It was excellent with corn-cakes and washed down with Hennessy and hot milk, but it is not an ingredient one can readily buy. For the same reason I have left out recipes for reindeer tongue and braised elk which I ate in Norway, and for the warming snake soup served to us one raw winter's day in Shanghai.

The diversity I describe does not, however, extend to the sausage. Nor do I write about ham, cured meat and other pork products, except in so far as they might appear in one or two favourite recipes such as the *tortellini*. This omission is deliberate in that *charcuterie* is an enormous subject that deserves a whole book devoted to it. Fortunately for us the late and much loved Jane Grigson wrote it, *Pork Cookery and Charcuterie* (Penguin), and it is still available. This excellent and authoritative book will tell you all you need to know on the subject and indeed is the source of information for most people who write about it.

The suppliers of real meat often make their own sausages and cure their own hams. These are the only ones worth buying on the whole. Much nastiness described as sausage has been foisted on the public.

25

It may be that you prefer to make up or adapt your own recipes? I have described different cooking methods for each type of meat and summarised the cuts available. I have also included my thoughts on suitable accompaniments to each type of meat, in the way of sauces, flavourings and vegetables. The 'meat maps' provide further guidance as does the section on carving and jointing meat.

Despite the fact that the chairman of Safeway and the directors of the British Organic Farmers and Organic Growers' Association have called for ten thousand more organic farmers in Britain to meet demand, farmers tell me a different story. One of the farms I visited produces not only beef for the Real Meat Company but free-range eggs for a large distributor who was supplying at least two of the large supermarket chains. "Send us more, send us more," they urged last year. More stock and extra space was acquired. The farmer was told this year, "Not so many, not so many," and he was selling 20% less, having made the investment in the previous year.

Others tell me that unless organic farmers sell at the farm gate, the premium by the time their product reaches the shop or supermarket can be as much as 70%. And whereas 90% of people questioned will say that they are willing to pay more for real meat, only about 10% actually do so. Who can blame them if they are trying to eat meat every day?

But producers of real meat are nonetheless flourishing. Their customers buy it as a treat and thus balance the cost of it against less expensive foodstuffs, just as enjoyable in their own right.

I found it encouraging to meet so many dedicated farmers during the writing of this book and I believe they represent a far greater number all over the country. I believe the consumer can seek them out, and I know that the farmers will welcome the contact with the consumer. After all, this is how we used to buy our meat long ago, from the neighbour's farm. That is not a practical solution for everyone, which is why I have listed some sources of supply of real meat and have given a little more background about some of the organisations who supply it.

Although there are quite separate organisations setting codes for the production of high quality meat reared to high standards of welfare and purity, I gradually came to feel that there was very little that separated them, but they seem, nevertheless, to be at odds in their views. What also struck me was that it is probably in the mainstream meat industry's interest to keep them separate, to encourage disagreements about the definition of organic standards, which physical interventions are inhumane to pigs, which chemicals are permissible – and so on.

Another factor also struck me. Many of the farmers and producers I spoke to commented on the different nutritional values of real meat. Like humans, animals are what they eat. There are exciting pointers which suggest that a healthy, natural diet for animals produces healthier meat, that cattle living a stress-free life and eating a grass diet will lay down less saturated fat and more polyunsaturated fat. Both Anne Petch and Sir Julian Rose, an organic farmer, have commented on this. Indeed Anne Petch did carry out a small-scale study, but as she says, the evidence is based on a relatively small sample and cannot thus be described as scientific. Professor John Webster at Bristol University thinks there is a possibility that such animals may have lower blood cholesterol. One can imagine the effect on the intensive meat industry if this was all found to be true. It would be brave of those in the industry to put up the money for such research.

In the long run the key to ending the system of intensive farming may lie in convincing governments and farmers and supermarkets that we do not want so much meat, just better meat.

WHERE TO FIND REAL MEAT; WHO SETS THE STANDARDS

THE SOIL ASSOCIATION is by far the oldest of the organisations which promote a pure food supply achieved through humane and sustainable methods. Founded as a charity in 1946, it encourages organic farming and food production as long-term alternatives to chemical farming, which damages the land and the environment. An ecological approach to agriculture cares for the soil and the land, which in turn affects the quality of the plants and animals raised on it. They, in turn, become the food on which our own health and well-being depend.

Livestock farmers who adhere to the organic standards laid down in The Soil Association Symbol Standards book may apply for the Soil Association Symbol, which licenses them as producers of certified organic meat.

Under the Symbol scheme permanent housing of breeding stock is prohibited, as is prolonged confining or tethering; the animals' behaviour patterns must be respected in terms of flock or herd size (for example, certain animals are kept in family groups rather than singly or in large herds). Animals should be put out to pasture during the grazing season. At all times, the animals' diet must be based on organic foodstuffs. This does not, however, mean that the diet must be wholly organic. Between 10% and 30% of non-organic foodstuffs is permitted, depending on the species. I am told that this is because there is not enough organic foodstuff to meet the demand. Certain organic farmers will, however, strive to maintain a feed supply which is 100% organic. Prophylactic drugs and almost all feed additives are prohibited under the Soil Association Symbol scheme. Some producers of real meat are not happy about the welfare aspect of the Soil Association code of practice. One organic farmer I visited would not treat a sick animal with antibiotics, but would use homeopathic remedies; when the animal is very small, frail and sick, more powerful interventions may be necessary administered under veterinary supervision.

Under their 'Campaign for Safe Meat', the Association produce a list of suppliers of organic meat, including those holding the Symbol. Regional lists are available from the Soil Association, 86 Colston Street, Bristol, Avon BS1 5BB, as are the details of the

28

Symbol Standard. Some of the farmers will sell directly to customers, at the farm gate as it were, some have local or national delivery services, and others will also sell through local butchers, or indeed, even further afield. Going direct, instead of buying in the wholesale market, means that the butcher is able to keep prices at a remarkably modest level. High quality farming with this level of commitment should attract a high premium which others have found the consumer is willing to pay.

The Guild of Conservation Food Producers, whose members hold the Conservation Grade Symbol, was formed in response to a need for an alternative somewhere between intensive and organic farming, which would provide consumers with food raised under acceptable conditions and the farmers with adequate recompense for their efforts. The Guild believes that the twentieth century has produced valuable advances in medical and veterinary science, including chemicals and medicines. It allows for the use of safe, degradable chemicals which have been identified with the help of Wye College. It allows animals the advantages of medical science from which human beings have benefitted. If a child catches pneumonia, it is given penicillin. So is the lamb. If a child gets worms, it is dewormed. So is the calf. On the other hand, routine medication is not permitted because it lowers the animal's defences and makes it much more difficult to treat a serious illness. Specifications are laid down as to how the animal is housed and managed, allowing it to 'work' under as near natural conditions as possible.

The Pure Meat Company is the largest company supplying meat to Conservation Grade Standards. It is available through mail order from 1 The Square, Moreton Hampstead, Devon, tel 0647 40321 and from a number of ASDA stores. Based on Jonathan Blackburn's own farm in Devon, the Company also buys meat from other farmers who are members of the Guild of Conservation Food Producers and subscribe to its code, which is maintained by spot checks. Details about the Guild can be obtained from The Guild of Conservation Food Producers, P.O. Box 157, Bradwell Common, Milton Keynes MK13.

The Real Meat Company have their own shop in Bath and two franchises in London who sell only RMC meat, plus authorised distributors throughout the country who sell the full range of RMC meat. At the time of writing, they are also supplying meat to several CRS (Cooperative Retail Services) food shops. In addition, meat can be ordered through their overnight delivery service, Real Meat Express. Telephone 0985 40501, for details and local stockists of their meat, or write to The Real Meat Company Ltd., East Hill Farm, Heytesbury, Warminster, Wilts BA12 0HR.

Heal Farm meat is available by mail order from Anne Petch, Heal Farm, King's Nympton, Umberleigh, Devon EX37 9TB, tel 076957 2077.

The Q Guild Ltd., the marketing group of independent retail butchers, produces a membership list by region. The list can be obtained from the Secretary, Q Guild Ltd., Meat and Livestock Commission, British Meat Quality Assurance, P.O. Box 44, Winterhill House, Snowdon Drive, Milton Keynes MK6 1AX. The organisation is sponsored by the meat industry.

The Supermarkets

*A*LL SUPERMARKETS stock their own non-premium, i.e. least expensive, range of meats.

ASDA

*C*ONSERVATION Grade beef, lamb, chicken, pork, veal and bacon is available in most of their stores.

CRS

*R*EAL Meat Company meat is stocked in a few of their food shops, the Leo Superstores.

GATEWAY

*T*HEIR own unpublished standards for 'traditional beef' and 'traditional pork' are applied.

MARKS & SPENCER

*I*N 1990 the company decided not to stock organic food any longer as there was 'insufficient' demand to justify shelf space. They have their own unpublished standards for their meat and poultry. Their free-range poultry will match the EC specifications (see p. 194).

SAFEWAY

*T*HEY stock organic beef and lamb holding the Soil Association Symbol and free-range poultry in all their stores.

They see a future for farming which produces this type of meat and they jointly sponsor an organic farming research centre in Perthshire to demonstrate that organic farming is a viable alternative.

SAINSBURY

*A*LTHOUGH this company has won several environmental awards, it sells organic meat in only a handful of its stores. Its traditional free-range chickens conform to EC standards. Otherwise it has its own unpublished codes for 'tenderlean lamb', 'tenderlean pork', 'traditional beef' etc.

TESCO

*T*HEY do not stock organic meat and have their own unpublished standards for their 'traditional' range of beef, lamb and pork.

WAITROSE

*T*HEY do not sell organic meat and have their own unpublished standards for 'traditional pork' and 'English country lamb'.

Ukrofs

THIS RELATIVELY NEW ACRONYM stands for the UK Register of Organic Food Standards. It was set up by Food from Britain in 1987 to provide a framework for assessing the various organic standards, and as a means of assuring the consumer that food is produced according to the standards claimed.

As well as the pioneering Soil Association with its symbol scheme, there are other organisations in Britain and abroad who have evolved their own standards such as Organic Farmers and Growers Ltd. In addition there is the International Federation of Organic Agricultural Movements and the standards they have set. Now we have the Ukrofs standards compiled with the advice of advisory committees of producers and processors (for organic standards can also be applied to processed food). Those farmers who are certified by one of the organic sector organisations, such as the Soil Association, but not exclusively the Soil Association, will also be eligible for the Ukrofs certification mark. However, the certification scheme is also available for producers who do not wish to participate in schemes operated by the organic sector organisations, provided they meet the Ukrofs standards. For me this confuses rather than clarifies the whole question of organics. And what is worrying is that whereas the Soil Association, which was the founder of the organic movement in Britain, was created by individuals with a passionate commitment to sustainable agriculture and animal welfare (a position which is maintained today), an official quasi-governmental body has no guiding founders to motivate it. This must make it vulnerable, by the lowest common denominator argument, according to which the lower limits of the standard are the ones chosen out of economic necessity, with no regard to the philosophy, integrity and dedication of those who founded the organic movement. I knew of a farmer, for example, who was withdrawn from the Soil Association Symbol Scheme for infringement of its Code on three counts, including using growth promoters and buying in stock from livestock markets. The farmer then applied for Ukrofs registration. The application is pending as I write. For almost two years a butcher was selling this man's meat as organic.

The EC Regulation for organic food production was approved in June 1991. After an adoption period which, at the time of writing, has not yet been confirmed, the regulation will prohibit the use of the word 'organic' for any food produced without Ukrofs registration, and Trading Standards Officers will be able to prosecute in case of false organic claims.

Meat Cookery

Buying Meat

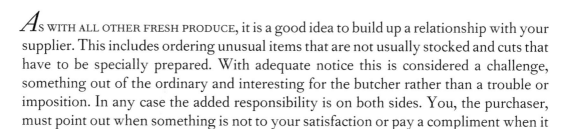

*A*s with all other fresh produce, it is a good idea to build up a relationship with your supplier. This includes ordering unusual items that are not usually stocked and cuts that have to be specially prepared. With adequate notice this is considered a challenge, something out of the ordinary and interesting for the butcher rather than a trouble or imposition. In any case the added responsibility is on both sides. You, the purchaser, must point out when something is not to your satisfaction or pay a compliment when it exceeds it.

It has to be said that there is not a great deal of difference in the outward appearance of intensively reared and free-range meat. There are two main exceptions. Properly reared chickens and turkeys appear a quite different breed to fast-growing, intensively reared broilers, and free-range pork smells differently from the intensive version. On the other hand, there is not a great deal of difference in appearance between wild and raised game.

Good butchers with a regular turnover and reputable stores are unlikely to sell poor quality meat, but here are a few pointers. Meat should always smell fresh, with no stale or off-taints. The cut surface should appear moist but not wet, and no part of it should feel slimy. Fat should be a whitish cream colour and firm rather than waxy in texture. Of course, there are variations: mature beef fat is darker than young pork fat while lamb fat looks crisp and brittle. Flesh colours are characteristic too. Free-range veal is pink, pork is a deeper pink, lamb is a light red, and beef a darker, richer crimson veering to crimson/brown when it is very mature. Kid meat is the colour of pork or young lamb, and more mature goat meat is the colour of one-year-old lamb.

When deciding how much meat to buy, it is probably best to be guided by the taste and appetites of those you are buying for. Recipes also provide a guideline. Current healthy diet guidelines recommend 3 oz/100 g portions. My recipes, which are designed for deliberately not eating meat every day, allow for 4-5 oz/110-140 g of fairly lean, trimmed meat off the bone. With meat on the bone, such as a joint or a chicken, it is usual to allow 8-12 oz/230-340 g for each person.

STORING MEAT

*I*F YOU BUY MEAT 'loose' from the butcher, it will probably be handed to you in a white polythene bag sealed with tape. When you get the meat home, take it out of this bag and loosely wrap it in foil, greaseproof paper or food wrap. Put it in the coldest part of the refrigerator until you are ready to use it. Never let the meat or any juices from it come into contact with any other food stuff. Wash your hands before and after handling meat, as well as any boards and utensils used. If you buy meat already in a plastic film covered tray or airtight pack, it can be so stored in the refrigerator but put it on a plate to safeguard against leaking.

It is difficult to give guidelines for storing uncooked meat in the refrigerator but remember that in particularly warm or humid weather meat, game and poultry will all deteriorate faster. Smaller cuts of meat such as chops have a relatively large surface exposed to the air and they will deteriorate faster than a large joint of meat. But roughly speaking, offal, sausages, loose mince and poultry portions should be used on the day of purchase. Pork, game, veal and whole poultry should be used within two to four days, and beef, lamb, mutton, goat and venison, depending on the size of the joint and whether it is being marinated, for up to a week.

Incidentally, a counsel of perfection that I usually forget to follow is to take a cool bag and ice-pack with you when you go shopping for meat, so that it can be kept as cool as possible on the way home.

THE HYGIENIC HANDLING OF MEAT

*B*ACTERIA ARE PRESENT EVERYWHERE: in the air, soil, water, food we eat, and in ourselves. Some are harmless; some, such as the lactobacilli which give yoghurt its particular characteristics are beneficial; some simply cause spoilage in food. Yet others, such as salmonella, listeria, botulism and campylobacter, can cause illness to the point of being life-threatening.

Whereas some foods, such as bread, milk or orange juice, simply become unpleasant, mouldy, sour or fermented when they go 'off' and are recognisably so by taste or appearance, which usually stop one from eating them, meat and poultry that have gone off are not always identifiably so and can cause food poisoning.

Whilst I remain unconvinced that the domestic kitchen is the major source of food spoilage – or contamination, call it what you will – I do believe from my own experience that it is an area open to improvement, and that this can be achieved with little extra cost and effort.

One such worthwhile low-cost investment is a thermometer to monitor the temperature in the refrigerator and freezer. When I used one for the first time I was horrified to discover that the temperature in my refrigerator was closer to 8-10°C/45-50°F rather than the recommended 5°C/41°F maximum. I was equally horrified to hear of someone whom I thought knew a good deal about cookery and domestic matters putting hot food into the refrigerator in an attempt to cool the food down quickly, while, in fact, doing this simply raises the temperature of the refrigerator and risks causing all the other food in it to start spoiling.

Refrigeration and freezing do not kill bacteria. Refrigeration, if the equipment is at the correct temperature (below 5°C/41°F), will slow the growth of most common bacteria. Temperatures from 10-65°C/50-150°F provide the best growing temperatures for bacteria. Freezing will stop the bacteria growing altogether if kept at the correct temperature – 18°C/0°F, but will not kill it. As soon as you begin to thaw food, whether in the kitchen or refrigerator, the bacteria will start to multiply again.

Bacteria such as salmonella and listeria, which may be present in much meat and poultry, will be killed if the meat is thoroughly cooked – that is, reaches 70°C/158°F at the very centre. Those who like their meat pink or even rarer, when the internal temperature of the meat is somewhere between 49-60°C/120-140°F, should be aware of the risk that not all harmful bacteria in the meat will have been destroyed.

The following steps should ensure that your meat and poultry is kept and prepared in a way that will minimise any risk of food poisoning.

1 Refrigerate all meat as soon as possible after getting it home. It should be carefully, but loosely, covered in a shallow container and placed as low down as possible in the refrigerator (this is the coldest part). Care should be taken to ensure that the meat juices do not drip into the salad drawer. The refrigerator temperature should not go above 5°C/41°F.

2 Before and after handling fresh meat, wash your hands. Utensils and knives should be thoroughly washed after preparing meat, whether raw or cooked.

3 Raw meat is best prepared on white non-porous chopping boards, which are easy to clean with bleach and hot water, rather than on wooden chopping boards, which are difficult to clean properly after use and tend to harbour bacteria. It is a good idea to use the practice followed in professional kitchens and keep separate boards for the preparation of raw and cooked food.

4 During storage and preparation, contact between cooked food and raw meat must be avoided as this helps to prevent cross-contamination.

5 Food which is either warm or at room temperature is an ideal breeding ground for bacteria. Any meat cooked for eating later should be cooled as quickly as possible, then carefully covered and refrigerated. Hot food must not be put into the refrigerator as this raises the temperature and you risk spoiling other food in there.

6 On whole uncut joints of meat, the bacteria are concentrated on the surface and are destroyed in roasting because the surface temperatures are high. With a rolled joint such as breast of lamb, or a stuffed joint, there has been much more handling and there will be bacteria in the middle of the meat. It is important, therefore, to make sure that the joint cooks for long enough at a high enough temperature to kill the bacteria: the internal temperature should be at least 70°C/160°F. For the same reason, I recommend that you do not stuff the body cavity of a turkey, but only the neck cavity.

A NOTE ON EQUIPMENT

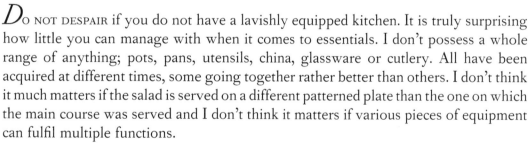

*D*O NOT DESPAIR if you do not have a lavishly equipped kitchen. It is truly surprising how little you can manage with when it comes to essentials. I don't possess a whole range of anything; pots, pans, utensils, china, glassware or cutlery. All have been acquired at different times, some going together rather better than others. I don't think it much matters if the salad is served on a different patterned plate than the one on which the main course was served and I don't think it matters if various pieces of equipment can fulfil multiple functions.

The wok is a good case in point. Since I have always had small kitchens and a wok takes up a lot of cupboard space, I thought long and hard before acquiring one. Subsequently I've discovered how many uses it has other than steaming and stir-frying. It works well as a jam pan, the large surface area putting more heat in contact with the bubbling fruit and sugar, which in turn encourages the jam to reach setting point quickly. I also use the wok for cooking home-made *ravioli* and other delicate stuffed pastas. Being broad and shallow, the pan allows the pasta to cook in a single layer without it being crammed close together with one piece on top of another.

On the other hand, as with most things, it is a false economy to buy cheap pans. Get the best you can afford and even be prepared to pay rather more than you can afford. It is worth it.

Here are most of the items I find useful for meat cookery together with a few suggestions for making do without them.

Casseroles and other ovenproof dishes

*L*IDDED CASSEROLES come in a variety of materials and finishes, from glazed earthenware to glass, taking in cast-iron, enamelled cast-iron and flameproof porcelain. Much of it can be used as oven-to-tableware and I think there is a great deal to be said for serving the food from the receptacle in which it is cooked. Transferring from a casserole to a serving dish cools the food, but, more important, it loses some of the immediacy and spontaneity with which food should be served.

I use both glazed brown earthenware casseroles, like the pot-bellied Dutch ovens, and the enamelled cast-iron ones of Cousances and Le Creuset. The former cannot be used on a direct heat and I have found from experience that with the latter it is also best to use a frying pan if you wish to brown the meat and vegetables first. By using too high a heat, I have cracked the enamel on more casseroles than I care to count.

Cast-iron casseroles are agreeable to use, but anything very acidic such as sorrel may cause a reaction and discolouration. It is important when cleaning them to dry them very thoroughly or they will rust. I often finish mine off with a little oil on a paper towel.

Charcoal grills and barbecues

*F*OOD COOKING OVER CHARCOAL has a wonderful smell as the juices caramelise and char on the outside. It is an ideal cooking method for many cuts of meat, and those who enjoy it and have the space will probably want to invest in a barbecue. In fact, the barbecue need not be a major investment. Small, single-use disposable barbecues are available in hardware shops. They are inexpensive and extremely efficient, lasting for up to 1½ hours, which is long enough to cook a butterflied leg of lam. For flat-dwellers and occasional barbecuers this is the answer.

Some of the more elaborate cookers and hobs are fitted with a grill over a lava stone base, which has a similar effect to a barbecue.

Clay pots, chicken bricks and Römertopfen

*M*ADE OF UNGLAZED EARTHENWARE or sometimes with an interior glaze, these are for use in the oven. I like them very much for slow-cooked casseroles and even for thick soups. They will also do a pot roast very well. It is important to soak the pot (top and bottom) in cold water for 15 minutes before using it. This keeps the food moist and also stops all the juices being absorbed back into the porous clay pot.

Clay pots are also good for cooking fish. However, here it is as well to have two separate pots to avoid transferring fishy flavours to meat casseroles. Whatever you are cooking in them, clean them by simply soaking and scrubbing. Their porosity means that any detergent or soap will linger into the next dish cooked in the pot.

Frying pans and sauté pans

I SOMETIMES THINK I could run my kitchen with just a battery of frying and sauté pans of different sizes and materials. My favourite is made of a matt, dark grey anodised aluminium, is 9½ in/24 cm in diameter and 2½ in/6.5 cm deep, with straight sides and a lid. It has a good solid feel to it and a bright, chrome-finished handle. Apart from being very good for the usual frying and sautéing, the pan is excellent for making casseroles, jam and risotto.

It is a good idea to have a sauté pan as well as a frying pan, especially if the former has a lid. Food can then be tossed and shaken in a sauté pan. Either pan is useful for reducing liquids and sauces because there is such a broad surface in contact with the heat; the liquid evaporates much more quickly than in a saucepan.

Stainless steel frying and sauté pans are very good indeed and excellent conductors of heat. Don't buy cheap stainless steel as it will be thin and buckle with heat.

Non-stick frying pans can be useful if you treat them kindly. Use them on a gentle heat and never use metal tools or scouring agents on them. Forget it just once and you'll start to get nasty black specks of non-stick coating in your food. The non-stick effect can be achieved with a well-seasoned cast-iron frying pan. To season a new pan, it should be rubbed or brushed all over the inside with a neutral edible oil such as groundnut oil. Pour in about ½ in/1 cm oil and put it on the lowest heat for about an hour. Turn off the heat and leave until cool, then pour off the oil and wipe with kitchen paper. This keeps the pan rust-free as well as preventing food from sticking. After washing, the pan should be oiled lightly before putting it away.

A word about copper pans. They are marvellous to cook with and will be found in all the best kitchens. They have only two drawbacks. One is their cost and the other is the work involved in cleaning them. Two of my stainless steel pans have thick copper bottoms as it is such an excellent heat conductor. That is about as much copper as I'm prepared to clean.

GRIDDLES

*F*LAT OR RIDGED, round or rectangular, a well-seasoned cast-iron griddle is a useful item in the kitchen. It is excellent for dry frying or grilling a steak, a chop, a noisette or a piece of calves' liver. Some are big enough to fit across two burners, electric or gas, and will hold enough for four to six people. Griddles cook entirely without fat, although it is a good idea to wipe them over with a screw of kitchen paper dipped in oil before heating them. The ridged versions give an effective striped appearance to meat, almost like that of a charcoal grill.

NEEDLES, THREAD AND SCISSORS

*N*O, I HAVE NOT INCLUDED these for emergency repairs to the starched pinny. They are indispensable items for meat cookery.

The larding needle is a long, thin pointed implement with a catch in the blunt end, which is designed to hold a small thin strip of pork fat for you to thread into, say, a fillet of beef. The action is not unlike taking a stitch in sewing and, like the thread in the cloth, the piece of fat stays in the meat. The larding needle will help determine how a bird or a joint is cooking if you do not have a meat thermometer. Pierce the chicken thigh with it to see that the juices run clear. Plunge it into the thickest part of the meat and leave it there for 30 seconds before pulling it out and holding it against your inner wrist as a rough temperature guide (see the roasting chart on p. 40). If you cannot get a larding needle, the very largest darning needle might work.

Kitchen string or twine is useful for trussing a chicken, for tying round a piece of beef fillet to be cooked *à la ficelle*, for tying boned loin chops into noisettes of lamb and for securing a crown roast of lamb.

Sturdy scissors are ideal for jointing poultry and spatchcocking small birds for grilling – that is, cutting along both sides of the backbone, discarding it and then squashing the bird flat by pressing down on the breast.

ROASTING PANS, RACKS AND BAGS

*M*OST OVENS COME with a large roasting pan and rack, which are often much too big for the size of roasts most of us cook. This burns the juices as they drip into the hot pan and caramelise on to it. It is always far better to use a roasting pan of approximately the same size as the roast.

The rack is useful so that the meat does not sit in the fat as it cooks. Something of the same effect can be achieved by setting the roast on a bed of roughly chopped vegetables and/or bones removed from the joint. Add a splash of water from time to time, but not enough to steam the meat, and you will have the beginnings of a very good gravy.

The clear roasting bag is remarkably efficient, roasting birds, particularly, to a marvellous golden brown, retaining the juices in the bottom of the bag and preventing any spattering of juices in the oven.

SKEWERS

*N*O BARBECUERS can do their job without skewers. In fact skewers are useful in the kitchen too because kebabs can also be cooked indoors under the grill.

Smaller wooden ones are more commonly used for oriental cooking, for satays and hot-pots. If using them under the grill or on the barbecue, they should be soaked in water for 20-30 minutes first to stop them charring.

Flat rather than round metal skewers are best because the meat chunks stay in place when the skewers are turned over. On round ones, the chunks tend to slip.

TERRINES

*F*OR *PÂTÉS* AND PORK PIES, it is possible to buy handsome enamelled cast-iron terrines. They are expensive, though they will last indefinitely. If you only make such dishes infrequently, I would be inclined to use a loaf tin lined with foil or greaseproof paper if necessary. It does the job quite well.

WOKS

*F*OR ORIENTAL STIR-FRY DISHES the wok cannot be replaced. The heat is applied in the right place to the right degree for this kind of cooking, and its shape lends itself to flicking and turning the ingredients with a spatula or shovel. It is also possible to fit tiers of bamboo baskets into the wok and steam a variety of delicacies one on top of the other. With the metal rack in it, a whole chicken can be steamed. And lined with foil, it can be used as a home-smoker (see the recipe on p. 240). Woks can be bought in all kitchenware sections of department stores, in a range of easy-to-care-for materials, and they usually come with instructions for care and use.

COOKING REAL MEAT

*I*T IS MORE IN THE CARVING than in the cooking that the difference between real meat and intensive meat becomes evident, and then, too, in the eating. Poultry and pork that has grown slowly to maturity does not contain much moisture, does not shrink in cooking and is firm to the carving knife. Real chickens that have run around will also need to cook longer, and more slowly, since they are often bigger than the intensive birds. On the other hand, the bones, too, are bigger and better developed and these act as a good conductor of heat. The smell of real meat as it cooks is a good one, just as it smells sweet in its raw state.

However I do have to say that not all free-range, organic real meat is impressive. If it is from an inferior breed, if the carcase has not been handled properly or matured after slaughter, this can have an enormous effect on the quality of the meat, which can be tough, tasteless and especially disappointing for the consumer who has paid dearly for it.

A Roasting Chart

*L*ET US CONSIDER THE QUESTION of roasting on or off the bone. A boneless joint is undoubtedly easier to carve, but there are those who maintain that a joint roasted on the bone has a better flavour and texture. Let me pass on a trick that chefs use. If, for example, you order a saddle of lamb, have it prepared by your butcher, or indeed, prepare it yourself, with the meat cut away from the bone for easy carving, but then tied back on to the bone in its original position so that the joint retains maximum flavour during cooking. For carving simply untie the string.

	Starting temperature °C	°F	GAS	Turn down after 15 min to °C	°F	GAS	Cooking time min per lb		Temperature** on meat thermometer °C	°F
Beef and some game*	250	475	9	200	400	6	Rare	12	51	125
							Medium	16	60	140
							Well done	18-20	70	160
Chicken	200	400	6	180	350	4		20	80	175
Duck	200	400	6	180	350	4		15-20	80	175
Goose	200	400	6	180	350	4		20-25	85	185
Lamb*	250	475	9	200	400	6	Rare	12	51	125
							Medium	16	60	140
							Well done	18-20	70	160
Pork	220	425	7	180	350	4		20-25	75	170
Veal	220	425	7	180	350	4		18-20	75	170
Turkey	200	400	6	180	350	4		20-22	80	175

*Apart from those meats asterisked, the rest should be cooked thoroughly.

**If you do not have a meat thermometer, the following is a reasonably accurate method of judging the internal temperature of meat. Insert a skewer into the thickest part of the meat and count to thirty. Remove the skewer and place it on the outside of your wrist, or back of your hand if very sensitive. The meat is not cooked if the skewer is cold. If the skewer is warm, the meat is still rare. If quite hot, the meat is medium rare. If the skewer is very hot indeed, the meat is quite well done.

CARVING

CARVING NEED NOT BE the terrifying exercise it is sometimes made out to be. Wynkyn de Worde's 'termes of a Kerver', set down in his *Boke of Kervynge*, which he had printed himself in 1508 and 1513, are worth repeating, if only as an indication that five hundred years later meat cookery presentation has become somewhat simpler. The list of terms also appears in the *Boke of St Albans* (1486) and even earlier manuscripts. Many of the terms come from Norman French since French was then, as now in many cases, the language of the great kitchens.

'Breke that dere
lesche the brawne
rere that goose
lyft that swanne
sauce that capon
spoyle that henne
frusshe that chekyn
unbrace that malarde
unlace that cony
dysmembre that heron
dysplaye that crane
dysfygure that pecocke
unjoynt that bittern
untache that curlewe
alaye that fesande
wynge that partryche
haunche that sturgeon
undertraunche ye purpos
tayme that crabbe
harbe that lopster

wynge that quayle
thye that pegyon
thye that wodcocke
breke that egryt
tyere that egge
chyne that samon
strynge that lampraye
splatte that pyke
sauce that playce
sauce that tenche
splay that breme
syde that haddocke
tuske that barbell
culpon that trout
fynne that cheven
transsene that ele
mynce that plover
border that pasty
tymbre that fyre
breke that sarcell . . .'

Today, with a sharp carving knife, a fork to secure the meat, a board on which to carve and a basic idea of the anatomy of the piece you are dealing with, anyone can do it.

Whilst it is true that to watch an expert carver at work on the Sunday joint gives extra pleasure to the meal, carving can just as easily be carried out in the privacy of the kitchen. Always allow the meat to rest when you take it out of the oven. This causes the meat to relax and the juices to flow from the centre into the rest of the meat. The meat should be loosely covered with foil and kept in a warm place for 10-15 minutes.

41

Slices need not be immaculately thin and uniform. If in doubt, slice rather more thickly, as this is easier to control. Send the plates to the table as soon as one is complete and do not wait until you have sliced everyone's helping; few things are less appetising than rapidly cooling fat on a slice of roast and congealing gravy. Plates should be warm, certainly, but not very hot, as this will further cook the slices of roast that you have timed so carefully.

Do not take the conventional wisdom of carving as dogma. I have to admit that I rarely carve a chicken as one is shown in diagrams. Usually I just ask who wants 'white meat or brown' and then cut each bird into pieces, either four large ones or eight smaller ones, halving each breast and dividing the legs into thighs and drumsticks.

With ducks, and indeed with a saddle of hare, one goes against the normal instruction of carving across the grain and instead cuts down the breast-bone (or backbone in the case of the hare), then cutting the meat into long thin strips or *aiguillettes*.

Usually one is instructed to carve turkey by cutting long thin slices the length of the breast. And what a dull dry slice that usually proves to be. My approach changed radically after I watched Ken Hom carve a Christmas turkey a few years ago. The Hom version is to remove each breast from the turkey and chop it across into short thick escalopes, which gives tender and juicy pieces of meat. By cutting across the grain, or muscle fibres, they are shorter and the meat more tender. Cutting along the muscle would give slices of long fibres which would be much more chewy. Of course, he had already marinated and basted it with a flavoursome bath of soy sauce, rice wine and sesame oil, with a hint of oriental spices, but the carving method, too, certainly enhanced the meat.

TO CARVE A BONED AND ROLLED JOINT OR A BONED
STUFFED BIRD

1 Put the meat on a carving board, spiked, if you wish, to help hold the meat in place, and preferably with a groove or depression in it to collect the juices which will run when you cut into the meat. Secure the meat with a carving fork in one hand.

2 With a well sharpened carving knife, slice with a gentle sawing movement down through the meat, across the grain.

TO CARVE A LARGE LOIN OR RIB JOINT ON
THE BONE

WHETHER A LOIN OF PORK, a sirloin of beef or a beef forerib, the joints are dealt with in a similar fashion. The joint should be chined, either by you or the butcher. That is to say the 'chine' bone, or half backbone should be 'loosened' from the rest of the carcase. This is best done by partially sawing along the bone lengthwise. The bone can then be easily removed after cooking and before you begin to carve.

1 Run the carving knife between the meat and the ribs to loosen it and then carve the meat in downward slices on to the rib bones.

In the case of a loin of pork, before loosening the meat from the ribs cut through the layer of fat between the crackling and the meat in order to remove the layer of crackling. Provided it has been scored through, the crackling can then be divided into pieces for serving.

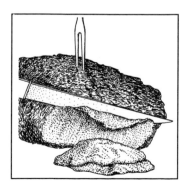

2 With a sirloin which still has the fillet attached, it is easier to carve the two portions separately, ie remove the fillet and slice it, then carve the sirloin as described above. Indeed, you may prefer to remove the fillet before cooking and use it on a separate occasion.

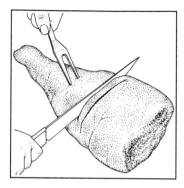

1 Grasp the shank or bone end or hold the meat firmly on the carving board with the carving fork. With the meatiest, crisp side uppermost, carve a narrow wedge-shaped slice from the centre of the joint, right down to the bone.

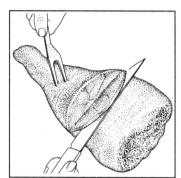

2 Continue carving slices from either side of the first cut, angling the knife to take slices as large as possible.

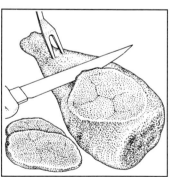

3 To carve the remains of the joint, hot or cold, turn it over and carve small or large horizontal slices according to the positioning of the bone. You can take longer slices from the leg than from the shoulder.

BEEF

IN THE EARLY SEVENTIES Tom and I visited Bern's Steak House in Tampa, Florida, more to have a look at their famous, Bible-thick wine list than out of a craving for steak. Steak is steak, after all, we thought. Up to a point. Here at Bern's they did seem to have made an art of cooking it.

This starts with the aging of the beef. We are lucky if we get beef that's been hung for two to three weeks, and that usually comes from the more specialist suppliers. A quick check around London butchers, for example, indicates aging of beef for ten to fourteen days. Only one stated that the aging time depended on the season, allowing two weeks in summer and just under three weeks in winter as the average aging period. By contrast, at Bern's steaks were aged for as long as eight weeks. This produces a unique steak, very tender, full of flavour but, it has to be said, not very juicy because moisture evaporates during aging. It is an expensive process for the butcher. Usually beef is not aged long and thus the customer pays for the water content; if the retailer ages, they have to pay for the water content lost through evaporation.

On the other hand, I've spoken to French chefs after enjoying the most tender and flavoursome fillet steak and heard quite a different story. In Bordeaux, I asked Jean Ramet how long the beef had been maturing.

'Oh, no time at all,' he said, 'the animal was killed at the end of last week.'

And what kind was it, I enquired. Angus? Charolais? He shrugged his shoulders. *'Je n'en sais rien,'* was the reply. He had simply asked his supplier for the best.

Beef from a mature animal, aged properly for at least two to three weeks, is a revelation to those who have got used to buying immature, fresh meat of a bright red hue. Meat of a darker reddish brown colour is often shunned, but wrongly so because it is usually better aged with a fuller flavour. The fat should be firm. Its colour may vary. Yellowish fat indicates a largely grass-fed animal. A mainly cereal and concentrated diet will give a white fat.

Other factors affect the quality of beef apart from the animal's diet, the treatment at slaughter and the aging of the carcase after slaughter. The breed itself is important.

Each breed has its own conformation, its own particular carcase structure and ratio of fat to lean accepted for its natural habitat, whether the rough grazing of open hillside or the lush pastures of the valleys. Different breeds mature at different rates and are slaughtered when ready. Continental and native breeds have been crossed to produce the leaner beef the consumer is said to want. However, much of the flavour of beef, as with any other meat, comes from its fat, particularly the intramuscular fat or marbling, which also tenderises it during cooking. In America particularly, and it will no doubt happen here in Europe, the notion of small (3 oz/100 g) helpings of lean beef eaten regularly is being heavily promoted. Rather than eat that kind of meat several times a week I prefer to eat a luscious piece of grass-fed real meat as an occasional treat.

The British Isles remain a rich source of recipes for beef, which, at its best, is one of Britain's most sought-after products. We use it economically in our pies and pasties, stretching it with other ingredients, but we can also be extravagant with it in our spectacular Sunday joints. '*Le rosbif*', as the French call it, and the beefeaters at the Tower of London are part of the image of traditional England.

So it is no accident that the first recipe in the book is for roast beef and Yorkshire pudding. This was the first recipe I relearned during my research and testing for the *À la carte* meat cookery series, and one that I was very proud to master. Fortunately, at about the time I was testing beef recipes I was invited to two dinner parties where roast beef was served, in each case cooked by very good cooks to accompany splendid wines. At the first one, a fillet of beef was roasted in a very hot oven for a very short time, then left to rest for a good while. When we came to help ourselves to the meat, it was tender, juicy and uniformly pink. At the second, the beef was cooked as I describe in the recipe here. The Yorkshire puddings were served first with gravy in the approved Yorkshire manner, then came the meat with roast potatoes and cauliflower cheese. This method of cooking beef gives something for everyone; crisp brown outer slices, grading to deep pink and rare at the bone.

HUSBANDRY

*B*EFORE DOMESTICATION, beef cattle roamed free across the wide open countryside. By putting a fence round a piece of the plain and using labour along with the climate and seasons to gather and store grass for winter as either hay or silage, we have a modified but still basically natural method of beef rearing. Food could be derived from grass, silage (fermented grass), hay or grains, usually barley. Other food sources might include potatoes or turnips.

Intensification and indoor keeping began as more sophisticated milk production systems required the separation of mother and calf so that all the mother's milk could be gathered for human consumption. The increase in popularity of milk, and of milk products like yoghurt and cheese, means that nearly three-quarters of the beef now produced in Britain comes from calves that are a by-product of the dairy industry and are reared in the intensive beef production system most favoured by the major suppliers and retailers, such as supermarkets, who require consistent shaped and sized cuts with minimal amounts of white fat. Called barley beef production because crushed barley forms the main part of the diet, it is low in labour costs and fast in terms of production time, although it gives a tasteless product, partly because of the monotonous diet but also because cattle bred for milk production do not produce the best beef.

Calves are born from dairy cows, separated shortly after birth and sent, usually by way of livestock market, to a specialist beef farm. This involves transporting a young and vulnerable calf for what can be a very lengthy and traumatic journey.

Individually, or sometimes in groups, calves are reared on milk powder which will contain an antibiotic growth promoter. This will be replaced by hay and a solid feed until, when aged four to six months, the animals are transferred to fattening accommodation. This may have straw bedding or slatted floors. Feed will consist of crushed barley and straw alone or a proprietary feed. Proprietary feed will contain an antibiotic growth promoter or the farmer may incorporate a product containing it.

Aged twelve to sixteen months, the animals will be ready for slaughter. Some calves started intensively may be put out to pasture during the summer months and some may be finished on grass. There are growth promoters and pre-emptive medication regimes specially geared to such semi-intensive production. Systems may often be mixed.

As cattle production has intensified, cheaper sources of essential ingredients for cattle feed have been sought. If indoor keeping was to work, they also had to be consistent in dietary balance. Protein sources now used include fish meal, soya and dried blood. In 1988, meat and bone meal made from processed slaughterhouse waste derived from sheep, pigs and, of course, cattle, was banned following the advent of a cattle disease called bovine spongiform encephalopathy (BSE). Despite investigation by a learned committee (the Southwood Committee), it is not known whether this disease poses a risk to humans consuming meat from infected animals. The committee felt that the chances were small, but admitted that its findings were based on very limited knowledge, and if it were proved to be wrong, the consequences would be very grave indeed. Dairy cattle, which consume vast quantities of the suspect food and, therefore, dairy derived beef, carry the greatest risk. The reason for this is that whereas meat from cattle reared for beef comes from animals of one to two years old, meat from dairy cattle comes from animals at least five years old or from their younger offspring when they are at the end of their life as milkers. The disease has a long incubation period and is not seen in calves and young cattle.

Other 'unusual' sources of fibre or protein are still used in order to manufacture cattle food at the cheapest price, with no regard to the fact that cattle are not omnivores or carnivores but vegetarians. One of the more bizarre ingredients is the innocuous sounding

DPM, which translates in full to dried poultry manure. This carries the risk of botulism from the chicken corpses and cattle have had to be destroyed as a result of contracting botulism after eating silage made from grass dressed with chicken litter.

Hormones were banned by the EC in 1986 after the apparently impossible happened when hormone residues turned up in human food, including baby food. However, they are still used illegally and are widespread outside Europe. The USA FDA (Food and Drink Administration) has determined that the use of hormones in beef cattle production is safe. They alter the fundamental metabolism of the animal to produce more muscle and less fat, and increase growth by 10%, thus keeping the price down and giving the customer leaner beef.

There are also half a dozen antibiotic growth promoters in common use; these are most common in intensive systems. Although no hazards to humans have been identified yet, the ominous warning 'keep away from children' is added to feed bags containing the product. Cross-species contamination provides a risk as one product, in particular, is fatal to horses.

There is a humane alternative to this system, which takes into account the fact that cattle are unwilling participants in intensification; their instincts are to be in wide open spaces. Calves can be left with their mothers at pasture to be reared on a natural supply of milk and to gradually switch to grass. If a calf is separated from its mother aged six months or more it can remain at pasture to be 'fit' in nature's own time at two to three years of age. If shelter is available, the farmer may bring the herd in to overwinter in strawed yards feeding it on hay or silage plus some solid food, which can be specified to contain no growth promoters.

This old-fashioned system is based on breeds of cattle which have been selected over the centuries for beef rather than dairy production. The longer lifespan, natural mixed diet, choice of breed and higher level of stockmanship produces the beef for which Britain was once famous.

After slaughter, the beef will need to be hung for at least two weeks, giving a dark maroon colour with yellowish fat indicating the grass in the diet.

CLASSIC DISHES

*R*OAST BEEF SERVED with Yorkshire pudding is not the only classic use of beef. Steak and kidney pie and the even more substantial steak and kidney pudding would have to be near the top of the list. Beef Wellington, in which a whole beef fillet is wrapped in pastry, is another favourite albeit expensive dish. Many steak dishes have become classics too. Among them I would place steak Diane and the wonderful carpetbagger steak stuffed with oysters (p. 65).

I have included fine beef dishes from France, Germany and Italy too. I love the *daubes* and other slow cooked dishes like the *stracotta* of Italy and the *sauerbraten* of Germany. The Far East has been another source of inspiration for my beef recipes, from the Chinese style stir-fries to the unusual sharp flavours of Filipino cookery as in the beef steak tagalog (p. 67). The Caribbean coast of Colombia is the home of one of the more unusual recipes in the book, beef cooked in rum and palm sugar (p. 74).

There are also recipes which include beef in the section of recipes for a crowd, those mighty meat dishes which call for several kinds of meat and lots of other ingredients. But not all the beef recipes are to feed multitudes. I have also included quick and simple recipes for one or two.

GOOD COMPANIONS

*W*HAT ELSE TO BUY if you're shopping for a piece of beef? It is, of course, possible to serve beef with any vegetable you like, or with any kind of sauce or seasoning, but just as lemon goes with fish, so there are a handful of ingredients which go supremely well with beef. On the vegetable front, celery hearts, celeriac, potatoes, Jerusalem artichokes, parsnips and fennel are all excellent, particularly when braised. And how appropriate these autumn vegetables are when you realise that beef is at its best between September and November. Gherkins and olives go well with cold roast or spiced beef. Mustard and horseradish are perfect flavour enhancers or relishes, whereas to serve fruit with beef, say in the form of a jelly or a purée, would be a culinary solecism of the highest order. It is difficult to explain why this should be so, but perhaps one or two examples will illustrate what I mean; fillet of beef with redcurrant jelly or a roast rib of beef with cranberry and orange compôte. Quite unthinkable, but excellent with lamb, grouse or pork.

Cooking Methods

THERE ARE NO COOKING METHODS which are unsuitable for all cuts of beef, although naturally, certain methods are best suited to certain cuts.

Steaming and Poaching

SURPRISINGLY, beef can be steamed or poached if it is a tender piece of fillet. Although this may sound very modern, poached beef, or *boeuf à la ficelle* (beef on a string) is a traditional French dish. The piece of beef is tied into a neat shape with a length of string and, attached to this, it is lowered into a pot of just simmering water or stock and left in it for about 15-20 minutes per lb. It is a less suitable method for beef on the bone.

Boiling

BOILED beef and carrots is a traditional English dish. In fact, *slow* boiling, which is closer to poaching, is the method used; it is particularly suitable for silverside and brisket, which are slowly cooked with vegetables and then often served cold and sliced. Sometimes the beef is salted or pickled first.

Roasting

THE dry intense heat of roasting requires prime quality meat. It must be a tender cut and, although lean, it should have a fine marbling of fat which will baste the meat as it cooks.

So, while a whole fillet can be roasted, it will need to be larded with pork fat if it is not to dry out. The larger joints, such as rib and sirloin, are those best suited to roasting.

Frying

A QUICK cooking method suitable for tender steaks, such as fillet and rump. A dry pan can be used since the meat has enough fat, or a non-stick pan, or a pan lubricated with just a little butter or oil. Depending on whether rare, medium or well-done meat is required, 1 in/2.5 cm steaks will take between 7 and 15 minutes to fry.

STIR-FRYING

*B*EEF is ideally suited to this method of cooking, commonly used in the preparation of Chinese recipes. Use tender cuts such as rump steak, or, for even better value, see if your butcher will sell you the tail end of fillet steak. (Often this will be a third of the price of the thicker end of the fillet.) This same method of cutting the beef into small strips and stirring it continuously throughout cooking is also used for making beef Stroganoff.

GRILLING

*A*PPROPRIATE for the same cuts of beef as for frying, grilling is a method which gets rid of any fat since the meat sits on a rack which allows the fat to drain away. This is only suitable for the tenderest cuts of meat as it is a fierce, dry heat. Steaks of 1 in/2.5 cm thickness will take 7-15 minutes, as for frying.

BRAISING AND POT ROASTING

*T*HIS is a very useful method for dealing with the less tender cuts of meat, such as the small lean joints of topside or silverside and blade or chuck steak. The meat is usually floured and fried all over first to seal it, then set on a bed of vegetables and herbs with enough liquid just to cover these. The pan is covered and the meat cooks in the gentle moist heat of the scented steam, absorbing flavours from the herbs and vegetables and giving its own flavours into the cooking juices, which make a rich sauce when the beef is served. *Sauerbraten* and *boeuf à la mode* are two of the most famous beef dishes

cooked by this method. Allow two to three hours in the oven at 170°C/325°F/gas mark 3.

CORNING

*C*ORNED beef has nothing to do with corn; it is so called because the coarse salt originally used in the preserving brine resembled grains of corn. Brisket, silverside and rump, in a piece, are suitable for this treatment, which is quite easy to do at home provided you have a nice large earthenware crock or other suitable non-metal container. Water, salt, sugar, bay leaves, peppercorns, mixed pickling spices and garlic make a bath in which the meat is immersed and weighted down for at least 36 hours. It can then be braised or boiled. Leftovers mixed with potatoes and beetroot make the famous red-flannel hash, or simple corn beef hash without the beetroot.

STEWING OR CASSEROLING

*W*ARMING and nourishing and full of appetising aromas which develop during the long slow cooking, some of the most famous beef dishes are based on stewing or casseroling recipes which use the least expensive cuts. For *boeuf bourguignon*, cooked in red wine, *boeuf gardien*, from the south of France and cooked in white wine, Hungarian goulash, rich with the colour and spicy flavour of sweet paprika, and *carbonnade* of beef, a Flemish dish cooked with beer, and even steak and kidney pie, you will find that shin and leg of beef, chuck and blade, neck and clod, skirt and flank are all suitable.

Cuts and Joints

W ITHIN EUROPE, there are wide regional variations in the way the carcase is butchered. In Britain, for example, the thick flank of beef has 27 different names.

English Cuts

BLADE BONE

F ROM the top forequarter of the carcase, the blade bone is a large, relatively lean joint which is usually boned and sold as chuck and blade steak. The meat has a little fat surrounding it and is well 'marbled' or streaked with thin seams of internal fat, which, when cooked, serves to baste and tenderise the meat. Chuck and blade are the best of the stewing meats and they can also be braised.

BRISKET

S OLD either on the bone or boned and rolled, the brisket comes from the lower part of the shoulder. It can be a fatty piece of meat, but it has a good flavour. Boiled, braised or pot roasted, it is sometimes salted or spiced first. Brisket is often served cold, thinly sliced.

CHUCK

S EE blade bone.

CLOD AND NECK

B OTH cuts of meat are from the neck part of the carcase, relatively lean, and usually cut up as stewing steak or stewing beef. Sometimes they are minced. They are leaner than chuck and blade beef and without the flavour of shin beef. Clod and neck, also called *sticking*, are amongst the most economic cuts of beef and make excellent stews provided you add plenty of flavouring and cook slowly.

FILLET

T HIS is a smallish (about 2-3 lb/900 g -1.35 kg) boneless joint of beef, the 'eye' taken from the inside of the rib bone or sirloin. It is extremely lean and tender and in prime specimens will be lightly marbled (this is particularly true of American prime beef). Although expensive, there is no waste on it and it cooks quickly, which makes it worth considering for a special occasion. It can be roasted whole in 20 minutes, or, for a more elaborate dish, beef Wellington, it can be wrapped in puff pastry and baked.

Fillet is also sliced to make steaks, called variously: fillet steak, *filet mignon*, Châteaubriand steak (although the whole roast fillet is properly called Châteaubriand as well) and tournedos.

The tail end of the fillet is narrow, tapers to a point and is unsuitable for cutting into steaks. You should be able to persuade your butcher to sell it to you much cheaper than the thick end of the fillet. It is excellent for cutting up into strips for stir-frying or for beef Stroganoff. My favourite way of preparing it is to trim it of all fat, chop it very finely, season it – with parsley, salt, pepper, Worcester sauce, capers, onions and whatever else takes my fancy – and serve it as *steak tartare*, raw chopped seasoned steak. It is very good. Fillet is the right cut to use for that other delicious and fashionable beef recipe from Italy, *carpaccio*, which is paper-thin slices of raw steak, laid in overlapping slices on a plate and dressed with virgin olive oil, sea salt, freshly ground black pepper, shavings of Parmesan cheese and a little greenery, which might be celery tops, peppery rocket or thin slices of raw artichoke.

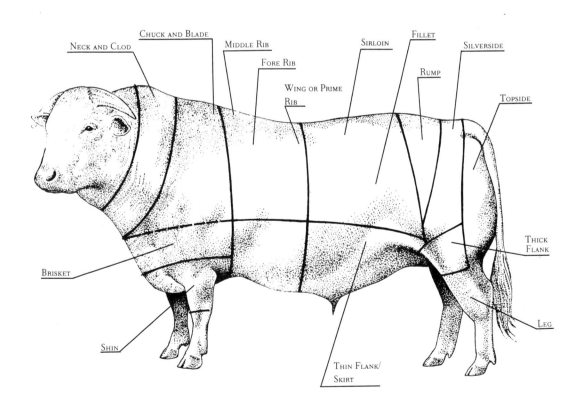

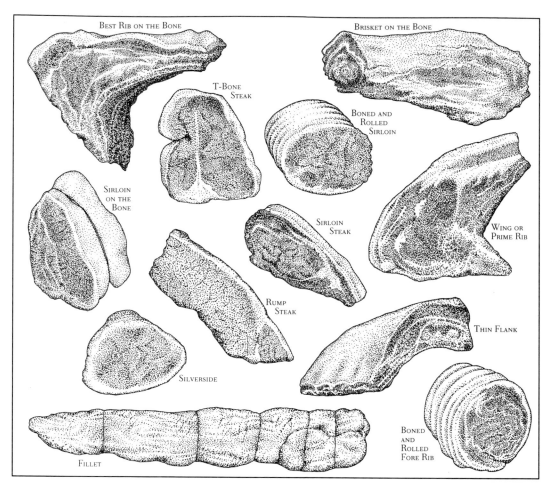

Best Rib on the Bone

Brisket on the Bone

T-Bone Steak

Boned and Rolled Sirloin

Sirloin on the Bone

Wing or Prime Rib

Sirloin Steak

Rump Steak

Thin Flank

Silverside

Boned and Rolled Fore Rib

Fillet

Flank

*T*HICK FLANK, or *top rump* as it is also known, comes from the hindquarter, the muscle at the front of the thigh. It is lean, like topside and silverside, and more suitable for pot-roasting and braising than roasting. When sliced, it can be fried slowly until tender.

Thin flank is the under muscle towards the belly. It can be rather fatty and gristly and is usually cut up or minced for stewing, and making pies or pâtés. When left whole, it can be salted or pickled and boiled.

Leg and shin

*T*HE leg comes from the back legs of the animal and the shin from the forelegs, which are slightly smaller than the legs. These are usually sold sawn into horizontal slices because the large shin bone is in the centre and surrounded by the lean tough leg muscle. Through this muscle run sinews and connective tissue which give the cooked meat its characteristically rich, flavoursome gelatinous quality. The bones contain marrow, which also adds to the richness of the stew. Shin and leg meat is perfect for stews and casseroles, and it is also used to make beef tea and stock.

Minced beef
*A*LSO called mince, this is beef which has been passed through the mincer once or twice. It is not always clear which part of the carcase has been minced, but as a general rule, if it is pale, it has a good deal of fat in it; if darker and more uniform in colour, it is probably leaner. There is much to be said for making your own mince by buying a piece of casseroling or stewing beef such as thin flank or neck, or the leaner chuck, trimming it of all fat (after all, you can always add extra fat in frying) and then mincing it in a table-clamped mechanical mincer or in a food processor. That way you decide how much fat your mince should have. Mince is ideal for cottage pie, meat sauce for *spaghetti* or *lasagna*, to mix with rice for stuffing peppers or aubergines, for making meatballs, meat loaf and hamburgers.

Rib
*T*HE *fore rib* or *best rib* is sold on the bone, or boned and *rolled* as a traditional roasting joint. It is a lean, tender joint.

The *middle rib*, which is the cut made up of the top and back ribs, comes between the fore rib and the blade bone; it is a large joint, usually divided into two, the top and back, and is often boned and rolled. They are lean joints, with less bone than the fore rib. The bone helps conduct heat to the centre of the joint and without it, the meat is best slow roasted. It can also be braised or pot roasted.

The *wing* or *prime rib* is one of the largest, most expensive and certainly one of the best roasting joints, with the perfect proportion of bone, lean meat and fat.

Rump
*I*F cut across the saddle with both back ends of sirloin, this becomes a large traditional joint, called a baron of beef. Now it is often sliced for steak.

Shin
*S*EE leg.

Silverside
*T*HIS is the lean, tough, outside thigh muscle. I do not find it roasts successfully unless you give it absolutely constant attention, basting it and checking the temperature. It is more successful when braised or pot roasted, as in the German *sauerbräten* or French *boeuf à la mode*. It can also be salted, spiced for corned beef and then boiled for pressing and slicing when cold.

Sirloin
*T*HIS is a fine majestic piece of beef for roasting, coming from the back or loin and therefore tenderest part of the animal. It is sold boned and rolled or on the bone. The lean tender fillet, which is the small 'eye' of meat inside the rib bone, can be removed for cooking separately.

Skirt
*Y*OU will be lucky to find skirt as it is usually the butcher's perk. It comes from the belly part of the animal: *thick* or *goose*

skirt, which is part of the inner muscle of the belly wall attached to the rump; *thin skirt*, which is the muscular part of the diaphragm, and *body skirt*, which is also part of the diaphragm. It can be a tricky cut to cook since it becomes extremely tough if not dealt with properly. The more you cook it the tougher it becomes unless you braise it very slowly. It can be treated like steak, cooked fast on a high heat and served rare when it is extremely tasty and juicy.

STEAKS

*C*HÂTEAUBRIAND – a thick cut from the fillet, which can be grilled or fried.

*E*NTRECÔTE – literally, between the ribs, this is a lean tender steak cut from the boneless sirloin, the name by which the steak is sometimes known. *Porterhouse* steaks are cut from the wing end of the sirloin and *T-bone* steaks cut right across the sirloin, to include the bone and the fillet.

*M*IGNON – a small steak cut from the fillet, sometimes called *filet mignon*.

*R*UMP steak – a large, long cut of steak taken from the top of the rump. It is tender and full of flavour when grilled or fried.

*T*OPSIDE – a lean boneless joint from the top of the inside hind leg, sometimes called *round* or *buttock* steak, it is inclined to be very dry as it is fine-grained with no marbling of fat. Braising or pot roasting is better than roasting.

French Cuts

AIGUILLETTE

*C*UT from the top of the rump or flank, this is the cut which the French consider to be the best for braising, being neither too fat nor too lean. It is used for *boeuf à la mode* as well as *boeuf braisé*; in each case it is usual to lard the beef by threading strips of thin pork back fat through the lean parts.

ALOYAU

*T*HE large joint from the loin, and marvellous for roasting for a special occasion.

CHÂTEAUBRIAND

*T*HE thick end of the fillet, this is usually roasted and served to two people.

CONTRE FILET

*F*ROM the sirloin, a tender and expensive roasting joint also called *faux filet*.

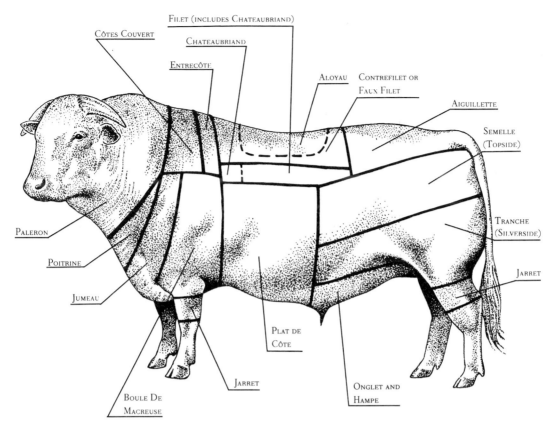

Côtes Couvert
Filet (includes Chateaubriand)
Chateaubriand
Entrecôte
Aloyau
Contrefilet or Faux Filet
Aiguillette
Semelle (Topside)
Paleron
Tranche (Silverside)
Poitrine
Jarret
Jumeau
Plat de Côte
Jarret
Onglet and Hampe
Boule De Macreuse

Côtes couvert

*T*HE rolled ribs are left on the bone as a roasting joint. Not as tender as the cuts from the sirloin, the *côtes couvert* are best roasted slowly rather than in a very hot oven.

Entrecôte

A THICK, juicy, well marbled steak, the *entrecôte* is cut, literally, from 'between the ribs'. Excellent for grilling, it is one of the classic French steaks, often served with a sauce such as *marchand de vin* or *à la bordelaise* with red wine and beef marrow, or simply with a flavoured butter as in *entrecôte grillé maître d'hotel*.

Filet

*T*HIS is the whole fillet taken along the backbone. It can be roasted whole, for about 15 mins per lb/455 g, usually larded, or it can be sliced into steaks.

Jarret

*T*HE shin is a very good cut of meat for slow cooked stews; the connective fibres break down to provide a rich gelatinous gravy.

Jumeau and boule de macreuse

*T*HESE cuts require slow cooking to break down the fibres; it should be noted too that they are lean cuts of meat.

Onglet and hampe

Cut from the breast or lower ribs of the carcase, the *onglet* and *hampe* are thick, juicy pieces of meat, somewhat like the skirt steak. Both are probably best braised as in a *carbonnade* or *daube* (see also steaks).

Paleron

Somewhere between the chuck and the neck, this is an excellent cut of meat for stewing or braising, whole or in pieces.

Plat de côte

Taken from between the ribs and brisket, the *plat de côte* is the equivalent of the short ribs or rolled ribs. Whether boned and rolled or on the bone, braise or pot roast it. One of the French cuts used for boiled beef.

Poitrine

A good lean shoulder cut, suitable for braising and pot roasting. Another of the French cuts used for boiled beef.

American Cuts

Brisket

The same cut as English brisket, this is one of the less tender but nonetheless tasty cuts of meat, inexpensive and an excellent meal when braised with herbs and vegetables and served with a good horseradish sauce. Brisket is also used for corned beef.

Chuck roast

The chuck, or shoulder quarter of the carcase (the blade in British cuts) is large and can yield a number of different cuts; inside chuck roll, chuck tender, blade pot roast or blade steak, boneless shoulder pot roast or boneless shoulder steak, chuck short ribs, arm pot roast or arm steak and Boston cut.

These are less tender cuts than the prime loin and rib cuts but are nevertheless extremely tasty and nutritious when properly cooked. A moist heat is required, which makes all these cuts suitable for braising and pot roasting as well as casseroling.

Foreshank

Cut from the shank or forelegs of the animal, this is the same as the English cut shin of beef. Use it for stocks, beef teas and well flavoured stews, but cook it slowly for a long time.

Rolled rib roast

The same cut of meat as the British fore rib, this has been taken off the bone, rolled and tied. Whether you choose this or the standing rib, bone in, is very much a matter of taste. Many people feel that the rolled boned joint is easier to carve, but perhaps it does not look quite as impressive as the standing rib.

ROUND ROAST

*T*HIS is the same cut of meat, the top of the hindquarter, which is used for the English cut of rump steak. With the bone, it is also called standing rump; without the bone it becomes *rolled rump*. From very tender, high quality beef, these joints can be roasted. Otherwise it is safer to pot roast or braise them.

SHORT RIBS

*F*ROM the short plate, rib or shoulder section of the carcase, short ribs are the equivalent of the English rolled rib joint. It is a good piece of meat for braising whole or in pieces.

STEAKS

*G*IVEN the Americans' reputation as steak eaters, the variety of cuts is no surprise. *Flank*, which has nothing to do with British flank although it is often seen on American menus as 'London Broil', is a narrow flat cut from the belly area below the loin. Inexpensive, boneless and easy to cook, it can be grilled or fried if from a tender animal.

From the loin come three types of steak: the *porterhouse*, cut from the large end, which has more tenderloin or fillet; the *club steak* from the small end, with no fillet; and the *T-bone*, which lies in between the two. Both the porterhouse and

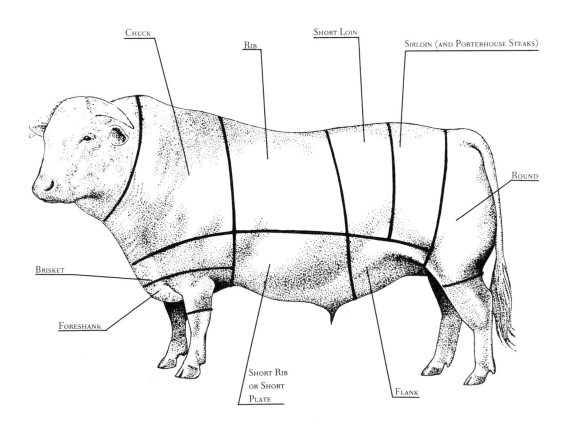

T-bone are usually cut about 2 in/5 cm thick and will feed two people. *Sirloin* steaks are tender, juicy prime meat, with the bone and an inner marbling as well as an outer layer of fat. Depending on where in the sirloin they are cut from, the steaks can be *pinbone, flatbone, wedgebone* or *boneless*. The New York *strip* steak is the boneless strip of loin left when the fillet or tenderloin is removed.

Rib steaks are large, usually one rib bone thick, and with quite a lot of internal marbling fat as well as an outer layer. The *Delmonico* or *Spencer* steak is the eye of the rib, with the bone, fat and coarser meat removed. Cut 1-2 in/ 2.5-5 cm thick, it is treated like fillet or tenderloin.

Finally, *round* steak, sliced from the top of the hindquarters, is very tasty but not very tender. It is suitable for panfrying, as in the so-called Swiss steak, in which flour and seasoning are pounded into the meat before it is fried with onions and then cooked very slowly until tender enough to eat with a fork. *Top round* steak is a more tender, prime cut towards the rump.

Beef (or Ox) Offal and Trimmings

THE BEEF animal and the ox are not different animals.
Ox is the term derived from Anglo-Saxon; beef the term
derived from Norman French.

CHEEK
NOT often found for sale any more, ox cheek is inexpensive and nutritious but requires slow cooking. It needs to be carefully trimmed and washed.

HEART
A VERY large organ, ox heart can be stuffed and braised, but it is best cut up or sliced and casseroled. The meat is dark, and more fibrous than other offal.

KIDNEY
DIVIDED into many small lobes, the whole kidney weighs about 1 lb/455 g. It has a strong flavour, which can be diminished by soaking in milk or water (or water and lemon juice) for half an hour before cooking. First, prepare it by removing any fat (this is suet and thus valuable for pastry making; you can grate it yourself after chilling it and then store it), peeling off the membrane and

cutting out all of the core and gristle. Ox kidney should only really be used for slow cooked dishes.

Liver

*C*OARSE, dark and strongly flavoured, this is an acquired taste. Like all liver it is highly nutritious, being rich in iron and protein. To minimise the flavour and texture, soak the slices or pieces of liver in milk overnight. It is best suited to braising or casseroling and it is as well to add other powerful flavouring such as pungent herbs or curry spices, and wine or cider for cooking it in.

Marrowbone

*M*ARROW is a soft, rich, fatty substance contained in the large shin and leg bones of the animal. It is a delicacy used for enriching sauces, for serving on toast or, traditionally, for eating with a long silver spoon from the roasted bones, served wrapped in a napkin. Your butcher will often give away marrow bones if you are buying your meat there and will saw them into lengths if asked. They are well worth having.

Oxtail

*O*NE of the best bargains on the butcher's counter, oxtail makes some of my very favourite winter dishes: oxtail soups, stews and terrines. The tail is usually chopped across into chunks. The thick bones can be used in a casserole, the small pieces added to the stock pot. The meat is richly flavoured and the gelatine released from the connective tissues enriches it even further after long, slow cooking.

Tongue

*T*HIS usually weighs 3-4 lb/1.35-1.8 kg, but can be more. Sold fresh or salted, the tongue is tough and needs soaking before cooking for 2-3 hours if fresh or 8-10 hours if salted. Cooking time will be about an hour or so for a salted tongue, otherwise long slow cooking is needed.

Tripe

*T*RIPE, from the ox family only, is the lining of the first three stomachs. It is wet, white and slithery and usually an acquired taste. Traditional tripe recipes are found all over the world – Mexico, Iberia, Taiwan, Normandy, Lyons and Lancashire, for example. In Britain almost all the tripe we buy has been scraped, bleached and pre-cooked, only requiring a further hour of cooking.

Roast Sirloin of Beef

If you can, use chestnut flour to dredge on the joint as this produces a delicious gravy. If there is clearly going to be plenty of meat for everyone, you may wish to cut off the flank end of the joint and use it in a casserole or for stock.

Serves 6-8 (plus leftovers)

1 sirloin of beef, weighing
6-8 lb/2.7-3.6 kg
1-2 tbsp olive oil
3-4 tbsp flour

salt
freshly ground black pepper
¼ pt/140 ml boiling water

*P*REHEAT the oven to 220°C/425°F, gas mark 7. Trim off any surplus pieces of fat and lay the sirloin, skin side up, on a rack in a roasting pan. Brush the olive oil over the meat, and allow any surplus to drip down into the roasting pan. Lightly dredge the upper surface of the meat with half the flour and some salt and pepper. Put it into the top half of the oven.

When the meat has been seared all over, after 20-25 minutes, quickly remove it from the oven and dredge with the rest of the flour and a little more salt and pepper. Return the meat to the oven. After 10 minutes, open the oven door and pour a third of the boiling water into the roasting pan. This will mix with any of the flour that has drifted into the roasting pan and browned to make the beginning of the gravy. Close the oven door and continue cooking the beef for the required amount of time.

When the sirloin is done, remove it from the oven to a carving dish and keep it warm. Pour off as much as possible of the fat in the roasting pan. Add most of the rest of the boiling water and stir it well to mix with the cooking juices and scrape up any bits stuck to the bottom of the roasting pan. Place the roasting pan on the stove and boil the gravy until it reduces by half. Pour in the last of the boiling water and boil again until thoroughly mixed and further reduced. Season the gravy and pour it into a heated jug.

For a more elaborate gravy, replace the water with red wine, preferably a decent one and ideally one made from the cabernet grape, which retains a good red colour when cooked (unlike many other red wines).

PLACE the joint on a board or suitable platter, with the backbone to the right. Loosen the meat from the bone by inserting a sharp knife between the meat and the backbone leading into the rib bone. Carve thin slices down to the rib.

Then turn the roast over and carve slices of fillet across the grain. If the joint is particularly large, the fillet can be removed and served cold the next day. Alternatively, you can remove it before cooking and prepare a separate dish from it as described on p.65.

TO ROAST POTATOES WITH THE SIRLOIN

CHOOSE main crop potatoes, that is 'old' rather than 'new' potatoes. Peel and cut them into even pieces about 1½ in/4 cm thick, allowing 6 oz/170 g prepared potatoes per person.

Quite simply place the pieces of potato in the roasting pan with the joint and roast for 50-60 minutes.

YORKSHIRE PUDDING

2 size-3 eggs
½ pt/280 ml milk
4 oz/110 g flour
½ tsp salt
1 tbsp dripping from the roasting pan

BEAT the eggs with the milk. Gradually beat in the flour and the salt until you have a smooth batter, then let it stand for 30-40 minutes. Place the dripping in a pie dish or other shallow roasting pan and place it in the top of the oven to heat up.

Pour the batter into the hot roasting tin and bake for 20-25 minutes until the pudding is well risen and golden. Cut it into squares and serve either before the meat course, with gravy, or alongside the meat.

BOEUF À LA FICELLE

This classic French dish makes an unusual and very simple
Sunday lunch. It is one of those dishes best carved and
arranged in the kitchen. Poaching turns the meat rather
grey, although it is an appetising rosy pink when sliced.
Serve it on a platter with a selection of boiled baby
vegetables, watercress, Maldon salt, mustard, horseradish,
gherkins and other pickles. Fillet or sirloin are the
tenderest cuts to use for this treatment. Rump will be
tougher but has plenty of flavour.

SERVES 6

*fillet or sirloin of beef, or rump
steak, weighing about
2 lb/900 g, in a piece
1 carrot
2 celery stalks
1 small turnip
1 onion
4 cloves
2 tsp sea salt
12 black peppercorns
1 bay leaf*

Tie the meat into a neat shape with sufficient string to suspend the meat from the handle of a spoon laid across the top of the pan. The meat should not touch the bottom of the pan, but should be fully covered by the water. Test this before you start to cook.

Peel, trim and slice the vegetables. Put them into the saucepan with the cloves and seasonings and enough water to cover the meat, but do not put the meat in yet. Bring the water to a full rolling boil and then add the meat. Bring the water back to the boil and then turn down the heat to the merest simmer. Poach the meat for 15 minutes per 1 lb/455 g.

Have a hot serving dish and all the accompaniments ready for the cooked meat. Before slicing it, trim all external fat from the meat.

CARPETBAG STEAKS

Now accepted as part of the 'classical' Australian culinary repertoire, the steak and oysters combination is probably rooted in English cookery. Hannah Glasse has a brief recipe for a leg of mutton stuffed with oysters and roasted. Steak and oyster pie, or pudding, was also a favourite English dish.

I ate the dish for the first time only recently, on my first visit to Pomegranates, Patrick Gwynn-Jones's welcoming cellar on the Embankment. Both experiences were long overdue and I am now making up for lost time. The steaks can be cooked individually, with a crisp, caramelised outer coating from a hot grill or frying pan and a tender pink middle into which the oysters have been inserted – or the fillet can be cooked in a piece. It makes a glamorous (and expensive) main course. Use the middle or thick end of the fillet, not the tail end.

SERVES 6

*fillet of beef, weighing about
2 lb/900 g, in a piece
12 oysters
freshly ground black pepper*

*pinch of mace
1 oz/30 g butter
1 tbsp olive oil
salt*

USING a sharp knife, make a deep slit down the length of the fillet, taking care not to separate it into two halves. Remove the oysters from the shells, sprinkle each with a little mace and pepper and stuff the fillet with them, spreading them out over the length of the fillet. Fold over tightly, so that the oysters are enclosed, and tie the roll round with string five times, at regular intervals (each steak will be formed by cutting between the strings).

Heat the butter and oil in a large frying pan and brown the meat all over. Transfer to the top half of a preheated oven and roast at 230°C/450°F/gas mark 8 for 15-20 minutes. Remove from the oven, cover loosely and let the meat relax for 15-20 minutes. Carve into six steaks.

This really needs no sauce, although you could serve a pat of herb butter with it. I like to serve it with a salad of young spinach leaves, watercress and rocket if I can get it. Carpetbag steaks would also be good with superlative chips or creamy mashed potatoes (see p. 352).

FILLET OF BEEF WITH ORIENTAL FLAVOURS

Warm or cold, but not from the refrigerator, this dish is full of flavour, and hints of Thailand and Malaysia. Serve it as part of an oriental meal or as a starter. It is particularly good with chilled glass noodles – the transparent ones made from mung beans. Hot, it is good served with rice.

A foray to your nearest Chinatown, or indeed a well-stocked branch of one of the high-street multiples, should provide you with the herbs, spices and condiments.

SERVES 4-6

fillet of beef, taken from the tail end, weighing about 1 lb/455 g, in a piece
For the marinade:
⅛ pt/70 ml coconut milk (see p. 227)
2 tbsp soy sauce
1 tbsp honey
1 tbsp rice vinegar or sherry vinegar
1 tbsp toasted sesame oil

2 or 3 green or red chillis, seeded and thinly sliced
2 stalks of lemon grass, thinly sliced
1 sprig of lime leaves or lemon verbena leaves
2 or 3 cloves of garlic, peeled and crushed

4 spring onions, trimmed and thinly sliced
1 in/2.5 cm fresh ginger, peeled and grated
1 tsp ground cumin
½ tsp ground coriander seeds
½ tsp ground cinnamon
¼ tsp ground allspice
For garnishing: *fresh coriander leaves and basil leaves, and green or red chillis*

*T*RIM any fat and sinews from the meat and put it in a bowl. Combine all the remaining ingredients, pour over the meat, cover and leave to marinate in the refrigerator overnight.

When you are ready to cook the meat, make sure that it has been brought back to room temperature. Heat a well-seasoned heavy iron frying pan until it is very hot. Remove the meat from the marinade, dry it very thoroughly and, if necessary, lightly oil the pan before you

put the meat in to stop it sticking. Press the meat well down with a spatula and fry for 10 minutes. Turn it over and fry until done to your liking. Remove the meat from the pan, cover it and leave it for 10 minutes or so before slicing it thinly and obliquely.

Meanwhile, make a sauce by boiling up the marinade, adding more coconut milk or a splash of rice wine if you wish. The meat can also be roasted at 200°C/400°F/gas mark 6 for 15 minutes.

BEEF STEAK TAGALOG

When I was guest cook at the Manila Peninsula Hotel, this was my favourite lunch dish in the chefs' dining room, where we would eat before service. Sourness is a very important element in Filipino cooking and there are many different words to describe it, depending on the type of sourness. As well as lemon juice the cook has coconut vinegar, palm vinegar, green mangoes, tamarinds and the small calamansi or Filipino lime. Here, ordinary lime juice can be substituted with no loss of flavour or authenticity.

In the Philippines, steak tagalog is traditionally served with garlic flavoured rice. It is a perfect combination.

SERVES 4

*4 beef rump steaks, each
    weighing 4-6 oz/110-170 g
2 mild onions, peeled and thinly
    sliced
3 tbsp soy sauce
2-3 tbsp fresh lime juice
freshly ground black pepper
1 tbsp groundnut or sunflower oil
3-4 tbsp water*

TRIM any fat and gristle from the meat and place it in a shallow dish on top of a rough quarter of the sliced onion. Mix the soy sauce, lime juice and pepper and sprinkle this over the meat. Cover it with a few more onion rings and leave to marinate for an hour or two, turning once or twice.

Heat the oil in a frying pan. Remove the steak from the marinade, letting the juices drip back into the dish, and fry it with the remaining onion until done to your liking.

Remove from the pan and keep warm. Pour the marinade and the marinated onions into the pan and cook, scraping up any residues on the bottom of the pan. Add the water, bring to the boil, sieve and serve the sauce poured over the steak and onions. Remove the meat from the pan and keep it covered in a warm place while you finish making the sauce.

FILLET STEAK WITH BALSAMIC VINEGAR

Modena is the home of balsamic vinegar, one of the world's most special condiments. Made from grape must and aged, in a solera system, somewhat like that used for sherry, in a succession of small barrels made of different fine woods, each barrel smaller than the one of the previous year, it is a complex, sweet yet sharp, richly flavoured vinegar. Some – the real thing – is very costly indeed and to be used sparingly, by the drop. The commercial preparations bear some resemblance to it, but cost only a few pounds rather than tens of pounds. An excellent ingredient for deglazing the pan after cooking liver, kidneys or chops, it is also used in Modena's best restaurants for this dish, *filetto ai balsamico*. This makes an instant yet luxurious main course.

SERVES 4

4 beef fillet steaks, each weighing
   4 oz/110 g
1 tbsp extra virgin olive oil
salt
freshly ground black pepper
2 tbsp balsamic vinegar

TRIM any fat from the meat. Heat the olive oil in a heavy frying pan and fry the meat on both sides until it is done to your liking.

Season and place on serving plates. Put the vinegar in the pan, boil and scrape up any residues and spoon on to the steaks. Serve immediately.

MARINATED GRILLED SKIRT STEAK

Meat that has undergone tenderising from a commercial product is very disagreeable, as you will know if you come across it in restaurants. However, a quick dip in pineapple juice, which contains the powerful tenderising enzyme papain, can do wonders for a piece of beef. I once had some lightly smoked beef fillet which had been marinated in pineapple juice. That seemed rather a pointless exercise given that the cut was naturally so tender, but I have adapted the idea and used it for skirt. This is an extraordinarily flavoursome piece of meat, but is always chewy and sometimes frankly tough. The secret is to cook it quickly and serve it rare since the longer it cooks the tougher it becomes. I think it is best to buy one large thick piece of meat and slice it for serving. A ridged cast-iron grill that rests on two rings on the hob is excellent for fast grilling, imitating the appearance, if not the flavour, of the charcoal grill.

SERVES 4-6

1½-2 lb/680-900 g beef, either thick skirt or goose skirt, in a piece
2 mild onions, peeled and thinly sliced

¼ pt/140 ml fresh unsweetened pineapple juice
4 juniper berries, crushed
freshly ground black pepper

REMOVE any thick membranes from the meat. Put a layer of onions in a bowl, the meat on top and another layer of onions on top. Pour over the juice and scatter on the juniper and pepper. Leave for 40 minutes, turning the meat once.

Heat the grill and, when it is very hot, remove the meat from the marinade, dry it thoroughly and grill it for 6-8 minutes on each side, turning it carefully once.

Remove from the grill and allow to rest in a warm place before carving it.

A little sauce can be made by frying the onion in butter until soft, adding the spices, pineapple juice and a little beef stock and cooking for several minutes while the beef is under the grill. Force the mixture through a sieve for a thick oniony sauce, or simply allow the liquid to strain through for a liquid one.

FOUR-PEPPER STEAK

A recent forage in my store cupboard yielded several jars
of pink peppercorns which date from the hey-day of that
fad for pink peppercorns placed at strategic points on
every white octagonal plate. I'm glad I kept them because,
fashionability aside, they do have a very good flavour.
Here they are combined with Szechuan peppercorns, black
pepper and green peppercorns, which are available fresh,
dried or in brine. This makes a quick tasty dinner for one.
If you want to serve it to two or more people, multiply the
ingredients accordingly. Fillet, sirloin or rump steak can be
used.

QUANTITIES PER PERSON

1 beef steak
*½ tsp each green and pink
    peppercorns (dried or in
    brine), crushed*
*pinch of crushed Szechuan
    peppercorn*
*½ tsp coarsely ground black
    pepper*

½ oz/15 g unsalted butter
2 tbsp red wine, port or Madeira
2 tbsp beef stock
1 tbsp double cream (optional)
salt
*fresh chives or parsley, chopped
    (optional)*

TRIM any excess fat from the steak. Mix the ground and crushed peppercorns together and press them into both sides of the steak. Melt the butter in a heavy frying pan and, when hot, fry the steak, turning it once, carefully, until done to your liking. A ¾ in/2 cm thick steak will cook in 2½ minutes on each side for rare meat, 4 minutes a side for medium-done meat, and 7 minutes each side for well-done meat.

Remove the meat and keep it warm while you deglaze the pan with wine and add the stock. Let it bubble down to 1-2 tablespoons, then stir in the cream, if using it, and season to taste. Some chives or parsley can be chopped and added with the beef stock or used as a garnish.

CARPACCIO

Said to have been invented in Harry's Bar in Venice, *carpaccio* is now a firm favourite in restaurants around Italy and elsewhere too. Although originally a description of a raw beef dish, *carpaccio* is now applied to salmon, tuna fish, scallops – indeed anything which can be served raw. I do not look forward to the day when we will be offered carpaccio of cucumber, but I fear it will happen. Already I have seen orange segments described on a menu as orange fillets.

One of the best buys for this dish is a tail end of fillet, which is usually cheaper than a middle cut. I slice *carpaccio* from the thick part and then use the rest for beef Stroganoff or a stir-fried beef dish (for example, the recipe on page 73). In order to achieve paper-thin slices, firm up the meat in the freezer first.

SERVES 4 AS A FIRST COURSE

*8-10 oz/230-280 g paper-thin
    slices of beef fillet
4 tbsp extra virgin olive oil
freshly ground black pepper
piece of fresh Parmesan cheese
small handful of watercress or
    rocket leaves, or 2 firm sweet
    celery stalks
coarse sea-salt*

*I*F not sliced thin enough, the meat can be flattened by rolling between two sheets of cling film. Arrange it in a single layer, with the slices only slightly overlapping, on large chilled dinner plates. Brush them all over with olive oil and grind black pepper lightly over the top.

Shave thin curls of Parmesan over the meat, then scatter a little greenery on top. If using celery, string it first then slice into transparently thin slices. The final touch is a few shards of coarse sea-salt on the meat. Serve the *carpaccio* immediately.

BEEF STROGANOFF

A dinner party favourite – one might almost say cliché –
in the sixties and seventies, along with smoked mackerel
pâté, potted kipper and crème caramel, this remains a
good stand-by dish, tasty and quick to cook if you do not
have a great deal of time and good served with quickly
cooked rice or broad noodles. Use the inexpensive tail end
of fillet steak or rump steak for it.

SERVES 4

1 lb/455 g fillet or rump beef
* steak*
2 oz/60 g butter, or 4 tbsp olive
* oil or sunflower oil*
2 tbsp finely chopped, trimmed
* shallots*
¼ pt/140 ml dry white wine
¼ pt/140 ml double cream
2 tsp lemon juice
seasoning
To garnish:
1-2 tbsp finely chopped parsley

Cut the meat into 2×½ in/5×1 cm strips. Heat half the butter or oil in a heavy frying pan and, a handful at a time, brown the steak strips all over on a high heat, adding more butter or oil as necessary. They should remain underdone inside. Put the meat in a sieve over a bowl as it is cooked.

Cook the shallots in the pan until soft and drain off the fat. Add the wine and reduce to a third. Add the cream and reduce the mixture until you have a thickish sauce. Pour in any meat juices and boil briefly. Add the lemon juice and seasoning with the pan off the boil and finally stir in the browned beef. Spoon into a heated serving dish and sprinkle with parsley.

STIR-FRIED BEEF

Stir-frying is a marvellous method of cooking when you're in a hurry: it takes longer, almost, to write this recipe than it does to cook it. Its other great advantage is the preservation of fresh flavours and colours because there is relatively short contact with heat. Have all your *mise-en-place* done before you start work. Use the tail-end of fillet steak, which is a prime tender meat, but because it is such an odd shape has remained inexpensive. Or perhaps it is better to say that it should be: if it becomes sought after, as so often happens with such cuts, the price is likely to rise!

SERVES 4 (OR MORE IF SERVED ALONGSIDE SEVERAL OTHER DISHES AS PART OF AN ORIENTAL-STYLE MEAL)

1 lb/455 g tail end of beef fillet, cut into thin strips
1 tbsp groundnut oil
2 carrots, peeled and cut into thin slices, or, if small and tender, simply stripped with a potato peeler
2 leeks, trimmed and thinly sliced on the bias

3 oz/85 g bean sprouts, blanched for 2 minutes
1 or 2 cloves of garlic, peeled and very thinly sliced (optional)
¼ lb/110 g Chinese leaves, sliced
2 tbsp dry Amontillado sherry or rice wine
1-2 tsp soy sauce
freshly ground black pepper

HEAT the oil in a wok or frying pan and when sizzling, not smoking, add the beef, stirring continuously over a high heat until just brown. Test the oil for sizzle point by dropping in a small cube of bread. The oil will foam and sizzle when it is hot enough. Add the carrots and leeks and cook for 2-3 minutes, still stirring all the time. Add the bean sprouts, garlic and Chinese leaves and cook for 2 minutes more. Then add the sherry, soy sauce and pepper, continuing to cook in the same way.

When the juices are bubbling nicely, serve immediately. Steamed or boiled rice is a perfect companion but this is also good with broad noodles, cracked wheat or rice.

SWEET BEEF POT ROAST

Rum and *panela* or palm sugar are the striking ingredients in this recipe from Cartagena on Colombia's Caribbean coast. If you cannot get palm sugar, molasses can be substituted, which will give the dish a similar caramelly flavour. The beef is marinated for several hours or can be left overnight.

SERVES 8

1 piece of top rump of beef (or
other suitable cut for pot
roasting), weighing 2 lb/900 g
3 onions, peeled and grated
1/2 tsp crushed allspice
4 whole cloves
1 bay leaf
1 tsp salt
2 tsp freshly ground black pepper
2 tbsp wine vinegar
4 tbsp molasses sugar
4 tbsp water
2 fl oz/60 ml rum
2 fl oz/60 ml red wine

TIE the beef into a round if this has not already been done. Leave only a very thin covering of fat.

Rub the meat all over with the onions, spices, salt, pepper and vinegar. Stick the cloves and bay leaf into the meat. Cover and marinate for several hours or overnight.

Mix the sugar and water and dissolve in a flameproof casserole that will just take the meat comfortably. Set it over the heat and turn the meat all over in the syrup. Add the rum, wine and any juices from the meat. Cover and cook very slowly until the meat is tender enough to cut with a fork. Add water from time to time to keep it moist.

This richly flavoured meat would be served with coconut rice in Cartagena (see p. 350). Mashed potatoes (see p. 352) would also go very well with it.

BEEF RENDANG

When we ate with Aziza Ali, one of Singapore's famous cooks, she was keen for us to try as many dishes as possible. I was particularly taken with this dark dry beef curry, which is, if anything, even better when heated up the next day. Make the coconut milk as described on p. 227 or buy it in tins or packets. Together with a platter of rice, a lentil curry, some curried vegetables, pickles, chutney and the Malaysian chicken curry on p. 227, you have a feast. Use one of the cuts of beef that responds best to long, slow cooking; flank or shin would be ideal.

SERVES 6

2 lb/900 g beef, in a piece
1 tbsp groundnut oil
5 cloves of garlic
2 medium onions
red chillis to taste
1 in/2.5 cm fresh ginger
1 in/2.5 cm freshly grated turmeric root or 1 tsp turmeric powder

1 tsp freshly grated galangal or ½ tsp dried galangal
1½ pt/850 ml coconut milk (see p. 227)
1 bay leaf or piece of pandanus leaf
2 stalks of lemon grass, shredded
salt

REMOVE any excess fat or gristle from the meat. Cut the meat into 2 in/5 cm chunks. Peel and chop the garlic and onions. Carefully seed and thinly slice the chillis and peel and chop the ginger. Grind the garlic, onion, chillis and ginger, turmeric and galangal in a mortar or food processor.

Heat a deep frying pan and smear it lightly with the oil. Seal the meat all over and stir in the spice mixture until the meat is well coated and the spices are releasing their aroma. Cover with coconut milk. Add the leaf and the lemon grass, and simmer uncovered for 1½-2 hours. Season the meat with salt towards the end of cooking, but use a light hand, as the mixture cooks almost dry and the sauce is very concentrated. The mixture will be dark and smell extremely good. The oil begins to separate from the coconut milk.

Cook for a further 30 minutes or so, stirring frequently to stop the meat catching, and until the oil and juices have been almost reabsorbed into the meat.

BEEF CARBONNADE

A robust, well-flavoured casserole cooked in beer and topped with triangles of bread rather than a pie crust, the *carbonnade* has its origins in Flanders. Beer is, I think, a better accompanying drink than wine.

SERVES 4-6

1½ lb/680 g braising beef, such
   as blade
1 tbsp olive oil
3 onions, peeled and sliced
2 tsp flour (plain or wholemeal,
   if you prefer)
⅓ pt/200 ml beef stock
2 tsp light muscovado sugar
1 tbsp sherry vinegar

⅓ pt/200 ml beer (brown ale or
   bitter rather than lager for
   preference)
salt
pepper
For the topping:
slices of crusty bread
garlic or parsley butter

Cut the meat into 2 in/5 cm squares about ½ in/1 cm thick. Fry in the olive oil until browned on all sides and put to one side. Fry the onions until nicely browned, which is what will give the casserole its rich colour, but do not allow them to burn. Scatter on the flour and scrape up any bits that have caramelised on the bottom of the pan. Gradually add the stock, stirring until you have a smooth sauce. Stir in the sugar, vinegar and beer. Bring it to the boil.

Put layers of meat and onions in a suitable casserole. Pour on the sauce, cover and cook for about 1½-2 hours at 180°C/ 350°F, gas mark 4. Season with salt and pepper.

Prepare the topping by cutting rounds or triangles of bread and buttering them (on one side only) with garlic or parsley butter. Remove the lid from the meat, and cover with the bread, butter side up. Return the casserole to the oven, now set at 200°C/400°F, gas mark 6, for 20 minutes or until the toasts are nicely browned.

CHILLI CON CARNE

Fashionable versions of chilli use venison. But succulent shin of beef cooked to a melting tenderness has as much flavour and texture, to tell the truth. Preparation needs to be started the day before required and two days is not too much because the chilli improves with a little keeping.

By the way, I am of the persuasion that *chilli con carne* should have beans with it; others believe that beans are a heresy. They can be left out of the recipe if you are of the second opinion. This also cuts down the preparation and cooking time. I also think that finely diced beef gives a better finished texture than minced beef.

SERVES 6-8

1½ lb/680 g boneless shin of beef
1 lb/455 g red kidney beans (dry weight)
1 large onion, peeled and chopped

2 tbsp olive oil
1 tbsp paprika
½ tsp cayenne pepper (or more to taste)
2-3 tsp ground cumin
2-3 tsp ground coriander seed

6 oz/170 g peeled, seeded and chopped tomatoes
½ pt/280 ml beef stock
salt
chopped fresh parsley or coriander

*P*UT the beans in a pan of water, bring to the boil and boil vigorously for 10-15 minutes. This rids the beans of certain toxins found on the skin of red and black beans to which some people are particularly susceptible. Drain the beans, cover with plenty of cold water and soak them for about 8 hours, or overnight. If you cover the beans with plenty of boiling water, 2-3 hours' soaking time will be sufficient. Drain the beans once more.

In a large flameproof casserole, fry the onion in the olive oil until golden brown. Dice the beef very small. Brown the meat all over then stir in the spices until the meat is well coated. Add the tomatoes, stock and beans, and then add enough water to reach the top of the ingredients. Bring to the boil, cover and simmer for 3-4 hours or cook in a very low oven.

Season towards the end of cooking, after the beans have softened, and stir in fresh parsley or coriander just before serving. Rice or bread are the things to serve with chilli, and perhaps a bowl of yoghurt to cool your mouth if you have made a hot one.

GULYAS

On our first visit to Vienna one February, this is the dish
we went in search of – rich, warming and filling goulash. I
always make more than I need for one meal so that there
will be enough for goulash soup later in the week. Use
Hungarian paprika if you can, for real authenticity,
choosing one of the sweet (ie mild) ones rather than
fiercely hot ones since what is important here is the
colour; the hot paprika can be used in place of the chilli or
cayenne. Since I do not like caraway seeds, I prefer to
substitute dill seeds.

SERVES 6 (PLUS LEFTOVERS)

*3 lb/1.35 kg braising beef,
such as flank or chuck
1 lb/455 g onions, peeled
and sliced
1 tbsp grapeseed oil
2 tbsp sweet paprika*

*2 tsp flour
pinch of chilli powder or
cayenne pepper, or hot
Hungarian paprika
1 tsp dill seeds
¼ pt/140 ml beef or veal
stock (see p. 344)*

*small can of tomatoes, approx
7 oz/200 g (optional)
¼ pt/140 ml red wine
salt
pepper*

FRY the onions in the oil in a large
flameproof casserole until golden
brown. Remove and put to one side.

Cut the meat into 2 in/5 cm pieces and
brown them in the oil. Sprinkle on the
paprika, flour, chilli and dill and stir in
well, continuing to cook. Pour on a little
stock and vigorously scrape up any bits
stuck to the bottom. Add the rest of the
stock, tomatoes, and the wine.

Bring to the boil, cover and simmer
very gently for about 3 hours, seasoning
after 2 hours. Sometimes potatoes are
peeled, cut up and added to the goulash
about half an hour or so before the end of
the cooking.

Serve with boiled or steamed potatoes, broad noodles or dumplings.

To make a *Goulash Soup* from the leftovers, cut up the meat into smaller
pieces together with any potatoes. Put
them and the gravy in a saucepan, together with a pint or so of stock. Stir
well, bring to the boil and simmer for 15
minutes. Serve with soured cream and
chopped parsley.

BRAISED BEEF WITH CHESTNUTS AND CELERY

A lovely warming autumn dish to cook when the first
frosts have given the new season's celery a good sweet
flavour and the glowing braziers for roasting chestnuts in
the street warm your hands on a cold day. It is also a
good-tempered dish, which will look after itself once
cooked in the oven, and so is excellent to cook for large
numbers. Serve it with jacket potatoes which will cook
alongside the casserole. Guinness, cider or brown ale seem
to me to be more appropriate than wine for cooking this
robust, earthy dish and indeed for drinking with it.

SERVES 6-8

3 lb/1.35 kg braising beef,
   either flank, blade or
   chuck, in a piece
2 dozen fresh chestnuts, peeled
2 rashers of unsmoked streaky
   bacon, rinded and cut into
   strips

1 oz/30 g butter
1 tbsp sunflower or groundnut
   oil
2 onions, peeled and sliced
1 tbsp flour
1/2 pt/280 ml Guinness, dry
   cider or brown ale
1/2 pt/280 ml beef stock

juice of 1 orange
1 tsp grated orange zest
salt
pepper
2 celery hearts
To garnish:
   chopped fresh parsley for
   garnishing

TRIM the meat of any fat and gristle
and cut it into 1½ in/4 cm cubes.
Peel the chestnuts by cutting a cross in
their flat sides, simmering them in water
for 8-10 minutes to soften their skins, and
peeling them while still warm. Brown
the beef and bacon together in the oil and
butter in a large flameproof casserole,
then remove them. Fry the onions until
just golden in the same fat and put the

meat back in the casserole. Sprinkle with
flour and stir to coat the meat. Pour on
the beer or cider and stock; add the
orange juice and zest. Bring to the boil,
add the chestnuts and season lightly.

Cover and cook at 170°C/325°F, gas
mark 3 for about an hour. Trim and slice
the celery and add it to the casserole.
Cook for a further hour or so. Serve from
the casserole, sprinkled with parsley.

BEEF IN BEAUJOLAIS

Although you can use new Beaujolais for this dish, and indeed serve the same to drink with the beef, a more stable single village Beaujolais is a better bet. Try a Fleurie or a Morgon. I like to use shin of beef for this, cooking it very slowly so that the connective tissues break down and release lots of lip-sticking juices. The marrow from the shin bone increases the richness and flavour.

SERVES 6

4 lb/1.85 kg shin of beef, sawn into 1½ in/4 cm slices
1 tbsp groundnut or sunflower oil
1 onion, peeled and sliced

2 large carrots, peeled and cut into batons
1 tsp finely grated orange zest
2 tbsp orange juice
1 clove
1 bay leaf

1 bottle/750 ml Beaujolais wine (see above)
salt
pepper
To garnish:
    a little finely chopped parsley

BROWN the meat in the oil heated in a heavy frying pan. Transfer it to a casserole. Fry the onion until golden brown in the same oil and put it with the beef, together with the carrots, orange zest and juice, clove and bay leaf. Pour the wine into the frying pan, bring to the boil, scrape up any cooking residues and reduce by a quarter. Pour it over the beef.

Cover and cook just below the centre of the oven at 150°C/300°F, gas mark 2 for 3½-4 hours, or at 180°C/350°F, gas mark 4 for 2-2½ hours. Season after a couple of hours. Remove from the oven and take out the beef bones, taking care to leave the marrow behind in the casserole, and remove the bay leaf.

If you prefer a thicker sauce, you can strain the juices into a saucepan and reduce them to taste or thicken them with a little flour worked into some softened butter (*beurre manié*, p. 345), cooking it into the sauce for 5 minutes or so before reuniting it with the meat. Serve from the casserole, scattering the meat with a little finely chopped parsley or a sprig or two of greenery, if you wish.

Barolo and Chinon are two other very good red wines that can happily give their name to a shin of beef casserole and be drunk with it too. I think potatoes are the perfect partner for beef. In this case creamy mashed potatoes or potatoes baked in their jackets fit the bill.

STEAK AND KIDNEY PIE

This English classic is a simple everyday dish that can be prepared in advance. Once the meat is cooking, it will look after itself and timing is not crucial. The pastry can be home-made or bought and the meat can be cooked and refrigerated overnight. All that remains to be done is to roll out the pastry, assemble and bake the pie, which in all should take no more than 45 minutes.

SERVES 6-8

2 lb/900 g lean beef, such as blade, chuck or topside
½ lb/230 g ox kidney, soaked in milk for an hour
1 oz/30 g flour
½ tsp freshly ground black pepper

¼ tsp salt
pinch of ground mace
2 tbsp sunflower or groundnut oil
1 onion, peeled and sliced
½ pt/280 ml beef stock (see p. 344)

½ pt/280 ml brown ale or dry cider
1 bay leaf
10 oz/280 g puff pastry
To glaze:
beaten egg and milk

CUT the beef and kidney into 1 in/2.5 cm cubes, snipping away any fat from the interior of the kidneys. Dry the kidney pieces. Put the flour and seasonings in a paper bag and shake a few pieces of meat at a time in it to give them a light dusting of flour.

In a heavy pan or flameproof casserole heat the oil and fry the onion until golden. Push to one side and brown the meat a few pieces at a time. Pour on a little of the stock and scrape up any residues stuck to the pan. Add the rest of the stock, the ale or cider and the bay leaf. Bring to the boil, reduce the heat to a simmer, cover and cook for about an hour until the beef is tender. Cool the meat quickly and either cover and refrigerate until required or transfer it to a pie dish.

Preheat the oven to 200°C/400°F, gas mark 6. Roll out the pastry and cover the meat in the pie dish with it, pressing down well to seal at the edges. Lop off any excess pastry and use it for trimming the pie. Slash the top to let the steam escape. Brush with the glaze. Bake for 30-35 minutes.

I would suggest serving this with a purée of celeriac (see p. 355) and a crisp green vegetable such as broccoli or Savoy cabbage.

CORNISH PASTY

This traditional recipe is a substantial dish, good hot or cold, which was originally devised to meet the requirements of miners and farmers who needed a portable meal. Children also used to take them for school dinners before the advent of the canteen. There is a surprising number of variants: some recipes include rabbit, some bacon and egg, others even liver and kidneys. And there are various permutations on the meat, potatoes, turnip and onion theme. Some are meat and potatoes only, some include onions and no turnips and some have everything. Pasties are still perfect for a picnic – not the elegant Glyndebourne type, I hasten to add, but an open-air meal in the middle of a country hike true to the pasty's rough and ready origins.

MAKES 2 INDIVIDUAL PASTIES

½ lb/230 g lean chuck or skirt beef, diced small
2 or 3 large potatoes, peeled and sliced or diced
1 onion, peeled and sliced or diced (optional)
1 turnip, peeled and sliced or diced (optional)
salt and pepper

fat or oil for greasing baking tray
For the pastry:
½ lb/230 g plain flour
pinch of salt
¼ lb/110 g fat (lard, soft margarine or butter, or use half and half)
iced water to bind the dough

SIFT the flour and salt. Rub in the fat and stir in enough iced water to bind it into a pastry dough. Leave to rest for 15 minutes.

Divide the pastry in two. Roll out one half into a circle about ¼ in/0.5 cm thick and in the centre build up a mound of potato, meat, onion and turnip. Season generously. Damp the edges of one half circle of pastry. Bring the bottom centre to meet the top centre and seal firmly, then seal all along the edge. Splits or holes should be patched with fragments of pastry. The finer the sealed edge, the neater will be the crimping. Mary Wright, in *Cornish Treats*, describes how it is done, from corner to corner. 'Make sure your hands are dry. Hold the edge with one hand and follow on with a firm fold down with the other hand. Hold and fold alternately and swiftly along to the end.' Line a baking tray with grease-proof paper, grease it and put the pasty on it, slitting the top to let the steam escape. Make the second pasty in the same way, using the rest of the pastry.

Meanwhile preheat the oven to 200°C/400°F, gas mark 6. Bake the pasties for 30 minutes, then reduce the heat to 180°C/350°F, gas mark 4 for a further 30 minutes.

This recipe can also be used to make a dozen *Miniature pasties* to serve with drinks. Bake them for 20-25 minutes in all, but fry the meat and vegetables for the filling briefly first.

MINCED BEEF

*H*AMBURGERS, steak tartare, *ragu* and meat loaf, as well as many other dishes, require beef to be minced. It can be bought ready-minced from the butcher or supermarket. Sometimes it will state on the package what percentage is fat, but often you will not know this. There must be a great temptation to put left-overs of various cuts into the mincing machine and occasionally I have felt that somebody has succumbed to this. Sometimes different grades of mince will be available, including minced steak. But which steak?

To my mind it is more satisfactory either to choose a piece of meat, have the butcher trim it of all fat and gristle (which you will pay for) and then ask for it to be minced, or to buy the meat, then trim and mince it yourself (see p. 55). In the end the second solution is the most advisable. Don't mince the meat until you are ready to cook it, for it deteriorates far more rapidly than meat in a piece.

The same general approach applies to buying minced lamb, pork and veal too.

HAMBURGER

Much unpleasant food masquerades under the name of hamburger, which is sad, for a real hamburger, made with good quality, lean, flavoursome beef, is a treat. It may not qualify as a 'serious' meal, with a beginning, middle and end, but, set against the realities of modern life, it makes a perfect snack, a lunchtime sandwich, something at the end of a busy day, especially for just one or two people.

The real creativity comes in what you serve with the hamburger. A slice of cheese to melt over the meat? Blue? Gruyère or cheddar? Slices of ripe tomato or sweet, mild onion? Pickles, sweet or sour? Lettuce? Mustard? Chilli salsa? Ketchup? And what kind of bun? I like a good chewy bun for a hamburger: sour dough or *ciabatta* are good. Half a pitta bread will also do the job well and is certainly preferable to a soggy, indifferent bun.

The tail end of the fillet, or a piece of rump steak or skirt, are good cuts to use. It is preferable to mince the meat yourself. A food processor should be used carefully and only briefly, otherwise it will make a meat paste.

QUANTITIES PER PERSON

4 oz/110 g trimmed beef
1¹/₂-2 tsp finely chopped
  trimmed shallots (optional)
1 tsp finely chopped fresh herbs
  (optional)

pinch of freshly ground black
  pepper
salt
bun

MINCE or finely chop the beef. Mix the meat with the shallots, herbs and pepper and shape it into a firm, neat patty shape roughly the size of the bun. Have the grill hot or use a well-seasoned cast-iron or non-stick frying pan. Cook the hamburger on both sides until done to your liking. Lightly salt it and serve hot on a toasted bun. Have all your accompaniments ready before you start.

RAGÙ

After I followed Marcella Hazan's method for making *ragù*, I have never needed another recipe for this wonderful rich Italian sauce. The flavour is achieved by a slow and subtle fusion of ingredients. In the early stages it needs watching if it is not to burn. To avoid this, use a heavy saucepan.

SERVES 4-6 (AS A SAUCE FOR SPAGHETTI; DOUBLE THE QUANTITIES FOR *LASAGNA*)

¾ lb/340 g lean beef, such as rump, skirt or feather steak, minced
1 onion, peeled and finely chopped
1 tbsp extra virgin olive oil
½ oz/15 g butter
1 celery stalk, trimmed and finely chopped
1 medium carrot, peeled and finely chopped

⅛ pt/70 ml red wine
⅛ pt/70 ml milk
freshly grated nutmeg to taste
1 bay leaf
1 sage leaf
large can of plum tomatoes, approx 14 oz/400 g
salt
pepper

*F*RY the onion gently in the oil and butter. When it is soft, add the celery and carrot. The vegetables need to cook on a very low heat for about 40 minutes and to be stirred from time to time. Then add the meat, break it up in the saucepan with a fork or spoon and fry it until it loses its raw look. Raise the heat and stir in the wine.

Cook until the wine has evaporated, then add the milk with the nutmeg. When the milk, too, has been absorbed on a gentle heat, add the herbs and rub the tomatoes through a sieve into the saucepan.

Lower the heat, partially cover and cook for 3½-4 hours, stirring from time to time. Season towards the end of cooking time, but not so near the end that the sauce does not respond to the seasoning.

FRESH BEEF HASH

An easy dish to make, this is good for supper, lunch,
breakfast or, indeed, any time.

SERVES 4-6

1 lb/455 g blade or rump beef
   steak
2 tomatoes, peeled, seeded
   and chopped
1 medium onion, peeled and
   finely chopped

2 cloves of garlic, peeled and
   crushed
salt
pepper
1 tbsp wine vinegar or sherry
   vinegar

1 lb/455 g potatoes, peeled
2 tbsp olive oil
drop of Worcestershire sauce,
   Angostura bitters or
   Tabasco (optional)

REMOVE any fat and gristle from the meat. Mince it coarsely and mix with the tomatoes, onion, garlic, salt, pepper and vinegar. Finely dice or coarsely grate the potatoes and mix them with the meat.

Heat the olive oil in a large heavy frying pan and cook the hash, stirring frequently, first on a high heat to brown the meat, then with the heat turned down, until the beef and potatoes are cooked. A little water can be added from time to time, as can a drop of Worcestershire sauce, Angostura and/or Tabasco.

This can be served with a fried or poached egg if you like.

OXTAIL

THIS bony, inexpensive extremity can be turned into some of the tastiest dishes imaginable. Like many cheaper cuts of meat, slow careful cooking is needed. The advantage with such dishes is that they can be cooked a day or two before required and then reheated. Here are the four dishes for which I use oxtail: a rich warming stew, a meaty soup, a rustic jellied mould or terrine and a hash. If you are making the stew anyway, it is worth cooking extra for the terrine.

On balance, I prefer to remove the bones after cooking rather than serve the meat on the bone. If you opt for the latter, finger bowls are definitely required.

OXTAIL CASSEROLE

SERVES 4

3 lb/1.35 kg oxtail, chopped into
    pieces
1 tbsp sunflower or groundnut oil
1 large onion, peeled and sliced
2 or 3 cloves of garlic, peeled
    and crushed
1 pt/570 ml good full-bodied red
    wine or brown ale

1 tbsp Dijon mustard
zest of ½ orange
1 bay leaf
4 crushed juniper berries
1-2 tsp potato flour or cornflour
1 tsp Demerara sugar
1 tbsp cognac or whisky
salt
pepper

TRIM as much excess fat as possible from the pieces of oxtail then brown them all over in the oil. Remove and put to one side while you lightly brown the onion, then add the garlic without letting it brown. Pour on a little wine or ale and scrape up any browned bits sticking to the pan. Stir in the mustard and add the orange zest, bay leaf and juniper berries. Return the oxtail to the pan, pour on the remaining liquid, bring to the boil, skim, cover and barely simmer for 3-4 hours.

Remove the oxtail from the sauce. Cool it rapidly, cover and refrigerate overnight. Do the same with the sauce, sieving it first.

Next day, lift off and discard from the sauce the fat, which will have solidified in a layer on the top. Remove the meat from the bone. Put meat and sauce together into a saucepan and reheat gently.

Slake the flour with a little water and stir it into the sauce together with a sprinkling of sugar, the spirit and seasoning to taste. Make sure the meat is thoroughly reheated and serve piping hot. Dumplings (see p. 351), rice or broad noodles are just the thing with oxtail stew, but mashed potatoes are very good with it too.

For an *Oxtail Soup*, for four people, follow the same basic method as for the casserole described above, but use an extra pint/580 ml liquid in the form of stock or water. On the second day, you could fry some finely chopped celery, potato, carrot, turnip and leek before adding the soup to it to heat through. Add the meat, too, if you want a hearty meat and vegetable soup, or keep the meat for an oxtail terrine.

HASH OF OXTAIL IN CABBAGE LEAVES

Based on a recipe from Jean-Marie Gautier, of the Grand Hotel du Palais in Biarritz, this dish uses oxtail which has been cooked, boned and degreased as described in the previous recipes. It is his own adaptation of the Basque *axoa* usually made with veal (see p. 110), a simple and inexpensive dish, unusual but homely and perfect for a weekday supper, or for a dinner party. To really dress it up, you can use chanterelles, ceps or other wild mushrooms, not to mention truffles, instead of the shiitake mushrooms I have suggested.

SERVES 4

12 oz/340 g cooked oxtail
2 or 3 shallots, peeled and finely
    chopped
2 tbsp walnut oil
¼ lb/110 g shiitake mushrooms,
    chopped or thinly sliced
⅛ pt/70 ml full-bodied red wine

1 pt/580 mls oxtail broth
sliver of orange zest
salt
pepper
8 or 12 large white cabbage
    leaves, with central rib removed

Gently fry the shallots in walnut oil until soft, then add the mushrooms. Fry them for 2-3 minutes, add the wine, ¼ pt/140 ml stock and the orange zest. Bubble the mixture until the liquid has reduced to about 4 tbsp, season and put to one side. When cool, stir in the oxtail and mix thoroughly.

Steam or blanch the cabbage leaves until quite tender. Dry them well with kitchen paper towel and use to line four greased moulds. Fill them with the oxtail mixture, folding in the overlapping leaves to close the parcel neatly. Stand the moulds on a baking tray and put in a preheated oven at 180°C/350°F, gas mark 4 for 15-20 minutes.

Meanwhile, reduce the remaining broth to make a gravy, adding some chopped parsley or chervil if you wish, and season to taste.

Turn the stuffed cabbage out on to heated dinner plates and pour the gravy over them.

OXTAIL TERRINE

SERVES 4-6

3 lb/1.35 kg oxtail
1 pig's trotter
generous splash of red wine
2 pt/1.15 l water
8 baby leeks

8 baby carrots
salt
pepper
1 pt/580 ml cooking juices

Cook the oxtail together with the pig's trotter, red wine and water. Separate the meat and cooking liquid as described in the oxtail casserole (see p. 87) and bone and degrease them the following day. You need 12 oz/340 g cooked meat, weighed off the bone, and 1 pt/580 ml cooking juices.

Cut the meat into small dice. Trim and peel the vegetables as necessary and steam or boil until tender. Place some of the meat in the bottom of a wetted loaf tin and arrange half the leeks and carrots on top, then more meat, the rest of the vegetables and a final layer of meat. Season the cooking juices quite well and pour over the meat. Chill until set, then turn out and slice.

This terrine will make a substantial starter or a cold main course if served with a lentil salad and salad leaves.

TRIPE

I was lucky enough to acquire the taste for tripe at a very young age when my father would bring home tripe as a supper-time treat, long before I had tasted Mexican *menudo* or Portuguese *dobrada* or had eaten dinner at Pharamond in Paris, where it is served, still bubbling, in an iron pot set on a charcoal burner.

In America and the south of England we tend to have become squeamish about this wholesome product. A pity, I think for it is easy to cook and prepare, and we are missing out on some wonderful popular dishes from European, Oriental and Latin American cuisines. In Istanbul, for example, there are whole restaurants devoted to tripe soup, which is a favourite evening snack for men returning home. At least in the north of England, where the inhabitants have a more robust approach to food, you can still find a few tripe shops in the markets and old mill towns.

Perhaps knowing that the ancient Romans considered it a great delicacy might tempt you to try it again. One of their recipes is given below. Another incentive is that much of the preparation has been done for us in Britain these days. In many countries, tripe is bought in its natural state, rather like folded lengths of clean unbleached dishcloths. But in Britain we are pampered. The tripe has already been washed, scraped, bleached and boiled before it goes on sale.

TRIPE WITH HONEY AND GINGER SAUCE

Sweet, spicy sauces, often enhanced with mint, were a feature of Roman cookery in classical times. Here is a most unusual version which will appeal to tripe-lovers.

SERVES 4

1½ lb/680 g honeycomb tripe
1 oz/30 g butter
¼ tsp freshly ground black
   pepper
¼ tsp freshly grated ginger
1 tsp celery seed
1 tsp honey
2 tsp sherry vinegar
½ pt/280 ml beef stock
1 tsp finely chopped fresh mint
salt to taste

RINSE and dry the tripe thoroughly and cut it into 2 in/5 cm squares. Melt the butter in a large frying pan, fry the tripe in it and sprinkle on the pepper, ginger and celery seed. Cook for 5 minutes then add the honey, vinegar and stock. Bring to the boil, skim the surface, and simmer for 20 minutes. Add the mint, season to taste and cook for 15-20 minutes more.

I like to serve this in shallow soup plates with triangles of fried bread. It is also very good with slices of grilled *polenta*.

TRIPE COOKED IN WHITE WINE

I much prefer the sticky brown tripe stews of Normandy, Spain and Portugal to the pale milk-cooked English recipes. This version, with its spices and sun-dried tomatoes, has a very mixed parentage, but is nonetheless extremely tasty, a good winter dish.

SERVES 4

2½ lb/1.1 kg honeycomb tripe
1 pig's trotter, chopped into 6-8
    pieces
1 pt/570 ml dry white wine
½ pt/280 ml water
1 onion, peeled and sliced
2 tbsp olive oil
2 cloves
¼ tsp ground allspice
1 tsp ground coriander seeds

4 cloves of garlic, peeled and sliced
3 or 4 pieces of sun-dried tomato,
    cut into strips) or 3 fresh ripe
    tomatoes, peeled, seeded and
    quartered
salt and pepper
To serve:
2 tbsp finely chopped parsley
grated zest of a lemon

*R*INSE the tripe, dry it well and cut it into squares. Put the pig's trotter in a small saucepan with the wine and water, bring to the boil and simmer gently for 3-4 hours. When you drain the pig's trotter, keep the stock.

Then prepare the rest of the dish. In a heavy-based pan, fry the onion in the olive oil until golden brown, add the spices and fry them for 3-4 minutes. Add the tripe and garlic to the pan and turn up the heat to evaporate all the moisture from the tripe. Add the tomatoes, the pig's trotter and about ½ pt/280 ml of the stock. Cover and simmer gently for 30-40 minutes, adding more liquid as necessary.

Transfer the tripe and pig's trotter to a serving dish. Reduce the liquid to a rich gravy. Season to taste and pour over the tripe. Sprinkle with the parsley and lemon zest.

BEEF CONSOMMÉ

Enriched and clarified beef stock becomes a clean, limpid beef consommé which can be served hot or cold, quite plain or garnished with tiny dumplings, julienne of vegetables or even caviar. Game consommé can be made in exactly the same way, using game stock and minced stewing venison or, for example, the minced meat scraped from pheasant drumsticks. Whatever stock you use, the same meat should be used for added depth of flavour.

MAKES 1½ PT/850 ML

½ lb/230 g lean beef from the
  shin, flank or skirt
1 celery stalk
1 small carrot
1 small onion
1 leek
2 egg whites
1 pt/570 ml beef stock (see
  p. 344)
½ pt/280 ml water
salt
pepper

TRIM the beef of all fat and mince it. Peel, trim and dice the vegetables as necessary. Thoroughly mix the meat with the vegetables and egg whites in a bowl.

Put the stock and water in a saucepan and stir in the meat and vegetable mixture. Bring slowly to the boil, stirring continuously and ensuring that none of the mixture has stuck to the pan.

Turn down the heat and simmer gently for 40 minutes. By this time the egg white will have coagulated into a crust, which will act as a filter for the consommé. Place a sieve over a bowl and carefully strain the contents of the pan through the sieve.

Season the consommé and serve, or allow to cool and refrigerate until required.

VEAL

WHEN I FIRST BEGAN to plan this book I had more or less decided to leave out veal since most of the meat sold in Britain has been imported from Holland, which, in turn, imports most of its young live calves from Britain to be reared in a system now banned here. This system houses the calf in a crate with no straw, insufficient space to turn round and a diet of milk powder to produce the white meat and tender flesh so highly prized by some people. Many others refrain from eating veal because of the regime suffered by these calves.

But it is now possible to find veal which is truly free-range and reared to high standards. The calves are not taken from their mother but pastured, or housed with them, depending on the conditions. Their diet is solely mother's milk, grass and hay, which produces pink flesh (not the white iron-deficient flesh of the crated calves). You may also find free-range veal sold as milk-fed beef or baby beef.

Thus there need be no restriction on our enjoyment of *osso buco*, *vitello tonnato* and *piccata di vitello milanese* or *blanquette de veau* and *jarret de veau printanière*, not to mention *ris et rognons de veau*. Just the names of these recipes illustrate that veal has never really been a traditionally British meat. English and Scottish cookery books from the Middle Ages onwards have given veal recipes, but the earlier ones bear very close resemblance to French recipes. It was the Normans who brought with them the practice of killing very young calves for food, along with many other early animal husbandry techniques. This was not something which found favour with Anglo-Saxon farmers, who regarded it as a waste of a perfectly good animal, and veal was thus more likely to be found served at the tables of the well-to-do rather than as a food of the masses.

More veal recipes were introduced after the French Revolution, when emigrés brought their cooks with them, but Hannah Glasse, writing ten years before the French Revolution, has many good recipes, including some for the cheaper cuts such as breast. In recent years, as more people have travelled in France and Italy, we have become more familiar with their modern recipes for veal. Here I have included some of the ones I used to enjoy when I lived in France as a young English teacher.

HUSBANDRY

*E*ATING VEAL as opposed to beef is equivalent to eating lamb as opposed to mutton: the meat is sweeter, more tender and, of course, all equivalent joints are smaller.

The big difference is that whereas lamb production is one of the least intensive production systems in modern agriculture, veal calf production is one of the cruellest and most intensive. Discovery of the unpleasant production methods made veal the first meat to experience consumer resistance. In Britain sales fell in the late sixties and seventies and today there are many people who simply refuse to eat veal on principle. Yet there are still those who seek out and pay highly for the whitest-fleshed veal, even though in reality that whiteness is a reflection of the degree of cruelty, not quality.

Intensive veal calf production uses the excess calves produced by dairy herds, which only need a small proportion of their calves to replace the parent stock. It also relies upon huge quantities of milk powder, produced by cheese processing plants. It is hardly surprising, then, that the Netherlands is the world leader in veal production.

There are various standards of production in use. Dutch crates, which are actually used all over Europe, including Britain, dominate in number. The construction of new Dutch veal crates is banned in Britain, but there is nothing to stop farmers from making their existing crates last longer. Calves spend their entire lives in a small crate with no room to turn around. The floors are slatted and no bedding is provided to prevent any intake of natural fibrous material. The calves never see daylight or a blade of grass. Reconstituted milk is provided in a bucket and is the sole source of sustenance for the calf. Although there is no indication that growth promoters or drugs are employed beyond curative use, iron intake is reduced to increase the whitening of the flesh by induced partial anaemia. This unnatural process causes rapid growth of a slightly anaemic calf whose stomach processes will not have been allowed to develop, as fibrous material is essential for this. Unspecified veal in Britain will be from Dutch crates, particularly in restaurants where the customer is unlikely to ask awkward questions.

The 'Dutch loose housed' or 'New British Standard' system is almost the same as fully intensive production. Slightly more space is given to the calves and latterly, the barriers are taken away so that the calves can at least mingle. Some fibrous roughage must be provided according to the rules, but there is no indication as to how much and no checking procedure. Most concerned welfarists think that this system has more to do with marketing than welfare – especially since retailers often label the meat 'loose housed' in very large letters. The famous higher welfare Quantock system came about as a response to British consumer resistance to intensive veal. It is an honourable attempt at a better system, with calves loose housed from birth, drinking from a mechanical milk bar. It produces pale pink flesh rather than pure white because it is not a solely milk-based diet. Bedding is provided. It is hard to specifically locate Quantock veal as it is often sold as an own-label supermarket product.

There is a second fully free-range alternative – that is, simply to use calves which would otherwise become beef cattle. Calves are kept with their mothers. At the time when they would normally be weaned and separated to grow on for beef, they are selected for slaughter. This means they have the freest life possible and are very much equivalent to lambs. Supplies of this fully free-range veal are very rare, but it is worth getting. While intensive veal is almost without taste, fully free-range veal, with its pink flesh, is a subtle, sweet and milder version of beef.

CLASSIC DISHES

FRENCH AND ITALIAN COOKERY BOOKS are usually the best sources of recipes for veal. *Fricandeau à l'oseille* is an old-fashioned French dish made from the small, plump, cushion-like muscle from the leg. It is barded and braised on a bed of carrots and onions and served with a purée of sorrel. *Paupiettes de veau* and veal birds are small stuffed parcels of flattened veal escalope. *Vitello tonnato* is another favourite of mine, a joint of roast veal sliced when cold and served with an unusual sauce, of tuna fish and capers. I make a version of the sauce with cooked salmon and often roast the veal especially to have it cold (see p. 106).

You are unlikely to find veal recipes in Indian, Chinese or southeast Asian cookery books.

GOOD COMPANIONS

ALTHOUGH VEAL IS LEAN, when cooked it has a gelatinous, sticky, suave quality, which is best complemented by sharp, piquant, fragrant scents and flavours. So lemons and other lemony-flavoured things, such as lemon thyme and lemon grass, should go into your shopping bag if you are buying veal. A sauce flavoured with lemon grass and nutmeg, for example, is a perfect match for braised veal. Summer savory, rosemary and lavender are also excellent herbs to flavour a veal roast. Sharp-flavoured greens such as sorrel, rocket, spinach and watercress provide the right sort of colour contrast and acidity with veal. Look, too, for the crisp textures of broccoli, green beans or stir-fried cabbage, instead of the softer texture of Jerusalem artichokes, salsify and other root vegetables.

COOKING METHODS

ROASTING

THE most memorable veal I have ever tasted was a whole leg, bathed in lemon juice and olive oil, stuck with slivers of garlic and encircled with sprigs of rosemary. It was roasted before an open charcoal fire in the homely kitchen of the Antica Trattoria Suban, a big stone barn of a restaurant high above the city of Trieste in north-eastern Italy. The veal was crisp and brown on the outside, tender and moist on the inside.

Veal should be roasted in a moderate oven, 180°C/350°F, gas mark 4 for about 35 minutes per 1 lb/455 g, if on the bone, and 40-45 minutes per 1 lb/455 g if boned and rolled. The leg, the loin and the rib joints are all suitable for roasting, as is the rolled shoulder. Veal should be thoroughly cooked and not served rare.

FRYING AND GRILLING

BECAUSE veal is so lean, great care needs to be taken when grilling it. In my view, the only cuts suitable for grilling are the massive Florentine chops, rather like a T-bone steak and cut from the loin, which you are sometimes served in good Tuscan restaurants. Even then, care must be taken to baste the meat, preferably with olive oil, during grilling to stop it drying out. Chops, fillets and escalopes cut from the leg are best panfried in butter or olive oil. They are sometimes breaded first, Milanese style, which gives an extra protection against drying out.

BRAISING AND POT ROASTING

SUCH a lean and tender meat lends itself very well to pot roasting and braising, in which the moist heat gently cooks the meat, and the herbs and vegetables which are added to the pot provide flavourings for sometimes frankly bland meat.

STEWING AND CASSEROLING

SOME of the cheapest cuts of veal make the tastiest stews. I think of the French *blanquette de veau* with its creamy, lemony sauce tasting of cloves and onions, or the Italian *osso buco* with its sticky, glossy sauce and piquant garnish of lemon, parsley and garlic.

Cuts and Joints

English Cuts

Best end

*T*HIS joint, also sold as *best end of neck*, corresponds to the ribs of the animal and is sold on the bone for roasting, like a smaller version of rib of beef, or in cutlets for grilling or frying. In either case it is best to remove the chine bone; this is the thick part where the rib joins the backbone. I like to roast this joint with a herb, mustard and breadcrumb crust pressed all over the thin outer layer of fat.

Breast

*T*HE thin underside of the body, corresponding to the belly, this is a marvellously economical piece of veal, with an excellent flavour and texture when carefully cooked. It can be roasted on the bone, braised on a bed of vegetables, diced for stew, minced for a meat loaf or, perhaps best of all, boned, stuffed, rolled and braised or roasted. It has enough fat on it to stop it drying out too much.

My favourite recipe combines the inexpensive breast with the more expensive kidney, but a 2½ lb/1.1 kg prepared breast and 1 lb/455 g kidney will feed six to eight people and thus it is still very good value. I like to leave some of the fat on the kidney, which then bastes the meat from the inside. Season the kidney, wrap it in spinach leaves and then roll the breast round it. It looks very good when sliced, and is absolutely delicious when cold and thinly sliced. The recipe is given on p.105.

Knuckle

*T*HE bonier end of the hind leg contains plenty of rich marrow and gelatinous connective tissue. The knuckle is sawn into 2 in/5 cm rounds to make *osso buco*. It can also be braised.

The *foreknuckle* or *shin* has very little meat on it but makes a fine, rich, pale stock.

Leg

*T*HIS is one of the largest, leanest, tenderest joints on the carcase, and consequently one of the most expensive. From a small animal, it is possible to buy and roast the whole leg, but it is more usually divided into several cuts from both the fillet end of the leg and the knuckle end of the leg (see diagram).

Loin

*E*ITHER left whole for roasting or cut into loin chops for grilling or frying, loin is another prime veal joint, which is taken from between the hindquarter and the ribs or best end. Sometimes it is sold boned and rolled around a stuffing. It is well worth boning a loin yourself, trimming it of as much fat as you wish and then mixing your own stuffing. If you buy the whole loin, you may or may not get the kidney with it (since veal kidney is a particular delicacy and therefore commands a high price, it is usually sold separately).

Middle neck and scrag

*B*OTH cuts come from the forequarter, between the head and the best end of neck. Bony but well flavoured, these can be chopped up for casseroles, the bonier pieces being used for stock, or the bones can be removed and the meat used for pies or mince.

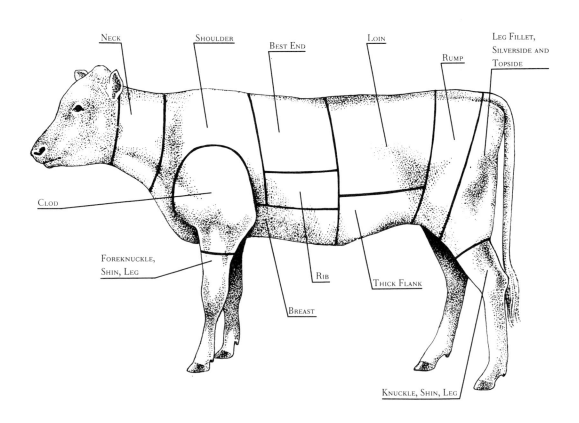

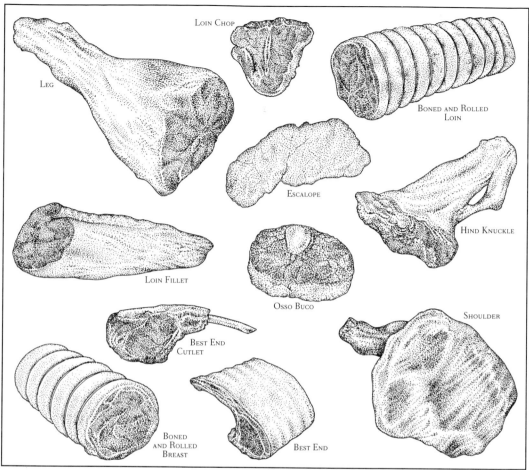

Loin Chop

Leg

Boned and Rolled Loin

Escalope

Hind Knuckle

Loin Fillet

Osso Buco

Shoulder

Best End Cutlet

Boned and Rolled Breast

Best End

Minced veal

*Y*ou will sometimes find this pale pink mince ready-made, although it is more usual to select your own piece for mincing. Minced veal combines very well with other minced meats, particularly pork and beef, as its gelatinous quality prevents the mixture from crumbling, which beef tends to do if used alone. Use minced veal in meat loaves, in pasta sauces – for example, as a filling for *cannelloni* or *lasagna* – and as a stuffing for cabbage leaves and other vegetables.

Pie veal

*T*his is the diced meat taken from the cheaper secondary cuts and is suitable for pies and casseroles. It usually comes from the scrag end or middle neck and includes, as well, the breast end trimmings after the carcase has been cut up.

Shoulder

*A*n awkward shape, the shoulder is nevertheless a good, inexpensive roasting joint. It can be roasted on the bone or boned and stuffed. Because of its round, flat shape after the knuckle has been removed, it is sometimes called the oyster.

STEWING VEAL

THIS is taken from the same cuts as pie veal. Both need slow, careful cooking with plenty of liquid and flavourings.

TOPSIDE

THE small, lean, cushion-shaped muscle from which escalopes, or very ¼ in/0.5 cm thick and then beaten even thinner, is also known as cushion of veal. It can also be larded and braised or pot-roasted.

Slices of veal, called either fillets or *escalopes*, are also cut from the top end of the leg for grilling and frying, or a large thick fillet can be removed for roasting.

French Cuts

These resemble English cuts quite closely.

CÔTE

THE ribs are divided into the *côtelettes premières*, the four cutlets from the best end of neck nearest the loin, and the *côtelettes secondes* or *découvertes*, which are the four cutlets nearest the shoulder. Both are excellent roasting joints, but are also cut up into cutlets for grilling or frying.

CROSSE

THIS is the heel end of the hind leg, suitable for the stockpot.

ÉPAULE, COLLET AND BAS DE CARRÉ

THE shoulder, neck and scrag end joints are not as tender as the prime cuts and are usually braised whole on the bone, or boned, rolled and braised. Neck meat is often cut up for casseroles.

GRENADIN

THIS is a small thick steak cut from the leg.

JARRET

THE knuckle or shin of veal, which contains the large leg bone and marrow and is surrounded by juicy succulent meat, can be braised whole with vegetables or cut into chunks.

POITRINE

THE breast of veal, which is also known as *flanchet*, is braised, boned or on the bone, and used for such dishes as *blanquette de veau*.

QUASI

ESCALOPES are cut from this lean rump piece, or the *quasi* can be roasted whole.

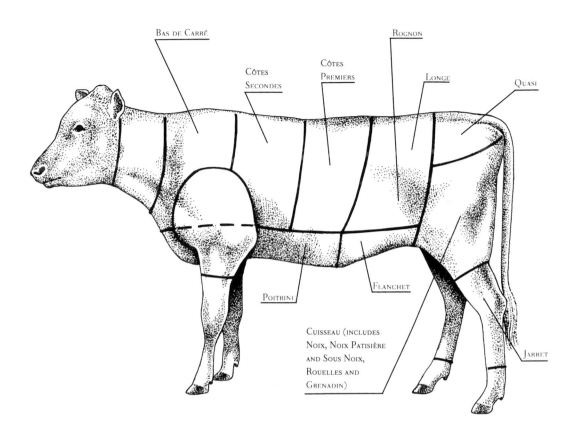

Bas de Carré

Côtes
Secondes

Côtes
Premiers

Rognon

Longe

Quasi

Poitrine

Flanchet

Cuisseau (includes
Noix, Noix Patisière
and Sous Noix,
Rouelles and
Grenadin)

Jarret

Rognon

*S*o called because it contains the kidneys. The *longe* (loin) and *filet* (fillet) are the prime roasting joints cut from this part of the carcase. *Médallion* is a small thick steak cut from the fillet in the loin.

Rouelles

*T*HE thick lean part of the leg between the *quasi* (rump) and the *jarret* (knuckle) contains the *cuisseau* or *noix*, which corresponds to the topside or cushion of veal, and the *noix pâtissière* which corresponds to the thick part of the flank. To roast successfully, it would be best to lard these cuts; otherwise they can be braised or pot-roasted.

American Cuts

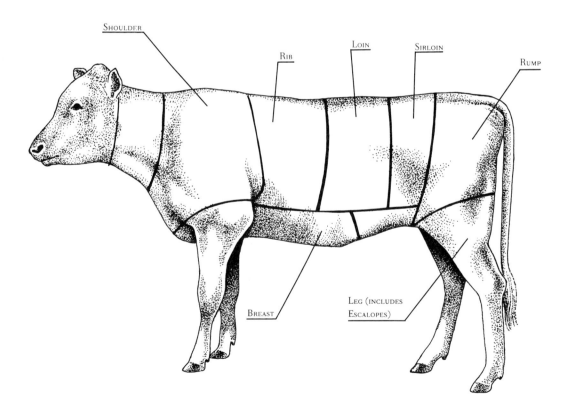

Because of the extensive Italian influence through immigration in the past and the present large cattle industry, veal is popular in America and a wide selection of cuts are available, both for roasting and for braising as well as smaller cuts for grilling and frying.

Breast
*B*REAST of veal, stuffed breast, stuffed chops.

City Chicken
*F*OR diced veal on skewers, the meat is usually cut from the lean part of the shoulder. For casseroles, braises and stews the following cuts are used: neck slices, riblets, foreshanks, brisket pieces and brisket roll, and the forequarter generally. For meat loaves, patties and sauces, the meat is usually cut from the lean part of the shoulder.

SHOULDER · RIB · LOIN · SIRLOIN · RUMP · BREAST · LEG (INCLUDES ESCALOPES)

LEG

STANDING rump, shank half of leg, rolled leg, centre leg, boneless cutlets, round steak, escalopes (*scallopini*), rolled cutlets (veal birds), heel of the round.

LOIN

LOIN roast, rolled stuffed loin, sirloin roast, roast double sirloin, loin chops, kidney chops, sirloin steak, cube steak.

RIB

RIB roast, crown roast, rib chops, Frenched rib chops.

SHOULDER

ARM roast, blade roast, rolled shoulder, arm steak, blade steak (these can also be braised).

OFFAL

MOST offal is a good bargain because there is not a great demand for it. Much veal offal, however, is an exception to this. Prices were always higher than those of other offal, simply because there is less veal about than beef and lamb, but they have been pushed further up by chefs, and discerning cooks, who particularly prize kidneys, liver and sweetbreads. Nonetheless, veal or calf's offal is worth buying, preparing carefully and turning into a dish for a special occasion.

BRAINS

REASONABLY priced, one brain, weighing about ½ lb/230 g, makes one serving. It should be soaked in very lightly acidulated water for about half an hour to remove all traces of blood and then it should be blanched (by bringing it to the boil in lightly salted water), drained, rinsed in cold water and allowed to rest. All traces of filament should be removed. Traditionally, brains are fried and served with black butter sauce, capers and lemon.

CALF'S FOOT

*T*HIS is a marvellous thing to cook with *daubes* and casseroles because the amount of gelatine it contains adds a rich, sticky quality to the dish. If you are making jellied meat terrines, it is a key ingredient.

CALF'S HEAD

*T*HE basis of mock turtle soup, brawns and *tête de veau vinaigrette*. It takes quite a lot of preparation to bone, blanch and trim, but the end results give a feeling of great satisfaction.

HEART

*T*HIS is reasonably priced and makes a good, inexpensive roast when stuffed and basted well. The meat has a good flavour and is pleasant and chewy, unlike most offal. It can also be sliced and fried, and cooked with spices and plenty of strong flavours.

KIDNEY

*V*EAL or calf's kidney is a great delicacy. As it is quite richly flavoured, I think one is sufficient for two servings. If you are ever lucky enough to find calf's kidneys in their suet overcoat, try the traditional French way of roasting them, *an naturel*. Kidneys can also be sliced and grilled or fried, always quickly so that the inner part is still just pink and juicy, or they are marvellous with a creamy sauce flavoured with mustard or Roquefort cheese and served with rice. Because they are so delicate, do guard against over-cooking.

LIVER

*C*ALF's liver is as fine and delicate as veal kidney. It should be lightly cooked, preferably grilled or fried in slices. A whole calf's liver can weigh 3-4 lb/ 1.35-1.8 kg and it is possible to turn it into a spectacular dinner dish by seasoning it and roasting it, basting it periodically and then carving it into neat slices at the table. A recipe is given on p. 113.

MARROW BONE

*T*HE hind legs of the animal have a thick sturdy shin bone which contains the rich marrow. It is excellent for lubricating sauces and casseroles, and can be used also as a garnish for other dishes. The roasted bones can also be served as a starter, the marrow being scooped out and eaten on toast.

SWEETBREADS

*R*IS DE VEAU is one of the classics of French cookery, mild, delicate and with an unusual texture which lends itself to a vast range of preparations and garnishes. The sweetbread consists of two parts of the thymus gland, the 'throat' bread which is long and the 'heart' bread which has a rounder shape. The pancreas, or 'stomach' bread, is not a sweetbread but is sometimes referred to as such. All need initial preparation in the same way (see p. 114). I like to cook them in butter with mushrooms, tarragon and cream and then use the mixture to fill a pastry case. Large slices can be breaded, fried and served with a wedge of lemon, or braised with a little bacon.

ROAST BREAST OF VEAL STUFFED WITH KIDNEY IN A SPINACH OVERCOAT

You need to plan this dish carefully by ordering the prepared meat well in advance from your butcher. If you tell your butcher exactly what you want, provided you give adequate notice, you are likely to get a beautifully trimmed piece of meat rolled around the kidney. Keep the bones to place in the roasting tin.

SERVES 6-8

1 prepared breast of free-range veal, weighing 2½ lb/1.1 kg, boned and trimmed to a neat rectangular shape, about 8×12 in/20×30 cm
1 lb/455 g free-range veal kidneys
salt and pepper
8 large spinach leaves

1 tbsp chopped fresh chives
½ tbsp chopped fresh tarragon
2 tbsp fromage blanc or 1 petit suisse
½ oz/15 g softened butter
1 clove of garlic, crushed and chopped fine
2 tbsp olive oil

LAY the veal on a flat surface. Trim most of the fat from the kidney and snip out the core. Lightly season both with salt and pepper.

Preheat the oven to 150°C/300°F, gas mark 2. Remove the central stems from the spinach. Blanch the leaves in boiling water, drain and run cold water over them. Pat them dry on kitchen paper and lay them over the meat. Mix the rest of the ingredients together (except for the olive oil) and spoon the mixture on to the spinach in a line. Lay the kidney on top and roll up the breast of veal. Tie at ½ in/1 cm intervals.

Place the veal roll in a roasting tin, on top of the veal bones, place in the oven and roast for about 3-3½ hours, brushing with olive oil, every 40 minutes.

Remove the meat from the oven and keep it warm while you prepare the gravy.

COLD ROAST VEAL WITH SALMON AND CAPER SAUCE

The roast stuffed breast of veal (see p. 105) is utterly delicious when cold and quite worth cooking specially to serve as part of a cold buffet. Any that is left over can be thinly sliced and served as *vitello tonnato* with a tuna fish mayonnaise sauce. You can also substitute cold cooked salmon for the tuna fish to make this *vitello salmonato*.

SERVES 4-6

1 lb/455 g cold cooked loin of
 free-range veal
For the sauce:
4 oz/110 g cold cooked salmon
1 small tin of anchovies
4 tbsp mild olive oil
2 free-range egg yolks
juice of ½ lemon
freshly ground black pepper
1 tbsp capers

SLICE the veal thinly and lay on a long platter in overlapping slices.

Combine the rest of the ingredients, except the capers, and blend or process until smooth and shiny like mayonnaise.

Roughly chop the capers and stir these into the sauce.

Pour over the veal and leave in a cool place for a couple of hours for the flavours to blend.

ROAST BEST END OF VEAL WITH HERB AND MUSTARD CRUST

Have the meat prepared by the butcher: the chine bone should be removed and the thick, fatty piece of meat removed from the rib bones, which should be scraped quite clean. The joint will now be easy to carve in slices across the grain of the meat, parallel to the rib bones. Keep the bones and trimmings for stock.

SERVES 4-6

3 lb/1.35 kg boned and trimmed best end of free-range veal
¼ pt/140 ml rich veal stock
splash of wine (optional)

For the crust:
4 cloves of garlic
2 shallots
4 tbsp finely chopped fresh parsley, with a little tarragon or chervil if available

2 tbsp Dijon mustard
4 tbsp soft white breadcrumbs
3 tbsp olive oil
juice of ½ lemon
salt and pepper

PEEL and finely chop the garlic and shallots and mix with the rest of the ingredients for the crust. Spread the mixture over all the meat except for the bones. Cover closely with plastic wrap or foil and refrigerate overnight so the meat takes on some of the flavours of the crust.

Next day, bring the joint to room temperature. Preheat the oven to 150-175°C/300-325°F, gas mark 2. Place the joint in a roasting tin and cook it in the middle of a slow oven for about 2 hours (40 minutes a lb). Every 40 minutes, pour on a tablespoon of veal stock.

Remove the meat from the oven and keep it warm while you make the gravy.

Gently pour any fat from the roasting tin, then set it over a low heat. Scrape up any caramelised cooking juices with a metal spoon, add a little water and the rest of the stock. Boil and scrape until you have a good mixture. A spoonful or two of whatever wine you are serving with the veal would not come amiss, but is not essential.

Carve the veal into thinnish slices and arrange on a serving platter with the gravy handed separately, or arrange a couple of slices on each heated dinner plate, pour on a little gravy and add whatever vegetables you are serving with the veal.

VEAL FILLET WITH SPICED SHALLOT AND KUMQUAT PRESERVE

There are no origins for this dish other than my tastebuds
and imagination, as fired by a hazy memory of a veal and
orange casserole that a friend used to cook twenty years
ago.
The shallot and kumquat sauce (see p. 360 for recipe) is
really more of a preserve and will indeed keep like one. It
is also very good served with grilled lamb, pork or
chicken.

SERVES 4-6

1 fillet of free-range veal
  weighing 1-1½ lb/455-680 g
1 mild onion, peeled and thinly
  sliced
2 tbsp orange juice
1 tsp freshly ground black pepper
1 tsp groundnut oil

½ oz/15 g unsalted butter
For the sauce:
⅛ pt/70 ml dry white wine
¼ pt/140 ml veal stock
2-3 tbsp shallot and kumquat
  preserve (see p. 360)
1½ oz/40 g unsalted butter

*P*UT a layer of onions in a shallow
dish. Cut the veal into four or six
equal steaks and brush them all over
with orange juice. Season with the pepper and place on top of the onions. Cover
with the remaining onions and marinate
for 30 minutes.

Remove the fillets from the marinade
and dry thoroughly. Heat a frying pan,
add the oil and the butter and fry the veal,
turning once, until done to your liking.

Transfer the meat to a warm place
while you finish off the sauce. Raise the
heat and deglaze the pan with the white
wine. Add the stock and the preserve.
Cook until reduced by half and strain
into a small clean pan. Bring to the boil
and swirl in the remaining butter, a piece
at a time, until amalgamated into a rich
sauce. Arrange the veal on heated dinner
plates and divide the sauce amongst
them.

Serve immediately. Asparagus, mangetouts, spinach, broccoli florets,
depending on the season, look and taste
very good with the veal, but keep them
to just a few stalks and sprigs, not a huge
heap.

VEAL WITH MUSTARD AND CAPER SAUCE

This piquant-flavoured casserole can be prepared a day
ahead and reheated gently just before you want to eat it. A
non-stick frying pan helps with the preparation.

SERVES 6-8

*2½ lb/1.1 kg free-range stewing
  veal
1 medium onion, peeled and
  sliced
2 medium carrots, peeled and cut
  into batons
¼ pt/140 ml white wine or stock
2 tbsp Dijon mustard
4 cloves
1 oz/30 g capers
salt and pepper
1-2 tbsp cream (optional)
To garnish:
  fresh parsley or coriander*

REMOVE and discard the fat, skin and gristle from the pie veal. Cut the meat into 1 in/2.5 cm cubes. Heat the frying pan and, taking a handful of cubes at a time, fry all the meat until sealed all over. Transfer it to a casserole.

Fry the vegetables together until the onion is translucent and add them to the meat. Mix the wine or stock and mustard and pour it over the meat and vegetables.

Add the cloves. Cover and cook in a moderate oven, 180°C/350°F, gas mark 4, for an hour or so. Fifteen minutes before the end, stir in the capers and season to taste.

If you like, just before serving you can stir in a spoonful or two of cream to enrich the sauce. Serve, surrounded by buttered rice (see p. 349) and garnished with parsley or coriander.

VEAL AXOA

Pronounced "ashoua", this is the Basque version of hash, *hâchis* or, indeed, *hachua*. Traditionally made with veal it is a useful way of using up smaller pieces of veal. It is also sometimes made with beef.

The indispensable ingredient is the red pepper, or local *piment d'Espelette*. Indeed, I have seen the dish for sale in Espelette itself. October is the *piment* season, when the houses of this little red and white Basque village in the foothills of the Pyrenees behind Biarritz are festooned with red peppers drying in the sun. So fundamental are they to local cooking that the *maître d'hôtel* of the Grand Hotel du Palais in Biarritz described the region as that of the trinity of the pepper, onion and tomato. I find the large mild sweet peppers from Holland extremely indigestible but the peppers from the Basque country and Galicia do not have this effect. If using Dutch peppers instead, skin them first by holding them over a gas flame or grilling them until the skin blisters. Put them in a polythene bag and let them steam for a while, after which the skin can be peeled off. Remove the seeds too.

SERVES 4-6

1½ lb/680 g stewing veal
1 onion, peeled and sliced
2 red peppers, peeled (see above) and diced

1 tbsp olive or walnut oil

2 or 3 ripe tomatoes, peeled, seeded and chopped
1 glass dry white wine or cider
salt and pepper

TRIM any fat and gristle from the meat and cut it very small, into dice about ½ in/1 cm square. Fry the onion and pepper in the oil until the onion is transparent. Stir in the meat. When it has lost its rawness, add the tomato and cook the meat and vegetables over a moderately high heat for 5 minutes. Add the wine or cider, turn down the heat and simmer until the meat is tender. Season to taste.

Serve with rice or boiled potatoes. The crisp local wine from Irouléguy is excellent with this, as is the Txakoli from just over the border in Spain, or indeed the local cider, which is why I have suggested it in the recipe.

Braised Knuckle of Veal

Often used for the familiar *osso buco*, knuckle of veal can also be left whole. I like to braise it slowly on a bed of vegetables. The bonus comes in the form of the marrow, which is marvellous stirred into a risotto to accompany the veal.

Serves 4

1 knuckle of free-range veal, weighing 3-3½ lb/1.35-1.6 kg
1 large onion
2 carrots
2 celery stalks
1 leek
1 fennel bulb
2 tbsp extra virgin olive oil

4 cloves of garlic, peeled and crushed
2 ripe tomatoes, peeled, seeded and chopped
1 bay leaf
3 in/7.5 cm twist of orange zest
sprig of fresh or dried thyme or rosemary
½ bottle of good dry red wine
salt and pepper

PEEL, trim, slice and dice the onion, carrots, celery, leek and fennel quite small. Sweat them in the olive oil in a flameproof casserole, cooking them slowly to achieve a full flavour without letting them burn.

Push the vegetables to one side and turn the veal all over in the oil, just so that it loses its raw look. Push the vegetables back to the middle of the casserole and arrange the veal on top. Add the rest of the ingredients, seasoning only lightly at this stage.

Bring the liquid to the boil, reduce the heat to the merest simmer, cover the casserole with a well fitting lid and cook gently until the meat is tender. About 2½-3 hours on a back burner or in the bottom half of a moderate oven should be sufficient.

Transfer the meat to a warm serving dish, strain the cooking juices and reduce slightly if necessary before pouring it over the meat.

Finely chopped garlic (1-2 cloves), parsley (1-2 tbsp) and the zest of a lemon – the Italian *gremolata* – makes a nice addition sprinkled over the top at the end. You can also serve the braised vegetables with the meat.

LIVER AND BACON

When properly made, as I had it one lunchtime at the Groucho Club in Soho, this is an excellent dish. The liver was well cooked, with charcoal stripes on the outside and a pink and tender inside; the bacon was so good that I could have eaten nothing but the bacon. Such a simple, unadorned recipe needs the finest quality ingredients. Use back bacon or streaky, smoked or green, according to what you prefer. The liver and bacon cook so quickly that if you want to serve a heap of fried onions with them, you should cook these first. It's a meal I like to cook for the two of us rather than for dinner parties.

SERVES 2

4 rashers of bacon, rinded
8-12 oz/230-340 g free-range
    calf's liver, cut into 3 or 4
    slices
1 tbsp flour
¼ tsp salt
¼ tsp pepper
½ oz/15 g butter or 1 tbsp olive
    oil
2 or 3 sage leaves (optional, for
    an Italian flavour)

I F the rashers of bacon are long, cut them in half. Fry them in a frying pan until done and just beginning to crisp. Meanwhile shake the liver in a bag with the flour, salt and pepper. Shake off any surplus flour. Remove the bacon from the pan and keep warm. Drain away the bacon fat.

Heat the butter or olive oil and fry the liver on both sides until cooked to your liking. Put it on heated plates with the bacon. Bruise the sage and stir it into the pan juices briefly before pouring them over the liver.

Creamy mashed potatoes are the only thing to serve with liver and bacon.

ROAST LIVER STUFFED WITH HERBS AND BACON

Angelo Lancellotti devised this recipe for *fegato di vitello al forno, ripieno di erbe aromatiche e pancetta*; that is, a whole liver, filled with aromatic herbs and a piece of unsmoked bacon. Wrapped in the thinnest slices of pork fat or unsmoked bacon, it is roasted whole and served sliced with a little of the pan juices and a fragrant, leafy salad.

SERVES 8-10

1 whole free-range veal liver, weighing 2-3 lb/900 g-1.35 kg
½ lb/230 g unsmoked streaky bacon, in a long piece
½ lb/230 g belly of pork, thinly sliced
about 2 oz/60 g bacon or Parma ham, in a piece
1-2 tbsp olive oil

⅛ pt/70 ml white wine
branch of thyme
4-5 tbsp brandy
For the stuffing:
2 oz/60 g fresh white breadcrumbs
3 oz/85 g finely chopped unsmoked bacon
2-3 cloves of garlic, peeled and crushed
6 juniper berries, crushed

2 tsp finely chopped fresh thyme
1 tsp finely chopped rosemary
1 tbsp finely chopped fresh parsley
1 tbsp finely chopped fresh chervil
1 onion, peeled and finely chopped
freshly ground black pepper

WITH a long, thin-bladed knife, make a tunnel-like slit through the length of the liver that is wide and deep enough to just take the bacon and stuffing. Remove and discard the rind from the bacon. Tie a long piece of string round one end of the bacon and the other end of the string on to a larding needle. Draw the bacon through the slit. If the bacon is thick and firm enough, it can be pushed, rather than drawn, through the centre.

Heat the oven to 220-230°C/425-450°F, gas mark 7-8. Mix the stuffing and, with the help of a teaspoon, push it as far as possible into the cavity evenly all along its length. Tie the slices of belly of pork around the stuffed liver to make a neat shape and put it in a roasting tin with the piece of bacon or ham, olive oil, white wine and thyme.

Put the tin into the oven and bake for 10 minutes. Turn the heat down to 180°C/350°F/gas mark 4, splash on the brandy, cover the roast with foil and seal it, then cook for a further 35-40 minutes. Remove from the oven and allow the meat to relax for 10 minutes before slicing it.

113

ROGNONS EN CHEMISE

When you can get veal kidneys still in their overcoat of crisp white suet, here is a very simple dish to cook! It is a very pleasant dish to serve for two, but rather wasteful unless you have the oven on for something else. Serve it with mashed potatoes (see p. 352) and the cooking juices.

SERVES 2

1 free-range veal kidney
6 sprigs of fresh or dried
rosemary or thyme

sea-salt
freshly ground black pepper

PREHEAT the oven to 180°C/350°F/gas mark 4. Put a rack in a roasting tin (or you can cook the kidney directly on the bars of the shelf in the oven, in which case put an overproof dish underneath to collect the drippings.) Place the herbs on the rack and the kidney on top, lightly seasoned. Roast for about 25 minutes, until all the fat has melted, by which time the meat should be just cooked.

Remove from the oven and keep warm for 10 minutes before slicing. Drain off almost all the fat, add a splash of white wine and boil up the juices, together with the juices that drain from the kidney.

PREPARING SWEETBREADS

BEFORE sweetbreads can be cooked they need initial preparation. First, soak the sweetbreads in lukewarm water for several hours to remove all traces of blood, changing the water from time to time. Rinse the sweetbreads and remove any pieces of fat and discoloured bits, as well as the tougher membrane. Leave the inner membrane intact or the sweetbreads will disintegrate. Put them in a pan of clean water with a pinch of salt and bring slowly to boiling point. Simmer gently for 3 minutes, then remove and plunge into cold water. Blanching them in this way firms them up and allows you to pull off gristle. The sweetbreads are now ready to cook.

BRAISED SWEETBREADS WITH SORREL SAUCE

I have a soft spot for this recipe since it appeared in the first part of the first series I ever wrote for a national newspaper, *The Sunday Times Magazine*. Unbeknown to me, my then editor, and now dear friend, Brenda Houghton, sent off my recipes to an experienced cookery writer to test, just to make sure that they would work for readers. It was Brenda who taught me the mechanics of recipe writing. One day she said to me, "You know, Frances, it would be such a help to the subs if you would write down the ingredients in the order in which you use them."

If sorrel is unavailable, use watercress and cook in the same way. It will not be a sharp sauce, but rather a peppery one.

SERVES 4

1 lb/455 g free-range calf's sweetbreads, trimmed, disgorged and blanched (see p. 114)
1 medium onion

1 celery stalk
1 carrot
3 cloves of garlic
3 oz/85 g butter
1 tbsp sunflower or groundnut oil
¼ pt/140 ml dry white wine

2 tbsp crème fraîche or double cream
3 tbsp shredded fresh sorrel
salt
pepper

*P*EEL and thinly slice the onion, celery, carrot and garlic. Cook them in 1 oz/30 g of the butter and all the oil in a flameproof casserole, until the onions are transparent. Push them to one side. Drain, rinse and dry the sweetbreads and fry them gently all over in the pan. Add the white wine, bring to the boil, cover and cook in the oven for 30-35 minutes at about 150°C/300°F, gas mark 2.

When cooked, strain the cooking juices into a shallow pan or small frying pan. Keep the sweetbreads warm in the pan, but away now from any direct heat. Reduce the cooking juices to about ⅛ pt/70 ml. Add the *crème fraîche* and the sorrel. Season to taste. Slice the sweetbreads on to heated serving plates and finish the sauce over a high heat, adding small pieces of the remaining butter, swirling it to emulsify into the sauce. Pour over the sweetbreads and serve immediately.

SWEETBREADS WITH WALNUTS

This is a marvellous dish to cook for a special occasion in the autumn when the new season's pears, leeks and walnuts are available.

SERVES 6

3 pairs of free-range calf's
    sweetbreads, trimmed,
    disgorged and blanched
2 juicy but firm dessert pears
    (such as the Italian
    Passacrassana)

1 lemon
12 fresh walnuts in the shell
3 leeks, white part only
5 oz/140 g unsalted butter
1 tbsp sugar

4 tbsp water
½ tsp freshly grated ginger root
    or ¼ tsp powdered ginger
1 tbsp walnut oil
salt and pepper
¼ pt/140 ml Madeira

SLICE the prepared sweetbreads. Peel the pears and sprinkle with lemon juice. Shell and roughly chop the nuts. Slice the leeks. Gently melt 4 oz/110 g butter in a small saucepan. Skim the foam off the top and pour it carefully into a bowl, keeping back the sediment which remains in the pan.

Take a third of this clarified butter and heat it in a frying pan or *sauteuse*, put in the quartered pears and let them cook until lightly golden on both sides. Sprinkle on a good tablespoonful of sugar, moisten with two tablespoons of water and add a couple of pinches of freshly grated or dried ginger. Remove from the heat and keep warm.

Take another third of the clarified butter and cook the leeks until soft, add two tablespoons of water, the walnut oil, chopped nuts, salt and pepper.

Finally, heat the rest of the clarified butter in a frying pan and cook the slices of sweetbreads for one minute on each side, on a high heat. Season to taste. Remove from the pan. Deglaze with the Madeira, let it bubble up a few times. Away from the heat whisk in the rest of the butter, a little at a time.

Spoon the leeks on to hot plates, arrange the slices of sweetbread on top of each, garnish with the pears and lightly coat the sweetbreads with the sauce.

PORK

'THE GENTLEMAN WHO PAYS THE RENT'. 'Everything edible but the squeak'. 'A meal on legs.' Such have been the friendly epithets attached to the pig, which has lived in close harmony with humans and allowed itself to become domesticated over thousands of years. How shameful, then, that we have not treated this intelligent and gentle animal more kindly.

Until the Industrial Revolution, when people left the land to seek work in Britain's cities and when more and more land became enclosed, many families relied on the pig as their main source of meat during the winter months. A spring-born piglet would forage under the trees on common land or feed on scraps in the farmyard until late November, when it would be killed. When the carcase was cut up, the first meals would be based around the fresh offal. The large joints would be packed into the brine tub or hung up to cure and the trimmings, blood and fat made into sausages. The intestines were thoroughly cleaned and used as sausage skins. The head would be turned into a tasty brawn, the trotters used to enrich a stew, and even the ears would be cooked until tender then dipped in butter and breadcrumbs and fried to provide a tasty crunchy morsel.

The annual pig killing, or *matanza*, is still an important part of social and culinary traditions in many parts of Europe, particularly Spain and southern Italy. Recently, I discovered that one did not have to look back very far to find *la matanza* in Britain. My father described how he was billeted with a family in Lincolnshire during the war. Anyone who had the space and means to do so would raise one pig per family in the same way as it had always been done, feeding the piglet from the spring onwards on potato peelings and household scraps until it was a well-grown animal by the autumn. My father happened to be at home the day the journeyman slaughterer came to call, after which the family's meat rations were enhanced for months to come.

It was the eighteenth-century French gourmet and philosopher Grimod de la Reynière who described the pig as 'an encyclopedia; a meal on legs', placing it firmly in the category of plebeian food, rather than that of *haute cuisine*. The classical French repertoire does, indeed, list very few pork recipes, and the ones it does describe are decidedly rustic and hearty, combining the meat with sauerkraut, red cabbage, Brussels sprouts, apples and mashed potatoes. Not a truffle or asparagus stalk in sight.

Since the pig has a long history of domestication in China, it is perhaps not surprising that this is a source of excellent pork recipes. However, pork is forbidden to Jews and Muslims alike and there are no pork recipes to be found in the cuisines of north Africa and the Middle East and other areas where Islam is the main religion.

Expect to find pork as a young meat, with firm white fat, pink flesh that is smooth and almost velvety, pale bones with a tinge of blue to them and a pale, pinky-fawn, smooth hairless skin. Avoid any meat that looks in any way damp or clammy, or that has oily, waxy looking fat. These days it is quite safe to eat pork all year round and not, as tradition used to have it, just in those months with an 'R' in them – that is, the winter months. Modern storage and refrigeration techniques mean that this restriction is no longer necessary. Nonetheless, it is still often seen as a winter food. It follows, therefore, that it is less in demand and often to be had at bargain prices during the summer.

HUSBANDRY

*W*ITH an IQ on a par with a dog the pig is certainly the most intelligent of all farm animals. It can recognise different human voices, learn to perform certain tasks and use more advanced problem solving techniques than any other animal used for meat production. Despite a reputation to the contrary, pigs in their natural state are also very tidy; they are the only farmyard animals to organise separate dunging, sleeping and feeding areas if enough space is provided.

The intelligence and survival ability of the pig has allowed it to become the most intensively reared mammal. As there is no need for grass in the diet – a pig can and will eat almost anything from chocolate, potato peelings and manure to yoghurt – it can be reared on anything from human food waste to cereals to fish, as long as the average ration provides the correct balance of nutrients. Food can therefore also be presented in a form which is effectively piped into troughs in front of the animal, doing away with the need for any human contact at this point.

In an intensive rearing system, sows are held in permanent position by a tether round the neck or waist or by use of a 'stall', which allows automated feeding and dung collection, minimises space requirements, and considerably reduces labour costs. Depression, which manifests itself in repetitive bar biting, sets in. To reduce stress, there are further specialist drugs available to partially tranquillise.

No straw or any other bedding is usually used in the most intensive systems. Instead growing pigs are kept on grids or slats, like ventilator covers found in pavements. Most of the dung drops through, leaving that which does not to smear on the pigs and that which does to be dragged away by a scraper. Effectively, the animals, which like to be clean, are living over an open sewer. Space is extremely restricted; if the pigs all lie down together, they cover the floor like pieces of a jigsaw. These conditions give rise to irrational fighting, including tail biting, which is combated by tail amputation at birth, and since automated feeding and dung collection keep labour and movement to a minimum, a pig's trip to the abattoir may be its first and only close contact with a human being and its first experience of natural daylight. This also causes great distress.

As a recent *Times* leader commented, 'the absence of wings is a design fault in the modern pig, although about the only one.' With wings it could escape man's swinish behaviour.

The efficiency with which the growing pork pig turns its food into weight gain is the key, and efforts to improve the food conversion factor are essential to intensive rearing. Pigs are most usually fed cereal in the form of wheat or barley (70-75%), protein in the form of soya or fishmeal (20%) plus trace elements and vitamins.

The economic importance of pork has given rise to more growth promoters being developed for pigs than for any other species. There are three basic types, of which two or more in combination are routinely used on intensively reared porkers. The first type are ionic salts, most commonly copper sulphate. It acts on gut bacteria, and it causes the characteristic and penetrating smell of modern pig farms. Manure from treated pigs is dangerous to other animals, and spreading it is restricted in certain parts of Europe. In conjunction with copper sulphate, one of ten or more different types of antibiotic will usually be used. All act on gut bacteria and cause hazards in that other farm species can be harmed by these materials. A hormone, Porcine Somatotrophin (PST), has also been cleared for use on pigs for human consumption, but it has yet to receive a product licence.

The unnatural living conditions of intensively reared pork pigs and the very early weaning practised – especially by outdoor sow farmers – are possible only when propped up by frequent use of curative drugs. At weaning, and frequently all the way through the rearing stage, an antibiotic will be introduced to the feed to combat a variety of conditions from scours to pneumonia.

In alternative systems of husbandy, sows and boars can be kept outside if ground conditions permit. However, this may not be appropriate as outdoor keeping can give rise to higher birth mortality and losses of young due to predators and exposure. In most areas in Britain the climate and terrain mean that this is not the best welfare choice for the porker, and in any case, growing porkers do not need to be kept outside. I was interested to hear from one farmer who advises on animal welfare cases that the worst conditions have been not from intensive pig farms but badly run outdoor units where the terrain and climate were entirely unsuitable for keeping pigs outdoors throughout the winter. Not only were the animals' conditions quite contrary to the practices of good stockmanship but the environment was being damaged by the pigs trampling and destroying the pasture.

With good husbandry, loose housing in strawed yards with plenty of space, daylight and fresh air is a good alternative. A covered building is more akin than is an open field to the woodland that a pig would seek out in nature. Straw bedding (to satisfy the rooting instinct) should be provided at all stages of growth in spacious indoor yards. Natural daylight and ventilation should be used and slatted flooring should only be used in a designated dunging area, which should not be more than a quarter of the floor space. The space allowed for each pig should easily allow room for the organisation of separate dunging, sleeping, feeding and exercise areas. The low stress of this system eliminates irrational fighting behaviour and, therefore, tail amputation is not necessary.

There is disagreement about the use of physical interventions such as farrowing crates, tooth-clipping and tail docking. Heal Farm does not allow any of these, finding none of them necessary. The RSPCA permit the use of farrowing crates and tooth clipping. The Soil Association do not allow farrowing crates to be used, nor tail docking to be practised. In principle, tooth clipping is not allowed but in cases where it is proved that the sow's welfare is at risk, then it would be permitted. Under the international standards of organic livestock management tooth clipping is not permitted, but in Norway, for example, where the breed of sow makes it more likely that damage would occur, it is permitted to file the piglets' teeth. Under the Guild of Conservation Food Producers' Code, tail docking and farrowing crates are not allowed. The sows farrow outdoors, in pens with plenty of straw, which means that the piglets can get away from the sow with little danger of being crushed. Only if there are sound, constructive reasons from a veterinary point of view relating to proven previous damage to a sow after farrowing, and that individual case is notified to the Guild, permission will be given for tooth clipping. The Real Meat Company's welfare code does not allow for tail docking. In certain circumstances, and for a limited period, special farrowing crates designed to minimise discomfort to the sow are permitted. If there is evidence that the sow or piglets would otherwise be harmed, tooth clipping is permitted.

In these conditions and with the average weaning age nearly double the intensive average, drug usage is reserved only for genuine illness, which is rare. Growth promoters are not used at any stage, as they should be regarded as an unnecessary adulteration of the food chain.

Pigs genuinely reared this way take nearly 20% longer to grow than intensive pigs. The reward is meat of an improved texture, flavour and smell, produced by the more mature animal living in stress-free conditions on a chemical-free diet.

CLASSIC DISHES

*A*PART FROM THE TRADITIONAL PORK ROASTS, there are many marvellous pork dishes from around the world that we can reproduce in our own kitchens. Amongst the countless Chinese recipes, some of my favourites are from the south, particularly the Cantonese *char siu*, a rich red roast pork which is marinated in soy sauce amongst other things, before cooking, then is used almost as a seasoning for other dishes, such as fried rice and noodle dishes. Barbecued spare ribs and stir-fried pork tenderloin are also dishes borrowed from China.

In European and American dishes, the pork often gives flavour to other ingredients. *Cassoulet*, from south-western France, has pork in it, as well as lamb and duck or goose. Boston baked beans, which is surely a first cousin of the *cassoulet*, has a piece of salt pork buried in amongst the beans. In Germany and Alsace, cuts of fresh and salt pork are served with sauerkraut and boiled potatoes.

The Iberian peninsula, too, is a rich source of pork recipes. Indeed, the Iberian pig is one of its great gastronomic treasures of the country, producing as it does cured ham (*jamón de Jabugo*) to rival that of Parma and San Daniele in Italy. Suckling pig is the speciality of Segovia, just north of Madrid. Clever Portuguese cooks invented what has become one of my favourite pork dishes – *porco alentejana*, pork in the Alentejo style.

GOOD COMPANIONS

*T*HIS PALE, RICH MEAT needs sharp, fruity or acidic accompanying flavours. Its single most striking accompaniment is fruit. Just as one would never serve fruit with beef, many pork dishes are unthinkable without it. In the Touraine in north-western France, it is traditionally served with prunes; due north in Normandy, it is served with apples, as it is in England and Germany; in New England it is served with cranberries, in Georgia with peaches, in Hawaii with pineapple. Experiment with other fruits, such as plumped out dried apricots or pears. Sauerkraut and spiced red cabbage are other perfect companions. Pickles also go beautifully with cold pork, in Szechuan and South Korea as well as in any Suffolk pub.

The pungent oily herbs such as sage, rosemary, myrtle, savory and thyme are right with pork, as are juniper berries, cardamom, ginger, allspice and nutmeg. For me, pork and Mediterranean flavours have little in common and I rarely cook it with tomatoes, olives, garlic or basil, for example. In Tuscany, on the other hand, it is slowly braised in milk, which eventually produces a rich brown sauce.

COOKING METHODS

BOILING

*T*HIS is something of a misnomer since the meat is never boiled, just allowed to simmer gently. It is a good method to use for a joint of salt pork. The meat should be soaked in water overnight, then put in a large saucepan of clean water together with vegetables, suitable herbs and spices, brought to the boil and simmered for 25 minutes per 1b/455 g.

ROASTING, GRILLING AND FRYING

*B*ECAUSE pork is young, tender meat, most cuts can be roasted, grilled or fried. It should always be well cooked and is never served rare or underdone. Whereas it was once considered too fat for many people's taste, it is now so lean that some of the cuts need basting as they roast. Alternatively, lean pork can be roasted in foil or a roasting bag to eliminate the need for basting.

For many people, the attraction of roast pork is that marvellous crisp, crunchy, golden mahogany crackling. To achieve perfect crackling, the skin must be scored in deep parallel lines, not too far apart, and right down through the fat.

Unless you have a very good knife, it is worth asking the butcher to do this for you. The rind can be removed and roasted separately or it can be left on the joint. Whichever method you choose, do not baste the skin and do not let it come into contact with any fat, liquid or cooking juices in the roasting tin. If it does, it will become like leather. When roasting, 30 minutes per lb/455 g plus 30 minutes, at 180°C/350°F/gas mark 4, will be sufficient.

BRAISING

*T*HIS is a suitable method for large, lean joints, which will benefit from the addition of lightly browned vegetables, herbs and well flavoured stock or wine.

STEWING AND CASSEROLING

*S*LOW cooking, either on top of the stove or in a heavy sealed pot in the oven, is an excellent method for this tender, succulent meat. A pork casserole is an extremely good tempered dish and difficult to spoil since it will just go on cooking gently until you are ready to serve it.

Cuts and Joints

English Cuts

Belly of pork

Also known as streaky and flank, this is the equivalent cut to breast of lamb. A thin cut of meat, it has approximately the same proportion of fat to lean in thin layers. The long rib bones can be removed and divided up for roasting or barbecueing. These are the *spare ribs*. The belly can then be stuffed, rolled and roasted.

This meat is also invaluable for terrines, and is the cut I buy for mincing when, as with terrines, a good proportion of fat is required. It can also be chopped up and added to casseroles, to which it adds flavour and richness. A tripe casserole, for example, benefits hugely from a few chunks of belly of pork.

Chops

Chump chops are cut from the hind loin and *loin chops* from the foreloin. These are best grilled or fried on a moderate heat rather than on a very high heat, as you would do for lamb. The skin and fat need cutting into at intervals with a sharp knife or kitchen scissors to stop them curling in the heat.

Foreloin

The rib end of the loin, this looks like a larger version of a best end of lamb. Boned, stuffed and rolled, it makes a marvellous dinner party dish and slices beautifully. It is also extremely good served cold, in thin slices with fresh bread, unsalted butter and homemade pickles. This is the joint that I stuff with apricots, walnuts, herbs and breadcrumbs.

Hind loin

This is the choice half of the loin, the prime roasting joint. It contains the kidney and the fillet or *tenderloin*. The hind loin will weigh about 4-5 lb/1.8-2.3 kg. If buying it to roast on the bone, have the butcher saw the chine bone (the half backbone) for easier carving. The *tenderloin* is now often sold separately from the hind loin. It is a lean, tender and very succulent piece of meat, weighing 10-14 oz/280-395 g, which makes it a perfect choice for two. It can be sliced into medallions and pan fried; or split lengthways, stuffed, tied and roasted; or marinated and cooked oriental style. If roasting it, a roasting bag is a good idea, to allow the meat to baste itself.

LEG OF PORK

*T*HIS is the largest joint of the carcase, weighing in excess of 10 lb/4.5 kg. It can be roasted whole, on the bone, or boned and stuffed. It is more usual, however, for the butcher to chop the leg into two large joints, the *knuckle half* (or *hough*, as it is known in Scotland) and the *fillet half leg*. Both are excellent roasting joints, the knuckle having rather more bone than the fillet end, which is the top half of the leg. This is sometimes sliced into *leg chops*, which can be braised or grilled.

NECK END

*Q*UITE an assortment of cuts come from this part of the pig. One of the best is the tasty and inexpensive *spare rib*, sometimes cut into *spare rib chops* (see chops) not to be confused with *spare ribs* (see belly of pork).

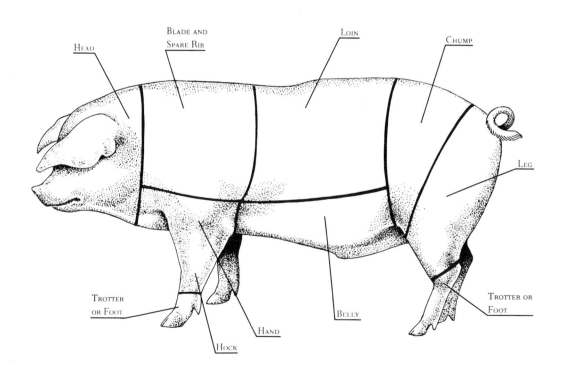

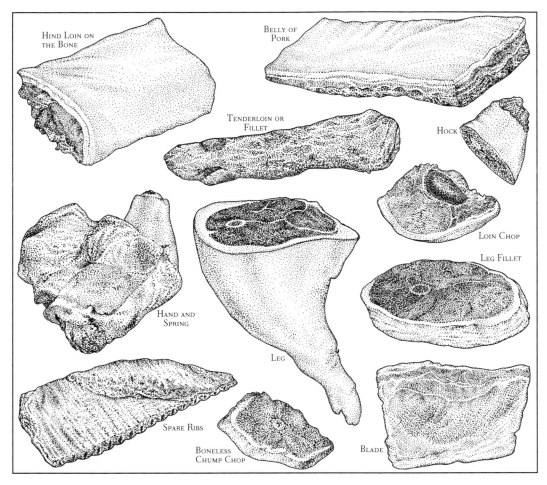

Hind Loin on the Bone

Belly of Pork

Tenderloin or Fillet

Hock

Hand and Spring

Loin Chop

Leg Fillet

Leg

Spare Ribs

Boneless Chump Chop

Blade

Spare rib chops are not quite as lean as loin chops because they have a good deal of marbling, but this is what helps to keep them sweet and succulent as they cook. The chops can be grilled or fried, cut into slivers for stir-frying, or the whole piece of spare rib can be braised.

SHOULDER

*T*HIS part of the forequarter is divided into the *blade bone, hand and spring* (also known as *shoulder*) and the *knuckle*. Either singly or together, these make excellent braising joints, inexpensive and with a very good flavour. The gelatinous content of the skin, bones and connective tissues give a wonderfully suave texture to casseroles. I find these pork cuts particularly good when cooked slowly, with beans, for example, in an unglazed clay pot. The *blade* can also be roasted, on the bone or boned, stuffed and rolled.

French Cuts

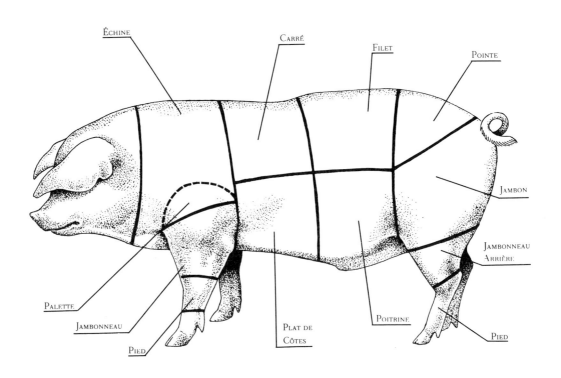

CARRÉ

*T*HE equivalent of the best end of neck, this joint is taken from the foreribs (*côtes*) and can be roasted on or off the bone, rolled and stuffed if the latter. The joint can also be divided into *côtelettes*, or chops, which are usually grilled or pan-fried, a marvellous combination served with the creamiest of mashed potatoes.

ECHINE

*T*HE top part of the shoulder has the equivalent of the spare rib joint, which is braised whole, pot roasted or cut into chops. The *palette* is the blade bone joint, which can be roasted on or off the bone.

FILET

*T*HIS is the prime roasting joint, the centre or middle loin, to which the kidney is attached. The *pointe de filet* is the tenderloin.

JAMBON

*T*HE *jambonneau* is the narrow, bony part of the hind leg between the trotter and the top end of the leg or *jambon*. It has plenty of flavour and gelatine and thus is good in soups and casseroles. It is also a nice piece to salt, then cook and serve with sauerkraut or beans. The *jambon* is usually roasted. The *pied de cochon* or *pied de porc* has little meat on it, but is a popular dish in its own right, cooked very slowly and sometimes boned.

PLAT DE CÔTES

THE forequarter flank is suitable for braising, pot roasting, or casseroles.

POITRINE

THE belly is sold whole or in slices and is a very versatile meat. It enriches other dishes such as stews and pâtés and comes into its own in the preparation of *rillettes*, that very superior potted meat made by slowly cooking belly pork until it falls apart, then shredding it and packing the meat loosely into pots, which are filled up with the clear liquid pork fat. When cool, it solidifies around the meat.

American Cuts

In the USA, the leg of pork is called the ham, whether it is fresh or cured. More of the cuts are sold cured or smoked than in Britain.

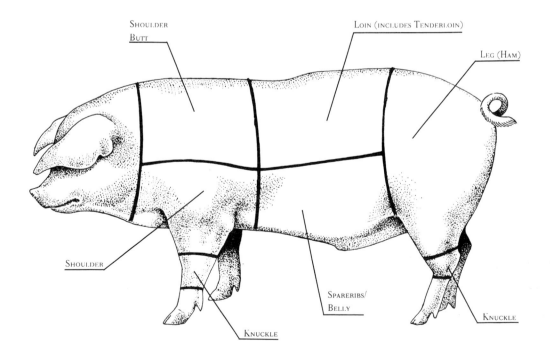

The main roasting joints are as follows:

Ham roast

*T*HIS is the leg of pork sometimes sold off the bone as *boneless ham roast*, a very large joint weighing up to 10 lb/4.5 kg.

Loin

*G*RILLING or frying cuts taken from the loin include chops such as the *butterfly pork chop, rib chop, loin chop, sirloin chop* or *top loin chop*. The *tenderloin* is cooked whole, or cut into *noisettes* or *medallions* and pan-fried.

Pork loin roast

*T*HIS is taken from the front or rear of the loin, or indeed can be the whole loin,

weighing about 10 lb/4.45 kg. The butcher will, of course, cut it at the weight you require.

Less tender cuts

*F*OR braising, pot-roasting or casseroling the main cuts are: the *shoulder slice, shoulder butt, spare ribs* and *pork knuckle*.

Ground pork

*T*HIS minced pork is usually taken from one of the forequarter or shoulder cuts, and is used as a stuffing for vegetables, or for mixing with other ground meats such as beef and veal to make excellent meat loaf.

Offal

*E*VERYTHING but the squeal, remember. Whilst some pork offal such as heart and liver is fairly coarse and a poor substitute for lamb's heart and liver, there are other parts of the pig that are unique and invaluable. One of the most important of these is pork fat.

Ears

*T*HESE are still very popular in France, but not often seen for sale here. When washed and singed, they are simmered for an hour or two to soften them, then pressed cold, cut in half, dipped in melted butter and breadcrumbs and fried to be served with a mustardy vinaigrette. Very nice they are, too, with that crunchy, gelatinous quality.

Head

*T*HIS shop used to be a popular dish, made into brawn (*fromage de tête* or *hure* in French). Like so many bits of offal and odds and ends, a pig's head needs a great deal of careful preparation, cleaning, singeing, scalding and soaking. Pig's cheek is sometimes sold separately; this is cooked until tender, then shaped and coated in egg and breadcrumbs to make a

Bath chap. If you ever find any brains for sale, these can be prepared like lamb's or calf's brains – soaked in cold water then blanched in lightly salted water – before being cooked.

Heart

Not often seen for sale, the heart, along with the lungs and melt, usually goes into commercial processing for pies and sausages.

Kidney

Pig's kidneys have a good flavour and texture. Usually they are divided and left attached to the loin chops, so are not often found separately. They can be grilled or fried.

Liver

Although not as delicate as lamb's liver, if soaked in milk first pork liver can be gently cooked or fried to make nutritious and inexpensive dishes. I have to say I have been put off pig's liver ever since eating a traditional Albigeois Christmas dish of sliced radishes and pork liver. It was truly one of the least enjoyable things I have ever eaten. Pig's liver is excellent, on the other hand, as one of the ingredients in terrines and pâtés.

Pork fat

The *back fat* is sliced into thin sheets that are used for barding – or wrapping around – lean joints of meat (pork or beef) and larding, or for inserting thin slivers of fat into lean pieces of meat such as a fillet of beef.

Back fat also makes *lard*, a fat used in cooking and baking. Flead, or leaf lard, is the crisp white flare fat from around the kidney. This is considered excellent for pastry making.

Caul fat is the thin, veil-like membrane around the stomach lining, through which run thin veins of fat. It is invaluable for making home-made sausages, faggots and *crépinettes* (from crépine, the French word for caul fat). It is stiff and needs soaking in warm water for 5 minutes or so to make it pliable.

Tail

Even this small pink curly object is worth having. Chop it up and add it to the stock pot as it is rich in gelatine.

Tripe

Pork tripe and intestine are the main ingredients of chitterlings (or tripe sausage, also known as *andouille* and *andouillette* in France).

Trotters

One of my favourite parts of the animal. I often buy a couple of trotters to cook in the stockpot. This way, they become tender and the stock takes in enough gelatine to allow it to set when cold. From this, you can make a good homemade aspic. The tender pig's trotters are then brushed with melted butter, rolled in soft breadcrumbs and grilled or baked until brown and crisp. Served with chips, watercress and a mustardy sauce, you have a dish straight out of the best French bistro. Pig's trotters have now become fashionable too, cooked by top chefs who bone, stuff, and braise them into rich, exquisite dishes.

ROAST LOIN OF PORK WITH APRICOT STUFFING

This is a dish that will wait for your guests and that cuts
very well cold. I have sometimes cooked a very large loin
for a buffet for twelve to fifteen people. Have the loin
boned or bone it yourself and keep the skin for wrapping
the meat to be cooked, and the bones for stock.

SERVES 4-6

1 loin of pork weighing
   3½ lb/1.6 kg (bone out)
3 sprigs of sage
stock, water or wine for deglazing
For the stuffing:
1 small onion, peeled
6 dried apricots, soaked in warm
   water for 30 minutes

3 oz/85 g soft brown breadcrumbs
2 oz/60 g pine kernels or chopped
   shelled walnuts
2 cloves of garlic, peeled and
   crushed
salt
pepper

REMOVE any excess fat from the meat and discard it. Finely chop any meat trimmings together with onion and apricots. Mix with the breadcrumbs, pine kernels, garlic and seasoning. Make a deep horizontal slit the full length of the loin, and open it out flat. Spread the stuffing over the meat. Roll it up and tie at intervals, tucking back any stuffing which escapes.

Preheat the oven to 180°C/350°F, gas mark 4. In a heated non-stick frying pan, fry the pork all over until well browned. Place a sprig of sage on a rack or crumpled foil in a roasting pan of a size just to hold the meat, place the meat on top, lay two sprigs of sage on top of the meat,

and cover it with the pork skin from which the fat has been trimmed. Place in the top half of the oven and roast for about 2 hours. Juices should run clear when a skewer is inserted into the centre of the joint; if the juices are pink, the meat is not yet cooked.

Remove the pork from the oven and keep warm. Skim excess fat from the roasting pan and then deglaze with a little stock, water or wine. Boil and strain into a jug or gravy boat.

A gratin of potatoes or a creamy potato purée is very good with roast pork. If the season is right, you might also consider a mixed purée of potatoes and turnips (see p. 352 and 355).

PORK TENDERLOIN WITH PRUNES

A little goes a long way with this rich and richly flavoured
dish with its origins in Touraine. The 'garden of France'
provides the full, almost sweet wine in which it is cooked,
but the prunes come from further south, Agen in Gascony,
if not from California where the Agen prune was
transplanted about a hundred years ago. I sometimes use
the same ingredients for pot-roasting a boned loin of pork.
An easy stove-top dish, this is perfect for two people.

SERVES 2

*1 pork tenderloin, weighing 8-10
    oz/230-280 g*
8 large prunes
¼ pt/140 ml Vouvray
1 oz/30 g butter
*2 shallots, peeled and finely
    chopped*
1 tbsp redcurrant jelly
1 tsp lemon zest
4 tbsp double cream
salt
pepper

SOAK the prunes in Vouvray for at least 6 hours. Remove the stones if necessary. Slice the pork into pieces 1 in/ 2.5 cm thick.

Melt the butter in a heavy frying or sauté pan and sweat the shallots until translucent and soft. Raise the heat slightly, add the meat and fry on all sides until it loses any rawness on the outside. Add about ⅛ pt/70 ml of the prune soak-ing juice to the pan as well as the prunes themselves and simmer until the meat is tender, gradually adding more juice as the liquid evaporates. Lower the heat to release some of the cooking juices and cook for 25-30 minutes.

Stir in the redcurrant jelly, lemon zest, cream and seasoning. Bring to the boil and cook only enough to amalgamate the cream with the cooking juices.

BRAISED PORK CHOPS

One of my reasons for cooking this simple recipe is to serve with it a wonderful dish of pear and potato purée. Arabella Boxer is the originator of this clever idea, suggesting it as an accompaniment to roast pork. The potatoes are peeled and boiled, then the pears peeled and poached in the same water after the potatoes have been cooked. The two are mashed together, seasoned with salt, pepper, butter and a little finely chopped crystallised ginger. The finished purée transforms the humble pork chop into something quite special.

SERVES 4

4 pork loin chops, with or
   without the kidney
1 oz/30 g flour
2 tbsp olive oil
1 mild onion, peeled and thinly
   sliced
1 lb/455 g tomatoes, peeled,
   seeded and chopped

¼ pt/140 ml chicken or vegetable
   stock
¼ pt/140 ml dry white wine or
   dry cider
salt
pepper
chopped parsley (optional)

TRIM most of the fat from the chops and dust them lightly with flour. Heat the oil in a frying pan and brown the chops on both sides. Transfer them to an earthenware dish. Fry the onion until golden brown and put them with the pork. Spoon the chopped tomatoes over the meat and onions. Deglaze the frying pan with the stock and cider and pour the liquid over the pork chops. Season and cover with foil.

Bake in the oven at 220°C/425°F, gas mark 7 for 30 minutes. Turn the heat down to 180°C/350°F, gas mark 4 and cook for a further 40-45 minutes, removing the foil for the last 15 minutes. A scattering of chopped parsley can be added just before serving.

GRILLED GLAZED PORK CHOPS

By no means a difficult or expensive dish, pork chops
seem to offer so little challenge that I rarely cook them.
When I do, I invariably think I should cook them more
often. Carefully grilled, they are juicy and full of flavour.
And they make the perfect meal for single diners. I see
them very much as an autumn kind of dish, to serve when
the weather is cold and you want something substantial.
Mashed potatoes or lentils go well alongside them then or,
for a lighter mood, grilled apple rings and green salad.
Loin chops, shoulder chops or chump chops can be used
for this recipe.

QUANTITIES PER PERSON

1 thick pork chop
1 tsp clear honey
2 tsp lemon juice
freshly ground black pepper
salt
2 tsp finely chopped parsley

MIX the honey, lemon juice and a good pinch of black pepper. Brush the chop all over with the glaze and let it stand for 15-20 minutes for the flavours to penetrate.

Have the grill very hot and put the chop under it. Turn it down after 4-5 minutes to continue cooking. Then raise the heat, turn the chop over – being careful not to pierce it with a fork and lose the juices – and finish the cooking, turning down the heat for the last few minutes.

Lightly season with salt and sprinkle with parsley before serving.

BAKED SPARE RIBS

This is the perfect food to serve for a Hallowe'en party or
some other informal occasion. Jacket potatoes can be
cooked in the oven at the same time to complete the meal.
You need to allow at least 1 lb/455 g ribs per person.
The meat can be marinated the night before required.

SERVES 6

6 lb/2.7 kg pork spare ribs,
cut into single ribs
a little wine or stock, for
deglazing the pan
For the marinade:
2 or 3 cloves of garlic, peeled
and crushed

2 tbsp tomato ketchup
2 tbsp clear honey or maple
syrup
2 tbsp soy sauce
2 tbsp Amontillado sherry
2 tbsp sherry vinegar
1 tbsp Worcester sauce

2 tsp Angostura bitters
2 tsp Dijon mustard
2 tsp freshly grated ginger
½ tsp chilli powder (or more
to taste)
salt
freshly ground black pepper

TRIM any excess fat from the spare
ribs and put them in a large shallow
bowl. Mix the marinade ingredients and
pour over the meat. Turn the ribs well to
make sure that they are coated, cover and
refrigerate until ready to cook.

Before baking the meat, bring it back
to room temperature. Preheat the oven
to 200°C/400°F, gas mark 6. Put a little
water in a roasting tin (this prevents the
meat juices burning on the pan and
makes the beginning of the gravy) and a
rack on top. Remove the spare ribs from
the marinade, letting as much of the
liquid as possible run back into the bowl.
Arrange the ribs on the rack in a single
layer. Roast them for about an hour.
Every 15 minutes or so, brush the ribs
with the marinade. Put them on a serving

plate and boil up the juices in the roasting tin with any remaining marinade and
some wine or stock, to make a gravy to
hand separately.

Another version of this is *Oriental
Spare Ribs*. The same amount of ribs are
marinated and cooked as described
above, but the marinade is given a more
oriental flavour. Rice wine and rice vinegar can be used to replace the sherry and
sherry vinegar, although this is not absolutely necessary. Replace the mustard
with toasted sesame oil, the bay leaf and
clove with a teaspoon of five spice
powder and slightly increase the amount
of ginger and soy sauce.

Sprinkle the spare ribs with sesame
seeds for the last 15 minutes in the oven.

PORK ADOBONG

I learned this method of preparing meat in a richly flavoured sauce which is sharpened by vinegar in the Philippines. Souring agents are vitally important in Filipino cooking, ranging through fruits such as the *calamansi* lime and green mangoes, to vinegars distilled from palm trees and coconuts. I particularly like coconut vinegar. You could also use cider vinegar, or, for a more pronounced sauce, a distilled vinegar. Aged sherry vinegars and antique balsamic vinegars would be wasted on such a dish. Short ribs of beef can be cooked in the same way.

SERVES 4

4 pork spare rib chops, trimmed
    of most of their fat
7 fl oz/200 ml vinegar (see
    above)
3/4 pt/430 ml water
3 tbsp soy sauce
6 cloves of garlic, peeled and
    sliced

1 medium onion, peeled and
    chopped
2 bay leaves
1/2 tsp coarsely ground black
    pepper
1/4 tsp salt
1-2 tbsp sunflower or groundnut
    oil (optional)

P UT the meat in a saucepan (not an aluminium one) with all the other ingredients except for the oil. Bring gently to the boil, lower the heat, cover and simmer for 40 minutes. (If possible, keep the kitchen window open to get rid of the smell, which is that of a pickle factory!)

Remove the meat and put it to one side. Skim and discard all the fat from the cooking liquor, bring it to the boil and reduce it to about 1/3 pt/200 ml.

Heat the oil in a frying pan (or use a non-stick pan) and when it is very hot brown the meat evenly all over. Put on a serving plate and pour the sauce over it. This is very good served with rice and steamed greens such as spinach or bok choy, the white-ribbed leafy green Chinese vegetable.

GALICIAN PORK CASSEROLE

This is not so much an authentic Galician dish – I never ate pork casserole there – but is inspired by the good things which come from this wet, green north-western region of Spain, particularly its fruity white wine Albariño. A varietal wine, it goes beautifully with the fish, shell-fish and high quality meat for which the region is famed. Use the new season's garlic when available. Apart from parsley, herbs are hardly used in Galician cookery.

SERVES 6

1½-2 lb/680-900 g pork from the shoulder or leg, off the bone
½ pt/280 ml Albariño (or other fruity dry white wine)
2-3 cloves of garlic, peeled and finely chopped
1 onion, peeled and sliced
2 tbsp olive oil

1 tbsp flour (optional)
3 small fennel bulbs (or 1 large one)
1 dozen black or green olives (optional)
1 green pepper, seeded and sliced (optional)

good pinch of saffron threads, soaked in warm water for 20 minutes
salt
pepper
1-2 lb (455-900 g) new potatoes (optional)
1-2 tbsp flat-leaved parsley, roughly chopped

C UT the meat into 2 in/5 cm cubes and put them in a bowl. Pour on the wine and mix in the garlic. Cover and marinate for at least 4 hours, or overnight if more convenient.

Fry the onion in the olive oil in a frying pan until just wilting and push to one side. Drain and dry the meat, reserving the marinade. Dust the meat with flour if you like and fry until browned all over. Trim the fennel, cutting small bulbs in half, or a large one into six pieces.

Spread the onion over the bottom of a casserole or soaked clay pot, put the meat on top and tuck the fennel around it. If using the olives and pepper, put them in. Deglaze the pan with the marinade and, when it is bubbling, stir in the saffron.

Pour the liquid over the meat, cover and cook in a low oven for 2-3 hours at 170°C/325°F, gas mark 3. Season towards the end of cooking time.

For a more substantial one-pot dish, put in a pound or two of new potatoes 40 minutes before the end of the cooking time. Stir in the parsley just before serving.

PORK AND CLAMS

This Portuguese dish stands like a signpost to my tastebuds, since it seems not yet to have become part of the anonymous international repertoire, a fate which has been visited on so many dishes – *paella, bouillabaisse* and *risotto*, to name but a few. I first tasted the dish over twenty years ago in Lisbon and have since enjoyed it on every visit to Portugal. Traditionally it is cooked in the *cataplana*, a copper cooking vessel with a deep domed lid, which can be shaken and tossed over the heat, but I have discovered that it can also be cooked in a wok.
It is best to choose not *too* lean a cut; diced shoulder or spare rib chops are good. The clams to use are the small sweet Venus clams. Mussels can also be used. As with many Portuguese dishes, the fresh coriander is essential and the dish is not worth doing without it.

SERVES 4

1½ lb/680 g mussels or clams
¾ lb/340 g diced pork
1 tbsp olive oil
1 onion, peeled and finely chopped

garlic cloves to taste, peeled and chopped
1-2 tsp ground coriander seeds

¼ pt/140 ml chicken or pork stock
1 glass of dry white wine
salt and pepper
fresh coriander leaves

THOROUGHLY scrub and rinse the shellfish, discarding any that do not close in the water.

Brown the pork in olive oil and add the onion, garlic and coriander. Add half the stock and all the wine. Bring to the boil, cover, lower the heat and simmer as gently as possible until the pork is tender. Add more stock if necessary. Raise the heat, put in the shellfish and cover with a tight-fitting lid After the heat has been full on for about a minute, season the dish and add the coriander, then replace the lid. Shake the pan vigorously (a real *cataplana* can be turned over and swung above the head). Return to the heat for a minute or two more and take to the table. Serve from the pan in which it was cooked. Rice is the best sop to serve with this.

BERZA

This filling stew of pork, beans, chick peas and black pudding comes from Andalucia. Not all sun and sea, it has mountains towards Granada which can be grey, bleak and chilling. We tasted this steaming, fragrant dish late one night in the tiny white village of Arcos de la Frontera. Soak the white beans and chick peas overnight. Use pork shoulder or spare rib chops.

SERVES 6-8

3 lb/1.35 kg pork, cut into
    2 in/5 cm pieces
1 onion
1 celery stalk
1 carrot
2 tbsp olive oil
4 cloves of garlic
1 oz/30 g flour
½ lb/230 g soaked chickpeas

½ lb/230 g soaked haricot or
    cannellini beans
2 pt/1.15 l stock
1 or 2 red peppers, charred and
    peeled
½ lb/230 g green beans, topped
    and tailed
½ lb/230 g black pudding,
    sliced
salt and pepper

TRIM, peel and thinly slice the vegetables. Fry in the olive oil until golden brown and then add the garlic. Toss the meat in the flour, add to the pan and fry all over. Add the chickpeas, beans and stock. Bring to the boil and cook for 5 minutes. Cover and cook in a low oven or over the lowest heat for 1½-2 hours until the pulses are almost tender.

Cut the peppers into strips and halve the beans if necessary. Add to the casserole and cook for a further 15 minutes before adding the black pudding and seasoning.

All it needs now is simmering for about 10 minutes before serving with plenty of crusty bread. This really is a whole meal in itself.

All you need before it is a green salad or a light vegetable dish – we had wild asparagus – and cheese and fruit after it. Cider is as good as anything to drink with this.

BIGOS

Punctuate this rich winter stew with small mouthfuls of
ice-cold vodka to recreate an authentic Polish experience.
Baked potatoes and rye bread are good accompaniments,
as is Polish beer.

SERVES 8

1½ lb/680 g boneless shoulder of
  pork or spare rib chops, cut
  into 2 in/5 cm pieces
1½ lb/680 g kielbasa or other
  spicy meaty cooking sausage,
  cut into 2 in/5 cm pieces
1 oz/30 g flour
½ lb/230 g onions, peeled and
  sliced
2 tbsp olive oil
½ oz/15 g dried porcini, soaked
  for 30 minutes
2 lb/900 g can or pack of
  sauerkraut

6 cloves
2 in/5 cm cinnamon stick
1 bay leaf
½ tsp dill seeds
½ lb/230 g soaked pitted prunes
4 canned plum tomatoes
water, beer or stock to cover
freshly ground black pepper
salt
2-3 tbsp soured cream (optional)
fresh dill or parsley

Toss the meat and sausage in the flour. Brown the onion in the oil and then brown the meat in the same pan. Add the mushrooms, sauerkraut, spices and prunes. Rub the tomatoes through a sieve into the mixture.

Cover with liquid, bring to the boil, cover and simmer gently for 1½-2 hours, or cook in a low oven. Uncover for the last 20 minutes to let the liquid evaporate as the stew should be fairly thick. Season and stir in the cream if using it. Serve straight from the cooking pot, brightened up with greenery if you wish.

PORK PIE WITH TRADITIONAL HOT-WATER CRUST PASTRY

The real pork pie is on its way to extinction if we're not careful. What is available commercially is one of the most degenerated of all food products – full of additives, cereal and scraps of meat recovered from the carcase, gristle, offal and so on. A home-made pork pie is a beautiful sight: tall and proud, with crisp, firm golden pastry, glazed on the top, encasing succulent tender meat in a flavoursome jelly.

Once when I was making this pie and had neither pig's trotter nor pork bones, I made the stock with a chicken carcase and then used gelatine to obtain a set. It worked very well and is, of course, quicker since the chicken carcase only needs an hour or so to simmer. For an even finer tasting jelly, you can replace some of the water with dry white wine.

GIVES TEN ¾ IN/2 CM SLICES

For the hot water pastry:
up to 1½ lb/680 g plain flour
1 level tbsp salt
9 oz/255 g lard
7 oz/200 ml water
For the stock:
1 pig's trotter, split in two
2 lb/900 g pork bones
4 pt/2.3 l water
1 carrot
1 celery stalk
12 peppercorns

For the filling:
1 lb/455 g fat belly of pork
¼ lb/110 g streaky bacon
1 lb/455 g lean pork meat, off
   the bone
1 tsp freshly ground black pepper
¼ tsp freshly grated nutmeg
1 tbsp finely chopped fresh
   parsley
½ tbsp finely chopped fresh sage
   or thyme

MAKE the stock. Simmer the ingredients together for 2 to 3 hours, strain and reduce to 1 pt/570 ml.

Remove the rind from the belly of pork and bacon (the rind can be added to the stock pot) and mince the two to-

140

gether. Fry quickly, in batches if necessary, just enough to remove the raw look. Dice the lean pork and fry it in the same way, draining off any cooking liquid into the stock. Mix the meats together and add the spices and herbs. Cover and stand it in a cool place.

Make the pastry, either in a bowl or on a marble slate or, as I make it, in a food processor. Sift together the flour and salt, keeping back about 5 tablespoons flour. Put the lard and water in a saucepan and bring them to the boil, stirring continuously and slowly adding the flour. When dry and liquid ingredients are thoroughly blended together in a hot, smooth (rather than sticky) mass, turn it out on to a worktop and knead, adding more flour as necessary to form a workable pastry.

Preheat the oven to 170°C/325°F, gas mark 3. Cut off a quarter of it to use as a lid and press or roll out the rest to line a 2 lb/approx 1 kg loaf tin, leaving about ½ in/1 cm pastry hanging over the rim of the tin. Fill with the pork mixture, slightly mounding it in the centre. Roll out the remaining pastry and use to cover the pie. Press the edges together, roll them over once inside the rim of the loaf tin (that way, it will be an easy matter to slide a palette knife all the way round the pie when cold to ease it out of the tin) and make a fluted edge by pinching together at intervals. Roll out the pastry trimmings to make stick-on decorations if you wish. Make a pencil diameter hole in the top of the pastry, and keep it open with a small roll of greaseproof paper. Brush the pie with milk or egg to glaze it, and lay two or three layers of greaseproof paper or foil on top so that the crust does not bake too brown.

Bake in the centre of the oven for 1¼ hours. Remove the paper for the last 15 minutes. Let the pie cool for 2-3 hours, and then slowly pour in, through the hole in the pastry, as much of the pint of rich stock as you can. Allow to cool completely. Then wrap in foil or greaseproof paper to store. Do not keep the pie for more than two to three days in the refrigerator before eating it.

PORK AND YAM PIE

Sweet potatoes or ordinary potatoes can be substituted in this Colombian dish if you cannot get yam. Many varieties of yam are available, but not usually in the same place and the variety is not important here.

SERVES 6

1 lb/455 g lean pork, minced
2 onions, peeled and finely
    chopped
2 cloves of garlic, peeled and
    crushed
1 oz/30 g butter
2 tbsp chopped fresh parsley
1 green pepper, seeded and
    chopped
salt

pepper
¼ pt/140 ml tomato juice
2 tbsp capers
3 tbsp raisins
4 tbsp Amontillado sherry or port
2 lb/900 g yam, peeled
butter or olive oil for mashing
    yam
1 egg
1 tsp baking powder

GENTLY fry the onions and garlic in the butter, add the parsley, pepper and pork and cook until the pork has lost its raw look. Add the salt, pepper and tomato juice and simmer together, covered, for 45 minutes. Remove from the heat and add the capers, raisins and wine.

Meanwhile, boil the yam until tender and mash with a little butter or olive oil. Mix in the egg and baking powder. Line a greased pie dish with half the yam mix-ture, pressing it down. Fill with the meat mixture. Spread the remaining yam purée on a sheet of greaseproof paper, shaping it to the same size as the pie dish. Turn it over the meat filling and neaten the edges.

Bake at 180°C/350°F, gas mark 4 for 35-45 minutes.

Steamed spinach or Chinese leaves can be served with this, but on balance I prefer to serve it on its own and follow it with a salad.

LAMB

LAMB HAS ALWAYS BEEN ASSOCIATED with springtime, in both a culinary and a symbolic sense. Signifying renewal and rebirth, the lamb featured in ancient Chinese spring rituals, as well as in the Jewish Passover, in Greek and Russian Orthodox Easter festivals, and of course the Christian Easter festival. Apicius, the Roman gourmet, recorded many fine recipes for lamb, some so elaborate that they must have been intended for festival food. In many Western countries it is still the traditional dish to serve on Easter Sunday. Today Romans will leave the city on Easter Sunday and head for the small towns in the hills, such as Frascati, where they will drink fresh young white wine and eat huge platters of simply roasted *abbacchio* (unweaned baby lamb).

The sheep is a rugged creature and thrives where other livestock and crops do not, on hillside and mountain pastures of temperate and cold climates. Since these are spread across both northern and southern hemispheres, mutton and lamb form part of the culinary traditions of many nations. Yet the different methods of cooking are not so very different, owing a great deal to the simple lifestyle of the rural communities supported by sheep farming. Irish stew and Lancashire hotpot are not very far removed in style from the *dabinlo*, or hot-pot of Mongolia, where lamb is simmered in a fragrant spicy soup to ward off the icy winds of the barren Asian steppes.

Human migration, too, led to culinary traditions being passed on. Basque shepherds from northern Spain and south-western France emigrated to California and the American West, imparting not only their skills but their cooking. Even today one can find Basque restaurants in San Francisco serving family-style meals at long trestle tables with communal jugs of wine, baskets of rough delicious bread and massive tureens of soup. One of my favourite lamb recipes, the Basque leg of lamb illustrated on p. 164, has its origins in Arizona rather than the Basque country.

British as well as Basque breeds of lamb have also found their way abroad. In Marin County, north of San Francisco, up in the hills west of Novato, a flock of Border Cheviots is to be found at Chalk Farm. This is a hardy mountain breed, from the border country between Scotland and England, and so does well in the high California terrain with its surprisingly chilly winters. This long-ribbed animal provided the meat originally used for the traditional Lancashire hotpot, its tall chops standing upright in the pot. Although the breed has been in the Borders since the fourteenth century, legend has it that these sheep, which are unlike other local breeds, swam ashore from a Spanish shipwreck. Even then, clearly, Spanish sheep and shepherds were renowned.

Of all animals, sheep and lambs are to be seen most as a part of our landscape rather than housed in 'units' away from their natural habitat. When one considers what the animal has fed on – the upland lamb nibbling on wild herbs and heather, the lowland lambs of Kent, Brittany and Texel in the Friesian islands feeding on lush salt marsh pastures – no wonder it tastes so good. This proximity to nature makes lamb a seasonal food almost in the same way that game is. Its breeding and growth season is affected by the climate to such an extent that we can work out which breeds, from which areas, are going to be available at a particular time of year.

The first of the English lamb is available in early spring, when it is a young, delicate meat from winter-born lambs raised in the milder south of England. Soon after that appear the lowland Scottish breeds, followed in the summer by lambs from the Welsh and Scottish hills. By the autumn the hardy mountain lambs from Scotland and the Islands, which give a lean, dark meat so unlike spring lamb, are available. After Christmas, until it is a year old, the lamb is known as a hogget. Much older than that and it becomes mutton, but only something like 4% of the national flock becomes mutton. It is very rare to find it for sale and I have not therefore included any mutton recipes. If you are lucky enough to come across any, the recipes for goat meat will suit mutton very well.

As a young meat, lamb is tender with a fine grain when you see a cut across the muscle. The younger the animal, the paler pink the meat will be. Its feeding also has a bearing on colour: some hill breeds have quite dark meat even when young. The fat is white, firm and brittle yet waxy. Lamb should be hung for about four days to mature it to the right degree.

Lamb is one of my favourite meats for roasting, probably because the unintimidating size of the joints is suitable for two people. It is also the meat most suited to roasting; because it is a young meat it will be tender, and because it is reared outside in a cold temperate climate the meat has a good covering of fat, which bastes as it cooks in the fierce heat of the oven, thus keeping it moist and full of flavour.

Husbandry

SHEEP ARE THE ULTIMATE go-anywhere, graze-anything animal. One man and his dog can keep large numbers on an open plain, as is the mode where such open plain still exists. For this reason, they have escaped most aspects of intensification and welfare problems are more concerned with neglect or poor husbandry practice caused by the vagaries of pricing systems.

Although fully indoor lamb production is possible, it remains rare. Usually grass, grazed directly, makes up the main part of the diet, although often it is provided as hay or silage in the winter months. If the flock is brought inside for the winter, hay and silage must be fed. Simple rolled (crushed) barley or a commercial 'nut', based on dried cereal or grass with soya protein, may also be used.

Where the animals are still out at full range – in Australia and New Zealand, for example – inspection for health problems will be lacking and the sheep can suffer from neglect. Overgrazing is common in Britain. Intentional starvation is sometimes used abroad to control numbers in the case of overproduction. Close attention at lambing time is vital, as is the condition of any accommodation provided. Too often, squalid and overcrowded conditions prevail.

While growth promoters are very few in number and are rarely used in sheep production, there are three categories of drug used to a fairly high level. Wormers, to kill parasitic worms, are needed to a greater or lesser extent, depending on how intensively the grassland is used. Extensive grazing greatly reduces the need for wormers. Coccidiostats, to kill a small parasite which causes trouble to sheep and poultry, are used routinely by many farmers where this condition is a problem. Finally, government-enforced annual dipping makes the sheep the only animal that carries compulsory drug usage. Some dips are more potentially harmful than others. Safe withdrawal time before slaughter must be observed.

In Europe particularly, the point of final sale of lambs can have a dramatic effect on price. This is in part caused by an unusual price-support system, which varies daily in the United Kingdom. It means that lambs may be shipped vast distances, from one end of the country to the other, passing through livestock markets more than two or three times to chase the best price. Even if food and water are provided, which is rare, the animals suffer unnecessary distress during these long journeys.

As a favourite food of the Jewish and Muslim communities and countries, some lambs meet ritual slaughter while still conscious, as required by those religions. Any extras killed this way are sold back on to the open market.

It is still possible to have flocks of sheep simply grazing on extensive pastures under the control of a responsible shepherd who will tend any sick animals, move the flock on to fresh pasture as needed and provide good accommodation and vigilance at lambing time. Good pasture management reduces or removes the need for worm treatment. If a fair price can be set, then there is no need to transport the animals for hundreds of miles trying to chase the best price. Taking the stock directly to slaughter removes the distress caused by live markets and allows control to see that pre-slaughter stunning takes place.

This traditional method causes less distress all round and provides the best possible finished product.

Classic Dishes

*L*AMB IS A CURIOUS MEAT. On the one hand, many lamb dishes are simple and rustic, tending to come in a direct line from areas where sheep are raised and are not in any way dressed up for the table. One of my very favourite lamb dishes is a Basque-style leg of lamb, well-cooked rather than pink, for which the leg is boned and the bone is replaced with a length of pork fillet. The whole is seasoned, tied and roasted. When sliced, you get a large tender piece of lamb encircling a small slice of pork fillet (see p. 164). I highly recommend this dish for those who like their lamb well done.

On the other hand, lamb has also found its way into the kitchens of top chefs. A loin or fillet of lamb, for example, will divide into the neat round pieces so well adapted to modern cooking, with its small portions of meat or fish sitting on a pool of reduced, glazed sauce, garnished with a sprig of this and a curl of that, and accompanied by a few squeaky green beans tied in a bundle with a chive stalk.

Thus you will find recipes for lamb in every kind of cookbook, from the masterworks of the European chefs through books on regional French, Spanish and Greek cooking, the rich, spicy cooking of the Indian sub-continent and, perhaps most abundantly of all, in the cookery books of the Middle East where lamb is the main meat consumed. There, tender cubes of lamb are charcoal grilled as kebabs, similar to the Russian Caucasian dish of *shashlik*; whole lambs are roasted with spices, nuts and fruit and served with light, dry rice; lean raw lamb is minced and mixed with cracked wheat in a flavoursome and savoury dish called *kibbeh*.

Apart from Lancashire hot-pot and Irish stew, not too far from home we can enjoy some of the delicious French recipes for lamb such as the *navarin d'agneau*, a light lamb stew with spring vegetables.

Good Companions

*A*s I think of appropriate accompaniments for lamb, the ones that come immediately to mind are the strong clear flavours of the Mediterranean: garlic, French mustard, tarragon, rosemary, tomatoes, olive oil, olives, aubergines. I think of a leg of lamb stuck with garlic cloves and rosemary, served with baked aubergine or ratatouille. But lamb also goes well with sweet tender young vegetables, new potatoes, baby carrots and kohlrabi, peas and beans.

Then I'm reminded of fragrant lamb *tagines* from North Africa, flavoured with cinnamon, coriander and cumin, combined with almonds and dried apricots or quinces and served with *couscous* or the spicy Middle Eastern, Indian and Persian lamb dishes served with golden saffron flavoured rice. In Britain we share the Middle East's fondness for lamb and mint; I wonder if crusader knights brought this combination back in the Middle Ages. Whilst I enjoy the flavour of mint, I am not keen on putting it with sugar and vinegar, which I find overpowers all else in the meal, particularly the sort of wine that goes with a fine roast leg of lamb. So instead, I tuck a few sprigs around the roasting joint for a more subtle effect.

Although lamb is not much featured in oriental cookery, its spices are marvellous with it. I have marinated a leg of lamb in soy sauce, rice wine and rice wine vinegar, fresh ginger, a little honey and some star anise, then brushed it with this marinade as it was roasting. There are those, too, who claim that lamb is best accompanied by the simple flavours of its natural habitat: rowan jelly with lamb from the Scottish mountains, samphire or laver bread with lamb from the salt marshes and thyme or rosemary with lamb from the Welsh hills.

COOKING METHODS

POACHING

*T*HIS is not a traditional cooking method for lamb, but it works with fillet, well-trimmed noisettes or other lean cuts, giving a tender, pink, fat-free piece of meat. One drawback of poaching is that it does nothing for the appearance of the meat, which emerges a dingy institutional grey. This is the cooking method of a Mongolian hot-pot.

STEAMING

*A*s with poaching, so with steaming. The end result is tender and low in fat, a dull grey on the outside but rosy pink and appetising when sliced. Fillet or a trimmed, boned loin can be steamed quickly, then allowed to rest without further cooking.

ROASTING

*B*ECAUSE lamb is a fatty meat, it needs to be well-trimmed before roasting, particularly if you are having prepared a special joint, such as a crown roast (see section on cuts). It is important to specify to your butcher how much fat to remove.

If you spit roast or barbecue lamb, the fat just runs off and is not a problem. This has to be the very best method of all for cooking a juicy, tender shoulder or leg of lamb. I have been lucky enough to eat it like that on several occasions and it cannot be bettered.

The English taste for lamb is said to be for well done meat, although I think that is changing. To well roast a leg or loin of lamb in the oven, it needs about 25 mins per lb/450 g at 180°C/350°F/gas mark 4, plus 25 minutes. If I am roasting a small best end of lamb for two people, I roast it at 200°C/400°F/gas mark 6 for 20-25 minutes, then let it rest in a warm place for 10-15 minutes or more, which relaxes the meat fibres and distributes the pink juices throughout the meat.

FRYING AND GRILLING

*S*MALL, neatly trimmed noisettes, loin chops and chops cut from the leg (known as gigots in Scotland) are all well suited to the hot, dry methods of cooking. Lamb usually has enough fat to baste itself during grilling.

BRAISING AND POT ROASTING

*L*AMB joints are on the whole so tender that they do not require this slow moist method of cooking to tenderise them, and indeed, with the amount of fat they contain, it is not a particularly good idea to braise them. However, some of the extremities such as the shanks are tougher and leaner as you would expect, and cook into tasty and inexpensive dishes.

STEWING AND CASSEROLING

*T*HE scrag and middle neck are often cut across the bone, or the shoulder boned and sold as casseroling lamb. Well trimmed of fat, it makes good stew with the addition of herbs and vegetables. The leaner best end chops are the foundation of some of our famous traditional stews such as Lancashire hot-pot and Irish stew.

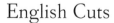

CUTS AND JOINTS

English Cuts

BEST END OF NECK

*S*OMETIMES called rack of lamb, this is the rib joint between the middle neck and loin and is one of the best value and most versatile pieces of lamb. It has six or seven small chops on it, which makes it a perfect joint to roast for two people. With two best ends and plenty of time, you can produce one of two rather spec-

tacular roasts. A *crown roast* is formed by joining two trimmed best ends together, ribs to the top and fatty side in. The cavity in the centre is usually filled with a stuffing and, when roasted and ready to serve, paper frills are slipped on the trimmed cutlet bones. A *guard of honour* is made by joining together two trimmed best ends so that they face each other, fat side out, ribs to the top and interlocking like hands at prayer.

If you want your butcher to prepare either of these cuts, you need to give several days notice.

Breast

*T*HIS is an inexpensive cut of meat from the belly of the animal. It is quite fatty and is best boned and well trimmed before stuffing, rolling and tying. Roasting is one way of cooking it – there is certainly enough fat on, and in, the meat to baste it. If well trimmed of fat, it can be braised.

Chops and cutlets

*C*HUMP or *loin* chops are cut from the loin to give thick chops of tender meat ideal for grilling or frying. *Best end* chops or cutlets are thinner than those from the loin or chump and, when trimmed of much of their fat, are used for Irish stew and Lancashire hot-pot as well as grilling. They can be replaced in stews and casserole by *middle neck* cutlets. Occasionally the top end of the leg is sliced across into *leg chops*, which grill beautifully to produce a quickly cooked, tender, juicy piece of meat. A garlicky green salad would be a suitable adornment.

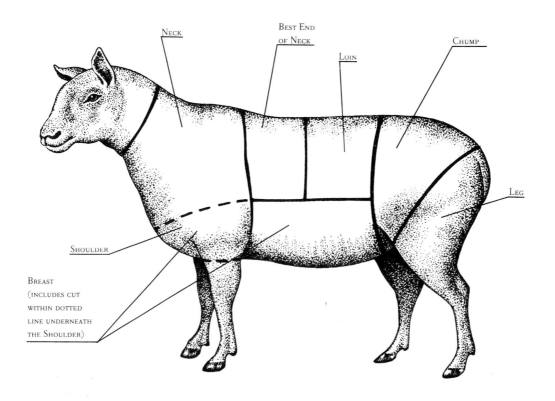

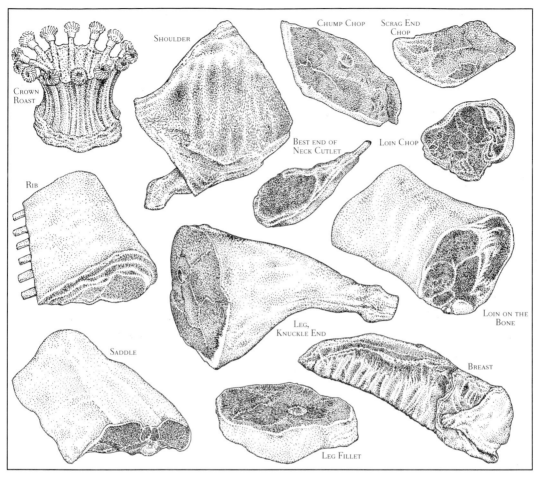

CROWN
ROAST

SHOULDER

CHUMP CHOP

SCRAG END
CHOP

RIB

BEST END OF
NECK CUTLET

LOIN CHOP

LOIN ON THE
BONE

SADDLE

LEG,
KNUCKLE END

BREAST

LEG FILLET

LEG

*C*ALLED by its French name *gigot* in Scotland, this is one of the prime roasting joints, and one of the largest, weighing 4-6 lb/1.8-2.7 kg. Often it is divided into two, the *knuckle* or *shank end* and the *leg fillet* which is the top of the leg. The leg lends itself to traditional treatments and can be roasted on the bone or boned and stuffed.

LOIN

*E*ACH loin divides into the *chump end* near the tail, and the *loin* at the *rib end*.

These joints can be roasted, on or off the bone, or stuffed, rolled and roasted (see above).

MIDDLE NECK AND SCRAG END

*T*HIS is the bony end of the forequarter nearest to the head, sometimes sold as one piece, sometimes chopped up and sold separately. With quite a lot of fat and a considerable amount of bone, these are cheap cuts which make exceedingly tasty casseroles when cooked on a gentle heat. They will take plenty of spices – I sometimes use them for lamb paprika or lamb *tagines*, and they can be used for excellent curries.

Occasionally the *neck fillet* is boned out and sold separately at a higher price. This is a nice lean piece of meat, suitable for grilling or frying and is the perfect size to cut up for kebabs.

NOISETTES

*T*HE eye of the loin is completely boned out and the resulting fillet is tied around, usually with a layer of fat, to be fried or grilled. This is an expensive cut of meat since there is much wasted bone. If you prepare noisettes at home, either from loin chops or the loin, you do at least have the bones from which to make a stock for sauce.

Noisettes can also be made by boning *best end chops* and tying them into rounds.

RIB

*T*HIS is the whole forequarter section, including the *scrag end, middle neck* and *best end*, but it is rarely sold whole as the three cuts within the rib are so different and not suited to the same cooking methods.

SADDLE OF LAMB

*T*HE large saddle area of the carcase between the leg and rib yields the tenderest and most expensive joints and cuts, the largest of which is the truly magnificent *saddle of lamb*. Weighing up to 8 lb/3.6 kg, this really is a special occasion joint and one which you will need to order specially. Whereas each carcase is usually divided into two sides and then cut into joints, the saddle is taken from right across the carcase and includes both loins, the kidneys and the tail, which are tied and skewered to the joint in a decorative fashion ready for roasting. With a good covering of fat, the saddle will need little attention in the oven, and is best cooked quite plainly.

SHOULDER

*T*HIS is a good, large roasting joint from the forequarter, weighing about 4 lb/1.8 kg. It has an excellent sweet flavour and, because it is fattier than the leg, it is ideally suited to being barbecued or spit-roasted. As it contains the blade bone and the shank, it is an awkward shape. Butchers now turn this to good use and, with some notice, will produce a *mock duck* for you. The shoulder is partly boned and the shank bone turned up and outwards, the whole being tied together and decorated so that it resembles a duck. Roasted, it makes a good centrepiece.

Boned shoulder can also be turned into *rosettes*. The opened out shoulder is stuffed (about 4 oz/110 g stuffing per 1 lb/455 g meat) then folded over and tied across three times, star-fashion, to give it a round rosette-like appearance. I use an olive, walnut and lemon zest mixture with some soft breadcrumbs and a little chopped ham (see p. 160). This makes a very good inexpensive roast.

Shoulder is also sold boned for kebabs or casseroles, and well trimmed boned shoulder can be minced.

French Cuts

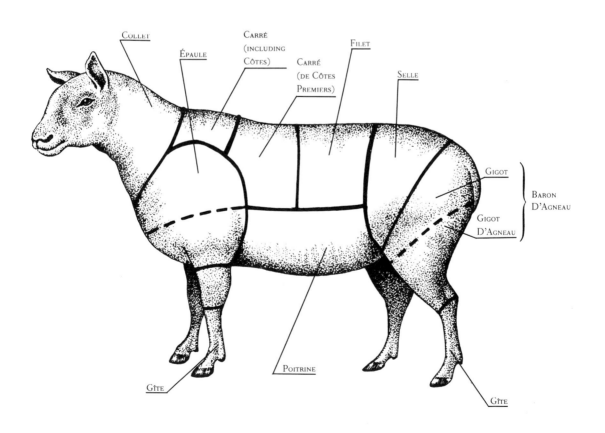

Baron d'agneau
The top end of the leg, this is suitable for roasting.

Carré
The rack or best end of neck is one of the most popular smaller roasting joints.

Collet
This is the scrag end of neck, also known as *collier*, and is used for casseroles or stews.

Côtes
The *côtes premières* or *côtelettes premières* are the four cutlets from the best end of neck nearest the loin; *côtes secondes* or *côtelettes secondes* are the four cutlets from the best end of neck furthest from the loin; *haut de côtelettes* is taken from the part between the best end and the breast; *côtes découvertes* are cutlets taken from between the *carré* and the *collet* or neck. The cutlets can all be grilled, or braised in a *ragoû*.

ÉPAULE

*T*HE shoulder of lamb is a popular French roasting joint, sold sometimes on the bone; sometimes boned, rolled and tied in a half shoulder, *épaule d'agneau roulée*; or a whole shoulder, *épaule roulée*. It may also be boned, stuffed and tied in a ball or melon shape, as in *épaule roulée en balon*.

FILET

*T*HIS is the loin of lamb, sold whole for roasting or as loin chops, *côte de filet* or *côtelettes dans le filet*.

GIGOT

*T*HE top end of the leg, suitable for roasting.

GIGOT D'AGNEAU

*T*HIS is the shank end of the leg suitable for roasting. A French recipe I like very much is *gigot d'agneau à l'anglaise*, for which the leg is wrapped in muslin and lowered into a large pan of boiling water. It is simmered for 15 mins per lb/455 g and served rare, as if it were roasted, with spring vegetables. A hint, given by the caper sauce served with it, indicates that it does indeed come from the traditional English boiled leg of mutton.

POITRINE

*T*HE breast of lamb is used boned and rolled as in the English cut and is also used to make *epigrammes*. The breast is cooked in stock, allowed to go cold, boned and cut into small pieces, breaded and baked in a hot oven or grilled. This is a delicious and inexpensive dish.

SELLE D'AGNEAU

*T*OGETHER with the *gigot*, this is the other prime roasting joint taken from the two sides of the carcase, the saddle.

American Cuts

*A*PART from slices from the neck, brisket pieces, shanks, ribs and breast, most of the other American cuts can be roasted. Some of the larger ones, such as the boneless, rolled breast and boneless rolled shoulder can be braised.

Joints for roasting and chops or cutlets for grilling or frying are as follows:

GROUND LAMB

*I*S taken from the neck, breast, shanks and flank and minced (ground) for patties and 'lamburgers'.

BREAST

*B*REAST rolled breast, breast with pocket, stuffed breast, stuffed chops.

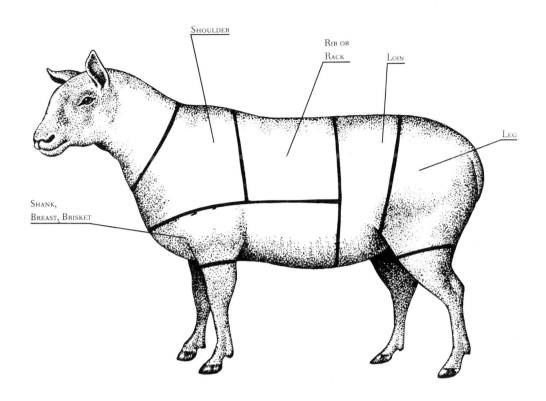

Leg

SIRLOIN half of leg roast, leg roast, sirloin on or sirloin off, American leg roast, centre leg roast, combination leg, rolled leg roast, French leg roast, leg chop, shank half of leg, hind shank.

Loin

SADDLE or loin roast, rolled double loin roast, sirloin roast, rolled double sirloin roast, English chops, loin chops, sirloin chops. From the rib: rib roast, crown roast, rib chops.

Rib or rack

RIB roast, crown roast, rib chops.

Shoulder

SQUARE cut shoulder roast, rolled shoulder roast, cushion shoulder roast, mock duck, Saratoga chops, blade chops, arm chops.

Stewing lamb

GENERALLY taken from the forequarter cuts, neck and shoulder.

OFFAL

BRAINS

SMALLER than calf's brains, weighing about 4 oz/110 g each, these are delicate and not expensive. Some maintain that they are not as good as calf's brains. They need to be soaked in cold water first to disgorge any blood, then blanched in boiling, lightly salted water before cooking them. One set (that is, two brains) is quite sufficient for one serving.

HEART

LAMB's hearts are small, inexpensive and make a very good homely casserole. Allow one heart per serving. They should be trimmed of excess fat and piping, then can be stuffed and braised or sliced and casseroled. The meat is full flavoured, dense and fibrous, producing a rich, meaty gravy. Cook it with plenty of spices or herbs and other full-flavoured ingredients such as nuts and dried fruit.

KIDNEY

TWO or three lamb's kidneys, quickly fried or grilled, make an excellent meal. Take care not to cook this tender meat too much as it becomes tough.

If the kidneys are still enclosed in their crisp, firm white fat (or suet), they can be roasted in this. Otherwise remove fat, thin membrane and, when you slice the kidneys in half, snip out as much of the gristly core as possible.

LAMB'S FRY

LOOKING rather like a white kidney, these are the lamb's testicles. Few butchers' shops in Britain sell them, but you may find them in continental butchers. Fry or grill them and serve as you would kidneys. They are delicious.

LIVER

ALTHOUGH not as tender and delicate as calf's liver, lamb's liver is not as expensive either. When gently cooked – by grilling, frying or braising – it is tender and full of flavour.

SWEETBREADS

FRESH lamb's sweetbreads are small, pale pink and delicate in flavour and texture. After soaking and blanching they can be turned into all manner of dishes, particularly creamy *ragoûts* and *fricassées* with mushrooms, lemon and herbs.

PAUNCH AND PLUCK

OF interest mainly to those who make their own haggis, the paunch is the lamb or sheep's stomach, which is used as the casing, and the pluck is the heart, liver and lungs (or lights), which are chopped up and mixed with oatmeal and spices for the filling.

TONGUE

AVAILABLE fresh or salted, lamb's tongues need soaking before cooking, skinning and pressing, or can be served freshly cooked. Each weighs 6-8 oz/170-230 g.

MUTTON

*I*F YOU HAVE COOKERY BOOKS of at least twenty years ago, then you will find them full of delicious sounding mutton recipes: chops baked with layers of potato and garlic; Hungarian sweet pepper stew made with mutton, bacon, potatoes, paprika and caraway seeds; mutton served with laverbread – a cooked seaweed – and with a sauce made from bitter oranges; braised haunch of mutton; *haricot de mouton* cooked with white beans and plenty of herbs and spices . . . all marvellously homely dishes for serving a hungry crowd.

Yet mutton is scarcely part of modern cookery at all. Even current Indian cookery books do not give mutton recipes, preferring to suggest instead the more universally acceptable lamb. Sheep are slaughtered much younger and in Britain only a small percentage becomes mutton, at two to three years old.

You will, however, occasionally find mutton in butchers serving Muslim and other ethnic communities. Or a local sheep farmer might on occasion sell it. Mutton comes from a larger carcase, a mature animal, and it should be hung like beef to allow its flavour to develop and its flesh to become tender to get the best out of it. The meat is darker and the fat yellower than lamb's. The joints, though larger, will look the same shape of course. You will find legs and loins of mutton as well as mutton chops.

It is a meat well worth trying. Trim it of as much fat as possible. Marinate it in wine or cider with herbs and spices, cook it gently, by braising or pot roasting, and serve it with other robustly flavoured food, perhaps some well-browned potatoes. If it is Welsh mutton, what better than a dish of laver, the dark rich seaweed. And if it is mutton from the salt marshes, then samphire would go very well with it. Or try a thick white onion sauce.

A well hung, trimmed, larded and marinated haunch of mutton tastes just as good, if not better than some of the rather insipid farm venison that is available.

I have also had delicious mutton ham, cured and thinly sliced.

GIGOT BOULANGÈRE

This classic French dish, a leg of lamb roast over potatoes,
is simple to cook, uses few ingredients and is a must for
the family Sunday lunch repertoire.

SERVES 4-6

1 leg of lamb, weighing
4-5 lb/1.8-2.3 kg
2-3 cloves of garlic
4 lb/1.80 kg maincrop potatoes,
peeled and sliced quite thinly
1 tsp dried rubbed thyme
2 bay leaves, crushed fine
½ tsp salt
good pinch of freshly ground
black pepper
1 onion, peeled and finely
chopped
up to 4 oz/110 g butter

PEEL and slice the garlic, then cut it into 'nails'. Insert these into the leg of lamb, all over, in slashes made in the fat with a sharp knife, between the muscles and around the bone.

Preheat the oven to 200°C/400°F, gas mark 6. Mix the herbs, seasoning and onion together. Butter an ovenproof dish and lay half the potatoes in it. Sprinkle on half the seasoning then the rest of the potatoes in a layer, topped with the remaining seasoning. Dot with half the rest of the butter. Pour on enough warm water to just cover the potatoes and put them in the oven for 1-1½ hours.

Mix the rest of the butter with a good pinch each of salt and pepper and smear this over the leg of lamb. Remove the cooked potatoes from the oven and place the lamb on top. Return it to the oven and cook it for 15-18 minutes per lb/455 g, depending on how well cooked you like the meat.

Switch off the oven, open the door and let the meat relax for 5-10 minutes before carving and serving.

OTTOMAN LAMB WITH AUBERGINE PURÉE

Of the many recipes that I have hoarded over the years, whether manuscript or typescript, torn from magazines or hastily jotted in a notebook while in someone's kitchen or restaurant, this is one to which I am particularly attached.
In the early eighties, I cooked side by side with Jeremy Round in a cookery competition. It was a delightful evening. Far more talking and laughing than cooking went on, and Jeremy fascinated me with his stories of Turkey. This was his winning recipe. After the competition he typed it out and sent it to me. I include it, with a couple of amendments that I know he would not object to, as a small memento of a friend who died much too young.

SERVES 6

1 leg of lamb, weighing about 6 lb/2.7 kg, trimmed of all fat and with the two bones at the haunch end removed
For the marinade:
½ pt/280 ml thick yoghurt
4 heaped tbsp tomato purée
8 generous tbsp dry red wine
2 fl oz/60 ml extra virgin olive oil

6 cloves of garlic, peeled and crushed
2 bay leaves
2 tsp fresh thyme
1 tsp sugar
1 tsp salt
pepper

For the aubergine purée:
3 lb/1.35 kg aubergines
2 oz/60 g butter
2 oz/60 g flour
¾ pt/430 ml milk
2 oz/60 g Cheddar cheese, grated
To garnish:
fresh bay leaves

BEAT the yoghurt together with the tomato purée. Still beating, dribble in the wine and oil. Stir in the crushed garlic, crushed bay leaves, thyme, sugar, salt and pepper. Make deep incisions all over the leg of lamb. Put it into the marinade, cover and refrigerate for 24 hours. Turn it occasionally.

Preheat the oven to 200°C/400°F, gas mark 6. Take the lamb out of the mari-nade and place on a baking dish. Cover and roast in a preheated oven, basting it occasionally. Forty-five minutes before the end of cooking, take the lamb out of the dish and place it on the bare shelf of the oven with a tray underneath to catch the drips. Save the juices from the original baking dish, strain and reduce down to almost nothing.

While the lamb is roasting, char the

aubergines on a naked flame or under a hot grill until black all over. Peel the cooled aubergines and leave to soak in slightly salty water. Squeeze as much liquid out as you can, then mash in a bowl.

Make a *roux* with the butter and flour and add the milk off the heat. Cook until you have a thick white sauce with no taste of raw flour. Stir in the mashed aubergines and cook for several minutes. Season, add the grated cheese, stir and pour the purée into a serving dish.

Take the lamb out of the oven and leave to stand for 20 minutes, covered with foil, in a warm place.

Carve into thick slices and lay on the bed of aubergine purée. Pour over the reduced pan juices. Garnish with fresh bay leaves.

ROSETTE OF LAMB STUFFED WITH OLIVES AND WALNUTS

Ask your butcher to remove the blade and thigh bones from the shoulder, but to leave in the leg bone. This makes for much easier carving.

SERVES 4-6

1 shoulder of lamb, boned as above, weighing about 3-4 lb/1.35-1.8 kg
For the stuffing:
4 oz/110 g fresh soft breadcrumbs
1 oz/30 g melted butter or 1 tbsp olive oil

1 small onion, peeled and chopped
10 stoned black olives, chopped
2 tbsps chopped walnuts
2-3 cloves of crushed garlic

grated zest and rind of 1 lemon
1 or 2 pieces of sun-dried tomatoes, finely chopped (if you have them)
1 tsp finely chopped fragrant herbs (whatever you have available)

*P*REHEAT the oven to 220°C/425°F, gas mark 7.

Mix all the stuffing ingredients together and place in the centre of the opened out shoulder. Fold the edges of the meat over, tie it round three times to form a rosette shape and place in a baking dish or roasting tin.

Roast for 1¼ hours for pink lamb, or for 1¾-2 hours if you prefer it well done. Allow it to rest for at least 10 minutes in a warm place before carving.

RACK OF LAMB WITH THREE MUSTARDS

Not many roasts are suitable for only two people but the best end of lamb, with six or seven small cutlets, is ideal and is one of my favourite dishes for a traditional Sunday lunch.

SERVES 2

1 best end of lamb, chine bone
*   removed*
2 cloves of garlic
1 tbsp Dijon mustard
1 tbsp tarragon mustard
1 tbsp grainy mustard
*   (eg Moutarde de Meaux)*
1 tbsp chopped fresh tarragon
salt
pepper
juice of ½ lemon
1 tbsp olive oil
1 oz/30 g fine fresh breadcrumbs

*I*F your butcher has not already done so, trim the ribs right down to the thick meaty fillet and remove the outer layer of fat. When carved, this will give an 'eye' of meat on each well-trimmed bone, and thus very little fat. Mix the rest of the ingredients with the exception of the breadcrumbs and spread all over the surface of the meat. You can leave it to marinate overnight or cook it immediately, as you prefer.

Make sure the meat is at room temperature when you cook it. Preheat the oven to 200°C/400°F, gas mark 6, and roast for 20 minutes altogether. After 10 minutes, sprinkle the meat with breadcrumbs and press them in lightly. Return the meat to the oven. When done, allow it to rest in a warm place for at least five minutes before carving.

This very classic lamb dish deserves a classic accompaniment: thinly sliced potatoes laid in a buttered dish with a little cream or seasoning and baked to a golden gratin (see p. 352) is just the thing.

POACHED LEG OF LAMB AND THREE SAUCES

My fish kettle just holds a thinnish leg of lamb, as I
discovered one Easter when I decided on a change from
cooking lamb with my favourite Mediterranean flavours. I
would treat the new season's English lamb to some
homely English accompaniments, caper sauce and onion
sauce. The iodine flavours of laver, the dark glossy
seaweed purée, also go well with poached or roast lamb.

SERVES 6-8

4 lb/1.8 kg whole leg of lamb
2 bay leaves
1 onion, peeled and stuck with
*   half a dozen cloves*

parsley stalks
1 carrot, peeled and sliced
1 small turnip, peeled and
*   sliced*
1 leek, washed and sliced

1 celery stalk, trimmed and
*   sliced*
salt
pepper

Trim and tie the leg of lamb to hold
its shape. Fill a large saucepan or
fish kettle with enough water to cover
the lamb. Test it first. Put in the seasonings, but not yet the lamb. Bring to the
boil, put in the lamb and when the water
comes back to the boil, turn down the
heat as low as possible and poach for 15
minutes per 1 lb/455 g. Remove the lamb
from the pot and put it to rest in a warm
place for about 15 minutes before carving.

LAVER SAUCE

To make a simple laver sauce, heat about ½ lb/230 g laver
with 1 oz/30 g butter and the zest of an orange or lemon.
Add ¾ pt/430 ml lamb stock, simmer for 5 minutes and
season to taste.

CAPER SAUCE

½ oz/15 g butter
½ oz/15 g flour
½ pt/280 ml lamb stock
4 tbsp cream
2-3 tbsp capers, rinsed
salt
pepper

MAKE a roux with the butter and flour and cook for 5 minutes. Gradually blend in the stock and cook until smooth and the flour no longer raw tasting. Stir in the cream and capers. Bring to the boil and season to taste.

ONION SAUCE

2 onions, peeled and chopped
½ pt/280 ml milk
1 bay leaf
4 cloves
1 oz/30 g soft white breadcrumbs
½ oz/15 g butter
freshly grated nutmeg
salt
pepper

COVER the onions with milk. Add the cloves and bay leaf and simmer until the onion is tender. Rub through a sieve and mix with the breadcrumbs and butter. Season to taste with nutmeg, salt and pepper.

163

ROAST LEG OF LAMB, BASQUE STYLE

This recipe, which is based on one that comes from the south-western states of America, Arizona, New Mexico and California, is of Basque origin. Many of the shepherds in that part of America were, and still are, of Basque descent and in San Francisco there are a number of Basque restaurants. The food is simple, rustic and tasty served family-style at long tables, as at the grill restaurants in the Basque country. Once upon a time this dish would probably have been barbecued. It is a dish for those who like their lamb well-cooked rather than pink.

SERVES 6

1 leg of lamb, boned, weighing about 4 lb/1.85 kg
1 pork fillet, about 8-10 oz/230-280 g, cut to the same length as the leg of lamb
1 tbsp olive oil
1 tbsp crushed black peppercorns

1 tbsp finely chopped fresh rosemary, thyme, oregano or lemon thyme
4 cloves of garlic, peeled, crushed and finely chopped
2 tbsp crushed pine kernels
1/2 tsp salt
1 lemon
2 tsp Angostura bitters

TRIM the sinews and excess fat from the lamb and pork. Mix together all the ingredients except for the lemon and Angostura and roll the pork fillet in the mixture (you should use it all up). Place the pork in the opened-out leg of lamb then fold it over so that the pork is enclosed. Tie it in several places and rub with the juice of a lemon and the Angostura. Allow to stand overnight, loosely covered, in the refrigerator.

When ready to cook the meat, allow it to come back to room temperature and place in a roasting tin on a rack. Preheat the oven to 180°C/350°F, gas mark 4, and roast the lamb for 3 hours. Keep covered in a warm place for 15-20 minutes before carving.

LEG OF LAMB ANDALUSIAN STYLE

This recipe comes from Fernando Bigote, who runs a famous fish restaurant on the waterfront in Sanlúcar de Barrameda, the home of the almost salty dry Manzanilla. He uses San Miguel beer, but any lager or light beer will do. Preparation begins the day before.

If you have a Römertopf or chicken brick, it will cook this dish to perfection. There is not enough surface area spare to evaporate and burn up the liquid ingredients too quickly. For the same reason, if you are using a roasting tin, the meat should just fit into it and no more.

SERVES 6

1 leg of lamb, weighing 4 lb/1.8 kg
2 onions, peeled and sliced
1/2 lemon
salt
pepper

4 cloves of garlic, peeled and sliced
1/8 pt/70 ml olive oil
1/4 pt/140 ml Manzanilla 'sherry'
1 red or green pepper, roasted, seeded and sliced

3 ripe tomatoes, peeled, seeded and chopped
1 bunch of fresh parsley (about 1 oz/30 g)
1/2 pt/280 ml beer

LAY half the onion slices on the bottom of the cooking pot. Place the leg of lamb on top of them. Remove the zest of the lemon in strips, and place them in the pot too. Rub the lamb all over with the lemon juice and season lightly with salt and pepper. Cut the garlic into slivers, and insert these under the skin of the lamb and around the bone. Brush the lamb with the olive oil, and pour on the Manzanilla. Cover carefully and marinate in the refrigerator overnight.

Next day, uncover the meat and let it come back to room temperature. Preheat the oven to 170-180°C/325-350°F, gas mark 3-4. Tuck the pepper and tomato around it. Reserve some of the parsley for decoration, but push the rest of it well down around the meat. Pour on the beer, put in the middle of the oven and cook for 30-35 minutes per lb/455 g. Allow to rest before carving.

Towards the end of the cooking, you can cover the lamb with the lid or with a sheet of foil, if you like a moist joint, or leave the meat uncovered if you want it browned.

LAMB AND POMEGRANATES

*Pomegranate juice makes an excellent, not too acidic,
marinade and the seeds provide an attractive decoration
for this now rather old-fashioned nouvelle dish.*

SERVES 4

*8 noisettes of lamb, together
   weighing about 1 lb/455 g,
   cut from the loin and trimmed
   of all fat and gristle
2 or 3 pomegranates (depending
   on size)
1 onion, peeled and thinly sliced
black peppercorns
pink peppercorns (optional)
garlic (optional, to taste)
4 tbsp rich meat stock (see
   p. 344)*

*P*LACE the noisettes of lamb in a single layer in a shallow dish. Cut the pomegranates in half. Pick the seeds out of one pomegranate half and keep these intact for decoration (about 1 dessertspoonful per plate). Squeeze the remaining pomegranate halves on a lemon squeezer and strain the juice over the lamb. Add the onion, crushed peppercorns and garlic to the marinade and pour it over the lamb. Stand for a few hours or overnight.

Remove the lamb from the marinade, which you strain into a small saucepan.

Heat up the grill and cook the lamb under quite fierce heat, turning it once, so that it is quite brown (but not burnt) on the outside and moist and pink inside.

Keep the meat warm while you finish off the sauce by adding the meat stock to the marinade and bubbling it hard until syrupy. Divide the sauce equally amongst four heated serving plates, place the lamb on top, scatter a few pomegranate seeds over it and serve with a few steamed broccoli florets and a purée of celeriac, carrot, garlic and cardamom (see p. 355).

BREADED LAMB CHOPS

Costine di agnello is a speciality from Romagna, the more austere half of Emilia Romagna. Quick to cook, it makes an ideal main course for an impromptu dinner party. The chine bone should be removed from the cutlets. Allow two per person.

SERVES 2

4 best end lamb cutlets, chine
bone removed
2-3 tbsp flour
1 egg, beaten
3 oz/85 g fresh soft breadcrumbs
grapeseed or olive oil for frying
1 lemon

B EAT the meat to flatten it slightly. Flour the cutlets then dip them in egg and breadcrumbs. Put about ½ in/1 cm oil in a frying pan and, when hot, fry the cutlets on both sides until done to your liking. Serve with lemon wedges.

In Italy, fried courgettes or potatoes would be served with the meat.

SPRING LAMB AND VEGETABLE CASSEROLE

Casseroles are often seen as winter dishes. But there is
many a spring and summer day on which a warming stew
would be welcome. To lighten it, I use spring vegetables
and white wine rather than root vegetables and red wine.
That made from the grassy, flowery currant-like
Sauvignon blanc is particularly good.
Use boned shoulder or neck fillet.

SERVES 4

1½ lb/680 g boned lamb (see
   above)
1 medium onion
garlic, optional and to taste
8 baby carrots
1 pt/570 ml Sauvignon blanc
8 small courgettes, peeled and
   trimmed
8 asparagus stalks, trimmed

¼ lb/110 g slim green beans,
   trimmed
8 baby leeks or spring onions
2 tbsp chopped fresh basil or
   parsley
beurre manié
salt
pepper

REMOVE as much fat and gristle as possible from the lamb and cut it into 2 in/5 cm cubes. Peel and thinly slice the onion. In a non-stick or well-seasoned frying pan, seal the meat all over and transfer it to a casserole. Lightly brown the onion and put with the meat, adding the peeled and crushed garlic (if using it) to the onion in the pan. Add the scrubbed, trimmed carrots.

Pour the wine into the frying pan, bring to the boil, scraping up any residues, and pour 4-5 tablespoons over the meat and vegetables. Cover and simmer on a low heat for about 45-60 minutes. After half an hour, add the rest of the vegetables and half the herbs.

If, once the stew is cooked, you want to thicken the sauce, do so by straining the cooking juices into a small frying pan and reducing them to the required amount, or stir a little *beurre manié* (see p. 345) into the casserole. Season to taste and stir in the rest of the herbs. Steamed or boiled new potatoes are the perfect accompaniment.

LAMB PAPRIKA

When I first came to live and cook in London, I lived in a house owned by two close friends, Ros and Pete, who also housed visiting friends and relatives. Usually about eight of us sat down to dinner every evening. Our contribution to food costs was £5 a week each, which shows how long ago it was. Lamb paprika, slow cooked, full of good smells and flavours to welcome us home and extremely economical was one of the house favourites. It still is a favourite. I use scrag end or middle neck of lamb. Best end can also be used. The bones give it flavour. Dry cider or beer can replace the stock.

SERVES 6

4 lb/1.8 kg neck of lamb,
   chopped
2-3 tbsp ground mild paprika
1 tbsp cumin seeds
1 tsp salt
1 tsp freshly ground black pepper

2 onions, peeled and sliced
3 tbsp olive oil
1 pt/570 ml lamb or other meat
   stock
potatoes, peeled and thickly
   sliced (optional)
chopped fresh parsley

TRIM any excess fat from the meat. Mix the spices and seasoning and coat the meat with them. The meat can be covered and refrigerated overnight or you can cook it straightaway.

In a heavy casserole, gently fry the onions in the olive oil until golden brown. Remove and put to one side while you brown the meat. Pour on the stock, put back the onions, bring to the boil and simmer very gently, covered, for 2 hours or so. The meat can also be cooked in the oven.

If you like, thickly sliced potatoes can be added to the casserole after about an hour. Serve sprinkled with chopped fresh parsley. If not using potatoes in the casserole, it can be served with plain boiled or mashed potatoes, rice or noodles.

MOROCCAN LAMB STEW

Dried fruit combines with meat and spices in a fragrant
tender stew, which is best accompanied by saffron
flavoured rice or *couscous* to soak up the juices. Boned
shoulder or fillet is suitable for this dish.

SERVES 4-6

1½ lb/680 g lamb (see above),
off the bone
1 tbsp olive oil
1 medium onion, peeled and
chopped
2-3 cloves of garlic, peeled and
crushed
½ tsp ground cinnamon
½ tsp ground cardamom
1 tsp cumin seeds
1 tsp coriander seeds, crushed
7 fl oz/200 ml lamb or veal
stock (see p. 344)

½ lb/230 g carrots or small
turnips, peeled and sliced, but
not too small (½-1 in/1-2.5 cm
chunks)
6 oz/170 g dried apricots, soaked
in warm water for ½ hour
½ preserved lemon (see p. 359) or
juice and pared zest of ½ lemon
salt
fresh ground black pepper
For decoration:
freshly grated nutmeg
chopped fresh coriander leaves

TRIM any excess fat from the lamb
and cut the meat into 1 in/2.5 cm
cubes. Brown them in the olive oil and
put to one side. Lightly brown the onion
then add 'the garlic and spices. Cook
these dry for 2-3 minutes then gradually
add the stock, scraping up the residues.

Put the meat in a casserole, pour the
spiced stock and onions over it, and add
the carrots, apricots and lemon to the
pot. Cover and cook at 180°C/350°F, gas
mark 4 for 1-1½ hours. Season for about
15-20 minutes before the end and, just
before serving, grind on some nutmeg
and scatter with the chopped coriander
leaves.

Two Recipes for Left-over Lamb

Moussaka, the Greek dish of minced lamb and gravy
layered with aubergines fried in olive oil and topped with
a thick béchamel sauce, is one way of using left-over lamb.
Here are two others, stuffed baked vegetables and
shepherd's pie.

Stuffed Baked Vegetables

Use blanched and hollowed-out courgettes, aubergines,
tomatoes, or peppers with the seeds removed. Peppers
should also be blanched. Onions, too, can have their
centres removed and should be blanched. Allow two or
three prepared vegetables for each person.

Serves 4

8-12 prepared vegetables for
stuffing, as above
For the filling:
*1/2 lb/230 g cooked lamb,
minced or finely chopped
3/4 lb/340 g cooked bulgar
wheat, couscous or rice*

2 oz/60 g finely chopped
onion
2 oz/60 g lightly toasted
almonds or pine nuts
2 oz/60 g raisins or chopped
dried apricots
2 oz/60 g fresh mint, chopped

1/2 tsp ground coriander seeds
1/2 tsp ground cumin
salt and pepper
2 tbsp extra virgin olive oil
a little white wine, lamb stock
or olive oil

*M*ix all the ingredients together, including the seasoning and olive oil,
and spoon into the vegetables. Place in an
oiled roasting tin or dish. Moisten with
wine, stock or oil and cover with foil.

Bake in the top half of a preheated
oven at 180°C/350°F, gas mark 4 for an
hour or so, or until the vegetables are
cooked. Tomatoes will take considerably
less time than this.

SHEPHERD'S PIE

These potato-topped pies can be made from scratch using raw mince, but they are ideal for using up the remains of a large joint. Grated cheese, egg yolks, herbs, cream and spring onions are just some of the ingredients which can be added to the mashed potato to dress it up if you think it needs it. Incidentally, cottage pie is the version using left-over minced beef.

SERVES 4-6

*1 medium onion, peeled and
   finely chopped
1 tbsp olive oil
1½ lb/680 g cooked lamb,
   minced or finely chopped
⅓ pt/200 ml lamb stock or
   gravy
2 tbsp port
1 tsp Worcestershire sauce
pinch of grated nutmeg
pinch of ground allspice
pinch of chopped fresh rosemary
1 tbsp finely chopped parsley
salt
pepper
2 lb/900 g mashed potatoes*

L IGHTLY brown the onion in olive oil. Mix with the rest of the ingredients except for the potatoes and spoon into an ovenproof dish. Spread the mashed potato over the top and score with the tines of a fork. Bake for about 45 minutes in the top of a preheated oven at 180°C/350°F, gas mark 4.

LAMB AND KIDNEY HOT-POT

SERVES 6

6 best end or loin lamb chops
3 or 6 lamb's kidneys (according
*   to taste)*
1 onion, peeled and sliced
1 lb/455 g potatoes, peeled and
*   sliced*
2-3 carrots, peeled and sliced
2-3 small turnips, peeled and
*   sliced (if liked)*
2 celery stalks, trimmed and
*   sliced*
2 leeks, trimmed and sliced
salt and pepper
4 cloves
1 bay leaf
½ pt/280 ml dry cider, ale,
*   white wine or stock (see*
*   p. 344)*
1 tbsp olive oil

TRIM excess fat from the chops. Remove the fat and membrane from the kidneys and, having sliced them in two horizontally, snip out the core. Use some of the fat, or use a non-stick frying pan, to fry the chops and kidneys all over to brown them. Put the meat to one side.

Arrange a layer of onions and potatoes on the bottom of a lightly greased casserole, put the chops on top, then a layer of vegetables, then the kidneys, and finish with a layer of potatoes. Lightly season each layer. Tuck in the cloves and bay leaf, pour on the liquid, brush the top layer with olive oil and cover.

Cook for 2 hours at 180°C/350°F, gas mark 4, in the middle or bottom half of the oven. Remove the lid, raise the heat, and finish off nearer the top of the oven for another 20 minutes or so to brown the potatoes.

LAMB AND KIDNEY KEBABS

Tender lamb fillet and lamb kidney both cook very
quickly, which makes this a recipe for easy entertaining or
for a family supper. In the summer the skewers of meat
can be barbecued. I like to serve this with bulgar wheat or
rice and a salad of tomato, cucumber and fresh mint.

SERVES 4

1 lb/455 g lamb fillet
4 lamb's kidneys
3 tbsp extra virgin olive oil
1-2 tsp lemon juice
½ tsp ground coriander
2 cloves of garlic, peeled and
  crushed
freshly ground black pepper

DICE the fillet into 1-2 in/2.5-5 cm cubes, trimming off any excess fat and gristle. Halve the kidneys lengthways and snip out the fatty core with a pair of scissors. Mix the rest of the ingredients and coat the meat with the mixture. The meat can be marinated for several hours or overnight if preferred, but leave it for at least half an hour before cooking.

Thread the lamb and kidneys on skewers and grill until done to your liking, under a pre-heated grill or on a cast-iron oven-top griddle.

ISCAS

Usually I do not enjoy liver in casseroles, preferring to grill it or sear it in a well-seasoned pan. This traditional dish from Lisbon is an exception. We used to order it, in the early seventies, in a tiny neighbourhood restaurant in the Barrio Alto. Some twenty years later, both the restaurant and the dish are still there. The liver is marinated overnight and cooking time is little more than ten minutes. It is best served with rice to sop up the very good juices. The crisp petillance of a *vinho verde* is a good match for the strong flavours, and you can also use it as the cooking wine.

SERVES 6

1½ lb/680 g lamb's liver, in a piece
¼ pt/140 ml extra virgin olive oil, and more for oiling the casserole
¼ pt/140 ml dry white wine

1 mild onion, peeled and thinly sliced
salt
pepper
chopped fresh coriander leaves

REMOVE and discard any piping from the liver and cut into little finger-size pieces. Put in a bowl and mix well with the oil and wine. Stir in the onion rings. Cover, refrigerate and marinate overnight.

A lidded casserole, not too heavy for you to pick up and shake, or a wide sauté pan, is best for cooking the liver. Strain the meat and marinade and reserve the marinade. Heat the casserole, add a tablespoon of olive oil, and, when it is very hot, put in the liver a handful or so at a time so as not to crowd the pan, which lowers the temperature and causes the meat to steam rather than fry. Put on the lid and shake the casserole vigorously. Return it to the heat and cook for 2-3 minutes to just cook the liver. Remove each batch as it is cooked and keep it warm in a serving dish.

When you have removed the last of the liver, pour the marinade into the casserole and boil until reduced by half. Season to taste and pour the sauce over the liver. Scatter the chopped coriander leaves on top before serving.

LAMB AND LIVER STEW

A thick, warming, rustic stew from Extremadura in the west of Spain, this will simmer away gently on the back of the stove and does not need to be cooked in the oven. The thickening agent in the stew is, unusually, pounded fried bread and lamb's liver. This would go well with rice or boiled potatoes. The bread should be a thick slice of firm home-made or country bread.

SERVES 6

3 lb/1.35 kg lamb, off the bone
(breast, leg or shoulder or
fillet, or a mixture of these)
⅛ pt/70 ml extra virgin olive oil
¼ pt/140 ml dry white wine
6 oz/170 g lamb's liver
1 tsp hot paprika
3 bay leaves
8 cloves of garlic, peeled
1 slice of real (not processed)
bread
salt to taste

Cut the lamb into 2-3 in/5-7.5 cm chunks. Heat some of the olive oil in a casserole and in it fry the meat until brown. Pour on the white wine, bring to the boil, skim any scum from the surface and simmer gently for 10-15 minutes. Add the liver in one piece, the paprika and the bay leaves. Cover and simmer until the lamb is tender.

Meanwhile, fry the bread and the garlic in the remaining olive oil without browning the garlic. Remove the liver from the stew. Cut it into pieces and put it, together with the bread, broken up, and the garlic, into the bowl of a food processor. Process until smooth. Stir the mixture back into the casserole, season to taste and cook for a further few minutes, stirring occasionally. Flat-leaved parsley and a fine grating of lemon or orange zest finishes off the dish nicely.

GOAT AND KID

*K*ID IS A FAVOURITE DISH to order when we go to Lisbon. There is a restaurant there, called Cabrinha in Cacilhas, across the Tagus near the huge shipyards of Lisnave, which specialises in succulent casseroles and pieces of roast kid. It is a popular trip for city dwellers on a Sunday. Kid is also popular in Spain, Italy, Malta and other parts of southern Europe, particularly the mountainous regions where goats are reared.

Although more goats are being reared in Britain for their milk and their hair, neither it nor young kid of three to four months old finds its way into the shops very often.

Kid is a delicacy, its pale, tender meat something between lamb and veal. Shoulder, leg or loin of kid can be roasted or treated as you would spring lamb. Barbecuing or spit-roasting would be excellent too. Whichever method you use, make sure the kid is frequently basted.

In order to keep it delicate and moist, you might prefer to braise it. For example, I have cooked pieces of kid in an unglazed chicken brick with stock, spices, almonds and dried apricots, and served it on a bed of saffron rice. It was extremely good. I have also come across an Irish recipe for casseroling it with mixed vegetables. If your imagination needs jogging beyond these ideas, you could use any lamb recipe for cooking kid.

Goat is another matter entirely, and in my view an altogether superior meat. Taken from a mature animal, say eighteen months old, and properly hung, it is a tender, extremely lean and very flavourful meat, a far cry from the rank, chewy stuff we are led to expect. It is also sometimes known as chevon, a term coined in Australia as an attempt to create a new interest in the meat. That name has been introduced to Britain but with little success. In America, with a large hispanic population, goat is often sold as *cabrito*. There are signs that it is gaining in popularity. The Angora Goat Society in Britain has now registered the name 'capra', which to me makes a great deal of sense; there is already an English goat cheese called Capricorn. A free-range, extensively reared animal, which produces excellent meat, means an entirely new addition to the meat cookery repertoire. For the recipes in this section, I have had great fun consulting a range of cookery books, from the Roman Apicius to the modern Italian cooks, and have also allowed myself free reign in the kitchen. I urge you not to be put off by received wisdom. This is a delicious meat and the basis for many exciting dishes. The cuts offered for sale are quite recognisable and are generally the leg, the shoulders and the loin, in cutlets or whole. The bones are slightly larger than lamb bones. With no EC subsidy the meat is considerably more expensive than lamb. On the other hand, for those who baulk at the idea of eating meat from the animals reared only for food, goat meat from angoras offers a real alternative; it is truly a by-product, the animals having been reared for their wool.

HUSBANDRY

GOAT MEAT IS NOT a traditional choice in Britain although it is very popular in many other countries of the world. This is probably because the requirement for goat milk or goat wool has, until recently, been very low. However, the increase in the demand for goat and angora wool brought about by the health foods revolution on the one hand and the popularity of natural fabrics on the other, has now firmly made goats a part of British agriculture.

If there is such a thing as conventional goat keeping, it involves the production of goat milk. The goats produce a kid and are then milked twice daily. The kids not required for herd replacements tend to be penned and reared on artificial milk in buckets. They may be kept at pasture at a later stage. The feed is principally grass and, in the winter, silage or hay. Although antibiotics may be found in artificial milk for kids, goats are generally spared the thrust of interest from the giant international drug manufacturers.

Angora goat herds are kept fully free-range, very much like sheep. All offspring are required for wool production, but only until two years of age after which the wool declines in quality. The culling out of the two (or less) year olds from the herd provides the supply of mature tasty chevon, capra or goat meat. This source, as specified fully free-range is unusual, and only certain shops will offer it.

CLASSIC DISHES

RECIPES FOR KID AND GOAT have never entered the classical repertoire and are generally few and far between in cookery books. These are rural dishes, cooked and eaten in those areas where goats mingle with the flocks of sheep or are reared for the milk which goes to make distinctive white cheeses.

Good Companions

*I*n Nigeria, we used to eat goat-meat pepper stew, sometimes with plantains or with a green vegetable such as calaloo. You can take this further and use the hot flavours of chillis and curry powders, but I prefer the subtler spicing of the Middle East, such as coriander, cardamom and cinnamon. Northern flavours do not seem appropriate; I would not even try goat or kid with beer and juniper berries, cabbage or sauerkraut. At a pinch, perhaps cider with apples, a cinnamon stick and a splash of Calvados would be good for cooking kid.

On the other hand, goat and kid marry well in a casserole with fruits such as apricots, or with Mediterranean flavours: tomatoes, garlic, olive oil, fragrant rosemary and thyme.

ROAST KID IN THE MALTESE STYLE

This dish is still cooked in the local baker's oven, along with roast beef, *timpana* (see p. 339), rabbit and all the traditional Sunday lunch dishes in Malta and Gozo. Beef and lamb are roasted in the same way – very simple and with extremely good results.

SERVES 4-6

1 leg or shoulder of kid
2½-3 lb/1.1-1.35 kg potatoes,
   peeled
3 large onions, peeled and sliced
2 or 3 cloves of garlic, peeled
   and slivered
salt
pepper
1 sprig of rosemary
⅛ pt/70 ml olive oil
2 tbsp soft fresh breadcrumbs

WEIGH the meat, allowing about 25 minutes per lb/455 g. Preheat the oven to 180°C/350°F, gas mark 4. Thickly slice each potato into three or four pieces. Insert slivers of garlic into the meat and lightly season it. Put it in a roasting tin on a bed of potatoes and onions. Tuck in the rosemary and dribble olive oil over the meat and potatoes. Sprinkle the meat with the breadcrumbs, pressing them in well before roasting.

ROAST GOAT WITH MINT SAUCE

The Romans used mint a great deal in their cooking and Apicius, the first-century Roman gourmet, records many such recipes, upon which this one is based. This is a far cry from the vinegary mint sauce so often served with lamb. Here the mint is used as one of the flavourings in an unusual sauce served hot with a plainly roasted joint of goat or kid. It is important that the goat has been hung for ten to twelve days, for maximum flavour and tenderness.

SERVES 4-6

1 leg or loin of goat, weighing
*   3-4 lb/1.35-1.8 kg*
3-4 tbsp extra virgin olive oil
2 or 3 sprigs of fresh mint
¼ tsp freshly ground black
*   pepper*
½ tsp celery seed
pinch of cumin seed
pinch of dried oregano
¼ tsp fennel seeds
2½ fl oz/70 ml red wine
1 tbsp plum or damson jam
2½ fl oz/70 ml cider vinegar
salt
pepper

P REHEAT the oven to 200°C/400°F, gas mark 6. Brush the meat with most of the olive oil. Strip the leaves from the mint, reserve them and place the stalks on a rack in a roasting tin. Roast the goat for an hour.

Put the mint, spices and herbs in a mortar and pound them. Put the wine, jam and cider vinegar in a saucepan. Scrape in the pounded herbs and add the remaining olive oil. Bring to the boil and simmer on a very low heat for 20-25 minutes. Strain into a heated sauceboat and serve with the roast.

LEG OF GOAT BOULANGÈRE

The first time I cooked this dish brought home to me the importance of using meat that had hung properly. It was one of the first samples of Richard Guy's new supply of goat meat, which came from mature animals raised for their wool. The leg came from an eighteen month-old animal that had been killed for nine days before I got it. I kept it in the refrigerator for another five days, loosely wrapped. Twice I wiped it over with a cloth dipped in sherry vinegar. There was probably no need, but it felt right, somehow, to freshen and sweeten the meat. I then prepared it in the following way, with no more herbs and seasoning than you might give a leg of lamb. With it we drank a 1981 Château Mouton Baronne Philippe. The meat was tender, fine-grained, juicy and full of flavour, quite the equal of the exquisite claret.

If you do not have a Römertopf or chicken brick, use a roasting tin into which the meat just fits.

SERVES 4

1 leg of goat, weighing 3 lb/1.35 kg
4 tbsp olive oil
1 head of fresh large-clove garlic
2 or 3 carrots, peeled and cut into chunky batons

2 large onions, peeled and thinly sliced
3 or 4 large potatoes, peeled and thickly sliced
sprig of thyme or rosemary

a few parsley sprigs, plus chopped fresh parsley for garnish
salt
pepper
glass of dry white or red wine

BROWN the joint all over in 1-2 tablespoons of the olive oil. Leave the garlic cloves whole, but separate and peel them.

Preheat the oven to 180°C/350°F, gas mark 4. Arrange the carrots, garlic, potatoes and half the onion in the bottom of a well-soaked Römertopf or chicken brick. Lay the meat on top and cover with the rest of the onions. Add the herbs, season lightly and pour on the wine and rest of the olive oil. Put on the lid and cook for 2-2¼ hours.

Serve sprinkled with chopped parsley.

CLAY-POT ROASTED GOAT

After you have cooked goat a few times with every imaginable herb, spice and flavouring, you may want to try it almost plain. It is very good. I like to spike it with garlic. You can also lard it with strips of fat pork or pork fat, which will keep it nice and moist. A chicken brick can be used instead of the clay pot.

SERVES 4-6

1 leg or loin of goat, weighing
3-4 lb/1.35-1.8 kg
several cloves of fresh garlic,
peeled and slivered
sprig of lavender or rosemary

2 tbsp extra virgin olive oil
4 tbsp white wine
salt
pepper

SOAK the clay pot or chicken brick, top and bottom, in cold water for 15 minutes.

Preheat the oven to 170°C/325°F, gas mark 3. Make incisions in the meat at 1 in/2.5 cm intervals and insert a piece of garlic. Put the rosemary or lavender in the bottom of the pot. Rub the meat with oil and sprinkle with wine, salt and pepper. Cover and bake for 2½-3 hours.

Serve with mashed potatoes and garlic.

CHANFANA

I've only ever visited Coimbra once, but we were lucky enough to try this local speciality on our first evening there. Kid and goat meat is popular in Portugal and will often be used rather than lamb to make this *chanfana*. It will look after itself once in the oven and can be served straight from the pot with thickly sliced boiled or steamed potatoes, with a little olive oil trickled over them.

4 lb/1.8 kg top leg of goat, in a piece
1 large onion, peeled and sliced
3½ fl oz/100 ml extra virgin olive oil

2 tbsp flour
2 cloves of garlic
6 cloves
1 bay leaf

2 pt/1.15 l good full red wine (such as a Bairrado, Garrafeira or Dão)
salt
pepper

*L*EAVE the meat whole or cut into chunks. Brown it and the onion in olive oil, in a flameproof casserole, sprinkle on the flour, add the garlic, cloves and bay leaf, half the wine and a little salt and pepper. Bring to the boil, cover and cook in a low oven or on top of the stove for 3-4 hours, adding more wine as necessary, but do not stir during cooking.

BRAISED LEG OF GOAT GREEK STYLE

SERVES 6

1 leg of goat, weighing 3 lb/1.35 kg
1 large onion, peeled and chopped
3 tbsp extra virgin olive oil
1 carrot, peeled and sliced

1 or 2 tbsp fresh coriander leaves, chopped
1 bay leaf
1 lemon, thinly sliced, without the pips
glass of full-bodied white wine

For the marinade:
1 tbsp coarse sea salt
1 tsp freshly ground black pepper
1-2 tsp thyme
1 tsp fennel seeds
3 tbsp wine vinegar
3 tbsp extra virgin olive oil

*R*UB the joint all over with the marinade, made by pounding together the seasoning and herbs and mixing them with the vinegar and oil. Loosely wrap and refrigerate overnight.

The following day, bring the meat to room temperature. In a large casserole fry the onion and carrot in the olive oil and brown the leg of goat in it. Add the coriander, bay leaf, a few of the lemon slices and the wine.

Cover and cook in a moderate oven (180°C/350°F, gas mark 4) or on top of the stove until tender. Garnish with the rest of the lemon slices and more fresh coriander.

CASSEROLED YOUNG GOAT, PIACENTINA STYLE

This is a well flavoured casserole, from Piacenza in Italy's
Po Valley, which I like to serve with steamed or mashed
potatoes or even a *risotto in bianco* (see p.348).

SERVES 4

*1½ lb/680 g shoulder of kid or
   goat, off the bone
1 onion, peeled and chopped
1 tbsp extra virgin olive oil
½ oz/15 g butter
¼ pt/140 ml dry white wine
¼ pt/140 ml lamb or veal stock
   (see p. 344)
¼ pt/140 ml fresh tomato sauce
   or* passata *(a thick purée of
   tomato, often sold in long-life
   cartons)
2 or 3 cloves of garlic, peeled
   and crushed
1 tbsp chopped fresh parsley
pinch of grated nutmeg or
    powdered mace
salt
pepper*

DICE the meat. In a flameproof casserole, lightly brown the onion and
then the meat in the olive oil and butter.
Add the wine, deglazing the pan and letting it cook until almost evaporated. Add
the stock and let it cook for 3 or 4
minutes, uncovered, before adding the
rest of the ingredients.

Let the stew bubble once or twice,
then lower the heat, cover and cook the
casserole gently until the meat is
tender.

ESTOUFFADE OF GOAT

This Provençal treatment of white wine, herbs, garlic and olives works particularly well with goat and other mature meats. The meat is marinated overnight in a cooked marinade.

SERVES 4

1 lb/455 g leg or shoulder of
goat, off the bone
12 stoned black olives
a few button onions or 1 onion,
peeled and sliced (optional)
seasoning
For the marinade:
1 onion
1 carrot
1 celery stalk
4 cloves of garlic (or more, to
taste)
½ pt/280 ml dry white wine
⅛ pt/70 ml extra virgin olive oil
1 sprig of rosemary or lavender
1 bay leaf
thyme or oregano

P EEL and chop the vegetables and put them in a saucepan with the wine and olive oil. Bring to the boil and simmer for 2-3 minutes. Remove from the heat and allow to cool down. Meanwhile dice the meat and put it in a bowl with the herbs. Pour over it the cooled marinade, cover and refrigerate overnight.

Drain the meat from the marinade. Wipe it dry and fry it all over in a flame-proof casserole to brown it. Add the olives and a few small onions (or sliced onion) if you like, and strain the marinade over it.

Simmer or cook in a low oven until the meat is tender. Season and serve with fresh broad pasta such as *pappardelle* or *tagliatelle* (see p. 346).

BLANQUETTE OF KID

With the right degree of spicing and other ingredients, a *blanquette* need not, despite its pale appearance, be an insipid dish. It must have a real underlying flavour of cloves. Make a stock with the kid bones first and use this for cooking the *blanquette*. The same method can be used for lamb and free-range veal.

SERVES 4

1 lb/455 g shoulder or leg of kid, off the bone
16 button onions
1 oz/30 g butter
1 medium onion, peeled and halved
8 cloves
1 bay leaf
½ pt/280 ml kid stock (see p. 344)

¼ pt/140 ml white wine
1 egg yolk
1 tbsp double cream
1 tsp grated lemon zest
salt
white pepper
To decorate:
chopped fresh parsley and grated lemon zest (optional)

Dice the meat, removing any visible fat and gristle. Peel the button onions and fry them gently in the butter without browning them. Remove and put to one side.

Fry the meat so that it loses its raw appearance, but do not let it brown. Stick each onion half with cloves. Put the meat, all the onions and the bay leaf in a casserole or saucepan. Pour on the stock and wine. Bring to the boil. Cover and simmer until the meat is tender and the onions done.

Remove the onion halves and cloves and the bay leaf. Carefully strain the cooking juices into a saucepan and put the meat in a warm serving dish. Cover and keep it warm. Reduce the liquid by half. Mix the egg yolk with a little hot liquid. Stir the cream, lemon zest and seasoning into the cooking juices and bring to the boil.

Remove from the heat and stir in the egg yolk. Mix thoroughly and pour over the meat. Serve immediately.

Parsley and grated lemon zest can be used to decorate the dish, which is good served with rice.

SPICED GOAT CASSEROLE

This is one of my favourite ways of cooking goat. I devised it after a visit to one of our local markets where there was a profusion of Indian, Turkish and Caribbean herbs, spices and vegetables. The fenugreek came from the Indian stall and adds a hint of bitterness, while the black cumin and sumac comes from the Turkish shop. The black cumin adds a mildly spicy flavour and the sumac an attractive dark red colour and agreeable sharpness that one might otherwise get from lemon juice.

SERVES 4-6

2 tbsp olive oil
1½ lb/680 g goat meat, off the
    bone, cut into 1 in/2.5 cm
    chunks
1 large onion, peeled and thinly
    sliced
1 tbsp ground coriander
1 tsp black cumin seeds (kalonji)

½ tsp ground cinnamon
6 cloves
½ pt/280 ml red wine
2 tbsp fenugreek (methi) leaves
3 in/7.5 cm strip of orange zest
salt
pepper
1 tbsp sumac

*H*EAT the oil in a heavy casserole and brown the meat all over, a few pieces at a time. Remove them and put to one side. Fry the onion and spices for 5 minutes then pour on half the wine, scraping up any caramelised residues.

Put the meat back in, add the fenugreek, orange zest and remaining wine. Bring to the boil, skim, then cover the pot, lower the heat and cook for 2-3 hours at 170°C/325°F, gas mark 3. After 1½ hours, season lightly and stir in half the sumac. When ready to serve, sprinkle on the rest of the sumac.

This is very good served with fluffy long grain rice mixed with almonds and seedless raisins, and perhaps lightly flavoured and coloured with saffron.

SPRING KID CASSEROLE

Early summer casserole would probably be a more accurate name for this recipe. It depends as much on the quality and freshness of the vegetables as it does on the meat: they should be young, crisp and full of flavour. If I can get fresh broad beans and the tiny purple navets I like to use them. Slim haricot beans, baby carrots, miniature Thai corn cobs, peas and shredded lettuce can all be added too. If using goat, as opposed to young kid, blanch it for 10-15 minutes first.

SERVES 6-8

1½-2 lb/680-900 g shoulder of kid, off the bone
1 heaped tbsp flour
¼ tsp salt
¼ tsp ground white pepper
1 oz/30 g butter
1 dozen small onions or fat spring onions, white part only
½ pt/280 ml lamb or veal stock (see p.344)

2 tsp grated lemon zest
1-2 tsp lemon juice
2 lb/900 g prepared spring vegetables (peeled, scrubbed, podded or trimmed as appropriate)
2 tsp finely chopped parsley
freshly grated nutmeg
salt and pepper to taste

Dice the meat and shake it in a bag with the flour, salt and pepper. Melt the butter in a heavy frying pan and fry the meat until it turns golden but not brown. Transfer the meat to a casserole and fry the onions too. Pour on the stock, bring to the boil and scrape up any caramelised residues. Add the lemon zest and juice and pour them over the meat.

Bring to the boil, cover and simmer for 1½-2 hours (longer if using goat) until the meat is tender. Add the vegetables about ½ hour or so before the end of cooking time, leaving them whole when possible (for example, the infant corn and carrots). Stir in the parsley, ground nutmeg and seasoning just before serving the casserole.

GOAT STEW FROM THE ABRUZZI

The Abruzzi, a province of Italy overlooking the Adriatic and bordered on its western flank by mountains, may be sparsely populated in human terms, but is an area with a high population of goats and sheep. This excellent goat stew also makes use of the region's other speciality, the chilli; the resulting tomato sauce is not an innocent one.

SERVES 6

2 lb/900 g goat meat, off the
*   bone*
3 tbsp olive oil
1 onion, peeled and chopped
3 or 4 canned plum tomatoes
2 red peppers
1 chilli pepper
pinch of rosemary
salt
pepper
1/4 pt/140 ml stock

*C*UT the meat into 2 in/5 cm chunks. Put into boiling water and blanch for 10 minutes. Drain, rinse and dry the meat carefully. Brown it in the olive oil and fry the onion until golden. Stir in the tomatoes. Halve and seed the peppers and chilli and cut into strips. Or leave the chilli almost split in two if you wish to remove it. Add to the meat together with the herbs, seasoning and stock. Bring to the boil, cover and simmer gently until the meat is tender.

If you were to mince the meat and cook it with the same ingredients it would make a suitable sauce for *spaghetti alla chitarra*, also from the Abruzzi.

Poultry

*F*ROM BEING, ALMOST LITERALLY, a backyard concern, poultry rearing is now such big business that chickens are referred to in terms of 'crops', with the aim being to 'harvest' at the right weight as early as possible. A cookery book published some twenty years ago describes the various categories of chicken broilers reaching a weight of three to four pounds at the age of six to twelve months. Under intensive rearing methods, they now reach that weight in five to six weeks. If you examine one of these intensively reared chickens next to a chicken of the same size that has had free access to range and has been fed on an additive-free diet, the differences are striking, perhaps more so than in any other comparison of intensively reared meat with its naturally reared counterpart. The whole skeleton of the free-range chicken, which is probably twice the age, is different; the bones are bigger and better developed, the legs are longer and better able to support the bird. When the birds are cooked, the flesh is less uniform in colour and texture in the free-range bird, the breast meat is paler and the leg meat darker. The flesh offers more resistance to the teeth, with an incomparably better flavour, and the skin is much thicker. When it comes to making stock from the carcase, that from the older free-range bird has much more flavour and body and sets to a firm jelly.

My favourite monarch is Henri IV of France, born Prince of Navarre, commemorated in one of Paris' most striking statues, the Vert Galant on the Île de la Cité. What has this to do with chicken, you may ask? It was this benevolent ruler whose aim it was to secure the economy to such an extent that each of his subjects could enjoy *la poule au pot* on Sunday. And today, a chicken is still one of the most popular meats for Sunday lunch, whether a roast, as often in Britain, part of a boiled dinner as it might be in New England, a *bollito misto* in Italy, or a French *poulet de Bresse à l'estragon*. The classical French repertoire alone includes one hundred ways of presenting sauté chicken and another fifty-four for chicken breasts, or *suprême de volaille*. *Poulet sauté Nouveau Siècle*, for example, is sauced with white wine and cooking juices and served with shaped cucumbers sweated in butter, small onions, ceps, diced tomatoes, fried aubergines, Japanese artichokes and cocotte potatoes.

But chicken is common to all cuisines, not just those of Europe and America. It is not surprising that the meat section of most general cookery books from any part of the world, devotes more space to chicken than any other meat, game or poultry. Chicken and pepper stew was a favourite Sunday lunch in Nigeria, served with a marvellous un-refined rice to mop up the fiery sauce. And think of the hundreds of ways chicken is pre-pared in all the regional styles of cooking in China, from the famous Kung Pao chicken of Szechuan cooked with chillies, ginger and roasted peanuts to the popular Hainan chicken, simply poached, carved and served with freshly grated ginger and salt. Singa-pore, Malaysia and Thailand all have wonderful ways of cooking chicken. From India we have learnt to appreciate the subtle flavour of Moghul chicken and the succulent tex-ture of a properly cooked *tandoori* chicken, first marinated in yoghurt and spices. In America chicken Maryland and, from the southern states, chicken gumbo have become classics. In Colombia and Peru chicken is cooked whole in a large pot with corn on the cob, local herbs and three kinds of potatoes in a dish probably not that different to the one the Spanish invaders adapted from the Indians. They used chicken, which they had introduced to South America, as the native wild turkey had become all but extinct.

This reminds us that poultry does not just mean chicken. It means all domesticated birds raised for the table, including ducks, geese, guinea fowl, quail, squabs and turkey. Originally some of these birds, like the turkey, guinea fowl and the quail, were wild. As man came to realise their value as a source of food he hunted them almost to extinction, but then he had the good sense to tame a few and raise them in the barnyard, taking par-ticular care of the goose or turkey that was to appear on the festive table, feeding it generously on carefully prepared mashes to supplement the scraps and scratchings on which it normally fed.

Thus were the modest beginnings of some of the objectionable practises which go on in order that we can have our Christmas turkey. A turkey I ate in America a few years ago was the nadir. Heaven knows how the turkey had been reared and slaughtered, but judging from the size and shape of its breast, hormones had been included in its feed. It had also been injected with a basting liquid, which contained salt, monosodium gluta-mate and vegetable fat. But more than that, it had embedded in it a thermometer, which popped out when the bird was cooked. I have Julia Child to thank for restoring my faith in America's favourite Christmas dinner. Last year I asked her advice on where to buy a decent turkey so that we could take it to Pittsburgh with us. Her own local food market, Savenor's in Cambridge, Massachusetts was the place, she said, and a bird was duly ordered. Collecting it involved such a lengthy detour from the centre of Boston to the airport, and our taxi driver was so intrigued by this famous bird, that he duly ordered one for himself. A good turkey needs nothing more than the simplest treatment, but I could not resist including the paper sack recipe on p.256.

Goose does not lend itself readily to intensive rearing. It is a marvellous bird to cook and serve, somewhat daunting because it is expensive, but very rewarding, and the fact that you can use every scrap of it greatly appeals to the thrifty housewife in me.

As for ducks, I fear that these are going to go the way of chickens. I have seen the huge duck farms and their small rectangular ponds just over the Chinese border from Hong Kong's New Territories. Yet we are also exporting ducks to China. Where and how are we raising them all? Nevertheless if you can get hold of a plump farmyard duckling, there are wonderful dishes to be made with it.

HUSBANDRY

*T*HE DRAMATIC SUCCESS OF intensive chicken farming has turned what was once a luxury meal into a cheap meat. But when poultry is termed cheap, this can only be a financial statement. In terms of welfare and drug adulteration, the bird itself pays a heavy price, leading a sub-standard life so that the customer can receive a sub-standard and largely tasteless product.

Indeed chickens are the most intensively farmed of all animals. Very sophisticated promotional activity is used to smokescreen production methods that remain well hidden from public gaze, so that the unwitting consumer is unlikely to react to the appalling conditions in which birds are reared. Probably the clearest example of this is 'corn fed' chicken, which is believed by most purchasers to be free-range or in some other way special. Although some corn (maize) is fed to the birds, the yellow flesh and fat colour comes from an artificial dye in the food. Other than that, the bird is reared as intensively as any other. In other words, the unwitting customer is buying a dyed factory farmed-chicken.

In the last few years almost all other fowl, with the notable exception of geese, are well down the slippery slope to full intensification. This fully intensive system has also come to dominate turkey, duck and even quail production, although chicken production is the most automated. It has even developed its own language: for example, 'crops' are the flocks of birds and 'harvesting' the name given to the often cruel catching process.

Under this system, parent stock is kept in percheries so that the cockerels can mingle, and the fertile eggs go to the hatcheries where they are incubated. Once hatched, the chicks are sexed and packed into boxes of a hundred. They will be let loose in a shed where they will spend their entire short lives. Numbers in each shed will vary: less than ten thousand would be below average, while fifteen thousand birds is more common. Since one person can control eight such fully automated units by mainly electrical means, a 'farm' will often house 120,000 birds. Space is carefully gauged so that at the target-weight the floor is virtually solid with birds – it is difficult to get room to put your feet between the birds to walk amongst them.

A heater broods the chicks whilst medicated food and water are provided. To bring about the astounding growth rate – chickens can be ready in less than five weeks – the birds are kept at a regulated temperature, movement is restricted and lights are left on twenty-four hours a day so that feeding can be continuous.

The livestock itself allows great versatility in devising rations because it is omnivorous. In nature the birds will eat most vegetation, insects, worms, grains and grit, the latter to form a natural 'mill' in the crop, a special organ in the neck which will grind seeds. Traditionally, wheat and barley became the usual ration, with fish meal, soy or beans used as a protein source. But as long as a balance of carbohydrate, protein, trace elements and vitamins are provided, usually in pellet form, the birds will grow. The farmer is usually a mere operative, with no choice or say in what feed is used, since the factory farm conglomerates own the feed mills and the feed millers own or control the factory farm and the slaughterhouse.

Light levels are carefully controlled to permit feeding, but to prevent over-activity or fighting. Mutilation of turkeys is universal to prevent pecking. Without medication, the birds would not survive. Many drugs are used to ensure that the birds can live in basically overcrowded conditions. There are a dozen routine anti-'blackhead' formulae for turkeys and more than twenty drugs to combat coccidiocis, a killer disease which was nature's original barrier to intensification. Then there are the growth promoters, which are antibiotic. Seven basic types sell under more than twenty different trade names. Not all of them are cleared for use in *all* poultry, although all are cleared for chickens. Several are hazardous to other farm animals and all of them warrant the feed carrying the ominous statement, 'Keep away from children'.

There is so much wrong with poultry production that it is difficult to know where to start or how far to go with alternatives. In addition each stage of restoring dignity and humanity to poultry production is expensive and requires considerable support, commitment and understanding from the consumer.

The most caring – and most expensive – system has the birds spending their entire lives on special free-range poultry farms with small houses, which can be moved to fresh sites to avoid disease building up. The birds have full access to range when feathered and plenty of room inside the houses. Only natural daylight is used. Birds are not mutilated as pecking is not a problem. No growth promoters are used and no drugs are administered unless there is specific illness. Birds are transported in special high-welfare modules or trailers, carefully handled and killed by hand so that there is no danger of machine failure. This system is operated by very few, very committed suppliers.

Other organisations will tackle one or more areas of welfare to give an appearance of free-range birds at a lower price. Consumer vigilance needs to be high to avoid buying a second-rate article. One might have hoped that once the European Community had decided to regulate the term 'free-range' that that at least would become an un-ambiguous definition. Not a bit of it. In Directive 6, Article 10 of EC Regulations

1906/90, which came into force in July 1991, there is not one definition of 'free-range' but three; 'free-range', 'traditional free-range' and 'free-range total freedom'.

The introduction of these definitions has caused a flurry of activity in the poultry industry. Some of the leading suppliers to supermarkets of broilers, or intensively raised birds, have diversified into producing, as a side-line, 'traditional free-range' chickens.

A closer look at the definitions is revealing.

Free-range

This allows for stocking rates of thirteen birds per square metre with no limit in the number of birds that can be kept in one poultry house. Slaughter age is fifty-six days (eight weeks). For at least half their lifetime, that is twenty-eight days or four weeks, the birds must have had continuous access to open-air runs, mainly covered by vegetation and allowing not less than one square metre for each bird. That access comes from 'popholes' which must have a combined length equal to or greater than that of the longer side of the poultry house. The feed used in the fattening stage must contain 70% of cereals and, if a specific cereal is mentioned, it must account for at least 35% of the total feed, except in the case of maize (corn) which should comprise 50% of the total feed.

Traditional free-range

This presents a wholesome image. In reality, birds are stocked at 'no more than' twelve per square metre and no more than 4,800 birds per poultry house. The farm, or 'production site', should not contain more than four such poultry houses. The 'mainly vegetation covered' open-air run should provide for at least two square metres for each bird. The same standards as for free-range apply to the formula of the feed. The traditional free-range bird will be one of a strain recognised as being slow growing; it will be slaughtered at eighty-one days (just over 11½ weeks) and will have had continuous day-time access to its open air runs from the age of forty-two days, about half of its life span. Free-range total freedom birds have the same regime, breed, slaughter age and feed criteria as the traditional free-range chicken but instead of having 'at least two square metres' of open air it has access to open air runs of unlimited area.

What questions all of this raises. Where do the birds live for the other half of their life? What is the rest of their feed made up of? How on earth does the bird get outside through one of the popholes to 'free range' if it lives, with twelve others in the same square metre, in the middle of a poultry house housing ten thousand birds? That is what you might be buying if you buy a bird labelled free-range. We are not told whether routine medication is permitted or not. Phrases such as 'drugs are never administered except for medical reasons under veterinary supervision' occur. 'Medical reasons' can include preventive medication, which is needed when livestock is kept in confined quarters. We are not told how the bird was slaughtered, but this was almost certainly done mechanically. Whilst this is swift it is not always efficient and painless. Slightly smaller birds might be missed on the conveyor belt and thus run the risk of being plucked alive.

CLASSIC DISHES

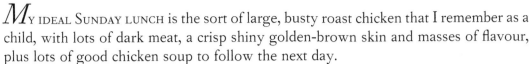

*M*Y IDEAL SUNDAY LUNCH is the sort of large, busty roast chicken that I remember as a child, with lots of dark meat, a crisp shiny golden-brown skin and masses of flavour, plus lots of good chicken soup to follow the next day.

Indeed, roasted fowl and other birds are classics within most of the world's cuisines, from the crisply roasted duck of the Peking kitchen to the American Thanksgiving turkey with all its trimmings. Such dishes have always been part of feasts and celebrations; take the roast goose of the Nordic Christmas and the great Yorkshire Christmas pie, with boned birds of different sizes tucked one inside the other. Grimod de la Reynière, the eighteenth-century French gourmet and writer, describes the turkey served at one of the Wednesday dinners of the Société des Mercredis held at the Restaurant Le Gacque in Paris. It was braised on a bed of veal bones, root vegetables, herbs and spices, and was stuffed with truffles, chestnuts and chipolata sausages. I have eaten the dish recreated by a London chef and it is excellent.

One of the most famous duck dishes also comes from Paris. For the *caneton à la presse* of the Tour d'Argent restaurant, the duckling is roasted rare, the breast fillets removed and the carcase pressed in a silver duck press which squeezes out all the juices that are then used to make the gravy. Each diner receives a numbered duck, a practice as old as the restaurant itself.

Not all the classic dishes are as elaborate as these. The jointed chicken, a most versatile fowl, can be turned into more relaxed classics: *poulet basquaise*, with the addition of red pimentos; chicken *chasseur* or *cacciatora* – both meaning hunter, the French version cooked with white wine and mushrooms, the Italian in Chianti (see p. 229); chicken Stanley, a satisfying dish of chicken and onions which cook down to a rich, velvety purée; or *waterzooi*, a Flemish or Belgian dish of chicken cooked with root vegetables and white wine.

The French *Repertoire de la Cuisine* is very succinct on the classic preparation of goose: 'it is generally roasted and stuffed in the English manner'. The young goose served at Michaelmas will be stuffed with sage and apple, and roasted. This, I am sure, is the very best way to treat this rich, fatty bird.

GOOD COMPANIONS

*I*T IS USEFUL TO CONSIDER the similarities between chicken and turkey and between duck and goose when thinking about accompaniments which will suit them.

On the whole the rich meat and crisp skin of duck and goose are best partnered with simple sharp flavours. Fresh green vegetables such as spinach, broccoli, broad beans or, best of all, fresh garden peas, are excellent with roast duck or goose. Sharp, fruity notes are added with an orange or cherry sauce, the classic *bigarade* or Montmorency. But note that it is Seville oranges and sour cherries, not dessert fruit, that should be used.

Herbs such as sage, thyme and rosemary also do well in cutting the rich fattiness. Oriental spices, such as ginger, lemon grass and anis are good with duck, as are marinades using soy sauce and rice wine prior to stir-frying or roasting. In classical times the Romans chose to emphasise the duck's richness by partnering it with honey and dates and each time I have tried it I have been surprised at how very good the combination is.

Chicken, on the other hand, is probably the most open-minded of all meats. Over the years I have discovered that it will go with almost anything. It can be cooked with beer, wine, champagne, cider or stock. It is good with all staples – rice, bread, potatoes, polenta – and, equally, with the most expensive ingredients, such as truffles and wild mushrooms. Both the delicately flavoured herbs such as chervil, chives and basil, and the more powerful ones, such as tarragon and rosemary, bring out the best in a tasty bird. Try it with oriental flavours or with Mediterranean ones. Cook it in curries and with spices from the Indian sub-continent. Chicken and chillis combine in Thai and Mexican food alike. Middle Eastern cooking methods and ingredients such as those for *tagines* and kebabs work well. Then, too, there is the broad American culinary repertory to be tapped: serve it with corn, with succotash, with mashed potatoes . . . the list could go on and on.

And I have found that turkey, too, will take the same accompaniments as chicken.

COOKING METHODS FOR CHICKEN

POACHING

A SUITABLE method for cooking the pale, tender flesh of chicken, poaching is used in the Oriental and Western kitchen. One of the simplest methods of making a one-pot meal; chicken, vegetables, herbs and seasonings are all cooked together. The broth can be eaten first and then the meat and vegetables. Alternatively, use this method (see p. 206) to cook chicken for salad, and freeze the strained broth for another occasion.

STEAMING

*U*NLIKE red meats which turn a fairly unappetising grey when steamed, chicken simply turns white and opaque. The whole bird can be steamed, as can the pieces such as breasts or leg. Thighs and drumsticks take longer to cook than the breasts and should be put in the steamer 8-10 minutes before the breasts. If all visible fat and skin is removed, this is a very low-fat cooking method.

ROASTING AND GRILLING

*W*ITH enough fat in the skin, chicken hardly needs basting when roasted or grilled. Both are excellent cooking methods for a succulent, well-matured, slow-growing bird full of flavour.

When grilling, the heat should not be set too high since cooking time is relatively long to ensure that the meat is cooked right through to the bone. This is not, of course, a suitable method for cooking whole chicken. Small ones can, however, be cut down the backbone and flattened or spatchcocked.

FRYING AND SAUTÉING

*S*LOW frying, almost braising, is the method to use for thighs and drumsticks, which need a good 30 minutes or so to cook through. One way of cooking chicken breasts quickly is to slit them lengthways into two flat fillets.

STIR-FRYING

A QUICK cooking method but which requires some advance preparation. Chicken is an ideal candidate for the wok, but the meat should be cut into slender, even pieces to ensure quick uniform cooking. With plenty of extra vegetables also cut into thin pieces, stir-frying is a good method of making a little meat go a long way.

Braising and casseroling

Cʜɪᴄᴋᴇɴ is not, unless you are lucky enough to find a real farmyard cockerel, a tough meat that requires slow cooking to tenderise it. However, one of the joys of these slow cooking methods is the way in which extra ingredients can be added to bring other flavours and textures to the finished dish, as in south east Asian curries. It is usual to joint the bird or to buy chicken portions for casseroles and curries.

To bone a bird

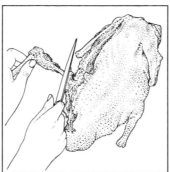
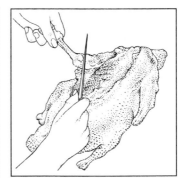

1 Place the bird breast side down on a clean work surface and make a cut from neck to tail down one side of the backbone. Using a sharp pointed knife, separate the flesh from the backbone, over the rib cage and down one side to the leg joint.

2 Carefully scrape the flesh from the thigh bone and drumstick, cutting through the ten-

dons. Pull the bone free and cut off through the joint.

3 Continue scraping and easing away the flesh from the whole expanse of the rib cage until you get to the wing. Cut through the tendons, pull the bone free and cut it off. Then scrape the flesh off down towards the breastbone.

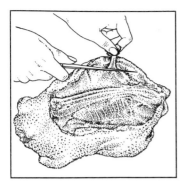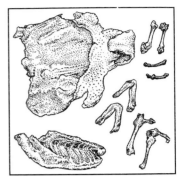

4 Turn the bird round and repeat the process on the other side of the bird, freeing the leg and wing bones and scraping and cutting the flesh away from the rib cage.

5 Lift the rib cage and then cut very carefully along the breastbone ridge to separate the carcase from the meat. Take care not to break the skin, which is fairly delicate on a chicken, for example.

6 Separate out any remaining tendons, scraping off the flesh. Turn the flesh of the wings and legs to the centre to give a neat, roughly rectangular shape, ready for stuffing, tying and cooking.

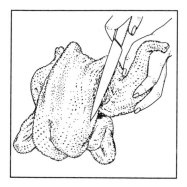
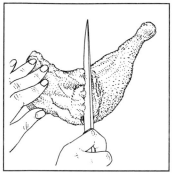
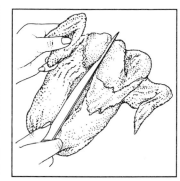

1 Place the bird on a cutting board, breast side up. Pull each leg away from the body and, using a sharp heavy cook's knife, cut down through the skin and through the joint between the carcase and thigh.

2 Divide the leg into two if you wish by cutting through the joint separating thigh and drumstick.

3 Pull each wing in turn away from the body and cut down through about an inch or so of the breast where it is attached to the wing, thus giving a more meaty portion than removing just the wing. Cut off and discard the wing tips.

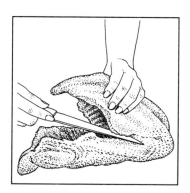
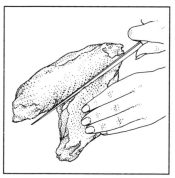
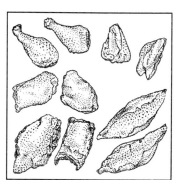

4 With your hand on top of the breast, split the carcase, then separate the whole breast from the backbone by cutting along the natural break in the rib cage.

5 Place the breast skin side down and, using first the knife point, cut down one side of the breastbone and then chop down with your other hand on the knife to divide the breast in two.

6 Cut the back into two pieces. There is little meat here, but these can be added to a casserole for extra flavour. The bird is now divided into eight. Large birds can be further divided up across the breast.

HERB-STUFFED CHICKEN

Judy Rodgers of San Francisco's Zuni Café is, as far as I know, the originator of this excellent method of roasting chicken with herbs under the skin. If you have a brick bread oven, as she has, the chicken will taste even better. Use plenty of fresh herbs, but avoid mint and too much of the stronger ones such as sage and rosemary. Tarragon, chervil and coriander are suitable, as is basil. The preparation starts a day or two before eating.

SERVES 4

3 lb/1.35 kg very fresh chicken
½ lemon
½ tsp salt
½ tsp pepper
pinch of ground mace

pinch of ground ginger
a handful of fresh herb leaves
2 oz/60 g softened butter
⅛ pt/70 ml dry white wine

REMOVE any fat from the cavity of the chicken. Rub the cut lemon over the chicken, then rub in the salt and spices. Put the lemon half in the chicken cavity. With your fingers gently ease the skin away from the flesh. It is much easier to do this than it sounds, but take care not to pierce the skin. Then, working with one leaf at a time, push the herbs under the skin and lay them flat on the flesh. When you have finished, smooth the skin flat again, over the leaves. Any remaining herbs can be put inside the cavity. Cover carefully but loosely and refrigerate for at least a day to let the chicken flesh absorb the herb scents.

When ready to cook the bird, have the oven preheated to 200°C/400°F, gas mark 6. Rub the bird all over, particularly the breast, with softened butter and place it on a rack in a roasting tin, lying on one side of the breast. Add the wine and put in the oven. After 20 minutes, turn the bird over on to its other breast and return it to the oven. After a further 20 minutes, turn it breast side up. Baste and continue cooking until the juices run clear when pierced by a skewer in the inner-most part of the thigh. Carve at the table or in the kitchen, and add the cooking juices.

Serve with roast or mashed potatoes (see p. 352) and a green salad after it.

ROAST CHICKEN WITH MUSHROOMS

After years of pot roasting chickens, which gives a lovely,
moist juicy dish, I began to miss the crisply roasted
chickens I remember from childhood. For these two things
are essential – or rather, one thing is essential and the
other is useful.

The essential element is the chicken. The best I had
tasted for many years was one given to me by François
Coolen, the young chef at the Grand Hotel Clement in
Ardres just outside Calais. . We had admired the delicious
poulet de Licques, served for dinner as a fricassée with beer
and in a more refined dish of *aiguillettes à l'orange*. It was a
marvellous bird, large and full of flavour. In the nearby
village of Licques we had seen the chickens running
around a number of the farmyards. Now such real free-
range birds are much more widely available in Britain.

The useful element is a chicken brick, one of the best
utensils for achieving a good crisp roast. I leave the lid on
for most of the cooking time and then take it off to let the
skin crisp.

Dried mushrooms are intensely flavoured and just a few
are needed to perfume the dish, which I would suggest
serving with roast jacket potatoes.

SERVES 4

3½-4 lb/1.6-1.8 kg chicken
sea-salt
freshly ground black pepper
1 oz/30 g sliced dried
   mushrooms (such as ceps or
   morels), soaked in warm
   water for 30 minutes

10 cloves of garlic
2 or 3 fresh tarragon (or other
   herb) stalks
generous splash of cream
   (optional for gravy)

SOAK a chicken brick for 15 minutes in
cold water. Preheat the oven to
190°C/375°F, gas mark 5. Remove any
fat from the cavity but do not throw it
away (save about 1½ oz/40 g for the
potatoes). Season the chicken inside and

out. Put the mushrooms in the bottom of the brick. Peel the garlic but leave the innermost skin to prevent the cloves from disintegrating. Put them in the brick and lay some of the herbs on top and put the rest inside the chicken.

Put the chicken in the pot, breast side down, cover and roast for ¾ hour. Remove the lid, turn the chicken over, cover and cook for another 15 minutes, then remove the lid, drain off the juices into a saucepan and roast, covered again, for a final 15 minutes. Reduce the juices to make a syrupy gravy, to which you could add some cream if you wished.

Carve the chicken and serve with a few cloves of garlic and the mushrooms.

Left-over roast chicken can be turned into a very good *Chicken Spread* for toast or sandwiches by putting it in the food processor with half its weight of butter (or sunflower margarine), half a teaspoon of grated nutmeg and a little salt and pepper. Process until smooth. Spoon into a dish, flatten the surface and pour on melted butter.

ROAST JACKET POTATOES

This recipe could not be simpler, and is excellent with roast chicken.

SERVES 4

1½ lb/680 g small potatoes
sea-salt
1½ oz/40 g rendered soft chicken
fat

SCRUB the potatoes well and prick each one with a fork. Place in a roasting tin or earthenware dish, sprinkle with sea-salt and put the chicken fat on top of the potatoes. Roast in the oven with the chicken for 1-1½ hours, depending on the size of the bird.

ROAST CHICKEN WITH LAVENDER HONEY AND CHINESE SPICES

In the course of my visits to Hong Kong, when I've been guest cook at the Mandarin Oriental, I've always made sure I spent time nosing around the kitchens to learn more recipes and techniques. This recipe is one of those, and is a delightful and apposite combination of eastern and western flavours.

SERVES 4

1 free-range chicken, weighing
    3¹/₂-4 lb/1.6-1.8 kg
3 tbsp clear honey
2 tbsp water
4 sprigs fresh lavender flowers
    or 1 tsp dried flowers
For the marinade:
1 tbsp ground coriander seeds
1 tbsp chopped fresh thyme
1 tbsp soy sauce

4 garlic cloves, peeled and
    crushed
¹/₂ tsp five-spice powder
¹/₂ tsp ground cinnamon
¹/₄ tsp sea-salt
¹/₄ tsp freshly ground black
    pepper
For the sauce:
¹/₂ oz/10 g butter
1 tbsp peeled and finely
    chopped shallot

1 tbsp port
2 tbsp red wine
remaining lavender honey
¹/₄ pt/140 ml chicken stock
    (see p. 344)
pinch of five-spice powder
1 tsp balsamic vinegar
salt
pepper
2-3 oz/60-85 g chilled diced
    butter

MAKE the lavender honey by bringing the honey and water to the boil and infusing the lavender flowers, off the heat, for several hours. Strain the honey and put half of it aside. Mix the rest of it with the herbs, spices and seasoning, and brush this marinade over the chicken. Cover it loosely and refrigerate overnight. Bring the bird back to room temperature before cooking it. Roast at 190°C/375°F, gas mark 5 for 20 minutes on one side, 20 on the other and 15 to 20 on its back.

Meanwhile make the sauce. Fry the shallots in butter until soft. Add the port, wine, honey, chicken stock, spices and seasoning to the pan, together with any roasting juices, from which you should have first skimmed the fat. Boil to amalgamate all the ingredients and reduce until you have a good concentrated sauce. Add the vinegar and season to taste, before whisking in the butter a piece at a time.

Carve the chicken and serve the pieces with the sauce.

POACHED CHICKEN

This is the best way to cook chicken that you plan to serve cold in a salad, and it also makes a very nice plain hot chicken dish. The broth produced is excellent and can be used either for soup another day, or as the basis for a sauce to serve with the chicken or to make a clear jelly to garnish the cold fowl.

SERVES 6-8

4-5 lb/1.8-2.3 kg chicken
1 carrot, peeled and chopped
1 celery stalk, trimmed and
chopped
1 onion, peeled and chopped
1 leek, trimmed and chopped
parsley stalks
1 tsp peppercorns
1 or 2 stalks of fresh tarragon (if
available)

T AKE the cleaned and prepared chicken and, instead of trussing it, insert four metal skewers into it, making sure that they go through the thickest, densest portions of the chicken's anatomy (thighs particularly). The skewers will conduct the heat most effectively right through the chicken.

Place the bird in a large saucepan and cover with water. Add the vegetables, including one of the inner layers of pale brown onion skin to give the stock a good colour. Add the rest of the flavouring ingredients.

If you will be eating the chicken cold, bring slowly to the boil and poach or simmer for only 20 minutes, remove from the heat and let the chicken go cold in the stock. To serve hot, poach the chicken for 10 minutes per lb/455 g, and serve with rice.

For a *Chicken Salad*, take the meat off the bones, leaving it in fairly large pieces, mix with freshly boiled new potatoes, chopped spring onion, diced avocado and home-made mayonnaise. Pile into a bowl lined with crisp lettuce and radicchio leaves.

HAINAN CHICKEN

Here is another version of poached chicken. My sister-in-law Bettina first cooked this dish for us in Hong Kong and it has since become a great favourite. Wherever there are Chinese cooks you'll find this dish on the menu. It originated in Hainan, the large tropical island off the coast of South West China, many of whose inhabitants have gone as cooks all over South East Asia. I've eaten this dish in Shanghai and in Singapore, but none so good as the dish that emerges from Bettina's kitchen. The chicken, although it can be served cold, is best freshly cooked and served. It does not taste nearly as good if it comes from the refrigerator.

Poach a chicken as described on p. 206 but replace the vegetables and seasonings given with the following:

SERVES 6-8

1 tsp five-spice powder
6 star anise pods
12 peppercorns, roughly crushed
1 medium onion stuck with 6 cloves

6 coriander stalks (keep the leaves for garnish)

6 thin slices of fresh ginger root
3 in/7.5 cm cinnamon stick
2 tbsp rice wine or Amontillado sherry
2 tbsp soy sauce

AFTER the chicken has cooked for about an hour in its stock, remove it from the pot and plunge it into a large bowl full of water and ice cubes for 10 minutes. This will set the juices in the chicken to a clear jelly. Remove the chicken and chop into small enough pieces to be picked up by chopsticks. Legs, thighs and breasts should be cut across the bone, so that each piece has both meat and bone, which some would say was the most flavoursome morsel.

Cook rice in chicken stock and garnish it with thinly sliced and fried onions.

Grate a piece of root ginger (about 2 in/5 cm) into a bowl and mix with a tea-spoon of sea salt.

Also in small bowls serve a chilli sauce made by mixing thinly sliced chillis with crushed garlic, toasted sesame oil, rice vinegar and soy sauce.

When you have removed the chicken from the pot, strain the stock, boil it and serve in soup bowls garnished with shredded spring onion. Broth, rice, meat and sauces are served and eaten together.

BEGGARS' CHICKEN

This classic Chinese dish makes a very grand party dish,
perhaps to be served as the centrepiece to an oriental feast.
The chicken is hermetically sealed, traditionally in lotus
leaves and clay, and cooked in a hot oven until the meat
falls succulently off the bone, which makes it very easy to
eat with chopsticks. Here, I suggest using a roasting bag
around the lotus leaves.

SERVES 6-8

3½-4 lb/1.6-1.8 kg free-
    range chicken
1 tbsp salt
1 tbsp dark soy sauce
1 tbsp rice wine or
    Amontillado sherry
2 tsp sunflower oil
1 tsp toasted sesame oil
2 in/5 cm piece fresh ginger,
    peeled and grated

4 spring onions, finely
    chopped
¼ lb/110 g lean pork, cut into
    matchsticks
8 fresh shiitake mushrooms,
    finely sliced
3 oz/85 g Chinese pickled
    cabbage, chopped

1 medium onion, peeled and
    finely chopped
1 tbsp light soy sauce
freshly ground black pepper
1 tsp five-spice powder
5 or 6 lotus leaves, soaked in
    hot water until pliable
1½ lb/680 g flour
water

REMOVE any excess fat from the bird. Rub all over with salt. Mix together the dark soy sauce, wine, half the oil, a little shredded ginger and the spring onions. Spread this over the chicken and let it marinate for an hour.

Fry the pork until crisp and add the mushrooms, cabbage, onion and remaining ginger, oil, soy sauce, pepper and a little of the five-spice powder. Cook over moderate heat for a few minutes. Drain off any excess oil and stuff the chicken with the mixture. Wrap the bird tightly in the lotus leaves, sprinkling the rest of the five-spice powder between the leaves. Tie if necessary. Put the parcel in a roasting bag, tightly closed to retain the juices.

Finally make a stiffish paste with the flour and water and use it to cover the parcel completely. Place it on a lined baking sheet and bake in the centre of a hot oven, pre-heated to 200°C/400°F, gas mark 6 for 2 hours.

To serve, crack open the dough and cut through the paper and leaves. The meat will be tender enough to eat with chopsticks.

ROAST CHICKEN WITH ORIENTAL SPICES

I first devised this recipe for a picnic, but the bird is
equally good hot, when I would serve it with rice and a
steamed green vegetable. If serving the birds cold, do not
stint on the seasoning; cold food always needs more
seasoning than hot.

SERVES 6

6 or 12 chicken portions,
depending on size
4 cloves of garlic
1/2 in/1 cm piece of fresh ginger
1 tbsp soy sauce
pinch of Szechuan pepper
freshly ground black pepper
pinch of five-spice powder or
ground cinnamon
a little sesame oil mixed with
sunflower oil

TRIM any loose fat and skin from the chicken pieces. Peel, slice and then sliver the garlic and ginger very thinly. Insert the slivers under the skin. Rub all over with soy sauce, peppers and spice and marinate for an hour before cooking.

Preheat the oven to 200°C/400°F, gas mark 6. For each chicken portion take a piece of foil large enough to wrap it completely and brush it over with the oil.

Wrap each portion carefully in the foil, with the fold on top. This is important to keep in the cooking juices, which will, when cold, turn into a delicious jelly.

Place the parcels on a baking tray and roast in the top half of a hot oven for about 35 minutes. Remove from the oven and allow to go cold. There is no need to unwrap the chicken until required.

STUFFED SPRING CHICKEN AND VEGETABLES

This is based on a favourite recipe that I first cooked for *À la carte*, as part of a dinner with a French flavour.

SERVES 4

3½-4 lb/1.6-1.8 kg chicken
For the stuffing:
4 oz/110 g lean bacon, rinded
6 oz/170 g black pudding
4 slices wholemeal bread
4 sprigs of fresh tarragon (if available, or 1 tsp dried)

2 cloves of garlic (or more if you like)
salt
pepper

2 measures of cognac
To serve:
1½ lb/680 g new potatoes
1 head of lettuce
1 large jar of petits pois or ½ lb/230 g fresh mangetouts

C UT the wing tips from the chicken. Cut the bacon into narrow strips. Render it in a frying pan until most of the fat runs. Meanwhile, cut up the black pudding and slices of bread into small cubes, removing the crusts from the bread. Put these cubes in a basin, drain most of the fat from the bacon and add the bacon to the bread and the black pudding. Chop the tarragon and add it to the stuffing. Peel and crush the garlic and mix into the stuffing together with a little salt and pepper. Moisten the stuffing with a measure of cognac and stuff the chicken with the mixture (much quicker to do with your fingers than fiddle about with a teaspoon). Secure the bird closed with cocktail sticks.

Preheat the oven to 180°C/350°F, gas mark 4. Heat up the pan in which you fried the bacon and brown the chicken all over. Pour on the second measure of cognac and light it. When the flames have died down, transfer the bird to a casserole, cover and cook in the oven for about an hour.

About 10 minutes before the chicken will be done, put the potatoes on to boil. Remove any wilted leaves from the lettuce, wash it and shake dry. Roughly chop the lettuce and stir-fry it quickly in the frying pan, moisten with water and stir until wilted. Heat up the petits pois, or boil the mangetouts rapidly for 2-3 minutes in plenty of salted water. When the chicken is cooked, drain off and reduce the cooking juices to serve as gravy.

Serve the chicken on a small bed of lettuce leaves with new potatoes and petits pois or mangetouts.

SALT-BAKED CHICKEN WITH WHOLE GARLIC CLOVES

SERVES 2

2½ lb/1.5 kg chicken
8-10 large unpeeled cloves of
garlic
3 lb/1.35 kg coarse rock-salt

WIPE and trim the chicken. Untruss it as this allows it to cook through more evenly. Trim the garlic cloves of their outer skin, but do not peel. Preheat the oven to 200°C/400°F, gas mark 6.

Line a roasting tin with foil. Spread half the salt in the bottom of the tray and make an indentation for the chicken in it. Lay the bird in it and press down well into the salt. Tuck the garlic cloves into the salt too. Cover the chicken and garlic with the rest of the salt, packing it well down to form a crust. Bake in the centre of the oven for 45 minutes.

Lift the foil out of the roasting tin and place on a serving dish, folding the foil back to display the salt crust. Crack it open and then carve the chicken.

CHICKEN AND ALMOND POTTAGE

This bland, soothing dish is based on a mediaeval recipe which became a favourite after I had researched a piece on the cookery of Britain during the early part of the Norman conquest. It is interesting to compare it with the chicken cream recipe, which follows. It has its origins in Italian cookery of a slightly later period.

SERVES 6

3 chicken breasts, off the bone, skinned and each cut into four pieces
6 oz/170 g shelled almonds

2 pt/1.15 l chicken or light veal stock (see p. 344)
2 small onions, peeled and finely sliced or chopped

1 oz/30 g butter
pinch of ground cinnamon
6 cloves

211

BLANCH the chicken pieces by dropping them into a pan of boiling water, bringing the water back to the boil, then draining the meat and refreshing it under cold water.

Put the almonds in a basin, pour boiling water over them and let them stand for 15 seconds. Drain the almonds and rub them hard in a damp cloth to remove the skins. Grind or pound the almonds until fine. Heat the stock in a pan, stir in the almonds and cook gently. Sweat the onions in half of the butter until golden brown and add to the pot. Add the chicken to the almond broth, with a pinch of cinnamon and the cloves. Simmer gently until the chicken is tender, stir in the rest of the butter and serve immediately in heated shallow soup plates as a starter.

CHICKEN CREAM

Based on a sixteenth-century Italian dish which I tasted in the Ceresole restaurant in Cremona, where the young chef, Lucia Giura, experiments with old recipes, this is a pale, delicate dish. It was described on the menu as *pietanza bianco.*

SERVES 1 AS A STARTER

¼ lb/110 g raw chicken breasts, off the bone
½ pt/280 ml milk

¼ lb/110 g real (unprocessed) white bread, crusts removed
white pepper to taste
pinch of powdered ginger

pinch of ground cinnamon
celery salt or sea salt to taste
a little cream (optional)

REMOVE and discard any skin and fat from the chicken breast. Pour the milk into a saucepan. Place the chicken in the milk, bring slowly to simmering point and poach gently for 10 minutes, until the chicken is cooked through. Remove from the heat. Place the bread in a basin and pour enough cooking liquor over to cover it. Let it stand for 10 minutes.

Cut the chicken into small pieces and put it with the soaked bread, all the liquid, spices and seasonings into a food processor or blender. Process until smooth. Rub through a sieve into a saucepan. Heat gently and serve this delicious warming gruel piping hot in a shallow heated soup plate. A little cream may be stirred in if you like.

BOODLES' STUFFED CHICKEN BREASTS

I came across a startling recipe in Florence White's *Good Things in England* for partridge stuffed with bananas. It sounded so unlikely that I had to try it. Since then I have cooked quails and a whole bird in the same manner and adapted the recipe here for chicken breasts.

SERVES 4

4 chicken breasts, skinned, off the
*   bone and with the fillets*
*   removed*
½ tsp salt
1 tsp freshly ground black pepper
⅛ pt/70 ml dry white wine
2-3 tbsp water
For the stuffing:
freshly ground black pepper
2 ripe bananas, peeled
2 thick slices wholemeal or corn
*   bread*
2 tsp finely chopped tarragon
1 tbsp finely chopped onion,
*   shallot or spring onion*

P REHEAT the oven to 190°C/375°F, gas mark 5. Lightly season the chicken breasts on both sides. Mix a little more pepper into the bananas, mashing them until fairly smooth. Cut and discard the crusts from the bread, and crumble it into the bananas. Mix in the tarragon and onion. With a sharp knife make a pocket in the chicken breasts. Spoon the mixture inside. Fasten closed with cocktail sticks.

Put the breasts on a rack in a roasting tin skin side up, and bake for 30-40 minutes in a fairly hot oven. When they are done, remove from the oven and keep warm while you make a little gravy. Skim the fat from the roasting tin, and pour in the white wine. Set it on the heat and bring to the boil, scraping up any bits of dripping stuck to the tin. Add the water and cook, stirring, for 5 minutes. When reduced to about half, it is ready to serve with the chicken.

Stir-fried cauliflower or Savoy cabbage are good served with the chicken.

CHICKEN WITH CUCUMBER

When we were first married and lived in a cold-water flat in the attic of a Victorian house, this was one of my favourite dishes to cook in the summer. I can remember cooking it once on Wimbledon Men's Final's Day for a great friend who had come to dine. It is inexpensive, easy to prepare and unusual in that the cucumber is cooked.

The cucumber is best prepared a few hours in advance, even the day before. Fresh dill goes well with both main ingredients. Those who do not like it may prefer to substitute fennel or chervil.

SERVES 4

4 chicken breasts, off the bone
2 large cucumbers
1 tbsp salt
1 oz/30 g unsalted butter (or use a non-stick frying pan)
4 tbsp dry white wine or chicken stock (see p. 344)

salt
pepper
1 tbsp fresh dill, plus a few fresh fronds to lay on the cooked chicken

REMOVE the skin and any fat from the chicken breasts. Shave the skin off the cucumber in thin strips and cut it in half lengthways. Scoop out and discard the seeds and slice as thinly as possible. Place in a colander, sprinkle with salt and mix with your hands to get all the cucumber salty. Leave to degorge over a bowl for several hours.

Rinse thoroughly and dry by wringing gently in a clean tea towel.

Fry the chicken breasts in half the butter on both sides, cover partially and cook until the juices run clear. Remove the chicken to a warm serving dish. Add the wine or stock to the pan juices, season lightly, scrape up any residues and add the dill. Cook for a minute or two and pour over the chicken.

Fry the cucumber in the remaining butter until you begin to see a few small patches of golden brown. The cucumber will brighten. Arrange it around the chicken and serve.

CHICKEN BREASTS WITH LIME AND LOVAGE SAUCE

An inexpensive, simple and flavoursome dish that I learned from Marion Maitlis in Sheffield during my cook's tour of Britain for the *Sunday Times*. It's one of those useful dishes to know about if you have the oven on for other things since the chicken is finished off in the oven. Lovage is a herb that you may well have running riot in your garden. It is not readily available in the shops, which is a great pity as I love its strong, yeasty, celery-like scent and flavour.

SERVES 4

4 chicken breasts, off the bone
1 tbsp flour
salt
pepper
1 oz/30 g butter
juice and zest of a lime

For the sauce:
1 oz/30 g butter
1/4 lb/110 g button
    mushrooms, wiped clean
    and sliced
1/2 pt/280 ml chicken stock
    (see p. 344)

2-3 tbsp double cream
handful of chopped fresh
    lovage (for which celery
    tops will make an adequate
    substitute)
salt
pepper

SKIN the chicken breasts. Flatten gently with a rolling pin between layers of cling film. Put the flour, salt and pepper in a paper bag and shake the meat in it to give it a light dusting of seasoned flour. Melt the butter in a frying pan and, when hot, lay the chicken breasts in it. Cook for about a minute on each side, enough just to firm them up but not to brown them.

Remove the chicken breasts from the pan and place them in a lightly buttered roasting tin or ovenproof dish. Sprinkle with lime juice and zest, then cover with foil. The dish can be prepared to this stage in advance if necessary, in which case the chicken breasts should be cooled rapidly, covered and refrigerated.

Put the chicken pieces in the top half of a pre-heated oven, 200°C/400°F, gas mark 6 and cook for 8 minutes. Meanwhile, make the sauce by cooking the mushrooms in the butter, pouring in the stock and cream and cooking over a high heat until reduced a little. Remove the chicken from the oven and transfer it to a serving plate, pouring any cooking juices into the sauce. Add the lovage to the sauce and check for seasoning. Serve spooned over the chicken.

Extra lime and lovage can be used to trim the dish.

POACHED CHICKEN BREASTS STUFFED WITH PARSLEY MOUSSE

Here the flavour of a chicken is enhanced, but not masked,
by the delicate flavour of parsley. A dinner party dish
rather than one for quick everyday cooking because
forcing raw chicken meat through a sieve takes time.
Nonetheless, airy texture which results is worth the effort.

SERVES 4

2 breasts from a 5-6
   lb/2.3-2.7 kg chicken (or
   4 smaller chicken breasts)
   off the bone
1 chicken liver

2 oz/60 g flat-leaved parsley
   (leaves only)
2 tbsp double cream
¼ tsp salt
pinch of white pepper

pinch of freshly grated nutmeg
1½ pt/850 ml chicken stock
   (see p. 344)
¼ pt/140 ml white wine

REMOVE the skin and the fillets from the chicken breasts. Discard the skin and the sinew from the chicken fillet. Trim the chicken liver of any threads and green parts tainted by the gall bladder.

Roughly chop the liver and the fillet and blend them in a food processor until smooth. Rub this mixture through a sieve. Blanch the parsley leaves in boiling water and refresh under cold water. Dry thoroughly and chop very finely. Mix into the chicken stuffing together with the cream and the seasoning.

With a sharp, long-bladed knife, make a pocket in the chicken breast, entering from the blunt rather than the pointed end and taking care not to pierce through to the outside. Spoon in the stuffing and close the end with cocktail sticks or by sewing it up.

Bring the stock and white wine to the boil, in a large pan and carefully lower in the stuffed chicken breasts, which will immediately take the stock off the boil. Let it come back to the point where the surface just breaks with a bubble or two, then turn the heat right down, and poach the meat very gently for 10 minutes.

Remove and put on a plate covered with foil to keep warm. Spoon about ½ pt/ 280 ml of the stock into a shallow pan and reduce by more than half to produce a well flavoured, not too syrupy, sauce.

Slice the chicken breasts and arrange on heated dinner plates. Spoon the sauce over the top. Decorate with a little greenery if you wish.

STEAMED STUFFED CHICKEN BREASTS

With no added fat, lots of fibre and cooking by steaming,
this is an exceedingly light and healthy recipe and quite
elegant enough to serve for a dinner party.

SERVES 4

2 large or 4 smaller chicken
    breasts (see previous recipe),
    off the bone
12-16 large round lettuce leaves
For the stuffing:
4 tbsp cooked brown rice
4 tbsp chopped, peeled, deseeded
    tomatoes
2 tbsp soft wholemeal
    breadcrumbs

2 tbsp grated apple (firm, sweet
    dessert apple)
2 tbsp dry sherry
pinch of fresh or dried marjoram,
    oregano or thyme
salt and pepper to taste
For the infusion:
a handful of fresh herbs or 1 dsp
    mixed dried herbs
zest of 1 orange

SKIN the chicken breasts. Slit each one almost in half and open it out butterfly fashion. Press it flat. Using a non-stick or well seasoned cast-iron frying pan, seal the chicken, cooking it on a high heat for 30 seconds on each side. Remove.

Blanch the lettuce leaves by arranging them carefully in a colander and pouring boiling water over them to make them soft and pliable for wrapping. Trim out the base of the hard central rib. Pat the leaves dry on kitchen paper towels.

Mix all the stuffing ingredients together and divide amongst the four pieces of chicken. Fold the edges of each one together, reform into the original neat pouch-shape and secure with half cocktail sticks. Now wrap each chicken breast completely in three or four lettuce leaves and place in a single layer in a steamer basket. Set this over a pan of water containing the herbs and orange peel, cover tightly with the lid (or foil) and steam gently for 20-25 minutes.

Serve each parcel, whole or sliced if you wish, on a heated dinner plate, with a little fresh pasta and a spoonful of tart fruit jelly, such as apple or quince (see p. 361), or some homemade apple purée.

CAJUN BLACKENED CHICKEN

Care needs to be taken with this popular style of cooking,
originally from Louisiana and now spread far and wide,
since it entails heating a sturdy well seasoned cast-iron
griddle or frying pan to almost white heat. A piece of fish
or meat, which has been dipped in melted butter and a
seasoning mixture, is then cooked by fast searing. More
suited to the professional restaurant than the domestic
kitchen though it may be, I include this recipe because
good results can be obtained, either with a frying pan or
on the barbecue. Flat cuts which cook evenly and
relatively quickly are best over such fierce heat.
You can make up your own seasoning mix and store it
in a jar in your spice cupboard. Many variations can be
made along the following theme.

SERVES 4

*4 chicken breasts, off the bone
and with the skin and small
fillet removed*
3 oz/85 g butter, melted
*3-4 tbsp Cajun seasoning
(below)*
For the Cajun seasoning:
2 oz/60 g cayenne pepper
1 oz/30 g fine sea-salt

*1 oz/30 g freshly ground black
pepper*
*1 oz/30 g freshly ground white
pepper*
1 oz/30 g ground coriander seeds
1 oz/30 g ground cumin
1 oz/30 g ground celery seed
*1 oz/30 g dried oregano or
marjoram*

*H*EAT the frying pan or griddle.
Thoroughly dry the chicken
breasts, flatten them and dip them in the
butter. Sprinkle liberally on both sides
with the seasoning, pressing it in well.
When the frying pan, or barbecue coals,
are as hot as you can get them, put on the
chicken pieces. Cook for 4-5 minutes on
each side and serve. A crisp cooling salad
and a baked potato with soured cream or
mashed potatoes (see p. 352), are good
accompaniments.

CHICKEN IN SALMOREJO

This is cooling summer food from the south of Spain.
Chicken, or often rabbit, is cooked and then left to
marinate in a thick sauce, not unlike gazpacho, made from
tomatoes, garlic, olive oil and vinegar. Perhaps I should
emphasise that this is *not* a way of using up cold meat; it
must be freshly cooked, char-grilled if possible for the
authentic flavour, and the sauce poured over while the
meat is still hot so that it absorbs the flavours. It can be
prepared in the morning and served for dinner.

SERVES 4-6

3-4 lb/1.35-1.8 kg chicken
2 lb/900 g ripe tomatoes, peeled
 and deseeded
6 cloves of garlic
¼ pt/140 ml extra virgin olive
 oil
4 tbsp sherry vinegar
salt to taste

ROAST the chicken or, if you have a char-grill or barbecue, joint it and grill the pieces. Skin after cooking; this keeps the flesh well basted during cooking. Removing it allows the sauce to penetrate. Put the tomatoes in a blender with the garlic, oil, vinegar and salt; blend until smooth. If you have roasted the whole chicken, joint it.

Put the chicken portions in a deep casserole or earthenware dish and pour over the sauce. Leave to stand for several hours, covered, in a cool place or, preferably, the refrigerator. Allow to come back to room temperature before serving.

Serve it as part of a cold buffet or with salad vegetables and perhaps a potato, or rice salad. It is also very good just served with big chunks of crusty bread, a jug of extra virgin olive oil and some lemons cut in wedges.

TANDOORI CHICKEN

Even without a *tandoori* oven, it is possible to cook a very tasty version of this restaurant and take-away favourite. Good *tandoori* mixes are widely available in supermarkets and grocers. This recipe is from a former colleague, Margaret Uppal, who taught me to make lots of Indian dishes.

SERVES 4-6

3-4 lb/1.35-1.8 kg chicken, skinned and jointed
For the tandoori paste:
5 oz/140 g plain yoghurt
½ tsp salt
½ tsp chilli powder (more, or less, to taste)

2-3 cloves of garlic, peeled and crushed
3 tbsp tandoori mix
1 tbsp tomato purée
To serve:
fresh mint leaves
1-2 lemons
salad leaves

*M*IX the yoghurt, salt, chilli, garlic, tandoori mix and tomato purée in a large bowl. Make two or three small cuts in each piece of chicken and put it in the tandoori mixture. Make sure each piece is well coated, rubbing in with your fingers if necessary. Marinate, covered and refrigerated, for at least 6 hours or overnight if more convenient.

Preheat the oven to 200°C/400°F, gas mark 6. Lightly oil a baking sheet. Remove the chicken pieces from the marinade and let the excess drip off. Place the chicken on the sheet and bake in the oven for 20 minutes. Turn down to 180°C/350°F, gas mark 4 and bake for a further 15-20 minutes. Pour off any excess juices which accumulate during cooking as the chicken should be slightly dry on the outside and juicy inside. The chicken juices should run clear when pierced with a skewer to test for doneness.

Serve with green salad and quartered lemons as a starter or main course. Fresh mint leaves provide the perfect garnish.

FRIED CHICKEN WITH CREAM GRAVY

It is in simple dishes like this one that the truth will out. A real, mature, fully-flavoured chicken, jointed and fried to a crisp golden brown under a light egg and flour dip, is a feast for the senses. Such simplicity is best avoided with a lesser bird.

Edith, my mother-in-law, cooks this for us by special request, usually on our last day with her in Pittsburgh. She always cooks pounds and pounds more than we can possibly eat, so the left-overs often become a delicious picnic on the flight back home. The gravy is a traditional American one made from the drippings in a frying pan or roasting tin. This is how cream gravy is made for the Thanksgiving and Christmas turkey.

SERVES 4

3½ lb/1.6 kg chicken, jointed into 8 small pieces
3 oz/85 g flour
1 tsp salt
½ tsp freshly ground black pepper

2 eggs, lightly beaten in a shallow basin
For the cream gravy:
1 oz/30 g flour
½ oz/15 g butter
¼ pt/140 ml full cream milk

¼ pt/140 ml chicken stock, warmed
2 tbsp double cream, optional
salt
pepper
To garnish:
parsley or watercress

*H*EAT a heavy frying pan over medium heat. Place the chicken pieces, skin side down, in a single layer in the pan. Cook gently for 10-15 minutes, turning once most of the fat has been rendered. Transfer the chicken pieces to a plate and, when cool enough to handle, skin the pieces. Sift the flour and seasoning together. Dredge the chicken in flour then dip in egg and finally in the flour again. Raise the heat under the frying pan and fry the chicken pieces

until golden brown and cooked through. Test with a skewer or knife point inserted into a thigh piece next to the bone. The juices should run clear.

Transfer to a heated serving platter, garnish with parsley or watercress and keep covered, but loosely so that the meat will not steam, while you make the cream gravy.

Sprinkle the flour on the drippings in the frying pan and cook until the flour is golden brown, adding a little butter. Add a little milk off the heat and mix thoroughly, scraping up any sediments stuck to the bottom of the pan. Gradually add the rest of the milk, stirring continuously to avoid any lumps, and cook the sauce for a few minutes. Stir in the stock until you have a smooth mixture. Bring to the boil and simmer gently for about 10 minutes, to completely cook the flour. Strain into a small clean saucepan. Bring back to the boil. Stir in the cream, if using it, and add salt and pepper to taste.

A mountain of mashed potatoes (see p. 352) with a crater lake of cream gravy is the perfect accompaniment to fried chicken.

ORIENTAL CHICKEN PARCELS

Subtly spicy and somewhat messy to eat, these small savoury parcels make a good starter for an informal meal. Finger bowls are necessary. The recipe is based on a dish I enjoyed in a small simple restaurant called Hsieh's Garden in Singapore's Holland Village. Hsieh would not give me the recipe but this is quite close.

1½ lb/680 g chicken joints, chopped into 2 in/5 cm pieces
4 tbsp rice wine or Amontillado sherry
2 tsp clear honey
1 tsp freshly grated ginger
½ tsp ground cinnamon
½ tsp ground coriander

¼ tsp five-spice powder
¼ tsp Szechuan pepper
2 tbsp grated orange zest
2 tbsp soy sauce
1 tbsp toasted sesame oil
2 spring onions, thinly sliced

1 tbsp fermented black beans, crushed
6 in/15 cm square of greaseproof paper
oil for frying
To garnish:
beansprouts, spring onions, star anise and fresh coriander leaves

*M*OISTEN the chicken pieces with half the wine and the honey, then sprinkle with the dry ingredients. Mix the soy sauce and sesame oil with the remaining wine and pour over the chicken. Mix in the spring onions and black beans. Cover and marinate overnight. Wrap each piece of chicken in greaseproof paper, making sure that it is well sealed. Heat the oil in a deep pan or wok to 180°C/330°F and lower in the parcels. Fry for 8-10 minutes, drain and pile up on a platter, garnished with oriental greenery and spices.

POLLO ALLA CONTADINA

Our friends the Lancellottis cooked this for us one Sunday
lunchtime. Literally translated, it means 'peasant woman's
chicken'. And it is, indeed, a simple rural dish, based on
the sort of ingredients the country-woman might have on
hand if company comes to call; chicken in the back yard, a
few potatoes in the garden, and some tomatoes on the
vine, if not dried or bottled in the store cupboard. Angelo
Lancellotti describes it as Italian fast food! The chicken
used should be a young one so that it will cook quickly. It
is traditional to serve the dish with vinegar (not balsamic)
sprinkled on the potatoes.

SERVES 4-6

*1 tender young chicken, jointed
into quite small portions (ie
the breasts cut in two and the
legs divided into thighs and
drumsticks)*
⅛ pt/70 ml olive oil
*2 lb/900 g potatoes, peeled and
cut into 1-2 in/2.5-5 cm
pieces*
*¾ lb/340 g ripe tomatoes,
quartered and seeded*
white wine or broth to moisten
salt
pepper

F RY the chicken in a third of the oil and
cook for 20 minutes. Fry the potatoes
separately in another third of the oil and
also cook for 20 minutes. Stir both pans at
intervals to stop the food sticking.

In one large frying pan, fry the tomatoes in the rest of the oil for 2-3 minutes,
then add the chicken and potatoes to it.
Cook for 10-15 minutes more, uncovered, until the chicken and potatoes
are tender. Moisten with white wine or
broth if it looks like drying out.

To serve, pile on to a heated serving
platter and season lightly.

COQ AU VIN

When I first began to write this book I had not planned to include a recipe for *coq au vin*. A real old farmyard cockerel is a rare commodity, even in France, judging from the disappointing versions I've eaten in recent years. More often than not the dish has turned out to be little more than pieces of broiler cooked and then served with a red wine sauce. Then I returned to Languedoc where I'd spent a very happy year in the late sixties, learning much more about cooking than literature. My friend Michèle invited us to Sunday lunch and cooked quite simply the best *coq au vin* I've ever eaten. It was one of her neighbour's cockerels that had led a long and happy life in the yard. A big bird, at least six months old in Michèle's estimation, it was cooked and served with Cahors wine, the most local of the big reds, which is what this dish needs; a Rhône or an Australian Shiraz would do very well. Suppliers can sometimes get you a cockerel if you give them enough notice.

SERVES 6-8

1 free-range cockerel, weighing
   6 lb/2.7 kg
½ lb/230 g belly of pork
1 large or 12 small onions
2 leeks
2 carrots
small glass of Armagnac
2 bottles of Cahors wine
1 bay leaf
sprig of thyme
2 or 3 parsley stalks

3 or 4 cloves of garlic, peeled
2 tsp black peppercorns
2 cloves
½ lb/230 g pork skin, cut into
   2 in/5 cm squares or 1 pig's
   trotter, chopped up
salt
For serving (optional):
fresh or dried parsley
triangles of bread
chicken fat or olive oil

JOINT the bird into eight pieces and chop the remaining section of carcase into two or three pieces. This cooks with the casserole to add extra flavour to the sauce. Cut the belly of pork (including the rind if it has been left on) into matchsticks. Fry gently in a large frying pan until the fat runs.

Meanwhile peel the onions and, if using a large one, slice it. Trim the leeks and slice the white part only, discarding the green tops or saving them for soup. Peel and slice the carrots. Fry the vegetables with the pork and when beginning to brown lightly, transfer to a large casserole. In the fat remaining in the pan brown the chicken pieces and transfer them to the casserole.

Pour a glass of Armagnac over the chicken and vegetables and light it. In another large pan bring the wine to the boil, light it and let it flame for a minute or two. Take care with this operation: make sure there is nothing inflammable near the pan before you pour in the wine. Cover with a lid to extinguish the flames. Pour some of the cooked wine into the frying pan and scrape up the cooking residues. Pour it over the chicken with the rest of the wine. Tie the herbs, garlic and spices in a piece of muslin (or put them in a coffee filter paper and staple it closed). Put this in the casserole together with the pork skin or pig's trotter. Bring to the boil, cover and cook in the oven at 150°C/300°F, gas mark 2 for about 3 hours, or cook on top of the stove on a heat-diffusing mat until the meat is tender.

When almost ready, drain the cooking juices into a frying pan and reduce over a high heat until you have the consistency and concentration of flavour you desire. The sauce can also be reduced less and thickened with *beurre manié* (see p. 345 and the note on pan sauces on p. 344). Salt the sauce at this stage.

Serve from the casserole or arrange the pieces of meat in a heated serving dish and pour the sauce over it. The *coq au vin* can be garnished with fresh or dried parsley and triangles of bread, fried in either chicken fat or olive oil.

Traditionally the dish is served on its own and is followed by a helping of fresh pasta to be eaten with more of the copious sauce. This is how Michèle served it. There is a recipe for pasta on p. 346. Some cheese followed by a *tarte aux pommes* or *tarte au citron* is how to end the meal. A platter of *crudités* or a bowl of green salad makes a good starter.

CHICKEN GUMBO

Okra is the essential ingredient in this creole dish.
Without it or filé powder you lose the rich, thick silky
texture which is the hallmark of a good gumbo.
Sometimes shrimps or prawns are added at the last minute
instead of oysters. Small sweet queen scallops would also
work well. Serve with plenty of steamed or boiled white
rice.
If you can get filé powder and not okra, cook the
casserole and stir in 1 tbsp filé powder at the end, but do
not let it boil again. Filé is the dried powdered young
leaves of the sassafras tree.

SERVES 6-8

3½-4 lb/1.6-1.8 kg chicken
1 lb/455 g smoked ham or
    bacon joint
2 tbsp groundnut or sunflower oil
1 large onion, peeled and sliced
1 lb/455 g tomatoes, peeled,
    seeded and chopped
1 lb/455 g okra, trimmed and
    sliced

salt
cayenne pepper or chilli powder to
    taste
parsley stalks
1 bay leaf
1 dried red chilli, seeded
3 pt/1.7 l water
12 shelled oysters

JOINT the chicken into 12 pieces and dice the ham into 1 in/2.5 cm pieces. Heat the oil in a flameproof casserole. Brown the chicken and ham together, then add the onion, tomatoes and okra. Cook over a high heat for about 5 minutes, season lightly and add all the seasonings and the water. Bring to the boil, skim the surface, cover and simmer for about 1½ hours.

Add the oysters and more seasoning if needed. Cook for 2-3 minutes more, remove the parsley stalks and serve immediately.

MALAYSIAN CHICKEN AND POTATO CURRY

Coconut milk is a feature of much of the cooking of south east Asia and here it is used to good effect in a dry chicken curry. The liquid found inside the fresh coconut is coconut water and not coconut milk.

SERVES 4-6

3 lb/1.35 kg chicken, skinned
1 tsp salt
4 red chillis, seeded and crushed
2 shallots, peeled and finely chopped
2 tbsp mild or medium strength curry powder
2 tsp freshly grated ginger

8 cardamom pods, split open and the seeds pounded
1¼ pt/710 ml hand-hot water
¾ lb/340 g desiccated coconut
8 tbsp groundnut oil
2 medium onions, peeled and sliced
1 lb/455 g potatoes, peeled and sliced
1 stalk of lemon grass

JOINT the chicken. Mix together the salt, chillis, shallots, curry powder, ginger and cardamom and rub into the chicken. Leave to marinate for half an hour or so.

Meanwhile, make the coconut milk. Put ½ pt/280 ml water in a blender with the coconut and blend for 30 seconds. Strain it through a sieve into a bowl, pressing down hard to extract as much of the coconut "essence" as possible. Put the coconut back in the blender with the rest of the hot water. Blend and sieve into a second bowl. This time the coconut milk will be thinner.

Heat the oil in a large heavy frying pan and fry the onions until golden brown. Remove them and put to one side. Fry the potatoes until golden brown and remove those. Drain the chicken and fry in the oil for 10-15 minutes, turning it from time to time. Add the thin coconut milk, lemon grass and any remaining marinade. Simmer gently until the chicken is almost done, then add the potatoes, onions and coconut milk. Cook, uncovered, over a low heat until the potatoes and chicken are tender and the gravy almost absorbed.

Serve with rice and heated flat bread such as *nan* or *paratha*, and perhaps a vegetable curry.

WHITE CHICKEN CURRY

In Sri Lankan cookery, the white curries are the mildest,
indeed so mild that they are eaten for breakfast with
hoppers, a thin pancake made of rice flour and coconut
milk. String *hoppers* use the same batter but are forced
through a die into long strings which are folded into a
circle on small bamboo mats and then steamed. The red
and the brown curries are much fiercer, using chillies and
mustard seed in abundance.

This is one of the dishes I learned to cook there, making
full use of the spices I bought in the market in Kandy and
the fresh cashew nuts from Cadjugama, or "cashew city".

Something of the same rich, bland sweetness can be
obtained by using pine kernels. Almonds are, I find, too
hard and not quite rich enough. More chillies can be added
for those who enjoy a high rating on the Scoville scale.
Since it is the kind of dish it's as easy to cook for eight as
it is for four, it makes a fine centrepiece dish for a curry
and rice dinner. At home I serve it with basmati rice, a
spinach and dhal curry, a fresh herb sambol (see p. 358)
and one or two tempered vegetable dishes, a technique
which is a mixture of braising and frying, another
technique I learned from my Sri Lankan cook friends.

SERVES 8

8 free-range chicken portions
(or more if you wish)
1 tbsp rice
1 tbsp toasted coconut
1 tsp sea-salt
4 cloves of garlic
2 oz/60 g pine kernels
seeds from 8 cardamom pods
6 cloves
1 in/2.5 cm cinnamon stick

1 in/2.5 cm fresh ginger,
peeled and chopped
1 tbsp ground cumin
1/2 tsp ground coriander seeds
1 tsp fennel seeds
1 tsp turmeric powder
1 onion, peeled and chopped
2-3 green chillis, seeded and
sliced

2 tbsp sunflower or groundnut
oil
1 bay leaf or sprig of curry
leaves
3 in/7.5 cm piece of lemon
grass, sliced
1 piece of pandanus leaf
(optional)
3/4 pt/430 ml coconut milk
(see p. 227)

TRIM the chicken of most of its fat. In a mortar or food processor grind the rice, coconut, salt, garlic, pine kernels and spices. Rub this paste into the chicken and leave it to stand for at least an hour. It can be left to marinate overnight, closely covered, in the bottom of the refrigerator.

Gently fry the onion and chillis in the oil until the onion is transparent. Add the leaves and lemon grass. Turn up the heat and fry the chicken until it loses its rawness.

Pour on half the coconut milk, bring to the boil, cover and simmer until the chicken is tender, adding more coconut milk if the curry shows signs of drying out.

POLLO ALLA CACCIATORA

A traditional rural recipe from northern and central Italy, called hunter's chicken, which sometimes includes mushrooms and sometimes not.

SERVES 4

3 lb/1.35 kg chicken, jointed
½ lb/230 g pancetta or piece of
    unsmoked bacon, diced
1 medium onion, peeled and
    chopped
2 tbsp olive oil
¼ pt/140 ml dry marsala or
    white wine
½ lb/230 g ripe tomatoes,
    peeled, seeded and chopped
salt
pepper

BROWN the chicken pieces in a heavy pan with the pancetta or bacon.

Separately, brown the onion in olive oil. Moisten the chicken with the wine and let it cook for a few minutes. Stir in the tomatoes and sautéed onion, season lightly and cook, uncovered, for half an hour or so until the chicken is cooked.

CHICKEN IN GEWURZTRAMINER

I am inclined to make this dish based on the famous
Alsace classic, *coq au Riesling*, with the other fragrant and
distinctive Alsatian wine, Gewurztraminer, for a good
practical reason. We like a glass of Gewurztraminer as an
aperitif, but do not necessarily drink it with the meal,
which leaves just the right amount in the bottle for
cooking. It is unlikely, however, that we would have any
left-over Riesling!

SERVES 4

3 lb/1.35 kg chicken, jointed
½ oz/15 g unsalted butter
16 small onions, peeled
2 tsp flour
½ bottle/375 ml
    Gewurztraminer d'Alsace

2 cloves
fresh chervil or parsley
freshly ground pepper
salt
4 tbsp double cream (optional)

IN a heavy lidded sauté pan place the chicken, skin side down, over a low heat. Cook gently until the fat runs and the skin browns lightly, about 10-15 minutes. Turn the pieces over and brown the other side. Remove and put to one side. Drain off the chicken fat and put the butter in the pan. Fry the onions until golden. Remove to one side with the chicken.

Sprinkle the flour in the bottom of the pan and stir in with the cooking residues. Moisten with a splash of wine and stir until lightly thickened, then add the rest of the wine, blending it in well. Put the chicken and onions back in the pan with the cloves and a little chopped chervil or parsley, leaving some to scatter on the dish before serving. Grind in some pepper; add a little salt. Bring to the boil, lower the heat, cover and simmer for about 30 minutes or so, until the chicken is done.

Put the chicken pieces in a heated dish. Boil up the sauce and add the cream if using it. Reduce to a nice sauce consistency and add more seasoning if necessary, including a squeeze of lemon juice if you like. Pour the sauce over the chicken and serve. Spaetzle, the small, stubby homemade pasta from Alsace, which I think of as a cross between a dumpling and a noodle, is a good accompaniment.

COCK-A-LEEKIE PIE

Using the same ingredients as the traditional Scottish soup of the same name, I like to make this simple, inexpensive pie, which is equally good hot, warm or cold. Ideal picnic food in fact. Left-overs from a large poached chicken can be used quite happily.

SERVES 4-6

1 lb/455 g thin leeks, white and
    pale green part only
12 prunes, soaked and stones
    removed
1 lb/455 g cooked chicken meat,
    off the bone
14 oz/395 g flaky or shortcrust
    pastry (see p. 347-8)
¾ pt/430 ml strong chicken
    stock (see p. 344)
3 tbsp Amontillado sherry
2 tbsp double cream
2 eggs
salt
pepper
pinch of ground mace

C UT the leeks into ½ in/1 cm pieces, wash and blanch for 2 minutes in boiling water. Refresh them under cold water and drain thoroughly. Drain the prunes and cut the chicken into 1 in/2.5 cm chunks. Preheat the oven to 180°C/350°F, gas mark 4.

Use half the pastry to line a pie dish about 9 in/22.5 cm diameter and put in the leeks, prunes and chicken. Beat the rest of the ingredients together and pour the savoury custard over the filling. Roll out the remaining pastry and cover the pie, sealing the edges well (any pastry off-cuts can be used to decorate the pie). Make one or two slits in the top for the steam to escape.

Bake for 30-40 minutes.

CHICKEN IN FILO PASTRY

If you have any left-over chicken – or indeed, goose, turkey or duck – here is an excellent way of using it.

SERVES 6

1½ lb/680 g cooked chicken meat off the bone
3 ripe tomatoes, peeled, seeded and diced
4 spring onions, trimmed and chopped
12 sheets of filo pastry (about ½ lb/230 g)
3 oz/85 g melted butter

½ lb/230 g quickly fried mushrooms
½ lb/230 g cooked potatoes, diced
3 size-3 eggs

⅛ pt/70 ml strong chicken stock (see p. 344)
⅛ pt/70 ml single cream
freshly grated nutmeg
2 tsp lemon juice
1 tbsp chopped fresh chives
salt and pepper
2 sprigs of fresh tarragon or fresh basil

C UT the chicken into small cubes, mix with the diced tomato and chopped spring onion. Lay the sheets of pastry on a damp tea-towel and make sure the top sheet is always brushed with melted butter before you use it.

Brush a shallow, rectangular oven-proof dish (about 8×10×2in/20× 25×5 cm) with melted butter. Lay two sheets of filo pastry in the dish, gently lining the dish with them; some pastry will overlap the edges of the dish. Lay two further sheets of pastry, cut to fit the base of the dish, on top. Put the mushrooms and potatoes, fairly well packed together, in the bottom of the dish. Beat the eggs, stock and cream together with the nutmeg and lemon juice and pour a third of it over the mushroom and potato mixture. Sprinkle on chives and seasoning.

Lay four more sheets of filo on top, cut to fit, each brushed with melted butter. Spread the chicken mixture on top of the pastry. Pour the rest of the egg mixture over the chicken. Chop up the fresh herbs and sprinkle these on top together with a little more salt and pepper. Cut two more sheets of pastry to fit the dish and lay these over the chicken. Fold the overlapping sides over the top to make a neat parcel shape and finally lay two more sheets, cut to fit exactly, on top. With a sharp knife lightly score the top layer into a diamond pattern.

Preheat the oven to 170°C/325°F, gas mark 3, and bake for 40 minutes. Increase the temperature to 200°C/400°F, gas mark 6, for the last 5-10 minutes to allow the pie to cook to a rich golden brown.

EMPANADILLAS

The *empanadilla*, a Spanish and South American favourite,
is an immensely versatile small or large filled savoury
pastry. Serve individually with drinks or serve several,
accompanied by a green salad, as a main course.
Left-over chicken, game or beef can be used to fill them.
Cook in batches, taking care not to let the oil get too hot.

SERVES 6

½ lb/230 g plain flour
5 oz/140 g butter; softenedsalt
14 fl oz (400 ml) oil for frying
For the filling:
2 onions, peeled
14 oz/400 g chicken livers

4 fl oz/100 ml olive oil
sprig of fresh thyme
4 tbsp dry white wine
salt
pepper
1 egg, beaten

*S*IFT the flour into a heap on the table, place the softened butter in the centre, add a pinch of salt and work with the fingertips, adding a little water to obtain a smooth pastry which doesn't stick to the fingers. Roll it into a ball, cover with a damp cloth and let it rest in a cool place for 3 hours.

Meanwhile, make the filling. Thinly slice the onions, cut the chicken livers into small pieces. Heat the olive oil and lightly fry the onions without browning. When transparent, add the livers, sprinkle with a few leaves of fresh thyme, moisten with the white wine, add salt and pepper and cook for 2 minutes over a high heat. Let the juices reduce to a glaze.

On a lightly floured worktop or marble slab roll out the pastry to a thickness of ⅛ in/0.3 cm. With a pastry cutter, cut out circles of pastry. On each circle place a teaspoon of the liver and onion mixture with a little of its glaze. Fold over the pastry to form small turnovers and press the edges together. Brush the top with beaten egg.

Heat the rest of the oil and deep-fry the *empanadillas* until golden. Drain on kitchen paper towels and serve very hot.

CHICKEN LIVER SAUCE FOR PAPPARDELLE

Pappardelle, those broad, flat noodles, are excellent with chunky meat sauces, especially if home-made and few sauces are as quick to cook as this one, using chicken livers flavoured with sage. If you make this type of sauce often, or the *ragù* on p. 85, it is worth preparing a batch of the *soffritto* and storing it in the refrigerator.

SERVES 4

1 onion, peeled and finely
*   chopped*
1 celery stalk, peeled and finely
*   chopped*
1 carrot, peeled and finely
*   chopped*
2 tbsp olive oil
½ lb/230 g chicken livers
2 or 3 fresh sage leaves, finely
*   chopped*
4 tbsp chicken stock (see p. 344)
*   or good red wine*

*M*AKE a *soffritto* with the onion, celery and carrot, cooking them gently in the olive oil until tender. Clean the chicken livers, cutting out any bitter green pieces and any strings. Separate and halve the lobes.

Raise the heat under the *soffritto*, add the chicken livers and sage and fry for 2-3 minutes. Add the wine, reduce the heat after a minute or two and cook for just long enough for the wine to lose it sharp flavour.

DUCK

*W*ITH WEBBED FEET, OILY FEATHERS covering a layer of down, and a layer of fat under the skin to protect it from the cold, the duck is ideally designed as a waterfowl. It swims and flies, is to be found in every continent except Antarctica, and in most climatic zones. The Ancient Egyptians enjoyed eating duck, the Chinese domesticated and bred it for food over 2,000 years ago, and the Romans introduced it all over Europe. Apicius, that first-century Roman gourmet, recorded many excellent recipes, one including a date sauce to be served alongside the bird. Not long ago, in a modish restaurant in San Francisco, we were served a most exquisite dish very little removed from Apicius's idea. On a purée of dates was arranged a fan of sliced duck breast, lightly brushed with hollandaise sauce and glazed under the grill.

A large proportion of the duck industry in America is said to be descended from three White Peking ducks and a drake brought from China in the 1870s, while domestic ducks, on the other hand, are descended from the mallard or the Muscovy duck, the first native to the northern hemisphere, the second from Central and South America.

In Britain duck production was traditionally centred around Aylesbury and the white birds bred there for the table were the best known breed, although there were others, such as the Orpington, White Pennine and Danish strains. The last forty or fifty years have seen duck production move to Norfolk, Lincolnshire and Wiltshire, so although the name Aylesbury continues to be used, it is only descendants of that breed which appear on our tables. As a neat twist in the story of food-ways, Britain has now also become a major exporter of duck to China.

Are we really talking about duck or duckling? A bird becomes a duck when it reaches the second feather stage at two months old, by which stage a duckling, depending on the breed, can have reached 7 lb/3.2 kg. It is still not a duck, but has the tender meat of a duckling. On the other hand 3-3½ lb/1.35-1.6 kg birds are available all year round, the larger sizes tending to be on sale around Easter and Christmas.

Serving: allow at least 1 lb/455 g per person eg 4 lb/1.8 kg for 4 servings, 6-7 lb/
2.7-3.2 kg for 6 servings

Roasting: unstuffed – 20 mins per 1 lb/455 g at 200°C/400°F, gas mark 6
stuffed – 30 mins per 1 lb/455 g at 180°C/350°F, gas mark 4

Braising: 60 mins at 180°C/350°F, gas mark 4 (jointed)

There are easy ways of dealing with the fat on the bird and, indeed, of making the most of it. Personally speaking, I like a good layer of fat on a duckling. It provides the bird with its own basting which I do not need to do, and it provides me with a lovely pot of solid white duck fat at the end of the day for me to cook potatoes in or to use in baking. To make sure that the fat drains away during cooking all you need to do is prick the skin of the bird all over with a larding needle or sharp pointed knife and stand it on a rack while it is being roasted. Periodically, say every 20 minutes or so, remove the duck from the oven and drain off the fat into a large bowl. That way, the fat will not burn, and you avoid the danger of having to drain away up to a pint of boiling fat. Let the accumulated fat cool, then refrigerate it for late use. Covered, it will keep well for weeks, if not months.

Whilst roasting is perhaps the commonest and one of the most popular methods of cooking duck, it is by no means the only method. The bird can be jointed (see p. 201) and braised or casseroled. The duck breasts can be grilled or pan-fried and served as a meal for two, or for four if from one of the largest birds. The legs can then be added to that delicious traditional Languedoc dish, *cassoulet*, fragrant with herbs, sausage, lamb and plenty of melting beans. Or they can be used to make a casserole with green olives and a little orange peel for flavouring. A single piece of duckling can be boned and finely sliced or chopped to use in an oriental-style stir-fried dish, with ginger, garlic and mangetouts perhaps, an interesting variation on the duckling with green peas tradition. Of course, there are wonderful Chinese recipes for dealing with duckling. Perhaps the best is the well known Peking duck, where the bird is allowed to dry out thoroughly, which produces the extremely crisp skin when roasted or deep fried. It is then served with pancakes, plum sauce and sliced spring onions. In Scandinavia and Northern Europe duckling is served with apples, spicy red cabbage or with sauerkraut. In France it is served with wild sour cherries or bitter oranges. Note how most of the accompaniments to duck in classic dishes are sharp fruits or vegetables. This combines perfectly with the rich, moist meat.

Other Ducks

Barbary

THIS is a French breed of duck, occasionally sold in Britain ready for the oven. It is most definitely a duck, slaughtered at up to three months old, well into its second feather stage. The flesh is drier and more fibrous than that of duckling, with an altogether more mature flavour. The bird also has far less fat on it and often reaches a weight of 6-7 lb/2.7-3.2 kg, which makes it a handsome meal for four or five people. It should be cooked more slowly than duckling, needs the addition of plenty of moist flavouring (such as a good stuffing) and should be basted over the breast from time to time.

Gressingham

A NEW breed of English duck which came on to the market only recently is already very popular with chefs and restaurateurs. A cross-breed of mallard and domestic duck, it is not yet widely available for general sale, but it is available for some butchers. Full of flavour and texture, with dark meat, the bird is lean but with the succulence of a domestic bird. It can be roasted or cooked according to any duck recipe. One will feed two people. Use the carcases and leftover trimmings for an excellent duck soup, and use the legs in a casserole, a *confit* or a *cassoulet*.

Nantais

NANTES is famous for its special breed of duck, a delicately flavoured bird, which usually weighs in at 4 or 5 lb/ 1.8-2.3 kg and will just feed four people. It is traditional in France to roast the duck at a very high heat (220°C/425°F, gas mark 7), turning it during cooking and serving it so that the breast meat is still slightly pink. Nantais duck is the origin of the traditional *canard* (or, more properly, *caneton*) *aux petits pois* since Brittany is famous for its peas – a large proportion of the French crop is grown there.

Unless specifically wild, duck are now being kept in conditions almost identical to intensive chickens. Growth promoters and preemptive medication, particularly against septicaemia, are used. Free-range keeping conditions without use of growth promoters or preemptive medication are still possible and provide an incredibly tasty, albeit more expensive, product.

ROAST DUCKLING WITH SAUERKRAUT

The origins of this dish go back to a bottle of Southern
Comfort we bought duty free at JFK airport, returning
from a trip to America. Glazing a duck is as good a way as
any of using this sticky liqueur. Other stickies that you
have lurking in your drinks cabinet could well be
substituted.
Raising and lowering the temperature for short periods
during the roasting encourages the skin to crisp and more
fat to be rendered.

SERVES 4

5-6 lb/2.3-2.7 kg duckling
3 cloves of garlic, slivered
small piece of fresh ginger,
   slivered (optional)
1 orange, halved
salt
freshly ground black pepper
mild paprika
2 tbsp honey
3-4 tbsp Southern Comfort
For the stuffing:
1 onion, peeled and finely
   chopped
knob of rendered duck fat

duck liver, gizzard and heart
3/4 lb/340 g fresh, canned or
   vacuum-packed sauerkraut,
   drained weight
1 dsp dill seeds, or fresh dill weed
   or fennel seeds
To garnish:
flat-leaved parsley
To serve:
green salad
wild rice
rhubarb or gooseberry jelly
   (optional)

*P*RICK the bird all over, particularly the fatty parts. (This is most important, as it allows the fat to drain off during cooking, leaving a crisp skin.) Insert the garlic and, if you wish, ginger, into some of the slits. Rub the cut orange all over the skin, then sprinkle with salt, pepper and paprika. Let it sit for an hour or two to absorb the flavours.

Meanwhile, prepare the stuffing. Fry the onion in a little rendered duck fat until brown. Trim the fat and gristle from the liver, gizzard and heart, and dice them. Fry with the onion until well sealed. Stir in the sauerkraut and dill or fennel, and cook gently for 10 minutes. Allow to cool before stuffing the duck. Squeeze the orange, and blend the juice with the honey and liqueur. Preheat the oven to gas mark 7, 220°C/425°F. Stuff the duck, and secure the cavities with toothpicks or kitchen thread. Brush with the orange juice mixture.

Place the duck on a wire rack in a roasting tin, laying it on its side. Cook at 220°C/425°F, gas mark 7, for 10 minutes. Turn the oven to 190°C/375°F, gas mark 5, for 20 minutes. Remove the duck from the oven and turn the heat back up to 220°C/425°F, gas mark 7. Drain off the fat from the roasting tin, brush the duck once more with the orange juice then turn it on to its other side. Return the duck to the oven and cook for 10 minutes, then for a further 20 minutes at the lower temperature. Remove from the oven again, raise the temperature once more to 220°C/425°F, gas mark 7 and drain off any more fat. Turn the duck on to its back, brush with orange juice, roast for 10 minutes and then a further 20 minutes at the lower temperature. Baste once more during cooking. Remove from the oven and allow to rest for 10 minutes, kept warm.

If there are more cooking juices than fat in the bottom of the roasting pan, use them to make a gravy, adding any remaining basting mixture.

Garnish with flat-leaved parsley and serve with a green salad, wild rice and, if you wish, a little fruit jelly.

DUCK BREASTS WITH RHUBARB

A few years ago, it became fashionable to cook rhubarb with savoury dishes. This made a good deal of sense because rhubarb has the same astringent quality as sorrel and green gooseberries, both of which have had long and respectable associations with rich meat and fish dishes. This recipe is one I developed from a dish I first tasted at Christian Proust's restaurant, La Charmille, in the Grand Hotel Moderne at Chatellerault, in the Vienne, France. This should be prepared the day before required.

SERVES 4

4 duck breasts
1 oz/30 g unsalted butter
½ lb/230 g rhubarb, cut into
  slender 2 in/5 cm batons
¼ pt/140 ml duck or chicken
  stock

salt
black pepper
For the marinade:
1 carrot
1 onion
1 celery stalk

a few sprigs of fresh thyme
¼ pt/140 ml dry white wine,
  vermouth or white port
To garnish:
fresh parsley or chervil
  (optional)

239

S LASH the skin on the breasts in three or four diagonals and place the breasts skin-down in a shallow dish. Slice the vegetables into a saucepan. Add the thyme and wine and bring to the boil. Remove from the heat and allow to cool. Pour this infused marinade over the meat and marinate overnight. Remove the meat from the marinade and dry thoroughly on kitchen paper towels.

Heat a heavy frying pan and fry the duck breasts, skin-side first, on both sides until done to your liking. The last bit of the cooking should be done on high to crisp the duck skin. Remove the meat and keep it warm while you finish the sauce.

Remove excess fat from the pan and melt half the butter in it. Gently fry the rhubarb until just tender, but do not let it colour. Remove and keep it warm with the duck. Turn up the heat, strain the marinade into the pan and add the stock. Boil fiercely until reduced by at least half. Season to taste. Remove the pan from the heat and beat in the rest of the butter.

Serve the duck breasts on individual plates with a few batons of rhubarb, and the sauce. Garnish with herbs if using them and serve immediately.

TEA-SMOKED DUCK BREASTS

Although I am a great fan of smoked fish, I had never really appreciated smoked meats until I tasted tea-smoked duck at Bruce Cost's restaurant in San Francisco, Monsoons. His book, *Foods from the Far East*, and his own explanations helped me in setting up my own smoker at home. As well as smoking duck breasts, chicken breasts, quail, belly pork and whole poultry, I also hot-smoke salmon fillets in the same way (which need no presteaming). Whereas the breasts will steam in twenty to thirty minutes, large whole birds should be steamed for an hour or so. I usually use Darjeeling or Formosa Oolong tea and have not yet tried any of the highly scented ones such as Earl Grey. If serving this dish as part of an oriental meal, two to three duck breasts will be sufficient.

SERVES 6

6 duck breasts
1 tbsp coarse sea-salt
1 tbsp Szechuan peppercorns
4 star anise
2-3 in/5-7.5 cm cinnamon stick
1-2 tbsp soy sauce
¼ lb/110 g uncooked rice
¼ lb/110 g sugar
2 tbsp fragrant black tea

WIPE the duck breasts. Crush the salt and spices and toast them in the wok. Allow to cool and rub them all over the meat. Put a few inches of water in the wok, put the meat on a rack, cover and steam for 20-30 minutes, depending on the thickness of the meat. Remove the duck and rub all over with the soy sauce.

Prepare the wok for smoking. Wash it out, dry and line with a double thickness of foil. Mix the rice, sugar and tea and spread in the bottom of the wok. Place the rack on top and arrange the duck breasts on it. Put the lid on and seal the edge either with a strip of foil or, as Bruce Cost suggests, with moistened paper towels. Have the heat medium-high, place the wok on the burner and once it has begun to smoke, which you will smell rather than see, resist the temptation to have a look, and leave the wok on the heat for 10-15 minutes. Remove from the heat and leave for a further 15 minutes, before removing and serving. If you wish to serve it cold or as part of a warm salad, thinly sliced, leave it until it has cooled to the temperature you require.

This is a marvellous technique to experiment with, especially in the herbs and spices you rub into the meat before steaming, and the ingredients used to cause the smoke. Rice and sugar are the base, but you can then add, for example, a large crushed cinnamon stick, or some sturdy cuttings off a rosemary bush. Vine prunings are another obvious candidate for the smoker.

DUCK BREASTS WITH SHERRY AND HONEY SAUCE

Hazelnut oil, sherry vinegar and honey make an unusual
warm marinade for the duck breasts, which are then
quickly roasted, grilled or pan-fried, whichever you prefer.
Marinate the meat for at least two hours or overnight if
more convenient. Depending on the time of year, serve
the meat with a green salad, a selection of stir-fried spring
vegetables or a purée of root vegetables and potato. The
breasts are best served whole rather than sliced and fanned
on the plate in the old-fashioned style. In Spain nuts are
used to describe the character of sherry; almonds for *fino*,
walnuts for *amontillado* and hazelnuts for *oloroso*. It makes
sense to use *oloroso* in this recipe, but a dry rather than a
sweet one.

SERVES 4

*4 duck breasts off the bone,
  with the skin left on*
pepper
salt
*⅛ pt/70 ml dry oloroso
  sherry*

For the marinade:
*2 shallots or 1 medium onion,
  peeled and chopped*
1 carrot, peeled and chopped
*3 cloves of garlic, peeled and
  chopped*
1 tbsp sunflower oil

3 tbsp cognac
*few sprigs of fresh or dried
  thyme*
2-3 tbsp clear honey
3 tbsp aged sherry vinegar
2 tbsp hazelnut oil

*P*REPARE the marinade. Fry the vegetables in the sunflower oil until light brown, add the cognac and flame it. Add the thyme, honey and vinegar and cook until the mixture caramelises slightly. Add the hazelnut oil and simmer gently for 10 minutes. When just warm, pour over the duck breasts in a bowl. Mix well, cover and marinate for 30 minutes.

Remove the duck from its marinade, letting it all drip back into the bowl. Dry the meat and season lightly. Fry, grill or roast until done to your liking, then place the meat, covered, to rest in a warm place while you finish the sauce.

Strain the marinade into the frying pan or roasting tin and bring it to the boil, scraping up any residues. Add a little water if there is not much liquid, then pour in the sherry. Cook until the sauce has a good flavour and texture. Arrange the duck on hot dinner plates.

DUCK AND OLIVE CASSEROLE

Green olives are an excellent match for the duck, their piquancy balancing the richness of the meat. This is delicious served with rice and any left-overs make a good sauce for pasta.

SERVES 4

4-6 duck thighs
1 onion, peeled and thinly sliced
2 cloves of garlic, peeled and thinly sliced
2 celery stalks, trimmed and sliced

1 sliver (about 2-3 in/5-7.5 cm) of orange zest
4 oz/110 g best quality green olives
¼ pt/140 ml duck stock (or, if unavailable, other stock, see p. 344)
¼ pt/140 ml dry white wine

sprig of thyme
1 bay leaf
3 cloves
salt
freshly ground black pepper
To serve:
boiled rice

REMOVE the fat and skin from the duck meat. Fry a small piece of skin in a heavy casserole until the fat runs. Fry the onion and garlic in the fat until golden brown. Remove and put to one side. Fry the meat until golden brown. Trim and slice the celery and add to the meat together with the onion and garlic mixture and the orange zest. Stone the olives if you wish (if not, remember to warn your guests) and add them to the casserole together with the stock and wine.

Tie the thyme and bay leaf together, stick the cloves into the bay leaf and tuck into the casserole. Season.

Cover and simmer very gently until the duck is tender, or cook in a moderate oven, 160-180°C/325-350°F, gas mark 3-4, for an hour or so.

DUCK RILLETTES

This recipe can also be made with pork alone, rabbit (in which case you will need to increase the proportion of belly of pork) or goose.

SERVES 8-10

½ lb /230 g belly of pork
4-6 duck legs
duck skin with plenty of fat on it,
*   plus any more fat from the*
*   cavity*
salt
freshly ground black pepper
freshly grated nutmeg
bay leaf
sage
about ½ pt/280 ml water

SLICE the belly of pork, chop the duck legs (leaving the meat on the bones for flavour) and put the two meats together with the duck skin and fat, in a casserole. Add the salt, pepper, nutmeg, bay leaf, sage and the water. Cook at the bottom of the oven for 3-4 hours, on a very low heat, until all the fat has melted and the meat is cooked.

Place a sieve over a basin. Discard the bones and any skin from the casserole and ladle some of the remaining meat and fat into the sieve. Take a fork in each hand and pull the meat apart – it should finish up in shreds, with most of the fat in the basin. Pack the *rillettes* loosely into a jar, pot or *pâté* dish and add a little of the melted fat. Continue until all the meat has been shredded and potted and all the fat poured around it; the top should have a good layer of fat to seal it once refrigerated.

Serve with hot toast or crusty fresh bread.

SPRING DUCKLING STEW

More often grilled or roasted because of its high fat
content, duckling is nevertheless very tasty when cooked
with young vegetables. The meat is fried first to render
some of the fat.
This is a very nice dish to serve for an Easter luncheon
or other springtime occasion.

SERVES 6-8

6 lb/2.7 kg duck, jointed into 8
    pieces
1 lb/455 g new potatoes, peeled
1 lb/455 g small purple and
    white turnips (or navets),
    peeled
1 lb/455 g young carrots, peeled
    if necessary
6 cloves of garlic, peeled
½ lb/230 g green beans,
    trimmed

2 bunches of spring onions,
    trimmed
bouquet garni, made of 2 or 3
    parsley stalks, 1 bay leaf, a
    sprig of tarragon and a sprig of
    thyme
½ pt/280 ml duck or chicken
    stock (see p. 344)
salt
pepper

HEAT a deep, heavy-based frying pan and put the duck pieces in it, skin side down, but with the body fat on. Once browned, turn them over and brown the other side. Pour off the fat.

Put the carrots, potatoes, garlic and turnips in the pan, cutting up the vegetables to the same size if necessary to ensure even cooking. Tuck in the *bouquet garni*. Pour on the stock, bring to the boil, cover and simmer gently for 30 minutes. Add the green beans and spring onions and simmer for a further 20-25 minutes until both meat and vegetables are tender. Season to taste and serve.

Of course, if you can also get fresh peas and broad beans, add a few of these about 5 minutes before the end of cooking time.

DUCKLING WITH RICE IN THE MINHO STYLE

Slow-cooked casseroles of meat or fish, rice and wine are traditional in Northern Portugal. One of my favourites is lampreys with red wine, which produces a richly flavoured dark stew, and rabbit is prepared in the same way. The rice also acts as an excellent foil for the rich duck meat in this recipe, *arroz con pato*. Use red or white wine, depending on what colour you want the rice to be. For preference bake this in a chicken brick or unglazed clay pot – well soaked in water first. It is a simple rustic dish in which the duck skin would probably be left on. A less fatty dish is produced if you remove the skin first.

SERVES 6

1 large mild onion, peeled and
   thinly sliced
2 or 3 cloves garlic, peeled and
   chopped
2 lb/900 g skinned duck
   portions, chopped into smaller
   pieces
½ tsp salt
½ tsp freshly ground black
   pepper

4 cloves
1 bay leaf
1 cinnamon stick
12 oz/340 g medium or long
   grain rice
¾ pt/430 ml red or white wine
¾ pt/430 ml duck stock (see
   p. 344)
To serve:
1 tbsp extra virgin olive oil
1 tbsp chopped fresh coriander

*P*REHEAT the oven to 180°C/350°F, gas mark 4.

Lay half the onion and garlic in the bottom of the pot and put the duckling pieces on top. Season with the salt and pepper. Tuck the cloves, bay leaf and cinnamon into the pot and add the rice, shaking the pot to distribute it evenly.

Lay the rest of the onion and garlic on top. Heat the wine and stock and pour on top.

Cover and cook in the middle of the oven for 1-1½ hours or for longer in a slower oven, until the meat is tender.

Sprinkle with olive oil and coriander leaves before serving.

Goose

*I*N BRITAIN, WESTERN AND CENTRAL Europe, all over Scandinavia, but less so in America, the goose has long been a favourite bird to grace the table on high days and holidays. Indeed, records show that the ancient Egyptians enjoyed goose. It was certainly a popular dish with the Romans: Apicius, the first-century writer, gives many recipes and Pliny describes how geese were force-fed, often on delicious sweet figs, to produce enlarged livers specially for the table, a practice not very different from that of today in producing *foie gras*.

A Michaelmas (29 September) goose on the table has long been an English tradition, said to ensure a prosperous year. Many tales and stories about barnyard geese similarly associating them with good fortune, are to be found in many literatures; the goose girl and the goose that laid the golden eggs, not to mention the countless tales about the goose's legendary abilities as a vigilant guardian which saved whole cities from conquest. Certainly geese do have a knack for making their presence felt, and heard, with their hissing attack and noisy honking at any sign of an intruder to the farmyard.

If they have been too long in the farmyard, geese will not make good table birds. A young goose, called a gosling or a green goose, is eaten at about six months of age and an adult bird is sold for the table up to eighteen months old, although they can live as long as forty years.

Goose is still very much a seasonal bird and animal husbandry techniques have not been able to change that. It has largely been spared intensification, hence its relatively high cost. Goslings are hatched in the spring and by late September are just ready for the table. By Christmas, the geese are that much maturer and larger, and the few that are sold at Easter will be even bigger and older. A young bird will weigh about 7 lb/3.7 kg. It should have soft, flexible legs and webs, a supple windpipe and a soft, pliable under-bill. As the goose matures, its various extremities will naturally harden. Around Christmas time you will find geese up to 18 lb/8.15 kg. This sounds large, but because the goose has such a broad rib cage, there is less meat on it, pound for pound, than a chicken or a turkey. For example, a 15 lb/6.8 kg goose dressed weight, when prepared for the table, will weight about 11 lb/5 kg, including giblets, and contain about 1 lb/455 g fat. This can be removed from the cavity before cooking, and another 2 pt/1.15 l or so of fat will be given off during cooking. With stuffing, a goose of this weight will feed six people amply, or eight at a pinch.

I recommend the custom of a Michaelmas or Christmas goose. Hatching in the spring, the goslings have five or six months to fatten up and feed on grass, although in some years of drought when the grass is not so lush, grain is used to supplement their feed. Nowadays, of course, the Christmas goose, which tends to be larger that the Michaelmas goose, accounts for 95% of those reared in England.

It might at first seem an extravagance, but there are so many dishes to be made from a single bird that I think of it as an investment. One year, for example, a Michaelmas goose weighing 12 lb/5.45 kg (dressed weight) fed four of us for dinner as a roast, provided about 1½ lb/680 g meat pickings from the carcase and 1 lb/455 g clean white fat from the cavity, another large pot of fat drained from the roasting tin, which was marvellous for roasting potatoes, the carcase for soup and the giblets for a rich sauce which I made to serve with pasta. The goose neck I could have boned and stuffed to make a sausage. The clean fat from the carcase I rendered, using some as a fine shortening for pastry and mixing some with shredded cooked goose, a little chopped sage and a pinch of mace to make a very passable version of *rillettes*. If you have thighs, drumsticks or sizeable chunks left over after all this, these can be used in a *cassoulet* (see p. 328).

This was a much better goose than another which lives in my memory. I was to cook Christmas dinner at my parents' home in Derbyshire and asked them to order a goose from their butcher. I roasted it carefully to a burnished golden brown, my father prepared the vegetables, my mother laid the festive table and my husband, Tom, opened and decanted the good bottles brought up from the cellar earlier in the day. We ate the first course, and my father took up knives and his carving position while the rest of us looked on with much expectation. But the bird was so tough that it was impossible to even pierce its skin. It turned out to have been an old farmyard goose, probably someone's guard dog, for they are an excellent deterrent to intruders. Look, then, for a goose born within the year.

Cold goose is excellent, in salads – with potatoes, fennel and walnuts dressed in walnut oil for example – or shredded and mixed with rendered goose fat as *rillettes*, the traditional potted meat from the French provinces of Touraine and Sarthe. Goose is not normally found casseroled, braised or in any other way cooked covered or in a container since it would be swimming in fat. The legs are, however, often added to a slow cooking *cassoulet*, where the fat is absorbed by and enriches the beans. In Germany, goose is often served with sauerkraut (fermented cabbage), in Denmark with red cabbage, in Italy with chestnuts, and in Normandy with apples and Calvados.

TO ROAST A GOOSE

COINCIDENTALLY, as I started to write this, I was served the finest roast goose I have ever eaten. Weighing about 15 lb/6.8 kg, the goose was stuffed with a mixture of breadcrumbs (7 oz/200 g), chopped rum-soaked apple, chopped semi-dried prunes, parsley, lemon, salt and pepper. It was first roasted, standing on a rack, at a high heat (220°C/425°F, gas mark 7) for 30 minutes in a preheated oven, then the heat was turned down to 180-190°C/350-375°F, gas mark 4-5, and the goose cooked for a further 3½ hours, the fat being drained off periodically. My friend used some of the rendered fat to roast potatoes in and also for cooking some spiced red cabbage. The bird was extremely tender, and the rich dark meat was moist and full of flavour.

Carving a goose is quite a shock for someone whose only experience of carving is the Christmas turkey. The breast-bone is reached much more quickly. Long slices the whole length of the breast should be taken.

This is how I cook a 12 lb/5.45 kg table weight goose and what I do with the rest of it. Incidentally, this may sound like far too big a bird for four, but the very broad rib cage means that, pound for pound, there is considerably less meat on it than on a chicken or turkey.

Fill the cavity with a bunch of mixed herbs or the ones that you plan to use in the stuffing. Line a large roasting tin with a piece of foil large enough to come up the sides of the goose, and cut an extra piece to lay lightly on top of the bird to stop the breast from browning too much. Swaddle the drumsticks with pieces of foil since they do not have a thick skin and layer of fat, so are liable to dry out. Prick the bird all over, particularly at the sides and at the neck and vent end where most of the fat is concentrated.

Preheat the oven to 180-200°C/375-400°F, gas mark 4-6, depending on the accuracy of your oven. Experts say to use the higher temperature, but in my oven I prefer to use the lower one. Put the goose on its back in the roasting tin and put the tin on a rack just below the centre of the oven. After an hour, turn the goose breast side down and roast it for another 2-2½ hours, then finally on its back for half an hour to brown it. Keeping it breast side down for most of the cooking time will keep it juicy. Once the bird is cooked, let it rest, covered, in a warm place for 15-20 minutes. It will make carving much easier. The fat should be drained off periodically during cooking time and stored in a bowl.

If you want a shiny bird you can glaze it with a mixture of honey and sherry vinegar.

APPLE AND CALVADOS STUFFING

According to Dorothy Hartley in *Food in England*, sage and onion is the mixture with which to stuff the bird and, to serve with it, 'apple sauce, bread sauce, plain boiled potatoes and greens are the right English usage.' She also recommends watercress salad for cold roast meat. Eliza Acton, on the other hand, maintains that a green goose – that is, a young grass-fed gosling – should never be stuffed. I disagree with her, since I find a little stuffing is just right with this richly flavoured and textured bird. But for safety's sake I would advise cooking the stuffing in a dish rather than stuffing the bird's cavity since this is a poor conductor of heat and the bird risks not being cooked through.

8 slices of wholemeal bread
  (crusts removed)
1 large crisp, firm dessert apple
  (such as a Russet or Cox),
  peeled and cored
4 tbsp Calvados
1 medium onion, peeled
1 tbsp roughly chopped skinned
  almonds or pine kernels
2-3 tbsp shelled unsalted
  pistachios

1 tbsp chopped fresh sage
1 tbsp chopped fresh lemon thyme
1 egg yolk, lightly beaten
2-3 tbsp goose stock (see p. 344),
  white wine or dry cider
salt
pepper

L ET the bread dry out for a day then tear it into small pieces. Grate the apple and soak it in the Calvados. Grate or finely chop the onion and mix all the ingredients together. Grease a soufflé dish with a little goose fat and spoon in the stuffing. Bake it for about 45 minutes-1 hour at the same time as the goose. Prunes soaked in rum make an excellent alternative stuffing, as do pears and *eau de vie de poire* or dried apricots soaked in *eau de vie de mirabelle*.

POTTED GOOSE

Here is another good use for goose, a sage-flavoured
version of *rillettes*.

MAKES 1¾ LB/800 G

1 lb/455 g freshly cooked goose
meat
2-3 fresh sage leaves, finely
chopped
¾ lb/340 g soft rendered goose
fat
freshly ground black pepper
salt
freshly grated nutmeg

SHRED the meat and stir together the meat, herbs and goose fat. Season to taste and pack into a jar or individual ramekins. Cover and refrigerate until required. A layer of melted fat run over the surface will seal the meat as it solidifies and help it to keep. Unbroached, it will keep for a week to ten days, in the refrigerator.

GIBLET SAUCE

A small winy stew made from goose giblets can be served
on toast, or in a hollowed out brioche or breadroll crisped
first in the oven, or with homemade *pappardelle* pasta (see
p. 346). Heart, gizzard and liver can also be fried, sliced
and served warm on a bed of fashionable salad leaves with
an exotic vinaigrette.

SERVES 4 AS A STARTER, 2 AS A MAIN COURSE

*2-3 cloves of garlic, peeled and
   finely chopped
1 onion, peeled and finely
   chopped
1 celery stalk, trimmed and
   finely chopped
1 tbsp goose fat
heart, gizzard and liver
1 tsp tomato or vegetable purée
¼ pt/140 ml red wine or goose
   stock (see p. 344)
1 bay leaf
salt
pepper
fresh parsley, finely chopped*

FRY the garlic, onion and celery gently
in the goose fat without browning
them. Remove any skin, membrane and
discoloured parts from the giblets before
slicing and dicing them, keeping the
gizzard meat separate.

Put the giblet meat in with the vegetables, brown it all over then lower the
heat and cook for 10 minutes.

Add the heart and liver and brown
these before adding the purée and liquid.
Add the bay leaf, bring to the boil and
simmer for 25-30 minutes. Season to
taste, stir in the parsley and serve.

TURKEY

*A*s far as I can tell, at Christmas the world divides into two distinct camps: those who always have turkey and would not dream of having anything else, and those who will go to great lengths to avoid it with 'alternative' Christmas dinners of wild boar, a baron of beef, roast goose, small game birds and all manner of other exotica. For a number of years I was firmly in the second camp, but now, after two or three very good turkeys, I hover between the two.

And there are clearly plenty of other turkey eaters around. In 1987 we ate over ten million whole turkeys around Christmas time in Britain. And in America the turkey enjoys the status of national dish, if not national treasure. The wild turkey was once to be found in large flocks over North America, Central America and the Andean belt of South America. The Pilgrim Fathers learned from the native American Indians how to rear the birds and the Spaniards introduced them to Europe from their conquests in Central and South America. Although wild turkeys are still to be found, the turkey in America today is like the one we know in Europe, and indeed some will have been bred from Europeanised strains.

Of those, most are the familiar white-feathered birds. In good condition they will have a firm, broad round breast and a white, unblemished skin with a faint blueish hue to the flesh underneath. The thighs and drumsticks will be meaty. Before being drawn the fresh bird should have a short neck, bright eyes and a red, fresh looking comb. The hen bird is said to be the better buy since it is somewhat plumper and has lighter bones than the male.

Before the white feathered turkey became popular, largely because when plucked it left the skin unmarked, the most commonly bred turkeys were the Norfolk Black and the Cambridge Bronze, so called because of their plumage. Both varieties are once again available and are well worth looking out for. The birds are reared on a small scale, according to traditional non-intensive farming methods, which means they take longer to mature. For the last two years these are the kind I have cooked and eaten. They are juicy and full of flavour – natural flavour.

Avoid birds that are described as self-basting. It is not at all difficult to baste a turkey. Either wrap it in foil or put it in a roasting bag if it is not too large. I do not approve of the method of laying slices of bacon over the breast since I cannot abide bacon-flavoured meat unless it is bacon, but a thin layer of pork fat – if you can coax some from your butcher – will do the trick. Most effective of all is the buttered cloth. Take a large square of cheesecloth or muslin, dip it in melted butter and drape it over the whole turkey, breast and drumsticks, then roast it in the usual way. A most unusual American recipe for roast turkey, which literally gives you a self-basted bird, is to take a large heavy brown shopping bag, the kind in which they pack your groceries in an American supermarket, brush it all over inside with groundnut oil (peanut oil), put the turkey inside, secure the bag closed and roast (see p. 255 for instructions).

When judging the size of the turkey you require, allow up to ¾ lb/340 g per person if the turkey is oven-ready (that is, plucked, drawn, head and feet removed). If you are buying a traditional farm fresh bird, it will simply be dressed (ie plucked). In this case allow 1 lb/455 g for each person to take account of the discarded weight when the turkey is eviscerated.

You do not have to roast a turkey. It can also be regarded as a collection of various cuts of meat, a good way of discovering that is far from boring. The darker meat on wings and drumsticks is perfect for casseroles and pies while the thighs can be boned, stuffed with an exotic filling, rolled, roasted or braised and then sliced. The light breast meat can be cooked in the same way or sliced into escalopes, marinated and grilled. One year I prepared two turkey dishes for Christmas dinner. All the dark meat went into a rich Provençal style casserole with thyme, garlic, olive oil, white wine and green olives; the breasts I sliced and marinated in hazelnut oil and fresh pomegranate juice before grilling and serving with a scattering of pomegranate seeds and a sauce made from reduced turkey stock and pomegranate juice. To make these dishes you can buy portions of turkey or joint a whole one yourself. The giblets and carcase will give plenty of excellent stock and the liver can be cooked to make a separate dish. For example, soak it in coconut milk, fry it, slice it and serve on a bed of salad leaves with fresh crabmeat or prawns and freshly grated coconut.

The traditional American way with turkey at Thanksgiving and Christmas is to roast it, but cookery books are full of ingenious recipes for using up turkey leftovers. In Mexico, where turkey is very popular, one of the best known dishes is turkey with a chocolate sauce, called *mole poblana*. The other ingredients are various types of chilli, herbs and spices, all items native to Mexico. It is a fascinating dish: rich, dark, fragrant, spicy, full of flavour but with the chocolate hardly discernible.

The important note on meat and poultry hygiene on p. 33 also refers to turkey.

Roasting Times for Turkey

WEIGHT (oven ready)	SERVINGS	WARM 170°C/325°F/gas mark 3	HOT 230°C/450°F/gas mark 8
6-8 lb/2.7-3.6 kg	8-10	3-3½ hrs	2¼-2½ hrs
8-10 lb/3.6-4.5 kg	10-13	3½-3¾ hrs	2½-2¾ hrs
10-14 lb/4.5-6.3 kg	13-18	3¾-4½ hrs	2¾-3 hrs
14-18 lb/6.3-8.1 kg	18-24	4½-4¾ hrs	3-3½ hrs
18-20 lb/8.1-9 kg	24-26	4¾-5¼ hrs	3½-3¾ hrs
20-24 lb/9-10.8 kg	26-32	5¼-6 hrs	3¾-4¼ hrs

When a skewer is inserted into the thickest part of the thigh and, in a large turkey, right into the breast, the juices should run clear. If at all pink, return the turkey to the oven for 15 minutes.

With the slow method of cooking turkey, stuffing the body cavity is *not recommended* because of the density of the stuffing and the relatively low internal temperature of the centre of the stuffing.

Suggested Stuffings for Neck Cavity

Basic bread stuffing: breadcrumbs with herbs, onion and celery (see p. 355)

Oyster stuffing: basic stuffing and chopped raw oysters

Chestnut stuffing: basic stuffing and skinned, cooked chestnuts

Sausage stuffing: basic stuffing and sausagemeat

Fruit and nut stuffing: basic stuffing and chopped apples, prunes and walnuts or almonds

Rice stuffing: raw or cooked rice (brown, white or wild) replace the breadcrumbs of basic stuffing

A total weight of 8-10 oz/230-280 g stuffing is sufficient for the neck cavity of an average 10-12 lb/4.5-5.45 kg turkey.

TURKEY IN A SACK

In America a sack is the large brown paper bag in which your purchases are packed at the supermarket checkout. It is *the* essential equipment for this extraordinary recipe which was passed on to me by a friend, Ted Thompson from Birmingham, Alabama. I am afraid I cannot credit the recipe further, although it had been published in a book since I do not know from whence it came before Ted. The author is quite adamant that only thick brown paper will work and that foil should not be substituted. He – I don't know why I think the cook/author is a 'he' except that it seems such a robust, macho recipe – also cautions against using any other oil but peanut oil which 'imparts a wonderful flavor (sic) to the fowl' and is the only one that will work. I am very tempted to tempt fate by using extra virgin olive oil. But here is the authentic recipe.

FEEDS A LARGE GATHERING

*1 turkey, 14-16 lb/6.3-7.2 kg
(and again, the author
specifies, 'must be at least 12
lb/5.45 kg')
1 tsp freshly ground black pepper
2 tsp salt
3 tsp mild paprika
4 tsp hot water
1 cup (8 fl oz/230 ml) peanut
oil*

COMBINE pepper, salt, paprika and water and let stand for at least 10 minutes. Add peanut oil and mix thoroughly. Select turkey carefully. It should not exceed 16 lbs/7.20 kg. Wash and dry. Rub some peanut oil mixture in-side the turkey and on the outer skin. Truss as desired. Pour remaining oil into large paper sack, with no holes. Rub oil into inside of sack until every pore in every inch of the sack is sealed with oil mixture. Place turkey in sack, breast up.

Fold end of the sack over and tie securely. Bake in a moderate oven, 170°C/325°F, gas mark 3, for approximately 10 minutes per pound. Since the sack is airtight, the turkey is cooked by live steam. Therefore, when the sack is opened, be careful. You will not have to baste this turkey since the oil-sealed sack is self-basting. You will not have to watch it carefully. The turkey comes out tender to the bone and golden brown. Your turkey is done, ready to serve, and you can wrap up the sack after the bird and the juices have been removed, and throw it away. There is not even a roaster to scrub and wash. It is a good idea, however, to rest the sack on a cookie sheet as some of the oil may seep through the outside of the sack.'

This turns out to be a wonderful traditional roast turkey which deserves all the trimmings; mashed or roast potatoes, cranberry sauce, a green vegetable and a gravy made from the accumulated juices, which you carefully pour into a saucepan and reduce to the required consistency, adding a drop or two of whatever wine you're serving with the bird.

TURKEY BREASTS WITH SCALLOPS AND CORAL SAUCE

This is a recipe I devised for a Christmas feature some years ago. I still enjoy the unusual partnership of the poultry and the shellfish, of which the classic chicken with crayfish sauce from eastern France is the best known example.

SERVES 4

2 breasts from a 5 lb/2.3 kg
    turkey, skinned
10 oz/280 g scallops
2 tbsp crème fraîche or double
    cream
1 tbsp chopped fresh chives
2 tbsp chopped, peeled and
    deseeded tomatoes

1 tbsp egg white
½ pt/280 ml turkey stock (see
    p. 344)
To serve:
10 oz/280 g broccoli florets,
    lightly steamed
fruit jelly (such as lavender and
    rhubarb, or quince and apple)

CAREFULLY remove the breasts from the carcase without tearing the meat (you want to use each piece of meat as a pocket to be filled). Slits and holes are no good as the stuffing will burst out when cooked. From each breast remove the club-shaped fillet which you can save for another dish, such as a turkey and vegetable stir-fry. At the oblique narrower edge of the breast make a deep slit, opening up the whole of the breast inside without piercing the edges.

Remove the coral from the scallops and set aside. Remove the small chunk of muscle from each scallop as well as any other inedible bits. Chop the scallop into small cubes. Mix with half of the cream, the chives, tomatoes and lightly whisked egg white. Spoon the filling into the turkey breasts, close the opening with cocktail sticks and flatten the breasts slightly. In a non-stick frying pan cook the stuffed breasts for 30 minutes, turning them several times to allow each side to brown gently. You can moisten them with a little stock from time to time. When done, remove the breasts and keep them warm while you finish off the sauce. Add the rest of the stock to the cooking juices in the pan and gently poach the scallop corals for one minute. Remove and put them in the blender with the rest of the cream and a tablespoon of the stock. Blend until smooth, sieve and set aside. Reduce the contents of the frying pan over a high heat until you have about 4 tablespoons of syrupy sauce. Remove it from the heat and pour it into a small basin over a pan of hot water. Whisk in the coral purée and keep it hot without allowing it to boil.

Have four heated dinner plates ready. Slice the turkey breasts across into neat diagonal slices. Spoon some sauce on to each plate. Arrange a few slices of turkey breast on each plate and garnish with lightly steamed broccoli florets. A little fruit jelly (see p. 361) can be handed separately.

BONED AND STUFFED TURKEY THIGHS

THIGHS FROM A 5 LB/2.7 KG TURKEY WILL SERVE TWO

2 turkey thighs, skinned
1/2 fresh mango
4 oz/110 g celeriac or celery,
 blanched and cut into strips
fresh chopped parsley
1 tbsp fresh wholemeal
 breadcrumbs
salt
pepper
1/2 pt/280 ml turkey stock (see
 p. 344)
pinch of saffron
To serve:
sliced or shredded leeks, steamed
 or stir-fried
purée of sweet potatoes and
 carrots flavoured with
 cardamom seeds

C UT a slit down the length of the thigh and carefully remove the bone, scraping all the flesh away. Open out the resulting square and flatten it with a rolling pin. Remove as many sinews as possible. Prepare the other piece in the same way. Preheat the oven to 180°C/350°F, gas mark 5.

Peel the mango and cut into long strips. Lay the mango and blanched celeriac down the middle of the boned thigh. Mix the parsley, breadcrumbs and seasoning with enough stock to moisten. Divide between the two boned thighs and press it down over the mango and celeriac. Roll up each piece of meat and tie round in four places with kitchen string. Place the two rolls in a roasting bag and seal.

Place the rolls in the oven for 35 minutes. Remove carefully from the roasting bag, pouring the cooking juices into the turkey stock. Keep the meat warm while you finish the sauce. Reduce the stock by half and strain on to the saffron in a small clean saucepan. Reduce further until syrupy. Remove the string from the rolls and slice each into five or six rounds. Arrange on heated dinner plates, with the leeks, the sauce and a little purée of sweet potato, carrot and cardamom.

TURKEY BSTILA

This is based on the traditional Moroccan dish, which, in
its original version, uses young pigeon and over a hundred
layers of tissue-like filo dough.

SERVES 6-8

1½ lb/680 g cooked turkey
    meat, off the bone
6 free-range eggs
7 fl oz/200 ml strong turkey
    stock (see p. 344)
5 oz/140 g butter, melted
18 sheets of filo pastry (about
    ¾ lb/340 g)

3 tbsp caster sugar
4 oz/110 g flaked almonds,
    fried gently in butter
1 tsp powdered cinnamon
5 oz/140 g chopped dried fruit
    (eg apricots, prunes,
    peaches or pears – or a
    mixture)

2 oz/60 g pickled lemons,
    chopped (optional)
1 tsp cardamom seeds
2 tsp cumin seeds
2 tsp coriander seeds
To garnish:
toasted almonds
black olives
fresh mint leaves

*B*EAT the eggs with the stock and cook
gently in a non-stick frying pan, as
if you were making scrambled eggs.
When the mixture has thickened slightly,
remove the pan from the heat and let it
cool. Preheat the oven to 160°C/325°F,
gas mark 3. Crush the spices.

Brush a rectangular, ovenproof dish
with butter (I use one 10 × 8 in/25.5 ×
20.5 cm). Brush the first two sheets of
pastry with butter and line the dish with
them so that the edges hang over the rim
of the dish. Cut the next four sheets to
the size of the dish, brush them with
melted butter and lay them in the bottom
of the dish. Sprinkle half the sugar,
almonds and cinnamon on to the pastry
and spoon on three-quarters of the egg
mixture. Cut six more sheets ofdough

to fit the dish, brush each with butter and
lay on top of the egg mixture.

Dice the turkey and mix it with the
dried fruit, pickled lemon, spices and the
rest of the sugar, almonds and cinnamon.
Spread this mixture in the dish and spoon
over the remaining egg mixture.

Cut four more sheets of dough to fit
the dish, brush them with melted butter
and arrange them on top of the filling.
Fold over the overlapping pastry as
neatly as possible. Then cut two final
sheets to fit, brush them with butter and
place them on top.

Bake for 40 minutes, raise temperature
to 200°C/400°F, gas mark 6 and cook for a
further 10-15 minutes until golden brown.

Serve hot, warm or cold, decorated
with olives, almonds and mint leaves.

GAME

THE TERM GAME ONCE EXTENDED much further than it does now, embracing every edible form of furred and feathered meat that was not raised on the farm, the duckpond or the barnyard. Thus our ancestors ate heron, swan, peacock, bittern and wild boar as well as the more familiar hare, rabbit, pheasant and venison. And in other countries, much else is eaten that we do not eat in Britain. My South American cookbooks give recipes for caveys (or guinea pigs) and my North American cookbooks give recipes for squirrel, hedgehog, raccoon, muskrat and braised bear chops. In Norway I have been offered bear, reindeer, elk and seal.

Over the centuries, many of these species have all but died out and are no longer for eating, but for preserving. In their place, some of the birds and animals which formerly lived in the wild are now reared for the table; quail, rabbits and boar, for example.

I, for one, will always prefer to eat wild game. The old saying that we are what we eat is equally true of animals and birds. A partridge that has fed on corn left behind after the harvest, a young grouse that has eaten nothing but heather shoots and a boar that has rooted around eating acorns, roots and crabapples are going to taste very different from the creature who has been fed a carefully formulated and processed feed. In addition, the game bird (or animal) takes exercise, both in searching for its food and escaping from its predators, and does not get contentedly fat sitting in a farmyard being fed regular meals. All this has an effect on the flavour and the texture of the meat. For this reason, I have given few pheasant and partridge recipes. You can also cook them according to many of the chicken recipes I have given.

I am not sure how I feel about frozen game. Whilst I would not buy it ready frozen, I have put partridge, pheasant and grouse in the freezer myself once they have been cleaned. Game birds will keep for about nine months in the freezer, furred game for no more than six. As with most things, the flavour and texture is not improved with freezing. On the other hand, if you have a glut of game birds, freezing is the only answer. After such treatment, a gentle cooking method such as braising or pot roasting will be more suitable than grilling or roasting.

HUSBANDRY

Once upon a time, when game was the term applied to certain semi-wild animals suitable for providing meat, it was either poached at great risk of fines, imprisonment and death, if caught, or was legally hunted on common lands as a means of supplementing a meagre diet, or was one of the privileges of owning an estate in the country.

Economic pressures and a changing social structure have caused this to change out of all recognition. Some species, which are particularly desirable as a source of meat, are farmed – very intensively in certain cases – even if they are sold on the 'pure' and 'free' image. Other species are still kept at least partially outdoors, but are heavily exploited as a source of income from the very high fees charged to join a 'shoot'. For the now commercially run estates, the right to a day's shooting, known as a 'gun', can be sold for a great deal of money.

Literally, only one or two species of game are still running wild. Since the position of the different species varies a great deal, questions must be asked to be sure that you know what you are buying. Some 'alternative' meat suppliers confidently sell game thinking that it is all free-range and pure. This is true of grouse, but of few other types of game today.

Rabbit, for example, is usually very intensively farmed in a manner similar to battery hens. Several growth promoters are available since the need for preemptive medication is high. A satisfactory alternative to ask for is clean shot (not snared or ferreted) wild rabbits. Obviously they are free-range. Hare, by contrast with most rabbit, is still wild and unmedicated.

The case of deer, and venison, is quite different again. Here there has been a new 'alternative' farming boom. Many welfarists feel that an animal with no history of domestication should not be fenced in. Slaughterhouses and transport adapted for deer are rare and those not properly designed are cruel. The alternative for deer farmers is to shoot the animals in lines on the farms. While this does eliminate the cruelty of transporting a semi-wild animal, it is not a pleasant sight. There are growth promoters for deer, but they are rare.

Wild venison of highly variable quality can be obtained from some butchers. Fallow deer are thought to provide the best quality meat. They should be shot by, or under the supervision of an expert deer stalker when they are due to be culled and are at the correct age.

Both pheasant and partridge are now very intensively reared, with drugs to stave off the poultry disease coccidiocis. Beak-restraints may be fitted or beaks cut to prevent feather pecking. The birds are released before the 'season' begins. Most supplies of pheasant and partridge available in the shops will be from those intensive systems, although you may be offered wild birds. But how will you know?

Similarly, the quail offered for sale is intensively reared for both its meat and eggs, kept in cages similar to those of battery hens. I have come across wild quail in America where it is still a game bird, but of course, there wild game is not for sale and is usually the hunter's perk or for the hunter's friends. For these reasons, I have included few quail and pheasant recipes in the book.

SOME OF THE MORE UNUSUAL GAME BIRDS

SNIPE AND WOODCOCK
BÉCASSINE AND BÉCASSE IN FRENCH

*T*HESE TWO BIRDS ARE VERY CLOSELY RELATED, the snipe being the smaller of the two. They are pretty birds, dappled brown and cream, the woodcock with slightly redder plummage and a deeper, plumper breast. Both birds have distinctive long beaks. Three days is considered sufficient time for hanging both birds. It is customary to cook the birds undrawn, that is, with liver and entrails still inside to add to the flavour of the bird. The head is usually left on and the neck bent to allow the beak to be pushed through the legs and body to truss it very neatly.

When cooked, the liver etc. is spooned out of the bird, spread on toast and the little bird served on toast.

Snipe and woodcock are rarely found on sale. I have seen snipe in a French butcher's and woodcock in one of the large multiples, but rarely in the average butcher's shop, supermarket or game dealers. You are more likely to come across them by way of friends who shoot.

If you are lucky enough to get some, roast them quickly and serve as described, on toast. Make sure that when you roast the birds you put them on a rack and a few pieces of bread brushed with melted butter under the rack to collect the drippings from the bird which, some say, makes the roasted bread even tastier than the birds themselves.

TEAL AND WIDGEON

*B*OTH MEMBERS OF THE LARGE DUCK FAMILY, the teal is smaller than the widgeon. Both are smaller than mallard, and, many consider, superior in flavour. Really only large enough to feed one person, the teal and the widgeon are excellent roasted and served quite rare, or they can be spatchcocked – that is, split down the back with the backbone cut out, and grilled. Being smaller than the mallard, they need no hanging at all. If they are older birds, that is, without the soft, pliable, thin feet of the new season's bird, then braise or stew them gently in butter and a little red wine or port.

GAME IN SEASON

FEATHERED GAME

Black game	20 Aug–10 Dec (1 Sept–10 Dec in Devon, New Forest, Somerset)
Capercaillie	1 Oct–31 Jan
Grouse	12 Aug–10 Dec
Partridge	1 Sept–1 Feb
Pheasant	1 Oct–1 Feb
Pigeon	No close season. Best in autumn after feeding on stubble fields.
Ptarmigan	12 Aug–10 Dec
Snipe	12 Aug–31 Jan
Wild duck	1 Sept–31 Jan (3 weeks later if shot in, or over, area below high-water mark of spring tides)
Woodcock	1 Oct–31 Jan (1 Sept–31 Jan in Scotland)

FURRED GAME

Hare	No close season, but cannot be sold between 1 March and end of July. Best from October.
Rabbit	No close season.
Venison	Depends on breed. Farmed venison available throughout the year. Close season generally the summer months.
Wild boar	No close season as it is raised and not wild in Britain, thus not hunted.

How to Tell Young from Old Gamebirds

*I*N general young birds have pointed flight feathers at the tip and edge of their wings, soft, pliable feet, short rounded spurs and downy feathers on the breast and under the wings. However, some young birds have rounded flight feathers, and even on older birds the flight feathers look pointed if they are wet.

The most conclusive way of judging an old from a young bird is to apply the bursa test. The bursa is a small opening found on all young gamebirds just above the bird's vent. In mature birds the opening becomes much smaller and may close entirely. A bursa open to a depth of 1 in/2.5 cm in a pheasant, ½ in/1 cm in a partridge or grouse is a reliable indication of a young bird, and you can gauge this by inserting a matchstick or cocktail stick. Obviously, you can only do this on birds that are not packaged and oven-ready on the supermarket shelf or in the butcher's display cabinet.

SELECTING OVEN-READY WRAPPED GAME

1 Examine it. Is it fresh or frozen? The latter will probably show traces of watery blood in the wrapping. Like fresh game, frozen game cannot be sold more than ten days after the season closes. If there are any particularly bloody patches, that may indicate where the animal or bird was shot and you will need to look out for small lead shot which can literally break a tooth if bitten on inadvertently. Avoid any with badly misshapen limbs as this is an indication that it was badly shot.

2 Look at the sell-by date. It is beyond the date on which you want to cook it?

3 Smell the package. It should not have any 'off' taints nor should it in any way smell rotten, rancid, putrid or offensive. Properly hung game will smell rich and 'ripe', but not in any way unpleasant.

4 For the age of a gamebird you will have to accept what the package states, and if something labelled young turns out to be old and tough take it back and complain.

STORING OVEN-READY GAME

*I*F you buy game ready-packed it will probably already have been hung, but I have yet to come across a label which tells me for how long.

Do not leave the game in its tightly sealed packaging once you get it home. Unwrap the meat. Feel over it with your fingers and, if you detect any shot, ease it out gently. Remove any bits of fur or feathers and loose fat. Paying particular attention to any bloody patches, wipe over with kitchen paper moistened with vinegar. Dry the meat, put it on a plate or dish and cover it loosely but completely, making sure that nothing can drip from it on to any other food. Or you can put the meat, whole or jointed, in a large bowl and marinate it. I have found that this is quite a good way of flushing out lead shot too.

HANGING GAME

*H*ANGING is a matter of preference. What the process does is to allow the various enzymes and microbes naturally present in the flesh to react with it, breaking down the tissues and tenderising it. Clearly the final result of this process is putrefaction and that must not be allowed to happen. It is nevertheless difficult to set hard and fast rules for hanging. Hanging a freshly shot pheasant for three days in mild autumn weather will be sufficient, whereas it might take ten days hanging in a cold snap in the winter to reach the same stage. Also, a badly shot bird will decompose quicker than one which has been cleanly shot. Waterfowl such as wild duck are not usually hung for more than a day or so. They have a covering of fat under the skin and fat goes rancid quickly.

After hanging, the game is cleaned. Whilst venison is paunched before hanging, rabbit and hare are skinned and paunched after hanging. Feathered game is plucked and drawn.

To Pluck, Draw and Truss a Game Bird

A chicken, duck or turkey can be prepared in the same way.

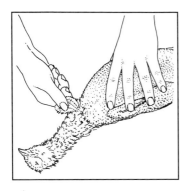

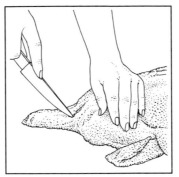

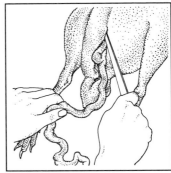

1 Hold the legs firmly in one hand and start plucking the breast area. Gently but firmly pull the feathers towards the head, being careful not to tear the skin. Pluck the rest of the body and the legs.

2 Turn the bird breast side down and cut off the head at the top of the neck. Slit open the skin down the neck and remove the neck.

Reserve for making stock. Hook your fingers just inside the neck cavity and remove the crop and discard it.

3 Make a small incision in the skin at the tail end and remove the intestines. Pull out the entrails, reserving the liver if you wish and the heart and gizzard for making stock. Make sure all has been removed.

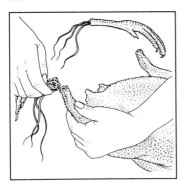

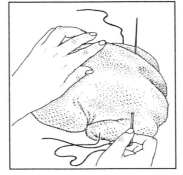

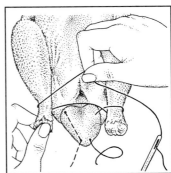

4 Run a knife around each leg just below the 'ankle', snap the bone and twist off the claw, pulling out the white stringy tendons.

5 To truss the wings, thread a trussing needle with string and insert through the second joint of one wing. Push through the body and into the second wing, and then back through the first joint where the wing

joins the body. Push through the body to the first wing and tie the ends securely.

6 To truss the legs thread the needle again, and push it through the right side of the parson's nose. Loop the string around the right leg and then around the left leg. Push the needle back through the parson's nose, pull the string tightly and tie the ends together.

 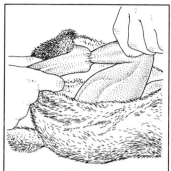 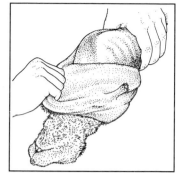

1 Cut off the ears and paws. With sharp scissors, cut open the skin along the belly and ease it away from the flesh around the body and along the cut.

2 Ease the skin over the hind legs, one at a time, to completely free the skin from the hindquarters.

3 Hold the hindquarters with one hand and with the other pull the skin up and over the forequarters and head. Cut off the head.

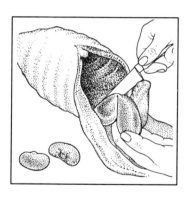 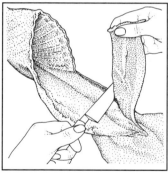 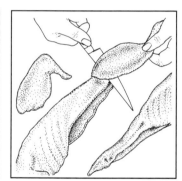

4 Carefully cut the belly open up to the breastbone. If preparing a hare carefully collect the blood in a bowl if you want to use it in cooking. Stir in a teaspoon of vinegar to prevent it from coagulating. Then proceed to remove the entrails, keeping only the heart, kidneys and liver.

5 Cut away the flaps of skin below the rib cage and, indeed, cut away the skinniest parts of the rib cage, using these trimmings for the stock pot or gravy. The animal can now be roasted whole or jointed for casseroling.

6 Cut the hind legs from the carcase at the joint.

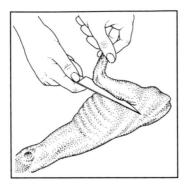 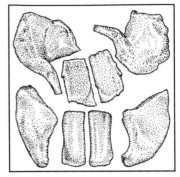

7 Remove the forelegs from the carcase at the shoulder joint.

8 If you wish to cook the saddle separately, leave it whole. If not, chop into two or three pieces across the carcase.

COOKING METHODS

*W*ITH PROPER HANGING TIME, game does not need marinating to tenderise it. Marinades give flavour, but often rather more than I feel the meat needs. I find myself marinating game less and less frequently, and then only if I am doubtful about how long it has hung. By its very nature game meat is lean and needs protecting during cooking if it is not to dry out. For this reason it is often barded: that is, a thin layer of pork backfat is tied over the breast to baste it as it roasts. You can also smear the breast with butter and tie on a butter paper (the greaseproof wrapping from a block of butter, which is usefully removed, folded up and put away in the refrigerator for just such a purpose). Roasting birds breast side down also helps keep them moist in that the juices flow into the breast rather than down towards the back, which is what happens when the bird cooks breast side up.

Young birds and furred game are best roasted: older game is best braised. Whether you serve game rare or well cooked is a matter of personal preference. For my part I prefer pale game, such as rabbit, partridge and pheasant, reasonably well done, and dark game, such as grouse, wild duck, hare and venison, rather rare, or at least pink in the middle. The same warnings which apply to the cooking of meat and poultry also apply to game in that it is just as susceptible to bacteria.

I have not included recipes for plover, snipe and woodcock. These small game birds are best simply roasted as described below.

Roasting Young Game Birds

Simply lard the bird after hanging, plucking and drawing (or smear with butter or olive oil), lightly salt and pepper inside and out, with perhaps a hint of mace, or a bay leaf or thyme sprig stuck in the cavity. Set the bird on a round of bread if you wish, and put it into the oven. After roasting, loosely cover and keep in a warm place for ten minutes before serving. This relaxes the flesh and tendons and makes it much easier to carve or dismember.

The shorter cooking time gives a slightly rare roast, the longer time cooks the bird through. For those above average size use the longer time. One cooking time is given if the bird is very small, but this method of cooking, at high temperatures, is not suitable for older birds.

Roasting Times

Bird	Temperature	Time
Capercaillie	200°C, 400°F, Mark 6	30-45 mins
Grouse	200°C, 400°F, Mark 6	30-45 mins
Mallard *(wild duck)*	200°C, 400°F, Mark 6	30-50 mins
Ortolan	220°C, 425°F, Mark 7	20 mins
Partridge	200°C, 400°F, Mark 6	30-40 mins
Pheasant	220°C, 425°F, Mark 7	20 mins per lb
Pigeon	200°C, 400°F, Mark 6	30 mins
Plover	220°C, 425°F, Mark 7	30-45 mins
Ptarmigan	200°C, 400°F, Mark 6	30-45 mins
Snipe	220°C, 425°F, Mark 7	20 mins
Teal *(wild duck)*	220°C, 425°F, Mark 7	20-30 mins
Widgeon	220°C, 425°F, Mark 7	30-40 mins
Woodcock	220°C, 425°F, Mark 7	20 mins

MALLARD AND WILD DUCK

*T*HE FIRST OF THE *chanterelles* coincide with the opening of the season for wild duck on the first of September. That is how I tasted them both for the first time in a small restaurant in Orleans: wild duck from the Sologne, roasted very rare and served with *chanterelles* and a gratin of potatoes. Since then I have cooked wild duck many times, as the mallard, weighing 2-3 lb/900 g-1.35 kg (dressed weight), is a perfect size for two. The smaller wild duck, the widgeon, weighs about 1½ lb/680 g and the teal about 14 oz/400 g.

All three are at their best in late autumn, between October and Christmas, once the weather has turned cold. Unlike some game, the wild duck should not be hung too long as it has such an abundance of fat that this may go rancid. With such lubrication, which denotes the wild duck as a waterfowl, it is not necessary to lard the bird or baste it during cooking.

The male mallard's handsome head, covered with irridescent green feathers and ringed by a white necklet, is a familiar sight on our ponds and lakes. The largest of all wild duck, it will feed two or three people. When ready for the oven, it resembles a duckling fairly closely, with broad, flat breast and quite light coloured legs but because it is a waterfowl there is a layer of fat under the skin. The flesh, however, is lean, dark and inclined to dryness if not properly cooked.

Many say that wild duck has a fishy flavour but that has never been my experience. If you are given a brace of wild duck, after they have been plucked and drawn, put a peeled halved onion and a halved lemon in the cavity, just to safeguard against any possible fishiness. Cover and refrigerate overnight. Remove the 'deodorisers' before roasting the duck. This is an American hunters' tip. I have never had cause to use it, but I pass it on because it sounds as though it would be effective. If the bird has already been plucked and hung and you still suspect it of fishiness, then it may be best to roast the bird with the lemon and onion in place. A raw potato, too, is a very good method of absorbing smells, in the same way as it will absorb salt from a too-salty soup.

A final word of warning. I have had more 'off' wild duck than any other game. After a day or so, it deteriorates quite rapidly. So buy from a reputable game dealer who will give you accurate information as to age and source, or check sell-by dates for ready packaged game, and smell before you buy. If in doubt, don't.

A medium sized bird will cook in a hot (200°C/400°F, gas mark 6) oven in about 30 minutes. It should be rested before it is carved to allow the blood and juices to redistribute through the flesh. It is a sad fact that a well roasted wild duck is rather a tough bird, so if you prefer the meat well cooked, it would better to braise it in a moist heat, having removed some of the fat first.

Since the meat is very rich, I often serve the duck at two meals, jointing the bird and marinating it, then serving the breasts at one meal, and the legs in some form at a second meal. The wings and carcase are chopped, browned and simmered in water and seasonings to make stock.

Wild duck and oranges are a good combination, especially in the form of a sharp sauce made with Seville oranges or kumquats roasted inside the duck's cavity with a little butter, herbs and seasoning, and perhaps a drop of port. After slicing the breasts off for the first meal, I usually take the meat off the legs and carcase, use the carcase to make a rich stock and then chop the meat finely and use it to make a delicious sauce to serve with pasta – either a chunky *rigatoni* or home-made *pappardelle*, the broad, flat ribbon noodles. Alternatively, pot the meat by processing it with an equal quantity of butter, some mace, a tablespoon of port and, after packing it into a ramekin, seal the top with a layer of clarified butter.

BREAST OF WILD DUCK WITH ELDERBERRY SAUCE

SERVES 2

2 wild duck breasts, off the bone
1 quantity of wine marinade, as described on p. 186 (using red or white wine)

½ pt/280 ml duck stock (see p. 344)
1 tbsp elderberry jelly

1 tsp eau de vie de sureau (elderberry spirit) or any other dry fruit spirit, especially plum, kirsch or mirabelle
salt
pepper

MARINADE the duck breasts for at least 3 hours and overnight if you wish. Remove and dry thoroughly. Slash the skin and fat in several places, taking care not to pierce the flesh. Heat a small heavy frying pan and put in the meat, skin side down. Let it cook for 5-8 minutes and drain off the large amount of fat that will be rendered. Turn the meat and cook on the underside until done to your liking.

The duck breasts take a surprisingly long time to cook; 12-15 minutes will still give pink meat. Meanwhile, heat the duck stock in a small saucepan and reduce by two-thirds. Stir in the elderberry jelly. Transfer the meat, when cooked, to a warm place to let it relax and then to heated serving plates. Skim any remaining fat from the frying pan and add the sauce. Boil it up, add the *eau de vie* and season to taste. Spoon the sauce on to the heated plates and serve.

I like to serve this wild duck with a little more elderberry jelly – redcurrant or blackberry jelly can be used if preferred – and a purée of potatoes and celeriac.

WARM DUCK LEG SALAD

Similar salads can be made from tame duckling if you use the breasts in another recipe such as duck breasts with sherry and honey sauce (p. 242).

SERVES 2

2 marinated wild duck legs (see previous recipe)
salad leaves
flaked toasted hazelnuts
2 tbsp hazelnut oil

1-2 tbsp raspberry vinegar (or other fruit, sherry or balsamic vinegar)
salt
pepper

DRY the duck legs and fry them, skin side down, in a heavy frying pan. Turn the meat over and continue cooking the other side. Arrange the salad leaves on two dinner plates and scatter on the toasted hazelnuts. Arrange the meat on top. Add the hazelnut oil to the frying pan, heat through and pour over the salad. Deglaze the pan with the flavoured vinegar and spoon over the salad. Season lightly.

An *Oriental Duck Salad* can be prepared by marinating the duck legs in rice wine, soy sauce and a little toasted sesame oil, together with garlic, ginger and lemon grass. Scatter the salad leaves with toasted pine kernels, heat a little groundnut oil in the pan, deglaze it with rice vinegar and splash a drop of sesame oil over each salad.

BRAISED WILD DUCK WITH KUMQUATS

Orange flavourings have a natural affinity with duck and none more so than the bitter Seville orange or the fragrant kumquat.

SERVES 2-3

1 oven-ready wild duck
salt
pepper

1-in/2.5-cm chunk of fresh ginger, peeled, sliced and slivered
12 pickling onions, peeled
12 kumquats
a few fresh coriander sprigs

¼ pt/140 ml fino sherry or dry white wine
To serve:
wild rice

REMOVE any fat from the duck's cavity, chop off the wing pinions and the very fatty parson's nose. Prick the skin all over and fry the bird in a frying pan for 10-15 minutes to render some of its fat. Remove the bird and wipe it with kitchen paper.

Preheat the oven to 180°C/350°F, gas mark 4. Lightly season the bird all over, insert slivers of ginger under the skin and put a few in the cavity. Fry the small onions all over until golden brown. Put them in a small casserole, put the bird on top and put the kumquats around it, together with some coriander stalks. Pour most of the fat from the frying pan, then deglaze it with the sherry. Pour the boiling pan juices over the bird. Cover and cook, for 35-40 minutes, in the oven.

Let the bird rest before carving it, surround it with the kumquats and onions and garnish with the fresh coriander leaves. Boil up the cooking juices, add more seasoning if necessary and hand separately. With dark game, like the wild duck, I like to serve wild rice.

GROUSE

THERE ARE MANY WHO CLAIM that the red or Scottish grouse is the finest of all game birds. It feeds on the young heather shoots of the Scottish, Irish, Yorkshire and Derbyshire moors, and it is this food which is said to give grouse its intense unique flavour. Much admired, not to say coveted, by the French, who have many breeds of game bird, it is called by them simply *la grouse*. I know of more than one French chef who has taken a dozen brace back with him, to cook, in guises far removed from our traditional roast grouse served with bread sauce, fried breadcrumbs, watercress and game chips.

A truly wild fowl, it does not lend itself readily to rearing and management techniques, so supplies fluctuate drastically. For example, if the heather has had a bad year, there will be little food to sustain the young birds. They are also disease prone. All this conspires to make grouse a rare treat for most of us, which means that it can be a little daunting, whether you are cooking it for the first time or trying to remember how you cooked it the previous year.

Although the grouse season runs from 12 August, known as 'the glorious Twelfth' by those who shoot, until 10 December the birds are at their best in the first half of the season. The glossy, dark feathered young birds have soft, downy breast feathers and pointed flight feathers at their wing tips. The spur at the back of the leg above the claws is soft and rounded.

One grouse will feed one person. The meat is dark red, rich and gamy in flavour, yet delicate and unusual at the same time. For me, the rule with grouse has to be the simpler the better. It is much better not to hide its qualities with sauces and too many accompaniments, and it should be quickly roasted and allowed to rest briefly before serving. Let it fly through a hot oven, as the French would have it. Although it is traditional to serve this tender meat on the rare side, it can be roasted more slowly if preferred, in which case the longer of the two cooking times should be used from the table on p. 269.

It really is best to roast young grouse, which are those shot in the same year they were born. An older grouse, one that has escaped the guns for a season or two, is not good for roasting. The meat is tougher and drier though it still has a good flavour.

274

There are several very good ways of dealing with old grouse. One is to marinate, then braise or casserole the birds. A *salmis* is an excellent method of dealing with grouse, wild duck and pheasant once past their first youth. Roast the bird in a fairly hot oven (190°C/375°F/gas mark 5) for 15 minutes. When cool enough to handle remove the breasts, make a stock from the carcase, reduce to a rich sauce, and then finish the meat off in the sauce, cooking it gently for 20-30 minutes. Otherwise, a mixed game pie would benefit very nicely from the diced breast meat of an older grouse.

In North America there are birds called grouse such as the ruffed grouse (also known as the partridge grouse or simply partridge, and, most confusingly as pheasant in the southern states), sage grouse, Canadian grouse and blue grouse. Although the last one is of the grouse family, none are comparable to the Scottish grouse.

Here are three grouse recipes. One is for roasting. The second, which is also for roasting, but with an unusual twist, comes from Michel Lorain, chef patron of La Côte St Jacques in Joigny, Burgundy. He works as consultant chef at the Oak Room Restaurant in Le Meridien, Piccadilly and on his autumn visits to London he has, over the years, come to appreciate English game cookery, especially grouse, which is not available in France. More than once, I'm sure, he has gone back to France with a brace or two in his luggage. When I asked him for a grouse recipe for *Times* readers, he was a little reluctant, as he put it, '*souhaitant ne pas choquer les fervents de la recette originale qui en fait un plat presque national*'. The bird's 'delicate flavour of pine shoots' gave him his inspiration. The third recipe is my own way of serving two grouse to four people when the grouse is getting quite high, in which case a marinade is not a bad idea.

CLASSIC ROAST GROUSE

An oven-ready grouse will probably still have its feet on,
tucked into the body cavity, to demonstrate by its sharp,
pointed spur that it is indeed a young bird. I prefer to cut
off the feet before cooking.

QUANTITIES PER PERSON

1 young grouse
thin layer of pork back fat
    (or, if unavailable, softened
    butter)
salt

pepper
1 oz/30 g butter
1 slice of real unprocessed
    (bread)

To serve:
sprigs of watercress
home-made fruit jelly
    (optional)

PREHEAT the oven to 200°C/400°F, gas mark 6. Tie a thin covering of pork back fat over the grouse's breast. If you cannot get back fat, rub extra butter over the breast and cover it with a butter paper before roasting. Whatever you do, do *not* lard the grouse with bacon unless you want a bacon flavoured bird. Lightly season the meat, put a little of the butter inside it and smear the rest on a piece of bread cut to the size of the grouse. Sit the bird upon it.

Put the grouse in a roasting tin and roast for 25-30 minutes, or longer if you like the bird well done. After removing from the oven, allow the meat to relax in a warm place. This will make cutting it up much easier.

Serve the grouse on its canapé. Sprigs of watercress are a nice accompaniment, as is a spoonful or two of home-made fruit jelly. Game gravy, game chips and bread sauce (see p. 353-4) are traditionally served with a grouse.

ROAST GROUSE WITH GRAPEFRUIT AND GINGER

SERVES 2

1 or 2 young grouse
2 grapefruits
1 celeriac weighing about 10 oz/280 g

½ pt/280 ml grouse or other game stock
4 courgettes

10 fl oz/300 ml game or other stock (see p. 344)
1 oz/30 g unsalted butter
1-2 tsp grated fresh ginger

THE grouse should roast for 20 minutes and rest for 10 minutes (see previous recipe).

Meanwhile, carefully peel the thinnest layer of zest from the grapefruit and, with a sharp knife, cut the zest into thin strips. Cook them in a little water to soften them. Squeeze the juice from one of the grapefruits. Peel the other one and cut out the segments, free of all pith. Peel the celeriac, cut half of it into thin batons and the courgettes into similar pieces.

Steam or boil them until just tender and put to one side. With the other piece of celeriac, make game chips: deep-fry them, then drain on kitchen paper and put to one side.

When you have taken the grouse out of the oven, deglaze the roasting pan with 4 tablespoons of the grapefruit juice and 7 fl oz/200 ml of the stock. Let it reduce by half, stir in the ginger then strain it through a fine sieve and reserve. Infuse the grapefruit zest in the remaining

3 oz/80 ml stock for a minute or two, then strain into the sauce.

Heat the butter in a pan and toss the celeriac and courgette batons until thoroughly heated through.

Arrange the grouse on heated dinner plates with the vegetables and celeriac chips.

Heat the grapefruit segments in the game sauce and arrange on the plate with the sauce. The zest is used to scatter over the dish. Serve immediately.

GROUSE IN PORT WINE SAUCE

This is a good way of making two grouse stretch to feed four.

SERVES 4

2 young grouse
2 tbsp sherry vinegar
⅛ pt/70 ml port
1 medium onion, peeled and
    thinly sliced
1 bay leaf

8 crushed peppercorns
3 crushed juniper berries
1 celery stalk, trimmed and
    sliced
about 1 pt/570 ml water

4 slices of bread
2-3 oz/60-85 g butter
1 tbsp fruit jelly (such as
    elderberry or blackberry)
salt
pepper

WITH kitchen scissors, neatly cut the back from the grouse and then cut in half down the breast bone. Moisten a kitchen towel with the sherry vinegar and wipe the breasts all over. Put them in a bowl with the port, onion, herbs and celery, reserving a little onion and celery for stock. Cover the grouse, after turning it well, and leave for several hours.

Meanwhile, chop up and brown the backbones in a saucepan, pour on the water and add a little celery and onion. Simmer until you have a well flavoured stock, strain and reduce it to half a pint and put to one side.

Preheat a hot oven. Trim the bread slices and spread a little butter on them. Remove the grouse from the marinade and pat it dry. Spread the remaining butter on the birds and put them on the canapés. Roast at 200°C/400°F, gas mark 6 for 25-30 minutes.

Meanwhile boil up the marinade, stir in the jelly and add the stock. Cook it for 5-10 minutes then strain, reduce a little if necessary and season to taste. Spoon the gravy on to heated plates and arrange the grouse on top.

Grilled *polenta* (see p. 350) and lentils go well with this dish.

PARTRIDGE

T HE "LITTLE RED GEMP'MUN", as the partridge is called in Kent, is a fine game bird. Young birds have soft feet and legs and pointed flight feathers. The flesh is pale, almost like that of a chicken, and has a very delicate fine flavour which should not be spoilt by allowing the bird to become too gamy. Three or four days hanging is sufficient if you are given freshly shot birds.

A shooting acquaintance of mine maintains that the little birds are at their best near the beginning of the season, having eaten their fill of grain left behind among the stubble in the harvested wheat fields. But he qualifies that by saying that they are good later in the season too, preferably eaten cold for breakfast on Christmas morning, with a half bottle of champagne.

Partridges are quite expensive, one bird being sufficient only for one serving, and it deserves the very best treatment. At the risk of sounding repetitive, let me say again that roasting and serving with plain accompaniments such as watercress, roast or fried potatoes and a gravy made from the cooking juices is the very best way of dealing with young birds. Incidentally, on a French menu, the term *perdreaux* indicates young birds and *perdrix* old ones, that is over six months old. Thus you can expect *perdrix aux choux* to be a slow-cooked casserole. Why the masculine should denote youth and the feminine maturity, I am at a loss to explain.

With older birds there are many excellent recipes; use them in *pâtés*, pies, casseroles and soups. Amongst the many recipes in the classical repertoire, perhaps the most famous is chartreuse of partridge, where the meat from two partially roasted old birds is layered with cooked cabbage in a chartreuse mould decorated first with slices of turnip and carrot. It is baked, turned out of the mould and served with a sauce of reduced cooking juices.

The partridge was one of the ingredients in the amazing Yorkshire Christmas Pie, a magnificent eighteenth century pie in which the pastry enclosed birds within birds – a pigeon inside a partridge inside a chicken inside a goose inside a turkey, all boned. The space between the crust and the turkey was filled with hare, woodcock and moorhens.

PARTRIDGE AND CABBAGE IN BRIOCHE PASTRY

Brioche pastry is relatively simple to make with a food
processor. Make it the night before required if for lunch or
in the morning if for dinner. Pheasants, quail, wild duck or
squab can be used in the same way.

SERVES 4

For the pastry:
1/8 pt/70 ml warm milk
1/2 tsp honey
2 tsp dried yeast
8 oz/230 g plain flour, sieved
1/2 tsp salt
4 oz/110 g melted butter
2 egg yolks

For the filling:
1 lb/455 g partridge fillets
    (from the breast and legs of
    three to four birds)
1 onion, peeled and sliced
2 oz/60 g butter
8 large cabbage leaves (white
    cabbage is best)
8 oz/230 g cooked rice (if
    possible use a mixture of
    basmati and wild rice for
    maximum effect and
    flavour)

1 tsp each of juniper berries,
    allspice and black
    peppercorns
1 tsp sea-salt
2 tbsp chopped fresh herbs
2 hard-boiled eggs
milk and egg beaten together
    (to seal and glaze the
    pastry)

*P*LACE the warm milk in a basin and stir in the honey. Sprinkle the dried yeast on top and let it work for five minutes. Sprinkle 2 oz/50 g of the sieved flour on top, stir in gently and leave the mixture for 30 minutes to let it double in volume and become spongy (say 30 minutes). Place the rest of the flour, the salt and the melted butter in the bowl of the food processor. Process until smooth. Continue processing and add the egg yolks one at a time. Finally add the yeast sponge and process once more until completely smooth.

Turn the dough out on to a floured board and knead for five minutes. Put it in an oiled bowl, cover with cling-film and leave for several hours. Knock back, that is, punch out the air in the dough, at least twice during this time to stop it rising too much.

Heat some of the butter and fry the partridge fillets in it for two minutes. Put to one side. Fry the onion until soft, golden and transparent in some of the butter. Remove from the heat. Cut the tough base and central stem from the cabbage leaves and drape them over a colander. Pour over enough boiling water to soften the leaves, then run them under cold water to cool them. Preheat the oven to 200°C/400°F, gas mark 6.

Roll out the pastry on a floured board to an approximate 14 × 14 in/35 × 35 cm square. Lay it on baking parchment or a baking tray. Dry the cabbage leaves and lay these over the pastry, leaving a ½ in/0.5 cm border all round. Spread the cooked rice on top.

Grind the spices and seasoning, and sprinkle these on the rice, together with the sautéd onion. Add the salt and fresh herbs.

Lay the partridge fillets on the centre of the filling in a small square, together with any cooking juices. Chop the hard-boiled eggs and spread over the meat. Brush the edges of the pastry with the milk and egg mixture, bring the corners to the middle, envelope fashion, and pinch the edges together. Make a couple of slits for the steam to escape.

Brush the parcel with the egg and milk glaze and bake in the top half of the oven, for 20 minutes, then turn the temperature down to 180°C/350°F, gas mark 4 for the rest of the time. This is delicious cold, as well as hot. It is best served on its own as a main course, but plan a nice green salad to follow.

PARTRIDGES IN THE MANNER OF PROVENCE

Olives and olive oil give this casserole a taste of Provence.

SERVES 6

3 oven-ready partridges, with
livers and gizzards
6 tbsp olive oil
4 oz/110 g green olives, stoned
removed
a few pinches of fresh thyme
a few fresh rosemary spikes
3 pieces of back fat
2 onions, peeled and thinly sliced
2 glasses of white wine
salt
pepper
cornflour or potato flour
(optional, to thicken)

S EASON the inside of the partridges. Heat a tablespoon of olive oil in a frying pan. Toss the partridge livers and gizzards in the hot oil until firm. Mix them with half the olives, two pinches of thyme and a few spikes of rosemary. Sew up the openings and tie a piece of bacon or pork fat around each partridge.

Heat two tablespoons of olive oil in a flameproof casserole. Brown the birds all over. Remove from the casserole and put to one side on a plate. Pour out the fat and replace with the rest of the oil. Gently sweat the onions and, when they are transparent, add the partridges and their juices. Sprinkle with more thyme and rosemary. Moisten with the white wine and add the remaining olives. Cover and let simmer gently for 15 minutes, turning the birds over twice during cooking. Remove them from the casserole and cut in two lengthways. Keep them warm on the serving plate.

Pour any juice back into the casserole, bring it back to the boil and check the seasoning. If you find the sauce too thin, add a little cornflour, or potato flour, which you have first mixed with a little water. Serve and pour the sauce over the partridges, decorating with the olives. This is very good with rice or boiled potatoes.

PHEASANT

THE COCK PHEASANT WITH ITS BEAUTIFUL PLUMAGE is a common sight in the English countryside in winter. Although native to the Far East, the pheasant was introduced to Britain hundreds of years ago. It is a very tame bird. You will often see one feeding by the roadside, at the edge of fields or in country parks, quite oblivious to people walking near by. Their tameness allows them to be reared by game-keepers and they even used to be hand-fed. This tameness has, of course, led to fairly intensive rearing practices to the point that such birds are not wild anymore and can hardly be classed as game.

Hen or cock, one pheasant will make four servings, dividing neatly and obviously into two legs and two breasts. Note that I do not say that it serves four people. To me, the meat on the breast – delicate and tender – is so different from that on the legs – darker, tougher and sinewy, even on a young bird – that it needs a quite different method of cooking. What happens if, when serving a roast pheasant to your guests, all want breast meat?

No, I would buy two pheasants to feed four. I would braise, pot roast or bake in foil the whole birds, with appropriate seasonings, serving only the breast meat. The meat left-over can be removed from the carcase and made into potted pheasant or chopped fine to make a rich sauce for pasta, and the carcase itself will make fine game stock. Another way to do it is to remove the breasts, marinate them and then shallow-fry them in a little butter and serve them with a good reduced pheasant glaze, some fruit jelly and a purée of celeriac and potato. Or, for a more elaborate dish, the breasts can be split open horizontally, filled with a stuffing (the one I have in mind is pheasant or chicken forcemeat with wild mushrooms), folded over and rolled up inside a piece of non-plasticised clear wrapper, with its ends twisted and folded, then steamed for eight minutes. Yes, it is quite possible to steam game. Unusual but very good. This particular dish looks very good when sliced and served with a clear pheasant gravy and spiced kumquats or quince compôte.

The legs can be casseroled, cooked in a Moroccan *tagine*, served *à la normande* with cream, apples and Calvados, added to a mixed game pie, or used to make a veal and pheasant pie. From this it follows that a pheasant is perfect for two meals for two. Cold pheasant is very good too. Mixed with chunks of new season English apples, some crunchy slices of celery, a few shelled wet walnuts and a creamy dressing, it becomes an English autumn salad.

POTTED PHEASANT

You can substitute other game, or indeed, rabbit, chicken or beef for the pheasant. Pot it in small, individual ramekins and serve with toast as a starter – or keep it in a container in the fridge and use it as a filling for sandwiches and rolls. Port, sherry or vermouth can be used instead of Madeira, but I find the latter goes particularly well in this dish.

SERVES 6 (AS A STARTER)

6-8 oz/170-230 g cooked
  pheasant meat, off the bone
2-3 fl oz/60-85 g Madeira
  (Sercial or Verdelho for
  preference)
seeds from 2 cardamom pods

1 tsp pink peppercorns
8 juniper berries
1 shallot, peeled and finely
  chopped
4 oz/110 g softened unsalted
  butter

salt
pepper
nutmeg
To seal:
3 oz/85 g butter (optional)

*P*UT the Madeira in a small saucepan. Tie the cardamom seeds, peppercorns and juniper berries in a small piece of muslin. Add the shallot and the muslin bag to the Madeira. Cook it over a low heat for 20-30 minutes, reducing it by a third and letting it reach no more than simmering point. Remove the spices and allow the liquid to cool.

Place it, with the pheasant and the softened butter, in the bowl of a food processor. Season lightly. Process until smooth and check for seasoning again. Pack into a suitable pot.

If you wish to keep the potted pheasant for a few days, melt 3 oz/85 g butter in a saucepan, allow it to cool slightly and spoon the clear butter (not the sediment) over the potted pheasant to seal it.

PIGEON AND WOODPIGEON

*A*LTHOUGH IT LOOKS AND TASTES LIKE GAME, and indeed behaves like it, the pigeon has no close season. Being considered vermin by farmers and land-owners, such is the damage it is said to do to the crops that it is considered 'fair game' all the year round. Precisely thanks to these feeding habits, eating the unripe and then the ripe corn, a pigeon in late summer makes for excellent eating. If it does not have soft, supple feet without scales, you can assume it is a wily old bird that has escaped the guns for a season or two and that its rich and highly flavoured meat will need careful cooking if it is not to be dry when served.

Just one small, scrawny old pigeon can make all the difference to a stockpot, the contents of which will form the basis of very good soups and sauces. A woodpigeon has a surprising amount of meat on the breast and is so dense and highly flavoured that I find one bird ample for one serving. If it is a young bird, it can be quickly roasted and served quite rare. Those who do not like rare game can take it out of the oven after roasting it on a high heat for 15 minutes, remove the breasts, slice them in half horizontally and finish them off in a frying pan, gently cooking them in a sauce and serving them as a *salmis* of pigeon.

Pigeon goes well with other strong flavours: gin and juniper berries; port and moscatel raisins or prunes; and, my favourite combination, chocolate, raisins and pine kernels which produce a dense, dark, savoury sauce, best highlighted with a little balsamic or wine vinegar. This is the basis of the classic Italian *agro dolce* (sour sweet) sauce. I once took the same ingredients and turned them into something quite different: pan-fried pigeon breasts served with chocolate ravioli stuffed with ground pine nuts, raisins and ricotta (see p. 285). The classical French repertoire includes a number of pigeon recipes. One of these, *suprêmes Saint Clair*, sounds particularly good: the fillets are fried in butter, arranged round a pyramid of fried cèpes, coated with Soubise sauce (a white onion sauce) and surrounded with pigeon *quenelles* (dumplings). However, these classical recipes were probably devised with squabs in mind, so unless you have very young tender birds, they might be safer to try on chicken, if not squab.

One of the very best staples to serve with pigeon and all the dark, richly flavoured game like wild duck and hare is *polenta*. For some reason it is even better than potatoes, rice or pasta. And the rich yellow cornmeal looks very good on the plate with the dark velvety sauce and meat.

One of the very best staples to serve with pigeon and all the dark, richly flavoured game like wild duck and hare is *polenta*. For some reason it is even better than potatoes, rice or pasta. And the rich yellow cornmeal looks very good on the plate with the dark velvety sauce and meat.

PIGEON BREASTS WITH CHOCOLATE RAVIOLI

Eight years ago I included this recipe in a series I wrote
for the *Sunday Times Magazine*. I think it was the one thing
that cost me my job. Not something to serve every day,
perhaps, but the chocolate pasta works extremely well
with the dark gamy pigeon meat.

SERVES 4

4 plump young wood pigeons,
  cleaned
1/3 bottle of good red wine
1 tbsp extra virgin olive oil
1 oz/30 g butter
2-3 pt/1-1½ l water
1 onion, peeled and chopped
2 shallots, peeled and chopped
2 cloves of garlic

1 carrot, peeled
1 celery stalk, trimmed
parsley stalks
salt
pepper
For the pasta:
6 oz/170 g strong plain flour
1 oz/30 g cocoa powder
2 eggs

2 oz/60g California seedless
  raisins
2 oz/60 g ricotta cheese
2 oz/60 g pine kernels, lightly
  toasted and crushed
salt
pepper
freshly grated nutmeg
a little melted butter

R EMOVE the breasts from the pigeons. Marinate them in half of the wine. Chop the carcases, brown them in a heavy pan in a little of the oil and butter, then add the rest of the wine, the water, the vegetables and parsley stalks. Bring to the boil, skim and simmer for a couple of hours or more. Strain. Keep half the stock to use for another day and reduce the remainder to about 1/3 pt/200 ml.

For the pasta, sift the flour and cocoa together, make a well in the centre and slide in the eggs. Work together into a smooth elastic dough. Let it rest, covered, at room temperature while you prepare the filling. Chop the raisins and mix with the ricotta cheese and pine nuts, together with a pinch of salt and pepper. Be generous with the nutmeg.

Roll out the pasta dough very thinly and cut it into rectangles or circles. Spoon a little filling into the centre and fold over and seal the edges by pressing them well. Put to one side on a clean tea towel.

Heat the rest of the oil and butter in a heavy frying pan. Remove the pigeon breasts from the marinade and dry thoroughly. Brown them on both sides for 2-3 minutes, then cook on a lower heat for 5-10 minutes.

Remove them and keep in a warm place. Pour the stock into the pan and scrape up any cooking residues and heat through.

Meanwhile, bring a large pan of lightly salted water to the boil and cook the pasta for about 7 minutes. Drain and toss in melted butter.

Slice the pigeon breasts in half and arrange on heated dinner plates with some sauce and a few pasta cushions.

PIGEON AND WALNUT CASSEROLE

Ideally, fresh wild mushrooms and 'wet' walnuts – the new season's picking before they are sent off to be kiln-dried – would be used to make this dark casserole full of autumn flavours. A few dried ceps which have been soaked in water first will make all the difference in the world to the flavour if you are using cultivated mushrooms. Use the freshest walnuts you can find and, if you have the patience to peel them, so much the better.

SERVES 4

4 wood pigeons
2 oz/60 g butter
1 carrot, peeled and sliced
1 onion, peeled and sliced
1 celery stalk, trimmed and sliced
1 pt/570 ml water

½ pt/280 ml good claret
3 shallots, peeled and finely chopped
3 garlic cloves, peeled and crushed
½ lb/230 g dried or fresh mushrooms (see above)

¼ lb/110 g shelled walnut halves
salt
pepper
To serve:
fresh parsley
fried bread triangles

*T*HOROUGHLY wash and dry the pigeons. Smear a little butter on the breast, put them in a roasting tin and roast them in a very hot oven for 10 minutes.

Meanwhile, put the vegetables and water on to boil for stock. When the pigeons are cool enough to handle, remove the breasts and legs and add the chopped carcases to the stockpot. Deglaze the roasting pan with half the wine and add this to the stock pot. Let the stock cook for 20-30 minutes. If you are using dried mushrooms, soak them in warm water for 30 minutes.

Meanwhile, in the rest of the butter, sweat the shallots and garlic until soft. Add the mushrooms (wipe clean the fresh ones) and pigeon breasts and legs. Pour on the wine, bring to the boil and simmer very gently, or cook in the oven, at 170°C/325°F, gas mark 3 for 20-25 minutes. Strain the stock into a clean saucepan and reduce to about ¼ pt/ 140 ml. Stir this into the casserole, add the walnuts and season to taste. Cook until the meat is tender and the flavours amalgamated.

Garnish with parsley or fried bread triangles before serving.

HARE

Hare is a very popular winter dish in Europe. In Germany a spicy stew called *Hasenpfeffer* is made; in France you will have a *civet de lièvre à la royale*; in Italy *pappardelle alla lepre*, a wonderfully rich dark hare sauce served with broad flat homemade pasta. In Spain hare is cooked with wine, wine vinegar, chocolate and pine nuts and in Belgium with beer, or with prunes and chestnuts. Our traditional methods with hare in Britain include jugged hare and roast saddle of hare. The latter, where the saddle is cooked quickly and carved into narrow strips for serving quite rare, is popular in fashionable restaurants.

I remember a jugged hare that I cooked for one of the first dinner parties we gave after we were married. On reflection I see now that it was a brave, some would say fool-hardy, thing to do. Hare was always a popular Sunday lunch dish in the autumn and winter when I was growing up, but I realise now that it is not everyone's favourite dish.

For that very reason, it remains one of the best of all bargains from the butcher or game dealer. It can be bought now in neat wrapped packs of joints, such as the saddle or the hind legs. Or you can buy the whole hare. A young one, unskinned and un-paunched, will weigh 6-7 lb/2.7-3.2 kg and will feed four people. An older larger animal will feed six to eight. Distinguish the former from the latter by its small white teeth (larger and yellow in the adult), its soft, easily torn ears and its soft pad and claws.

In Britain the breed of hare will be either the English brown or the Scottish blue. On the continent are many breeds; blonde French and huge Belgian hares weighing more than 12 lb/5.45 kg, to mention but two. In America the hare is not known, but the large jack-rabbit will be a good substitute in most recipes.

In former times, the hare was left whole for roasting and brought to table with its head on, trussed as if in the running position. You may even find instructions to that effect in relatively recent cookery books. Unless your aim is to create a historical banquet, I do not recommend this practice. We have all become much more squeamish about the food we eat and do not like to see flesh, fish or fowl too closely resembling its original state, at the moment of eating it.

The adult hare is hung for about seven days before skinning and paunching. Although it is a nice story, it is unlikely that Hannah Glasse, the eighteenth century cookery writer, ever instructed her reader to 'first catch your hare'. What she probably wrote was 'first case your hare', case meaning the same as skin. Most hares on sale nowadays are such adults. Leverets, or young hares, you are more likely to find in the country and if you know a farmer or gamekeeper who shoots. They have a delicate pale meat and can be roasted provided they are basted frequently to stop the outer flesh from hardening. A stuffing helps to keep the meat moist and bastes from the inside. It does not need hanging and should be skinned and paunched for immediate cooking.

An adult hare is a very economical buy. The saddle can be roasted and, if served with plenty of vegetables, will serve four; the massive hind legs can be jointed and 'jugged' or casseroled to serve four. The meat from fore-quarters or shoulders will make good sauce for pasta, a terrine or coarse *pâté* or potted hare, while the carcase and head make a rich stock. Hare soup with celeriac and dumplings is another fine winter dish. For an authentic jugged hare or *civet de lièvre*, the classic French dish. The blood is essential. It is added to the dish only about five minutes before the end, stirred in then heated through *without boiling*, which would curdle it. It enriches and thickens the sauce perfectly. If you order a hare, ask for the blood to be put to one side. When you have got it home, stir in a teaspoon of wine vinegar to stop it coagulating, cover it and refrigerate it until required.

Both young and mature hares benefit from a marinade, the first for flavour, the second for tenderness. Oil, wine and wine vinegar should be the basis, then add herbs, spices and vegetables according to your taste and what you have available. On an older hare the legs will be considerably tougher than the saddle or back, and whilst the saddle can be casseroled, braised or roasted, the legs should only be subject to slow, gentle heat with plenty of lubrication, and not roasted.

ROAST SADDLE OF HARE WITH SPICED PEARS COOKED IN SHERRY

Buy the whole animal for this recipe and have your
butcher joint it, leaving the saddle whole. With the rest –
forelegs, hindlegs and giblets – you will have plenty of
ingredients for excellent *pâté*, game soup or a sauce for
pasta.

SERVES 4

1 or 2 saddles of hare
  (depending on their size)
4 sound Conference pears
1/4 pt/140 ml dry Amontillado
  or oloroso sherry

2 tsp honey
blade of mace
2 tbsp sherry vinegar
1/4 pt/140 ml game stock (see
  p. 344)

For the marinade:
1/2 pt/280 ml organic apple
  juice
1 onion, peeled and sliced
1 dsp juniper berries
fresh marjoram, thyme and
  sage

MARINATE the hare overnight in the organic apple juice together with the onion, juniper berries and herbs. Remove the hare from the marinade, strain and set aside to use a little for the sauce. The hare takes very little time to cook – 15 minutes or so to roast and 5 minutes or so to rest – so prepare the pears and everything else that you might be serving with the hare beforehand.

Peel the pears and put them in a saucepan with the sherry, honey, mace and sherry vinegar. Cover with a lid and cook gently until the pears are just tender. Meanwhile, prepare any acccompanying vegetables.

Heat the oven to 230°C/450°F, gas mark 8. With a sharp knife ease the fillets gently away from the chine bone, without removing them. This makes carving easier. Put the hare in a roasting tin and place it in the top half of the oven. Roast for 15 minutes.

Remove the meat from the oven and let it rest in a warm place while you prepare the sauce.

Pour the stock into the roasting tin and cook it over a high heat until bubbling, scraping up any residue from the tin and adding a little of the marinade and the juice that the pears have cooked in. Stir vigorously and reduce by half until quite syrupy. Serve with the hare, sliced into thin diagonal slivers, and the spiced pears, which you can slice or leave whole, as you wish. A purée of celeriac and potatoes (see p. 355) makes a perfect accompaniment.

JUGGED HARE

This is one of the dishes I most distinctly remember from my childhood. I immediately associate it with the rich gamy smell which drifted out of the kitchen all morning, the dark flavoursome gravy soaked up by the mashed potatoes and the braised celery, still one of my favourite vegetables.

Hare is at its best in October. When you order your hare, ask the butcher to skin it for you, to joint it and save the blood.

A mature hare can be used for this; save the younger leverets for roasting. Any left-overs of jugged hare can be chopped up, mixed with the gravy and served with the pasta.

SERVES 8

1 mature, well-hung hare, jointed and with the blood reserved
1 tsp wine vinegar
2 oz/60 g flour
2 tsp freshly ground pepper
1 tsp salt
1/2 tsp ground mace
1/4 tsp ground nutmeg
1/4 tsp ground allspice

1 tbsp sunflower oil
1 oz/30 g butter
1 pt/580 ml game, light meat or poultry stock (see p. 344)
1 onion, peeled and sliced
1 celery stalk, trimmed and sliced

1 in/2.5 cm piece of fresh ginger
2 bay leaves
sprig each of fresh thyme, parsley, chervil and tarragon
3 tbsp home-made hedgerow or other fruit jelly
1/4 pt/140 ml port or red wine
salt
pepper

WIPE the hare joints all over. Stir the vinegar into the blood to prevent it from curdling, cover and store in a cool place until required. Mix the flour and ground spices in a paper bag and shake the hare pieces in it, one or two at a time, until they are well coated with the seasoned flour.

Heat the oil and butter in a heavy frying pan and brown the meat all over. Transfer it to a casserole. Deglaze the pan with the stock and pour it over the meat. Add the onion, celery, and ginger. Tie the bay leaves and herbs together, tuck into the casserole and cover.

Cook just below the centre of the oven

291

at 170°C/325°F, gas mark 3 for 3-3½ hours, or until the meat is tender. Transfer the meat to a heated serving dish. Strain the cooking juices into a pan with the fruit jelly and wine. Bring to the boil and reduce a little. Mix a little of the gravy with the blood and stir it thoroughly. Without letting it boil, stir the blood into the gravy, letting it heat through and thicken. Season to taste and pour it over the meat.

If you do not want to use the blood, *Beurre manié* can be used to thicken the sauce, as described on p. 345.

RICH CASSEROLED HARE

A favourite autumn recipe, this is based on the Spanish and Italian *agrodolce* dishes which use a small amount of chocolate to provide a subtle and mysterious flavour to the sauce.

SERVES 4-5

1½ lb/680 g hare meat, off the bone
1 dsp olive oil
2 onions, peeled and sliced
½ pt/280 ml game stock (see p. 344)
1 tbsp red wine, balsamic or sherry vinegar

1 oz/30 g seedless raisins
1 oz/30 g pine kernels (or walnuts)
2 squares of plain dessert chocolate seasoning

TRIM the hare of any sinews and gristle and cut the meat into even-sized pieces. Fry the meat very quickly in the olive oil until it is sealed all over. Put it in a heavy ovenproof casserole.

Fry the onions until browning, and pour the stock over them. Bubble until it is slightly reduced, scraping up any bits stuck to the pan. Add the wine vinegar, raisins, nuts and chocolate. Stir until the chocolate has melted, pour on the meat. Cook in a low oven, 170°C/325°F, gas mark 3 for 40-50 minutes. Season to taste.

Braised red cabbage is delicious with game and so, too, are sliced Jerusalem artichokes baked in a little stock.

Rabbit

*O*F THE SAME FOUR-LEGGED RODENT family as the hare, the wild rabbit is a smaller animal, weighing 3-4 lb/1.35-1.8 kg before skinning and paunching. In Europe tame rabbits have been raised as a source of food since Roman times, after they were spread around the Roman Empire from their native home in the Iberian Peninsula. The rabbits, or coneys, as they were known, were kept enclosed in warrens, but even in those days they escaped into the wild; the island dwellers of Majorca and Ibiza had to appeal to the Romans to send them assistance to control the rabbit population.

Nowadays there are wild and tame rabbits available. Larger animals are bred, often very intensively, for the table in Britain, in continental Europe and, particularly, in China. It puzzles me that whilst much frozen tame rabbit is imported from China, I have yet to see rabbit on the menu in a Chinese restaurant, whether in the West, in Hong Kong, Taiwan or China.

On the other hand, you will find excellent recipes for rabbit in European cookery books. It is a delicate, well flavoured meat which remains inexpensive. It can be grilled, fried, barbecued or roasted, but care must be taken to keep it well basted and thus moist. Wild rabbit is, as you would expect, tougher and needs slower gentler cooking. In fact, whether wild or tame, my preference is for a rabbit casserole. Cook it in red wine with prunes, in white wine with baby onions and mustard, in beer with celery or chunks of celeriac. Cook it like a *blanquette de veau*, the creamy veal dish flavoured with an onion stuck with cloves. Tarragon is the perfect herb for rabbit. In summer, serve a cold jellied rabbit terrine using white wine and tarragon.

The clay chicken brick is an excellent way of cooking rabbit. I soak the pot, put a layer of small onions on the bottom, place the rabbit pieces on top, scatter uncooked rice into the spaces (enough for the right number of servings), add twice the volume of rice of stock or white wine, and saffron threads soaked first in a tablespoon of hot water. Extras such as chopped apricots, almonds and cumin seed give a faintly Middle Eastern or North African touch to the dish. A similar Portuguese dish involves rice, rabbit and red Dâo wine, which produces a dark, rich purple dish.

PAN FRIED RABBIT WITH HERBS

For this dish use the back and hindquarters of a rabbit.
The forequarters can be used for stock or minced up with
other ingredients for a terrine. Start the dish the day
before required.

SERVES 4

3-3½ lb/1.35-1.6 kg rabbit
   pieces, on the bone
1 oz/30 g seasoned flour
2 tbsp extra virgin olive oil
1 tbsp chopped fennel (if
   available)
salt and pepper to taste

For the marinade:
½ pt/280 ml white wine
2 cloves of garlic
1 onion, peeled and sliced
1 carrot, peeled and sliced
1 celery stalk, trimmed and sliced
To garnish:
fresh herbs

TRIM any fat and gristle away from the rabbit joints. Lay them in a single layer in a china or earthenware dish. Pour over the wine. Add the vegetables, except for the fennel, and some of the herbs. Marinate overnight.

Drain and dry the rabbit, reserving the marinade. Heat a heavy iron frying pan, sauté pan or casserole. Shake the rabbit joints with the seasoned flour in a paper bag. This will give them the required light coating.

When the pan is hot, add the olive oil.

When this is hot, place the rabbit joints in the pan in a single layer. When nicely brown on one side, turn and brown on the other side. Lower the heat. Moisten with a little of the strained marinade, add the fennel and the rest of the herbs and cook very gently, partially covered. You will need to add more marinade from time to time to stop the pan from drying. When the meat is tender, taste for seasoning. Arrange the rabbit on a suitable serving dish and garnish with bunches of fresh herbs.

RABBIT IN SAFFRON AND ALMOND GRAVY

The use of saffron and almonds indicates the mediaeval origins of this recipe. It is based on one from *The Form of Curye*, the oldest English cookery book, itself based on a collection of fourteenth-century recipes. If you cannot get rabbit, chicken is very good cooked in this way.

SERVES 4-6

*1 good size rabbit, jointed into
    6 pieces
1 pt/570 ml chicken or veal stock
    (see p. 344)
¼ lb/110 g shelled almonds
6 cloves
1 blade of mace
pinch of ground cinnamon
2 oz/60 g pine kernels
1 dsp sugar
pinch of saffron
1 tbsp wine vinegar*

CLEAN and wipe the rabbit. Blanch it by dropping the pieces into a pan of boiling water, bringing the water back to the boil then draining the meat and refreshing it under cold water. Put the rabbit in a flameproof pot with half the stock and simmer gently.

Blanch, peel and finely grind the almonds. Mix the rest of the stock with the ground almonds and set over a low heat to cook. Add the rabbit pieces and strain the rabbit broth over them. Add the three spices, pine kernels and sugar and cook gently until the rabbit is almost tender. Cooking time will depend on whether you are cooking a wild or a tame rabbit. Meanwhile, soak the saffron in warm water for 20 minutes.

Stir in the saffron to colour the dish and just before serving, add the wine vinegar. Reboil and let the stew bubble a few times before serving.

CONIGLIO ALLA REGGIANA

This is a simple Italian rabbit stew from the region of Reggio, flavoured with celery, white wine and tomato.

SERVES 4

1 rabbit, jointed
½ oz/15 g butter
½ oz/15 g lard or bacon fat or olive oil
1 onion, peeled and chopped
1 or 2 cloves of garlic, peeled and crushed
1 celery stalk, trimmed and sliced
½ lb/230 g ripe tomatoes, peeled, seeded and chopped
½ pt/280 ml dry white wine
salt
pepper
To serve:
fresh parsley or chervil

IN a deep frying pan or flameproof casserole, brown the rabbit pieces in the butter and lard, remove and put to one side. Lightly brown the onion, then add the garlic, celery and tomatoes. Simmer for 5 minutes, then put the rabbit pieces on top, pour on the wine and season lightly.

Bring to the boil, then reduce the heat, cover and simmer until the meat is tender. Serve sprinkled with parsley or chervil.

RABBIT PIE

As well as making an excellent main course, this is superb
picnic food when cold.

SERVES 4-6

2-3 lb/900 g-1.35 kg wild
   rabbit
1 medium onion, peeled and
   sliced
3 tbsp sunflower or extra virgin
   olive oil
1/2 lb/230 g fennel bulbs
3/4 pt/430 ml rabbit stock, water
   or white wine, to cover
salt

pepper
3/4 lb/340 g field mushrooms
6 oz/170 g soaked prunes, stones
   removed (optional)
sprig of tarragon
grated zest of 1/2 lemon
6 oz/170 g short or puff pastry
milk or cream, to glaze the pastry
   (optional)

*R*EMOVE the meat from the rabbit bones, keeping these to make the stock. Fry the rabbit and onion in 2 teaspoons of the oil until golden brown. Trim the fennel, slice it into 1/4 in/0.5 cm pieces and put it with the rabbit and onion. Cover with stock and bring to the boil. Season very lightly, and turn the heat down to the merest simmer. Cover and cook gently for about 45 minutes. Remove the rabbit and vegetables from the cooking liquid. Strain and reduce it to about 1/4 pt/140 ml and refrigerate until required. The dish can be prepared to this point the day before.

Heat the oven to 190°C/370°F, gas mark 5. Wipe and quarter or slice the mushrooms. Fry them briskly in the rest of the oil until they give off most of their moisture. Lightly oil or butter a pie dish. Lay in the bottom the pieces of rabbit, on or off the bone as you prefer, then a layer of mushrooms, a layer of fennel and onion and finally the rest of the mushrooms. Tuck a few tarragon leaves into the filling, and put the grated lemon zest on the top. Spoon the by now jellied stock over the filling, roll out the pastry and cover the dish, pressing down well around the edges to seal it. Make a hole in the top for steam to escape and decorate with pastry leaves or other suitable trimmings.

Brush with milk or cream to glaze, if you wish, and bake in the top half of a pre-heated oven for 35 minutes.

Serve hot or warm with green vegetables or a crisp salad.

VENISON

*I*N BRITAIN WE ARE LUCKY to have such excellent venison. In our case it comes from one of four types of deer: the roe, the fallow, the red and the sika deer. Some of the venison comes from truly wild deer, some from park or farm deer. Whether the animal is male or female depends on the season and varies from one part of the country to the other. Scotland, Wales and the New Forest in Hampshire are the major sources of deer in Britain, while imported venison reached us from New Zealand. It is an extremely popular meat in Europe, and much of our venison is still exported to Germany. French and Scandinavian recipes abound, and you will also occasionally come across recipes for elk (and its American relative the moose) and reindeer in Scandinavia.

As with all other game, venison from the older animal needs slow careful cooking while meat from a young animal can be roasted. The different parts of the animal require different treatment too. Meat from the loin and saddle does not come from such hard working muscles as the shoulder and leg. It follows, therefore, that a saddle can be roasted and loin chops or medallions cut from the fillet can be grilled or, best of all, pan fried in butter.

Venison meat is quite unmistakeable, being a very fine-textured, dense dark red meat which has little fat on it and little marbling of fat in the flesh. What fat there is will be white if the animal is young, yellower if mature. The meat is sold jointed as a saddle, loin steaks, a leg, leg steaks or stewing venison, for example.

Because it is high in protein and low in fat, it is a meat with good nutritional properties. Covering it with a rich cream sauce or basting with lots of butter will change the balance entirely. I have, however, sometimes been disappointed at the lack of flavour in venison when I have cooked fillet, for example. True, it has been tender, but really one was just eating a lump of protein. On the other hand, two of the finest roasts I have ever eaten have been venison. One was a 7 lb/3.25 kg haunch cooked by a Scottish doctor (see p. 299). She had marinated it overnight in olive oil and lemon juice (truly Scottish ingredients of course) and then roasted it in a slow oven, 150°C/300°F, gas mark 2 for 30 minutes a pound. She advised against larding it as she felt that would spoil the fine flavour of this wild red deer. It was magnificent, as was the saddle of venison, which *was* larded, marinated in port, olive oil, wine, herbs, spices and all manner of other good things, then roasted in a hot oven for about 15 minutes a pound, frequently basted, and served rare.

Stewing venison, diced from a boned shoulder or leg, makes a marvellous game pudding, cooked with Guinness inside a suet crust. Or chop it very small and use it to make a venison chilli. The lean medallions or *noisettes* cut from the fillet cook very quickly and are fine for one of those dinners where your guests can be left for a few minutes while you fry the meat, deglaze the pan and swirl up a few tablespoons of delectable meat juices into a sauce enriched with redcurrant jelly, butter and a little cream.

Pot Roast Haunch of Venison

My *Sunday Times'* cook's tour in 1986 took me to Scotland where Elise Andrews entertained me and her friends to a magnificent haunch of venison for Sunday lunch. The slow cooking of the venison made it very tender and well cooked, with plenty of cooking juices to make a good gravy.
In Scotland, a traditional accompaniment to roasts is skirlie (see p. 351), a flavoursome 'stuffing' made from pin-head oatmeal.

Serves 8-10

7 lb/3.25 kg haunch of
  venison
For the marinade:
1 pt/570 ml olive oil
¼ pt/140 ml lemon juice

1 onion, peeled and sliced
8 crushed juniper berries
For the sauce:
2 tbsp freshly grated
  horseradish

6 tbsp dry Oloroso sherry
To serve:
rowanberry or crabapple jelly

*M*IX the marinade ingredients, pour them over the venison and leave for 12-24 hours, occasionally basting.

Remove the joint from the marinade, dry it and sear it all over in a frying pan.

Put the joint in a large casserole. Boil the marinade to reduce it a little then pour it over the joint. Cook it at 150°C/300°F, gas mark 2 for 30 minutes per pound/ 455 g.

Remove the venison from the casserole and put it on a carving dish, covered, in a warm place, while you finish off the sauce. This relaxing time for the meat will make it easier to carve.

Add the sherry to the juices in the casserole and boil to reduce and thicken. The horseradish should be stirred in just before serving. Rowanberry or crabapple jelly are ideal companions to venison.

NOISETTES OF VENISON MARINATED IN FRUIT JUICE

The loin of venison, from which the noisettes are cut, is meat of such good quality, texture and flavour that it needs only the lightest marinade if any. This marinade is based on passion fruit, which gives the finished sauce a delicate and interesting light fruity flavour. I have used the same method for preparing breast of wild duck and lamb fillet. If the juice is clearly not going to go very far, add a little more organic apple juice.

SERVES 4

4 slices of loin of venison, about 2 in/5 cm thick, each weighing 3-4 oz/85-110 g

4 large passion fruits
4 tbsp organic apple juice
freshly grated nutmeg
seasoning to taste

CUT the tops off the passion fruit and scoop out the pulp. Keep back a little to provide an attractive garnish. Rub the seeds through a sieve into a bowl and stir in the apple juice. Grind a little fresh nutmeg over each piece of venison, place in a dish and pour the fruit juice over it. Stand in a cool place for a couple of hours. Remove from the marinade and dry each piece.

Heat a non-stick frying pan and, when hot, put in the venison. Cook on a high heat on both sides until it reaches the stage of doneness you require. Remove and keep warm. Pour the juice into the hot pan and reduce a little. Season to taste. You can slice the venison or serve it whole, surrounded by a little light sauce and a scattering of the passion fruit seeds.

300

MEDALLIONS OF VENISON

Here is another method of cooking venison which can be adapted to suit the number of guests you're feeding and is well suited to the various accompaniments such as skirlie and rowanberry jelly. Use a non-stick frying pan for even healthier results.

SERVES 4

4 medallions of loin of venison,
about 1½-2 in/4-5 cm thick
¼ pt/140 ml game or beef stock
(see p. 344)
2 tbsp dry sherry, port or
vermouth
1 tbsp freshly grated horseradish
For the marinade:
2 tbsp olive oil
juice of one lemon
1 onion, peeled and thinly sliced
1 tsp crushed juniper berries

*M*ARINADE the venison overnight. As the medallions cook in little more than 10 minutes, you need to have all the other ingredients to hand. Dry the venison.

Heat the pan and, when it is very hot, add the medallions in a single layer. Cook for 3-5 minutes, depending on how well done you like the meat. Maintaining a high heat, turn the venison over and sauté for 2-3 minutes more. Ideally the meat should be dark and almost charred on the outside, pink and tender on the inside.

Remove the venison from the pan and keep it warm on a plate. Pour the stock into the pan and allow to reduce a little. Add the sherry and horseradish and cook for 2 minutes, enough to allow the alcohol to evaporate. Put a spoonful of sauce on each heated plate and lay the medallion of venison on top.

STALKER'S PIE

The credit for this idea must go to Derek Cooper, in
whose house I was eating wonderful roast deer sent down
from Scotland one day. As we finished second helpings of
the succulent meat, there was still plenty left over.
'We'll make a shepherd's pie with it', said Janet Cooper.
'Nay, stalker's pie', said Derek.
Instead of a mashed potato topping, I suggest mashing
celeriac or parsnips with the potato, as well as plenty of
garlic.

SERVES 4-6

1 lb/455 g cooked venison
¼ pt/140 ml venison gravy
1 onion, peeled, chopped and
  fried
2 oz/60 g butter
2 lb/900 g root vegetables,
  peeled (see suggestions above)
10 cloves of garlic, peeled
seasoning

C HOP the venison very small and mix
it with the gravy and onion. Grease
an ovenproof dish with half the butter.
Spoon the venison into the dish.

Boil and mash the root vegetables.
Mix in the remaining butter. Season and
spread over the meat. Bake in the middle
of the oven, at 200°C/400°F, gas mark 6
for 20 minutes, covering the pie for the
first 15 minutes with foil, then uncover-
ing it to let the vegetables brown on
top.

VENISON CHILLI

California must have been the first place I tasted this, for it
was then newly fashionable. The venison can, of course,
be replaced with beef, in which case use shin, chuck or
flank. It is a dish that is even better served the following
day. Try it also in scooped-out baked potatoes.

SERVES 8

2 lb/900 g venison meat from
  the shoulder, off the bone
1 lb/455 g kidney or borlotti
  beans, washed and soaked
  overnight
2 tbsp sunflower or groundnut oil
1 medium onion, peeled and
  sliced
3-4 cloves of garlic, peeled and
  sliced
cayenne pepper or chilli powder,
  to taste
1 tbsp mild paprika

1 tbsp cumin seeds
1 tbsp fresh marjoram or oregano
  (or 1 tsp dried)
2 bay leaves
stock or water, to moisten
1 large can of peeled plum
  tomatoes, about 14 oz/400 g
2 oz/60 g sun-dried tomatoes,
  soaked in hot water and cut
  into strips
salt
pepper

TRIM the meat and dice it very small
(I do not like the texture of chilli
made from meat that has been minced).
Put the beans in a saucepan with plenty
of water and boil them briskly for 15
minutes. This destroys the surface toxins
which can cause indigestion. Drain,
rinse, put back in the pan with fresh
water and simmer for an hour.

Using a little of the oil, brown the
meat all over and transfer it to a
casserole. Fry the onion in the remaining
oil until golden brown. Add the garlic,
spices and herbs, moisten with a little
stock or water and scrape up any residues stuck to the pan. Put the onions
and flavourings with the meat, add the
tomatoes, beans and their cooking
liquor. Stir well, bring to the boil and
simmer gently, partially covered, for an
hour or so until meat and beans are
tender. Season to taste and serve.

VENISON CRUMBLE

SERVES 4-6

1½ lb/680 g venison meat, off
    the bone
½ oz/15 g dried wild mushroom
    or 4 oz/110 g fresh
    mushrooms
¼ pt/140 ml stock (see p. 344)
2 cloves of garlic, crushed
½ tsp salt
½ tsp ground mace

5 oz/140 g plain flour
1 tsp rubbed dried thyme
3 oz/85 g butter
For the marinade:
1 tbsp olive oil
1 carrot, peeled and sliced
1 onion, peeled and sliced
1 celery stalk, trimmed and sliced
1 glass red wine or port

*C*UT the meat into small chunks. Make the marinade. Heat the oil and gently fry the sliced carrot, onion and celery until they begin to brown. Pour on the wine, and then remove from the heat. Cool the marinade and then pour it over the meat. Leave overnight or for at least a few hours. If using dried mushrooms, soak them in a bowl of warm water until plumped out and soft. Drain and dry the meat. Strain the marinade and set it aside.

Heat a non-stick frying pan. Taking a few pieces of meat at a time, sear them all over, and transfer to a casserole. Pour the stock and the marinade into the frying pan and boil, scraping up any residue. Pour the liquid over the meat and add the drained, sliced mushrooms. Season lightly and add the crushed garlic. Cover and cook in the oven at 150-170°C/300-325°F, gas mark 2-3 for 1½ to 2 hours. You can prepare the dish to this stage the day before. Indeed, like most casseroles, it benefits from the blending of flavours overnight.

For the final preparation, transfer the meat to a shallow dish, leaving at least ½ in/1 cm for the topping. Heat the oven to 200-220°C/400-425°F, gas mark 6-7.

Sift the salt and mace with the flour and stir in the herbs. Rub the butter into the flour until it resembles fine bread-crumbs. Spoon evenly over the meat and press down a little. Bake in a hot oven for 15-20 minutes.

VENISON AND GUINNESS PUDDING

If you use a good proportion of breadcrumbs in suet crust
pastry, it remains light and spongy in texture.
Approximately 8 oz/230 g pastry will line a 2 pt/approx 1
litre pudding basin, which will serve 4 to 6 people.

SERVES 4-6

*1½ lb/680 g lean venison meat,
  off the bone
12 small onions, peeled
8 oz/230 g celery hearts or
  celeriac
1 tbsp good olive oil
1 sprig of fresh marjoram
1 bay leaf
1 tbsp chestnut flour (arrowroot,
  potato flour or cornflour can
  be substituted)
¼ pt/140 ml Guinness*

*¼ pt/140 ml game stock (if
  available, or Guinness)
salt and pepper
For the pastry:
4 oz/110 g self-raising flour
4 oz/110 g soft fresh
  breadcrumbs, white or
  wholemeal
a little salt
4 oz/110 g shredded fresh suet
up to 5 fl oz/140 ml water*

*M*AKE the pastry. Sift the flour into a
basin and add the breadcrumbs
and salt. Stir the dry ingredients together
with a knife. Add the suet and sufficient
water to make a firm but springy dough.
Turn the dough out on to a floured
board. Knead the dough lightly and form
into a ball. Cover and leave to stand in a
cool place while you prepare the filling.

Cut the venison into 1 in/2.5 cm cubes.
Peel and trim the onions and celery; cut
the peeled celeriac into ¼ in/0.5 cm dice if
you are using it; the celery should be
sliced no more than ¼ in/0.5 cm thick.

Heat the olive oil in a heavy based
pan. Fry the vegetables until just beginning to colour lightly. Add the venison
and herbs. Seal the meat all over. Moisten the flour with a little of the Guinness
and stir it into the rest of the Guinness
and stock (if you are using it). Add this
all to the pan and bring to simmering
point. Season to taste and remove from
the heat. Leave the meat to cool.

Grease a 2 pt/approx 1 litre capacity
pudding basin. Roll out three-quarters of
the pastry and use this to line the pudding basin. Spoon in the cooled meat

mixture. Roll out the remaining quarter of the pastry and place this on top of the basin. Seal the edges. Cover the basin with a sheet of greaseproof paper, which you must first pleat in the middle to allow the pastry to rise slightly, bearing in mind that it contains raw flour. Tie the paper securely round the top of the basin. Cover the pudding with a clean tea towel and tie it round the rim of the basin. Bring the ends up over the pudding and tie it into a knot. Put the basin in a large saucepan, standing it on an upturned saucer or steamer tray. Pour in boiling water until it reaches half way up the basin, cover the saucepan with a lid and simmer for 2 hours.

For a *Steak, Kidney and Oyster Pudding*, substitute rump steak and veal kidney for the venison. Substitute red wine for the Guinness. Put fresh oysters on top of the meat mixture before covering with pastry.

For a *Game and Cider Pudding*, substitute pheasant, rabbit, partridge and hare, for the venison and cider for the Guinness.

POTTED VENISON WITH JUNIPER BERRIES

This recipe is a good way of using up left-overs from a roast, haunch or saddle of venison. It makes a good starter served with hot toast and a little redcurrant or gooseberry jelly, and is also an excellent present. It should be eaten within seven days.

MAKES ABOUT ¾ LB/340 G

½ lb/230 g cooked lean venison, off the bone
¼ lb/110 g unsalted butter

2 tbsp red vermouth
1 dozen crushed juniper berries

salt and pepper to taste
To seal:
clarified butter

TRIM any fat and gristle from the venison and cut into small cubes. Put into the food processor with the butter, vermouth and juniper berries. Process until smooth. Season to taste and pack firmly into suitable small containers. Pour on clarified butter to cover and seal the surface. Cover and store in the refrigerator and eat within a week. If you are giving the venison as a present, do not forget to label it with contents and date.

WILD BOAR

*T*HESE HANDSOME, AGGRESSIVE LOOKING BEASTS have been extinct in Britain for about three centuries, although they are still found in the more remote hilly areas of Italy, Southern Germany and Eastern France amongst our close neighbours.

You will find recipes for it in French cook books – for *sanglier*, or *marcassin* for the young boar – and German, Italian and Spanish books. In the winter, driving through snow and sleet to Casteznuovo in Garfagano, in the unfashionable and remote part of north-western Tuscany, a hot steaming, rich, gamy stew of wild boar heaped over freshly cooked polenta was one of the most welcoming dishes we ever consumed.

In recent years, some enterprising farmers have reintroduced the breed to Britain, so that the name wild boar now refers to the breed rather than their lifestyle. They are not allowed to wander unpenned and at will because they are classified as dangerous animals. About five years ago I visited a herd of wild boar in North Wales. They were fine animals and excellent food. Our host had made us a huge raised hot-water crust pie full of wild boar, grouse, pork, chicken livers, pistachio nuts and plenty of seasoning, served cold with some spiced plums. It was a marvellous dish (see the recipe on p. 332).

Sometimes wild boar is available in butchers. It looks like a slightly denser, darker version of pork and should be cooked in the same way; roasted for the lean or tender cuts and casseroled for the tougher cuts, with the trimmings turned into soups and *pâtés*. Unlike venison, boar should always be well cooked.

GAME TERRINE

Use pheasant, rabbit, wild duck, hare or pigeon off the
bone. If you cannot get the pork back fat to line the loaf
tin, thin rindless rashers of unsmoked streaky bacon can
be used, but remember that the saltpetre in the bacon will
give a pink tinge to the *pâté* and will also change its
flavour.

MAKES ONE 2 LB/1 KG TERRINE

¾ lb/340 g game meat, off the
   bone (see above)
½ lb/230 g lean pork or veal
1 lb/455 g fat belly of pork, rind
   removed and reserved
12 crushed juniper berries
1 tsp ground allspice
½ tsp ground cumin seeds

1 tsp freshly ground black pepper
1 tsp sea salt
¼ pt/140 ml red or white wine
4 tbsp gin, grappa or eau de vie
   de poire
½ lb/230 g pork back fat, cut
   into thin slices or sheets
1 size-3 free-range egg
½ oz/10 g potato or corn flour

CHOP the game into small dice (about
¼ in/½ cm), removing any sinews.
Mince the lean meat with the belly of
pork, mix it with the game, spices, seasonings, wine and spirits and marinate it
overnight, covered, in the refrigerator.

Next day, line a 2 lb (approx)/1 kg loaf
tin or terrine with similar capacity, with
very thin slices of pork fat.

Preheat the oven to 180°C/350°F, gas
mark 4. Beat the egg and flour until
thoroughly blended and strain it over the
marinated meat. Mix thoroughly and
pack into the lined tin. Push it well down,

excluding any air bubbles, and heap up
the top as the mixture will shrink down
as it cooks. Cover with foil, and stand on
a trivet or rack in a roasting tin deep
enough to allow boiling water to be
poured in to come at least halfway up the
loaf tin. Cook in the middle of a warm
oven for 2 hours. Remove from the heat,
allow to cool completely, weighted
down, and cover the surface with melted
lard or pork fat to preserve it.

This will keep for a week, covered and
unbroached, in the refrigerator.

GAME CRUMBLE

For this recipe, you can use any or all of the following: venison, hare, pheasant, wild rabbit or pigeon. Explain to your butcher that you are casseroling the meat. It is a very easy recipe to make for a large party, and can be prepared – except for the crumble – the day before.

SERVES 8-10

4 lb/1.8 kg game meat, off the bone (see above)
1½ oz/40 g dried ceps or 8 oz/225 g fresh mushrooms
¾ pt/430 ml stock (see p. 344)
seasoning

3 cloves of garlic, peeled and crushed
For the marinade:
⅛ pt/70 ml olive oil
2 carrots, peeled, trimmed and sliced
2 onions, peeled, trimmed and sliced

2 celery stalks, peeled, trimmed and sliced
½ bottle of port or red wine
For the crumble:
14 oz/400 g plain flour
8 oz/230 g butter

*C*UT the game meat into small chunks. Heat the oil and gently fry the sliced carrot, onion and celery until they begin to brown. Pour on the wine and remove from the heat. Cool the marinade and pour it over the meat. Leave overnight, or for at least a few hours. If using dried mushrooms, soak them in a bowl of warm water for about 30 minutes until plumped out and soft. Drain and dry the meat. Strain the marinade and set it aside.

Heat a non-stick frying pan. Taking a few pieces of meat at a time, sear it all over and transfer it to a casserole. Pour the stock and the marinade into the frying pan and boil, scraping up any residue with a wooden spoon. Pour over the meat. Add the drained, sliced mushrooms. Season lightly and add the crushed garlic. Cover and cook in the oven at 150-170°C/300-325°F, gas mark 2-3, for 1½-2 hours.

You can prepare the dish to this stage the day before. Like most casseroles, it benefits from the blending of flavours overnight.

For the final preparation, heat the oven to 200-220°C/400-425°F, gas mark 6-7, and transfer the meat to a shallow dish, which leaves at least ½ in/1 cm for the topping.

Rub the butter into the flour until it resembles fine breadcrumbs. Spoon evenly over the meat and press down a little. Bake in a hot oven for 15-20 minutes.

309

CHIPPEWA GAME SOUP

This is an excellent soup for left-overs. Wild rice, which is a very good accompaniment to all types of game, used to be harvested in the lake country of northern Minnesota by the Chippewa Indians. The recipe is also very good with left-over roast duckling, and stock, which is how I first tasted it.

SERVES 4

1 small onion or 2 shallots,
    peeled and finely chopped
2 tsp rendered duck fat
1 medium carrot, peeled and
    diced
1 small turnip, peeled and diced
1½ pt/850 ml game stock (see
    p. 344)
2-3 oz/60-85 g cooked game
    meat, off the bone
3 oz/85 g cooked wild rice
2 tbsp dry sherry or Madeira
salt
freshly ground black pepper
To serve:
fresh coriander or flat-leaved
    parsley
bread fried in duck fat

IN a heavy-based pan or casserole fry the onion in the duck fat until golden brown. Add the carrot and turnip and fry for 2 or 3 minutes. Pour on the stock, bring to the boil, and simmer until the vegetables are tender. Add the meat, rice and sherry, and cook for a further 5 minutes. Season to taste, garnish with coriander or flat-leaved parsley and serve immediately.

This is wonderful served with small squares or triangles of bread that have been fried in duck fat.

DISHES FOR A CROWD

There are certain types of dishes which simply do not lend themselves to small-scale dining. To enjoy them in their full glory, and they are indeed glorious dishes, it is imperative to cook them in the quantities used in the traditional recipe. For these are, without exception, traditional dishes. Who now would dare devise a recipe which required several pounds of different types of meat? Here are the *pot-au-feu* and the *bollito misto* of French and Italian bourgeois homely cooking, the Spanish *cocido*, the North African *couscous*, but also cobblers and crumbles from Britain. Some, such as the *pasticcio*, are ample demonstration of the fact that you do not need much meat in a recipe in order to create something really special. Here it is used as one of the many components in an elaborate dish.

Many of the recipes have been collected on our travels over the years. When I cook an *ajiaco* it brings back far more vivid memories of Colombia than does a glance through our photographs. When I cook a *baeckenoffa* from Alsace, I can almost taste the onion tart served before it, the pungent Munster cheese and the *tarte aux mirabelles* served after it, as well as the beautifully balanced, crisp Riesling and the heady *eau de vie* we drank in a little restaurant in Eguisheim.

These are not meals to prepare in a hurry, but ones to take your time over, in both the shopping and cooking. I enjoy all the rituals involved, down to preparing or hunting out all the very particular and traditional appurtenances which are served with them: bowls of capers and *aji* for the *ajiaco*; *harissa* for the couscous, gherkins and coarse salt for the *pot-au-feu*. Although this side of the preparation will be time-consuming, the dishes, on the whole, look after themselves once cooking is underway and do not need your constant attention. Indeed, many were devised for their practicality in a particular set of circumstances: the busy housewife in Alsace wanting to feed her family on Monday as well as get through the household wash, the housewife in Gozo preparing a sturdy dish to cook in the baker's oven that would not get spoiled carrying it back home.

And, of course, the dishes are all served straight from the pot in which they are cooked – no need to worry about time consuming and food-cooling plate service. Indeed, these recipes are a marvellous excuse for buying lovely pots on holiday. I yearned over large, bulbous half-glazed earthenware in a shop next to the market in Galicia, but did not buy it. Determined not to leave Ireland with regrets of this kind we wound our way down country lanes near Ballymaloe in Co. Cork to find the Stephen Pearce pottery, where we bought a lovely pot, square sided on a round base. It will sit next to the deep rectangular earthenware dish we bought in Lisbon, which has miraculously survived twenty years of hard labour, and a round handled and lipped pot from Catalunya which has survived even longer.

With such a centrepiece for the main course, aim for maximum simplicity to top and tail the meal. A vegetable rather than a fish or meat starter would be most appropriate; if the dish is not too soupy, a hot or chilled vegetable soup, or a plate of crudités. *Hummous*, a creamy dip made from chick-peas crushed and mixed with olive oil, garlic and lemon juice, and pitta bread seem just right before the *couscous*. Hot or cold marinated mushrooms, depending on the weather, is another easy, appropriate starter. Recipes based on eggs or cheese pile on the protein unnecessarily, I feel. Fruit ends such a meal perfectly. In the summer I would serve a *compôte* of berry fruits, or peaches or nectarines sliced in orange juice, in autumn and spring perhaps a fruit tart and in the winter a platter of sliced tropical fruits, including pineapple or papaya for their digestive enzymes, to help deal with the ample portions of protein.

FAJITAS

South-western and Mexican foods still seem to hold their own in California despite the growing interest in 'Pacific Rim' cooking. My most recent visit there took place at the end of the summer, just before the Labour Day weekend, which seems to be the last fling for outdoor grills and barbecues. *Fajitas* were much in evidence, both in cookery columns and bathed in a spicy marinade in cling-wrapped boxes in the supermarkets.

There are two ways of preparing *fajitas*. One is to slice the meat thinly, marinate then cook. The other is to marinate, cook, then slice thinly. I prefer the latter. The tail end of the fillet is ideally suited to this, as is the tougher but supremely tasty skirt, which is certainly helped by the marinade. Chicken or pork can also be used, or indeed lamb. *Fajitas* are a good party dish since they are easily served to large numbers.

Refried beans would be a traditional accompaniment. These are quickly made by draining, rinsing and mashing a can of red kidney beans and frying them with a little finely sliced onion in olive oil, or a non-stick frying pan, until they are just browning. A bowl of cooling, fresh-tasting *salsa* would also be a good idea. I have given two recipes below.

Best of all cooked on a barbecue and eaten outdoors, *fajitas* can also be cooked on a heavy, well seasoned and grooved cast-iron griddle.

SERVES 6-8

2 lb/900 g tail end of beef fillet steak, flank steak or goose skirt, in a piece
4 green or red chilli peppers
fresh coriander leaves
For the marinade:
2 tbsp soy sauce
juice of 1 or 2 limes

1 tsp Angostura bitters
1/8 pt/70 ml tequila
3 tbsp extra virgin olive oil
2 or 3 cloves of garlic, peeled and crushed
1 or 2 ripe tomatoes, peeled, seeded and chopped

1/2 tsp freshly ground black pepper
1/2 tsp sea salt
pinch of chilli powder or dried pepper flakes
To serve:
flour tortillas or pitta bread

313

IX together all the ingredients for the marinade. Slash the meat two or three times on each side and put it in a shallow bowl with the marinade. Leave for 2-4 hours.

Heat the grill. Reserving the marinade, remove the steak from it and, depending on the thickness, grill it for 5-6 minutes on each side if you like it rare, 8 minutes for medium and 10-12 minutes for well done. Grill the peppers until charred. When cool enough to handle, skin them, cut them in half, remove the seeds and shred the flesh finely. Slice the steak thinly across the grain.

Mix the steak and peppers with a little of the reserved marinade and pile on a serving platter, garnished with fresh coriander. Serve with warm tortillas or pitta bread.

SPICED TOPSIDE BRAISED IN CIDER

Not unlike the traditional German Sauerbraten, this is a dish for a large gathering unless you want a lot of leftovers. It is also a good-tempered dish and can be left for several hours to cook in a slow oven – perfect for Sunday lunch after a long tramp in raw November weather. Serve it with dumplings, noodles, boiled or mashed potatoes, or a purée of root vegetables. Start the preparation at least the day before or earlier if you want – it can marinate for up to 72 hours.

Left-overs are delicious in sandwiches, salads or as potted beef.

SERVES 8-10

4 lb/1.8 kg topside or silverside of beef, boned and rolled
2 tsp salt
2 tsp ground ginger
2 tsp ground cardamom seeds
1/4 pt/140 ml cider vinegar
3/4 pt/430 ml dry cider
1 medium onion, peeled and sliced

1 medium carrot, peeled and sliced
1 leek, trimmed and sliced
1 celery stalk, trimmed and sliced
2 bay leaves
1 small cinnamon stick
6 cloves

1 tbsp allspice
1 tbsp black peppercorns
1 tsp powdered mace
2 tbsp olive oil
1 tbsp Calvados (optional)
For the ginger beurre manié:
1 tsp flour
1/2 oz/15 g butter
1 tsp ground ginger

314

*T*RIM and wipe the piece of beef. Rub it all over with salt, ginger and cardamom and place it in a large bowl. Place the cider vinegar, cider, vegetables, herbs and spices, in a saucepan, bring them to the boil and pour them over the meat. Cool quickly, then cover and refrigerate for up to 72 hours, turning the meat occasionally. When ready to cook the meat, choose a casserole only slightly bigger than the joint. Remove the meat from the marinade and dry it all over.

Heat the oil in a frying pan, or in the casserole if the latter will take it. When the oil is smoking, sear the meat all over until browned. Put it into the casserole and add about half the marinade and vegetables. Cover and cook in a slow oven, 170°C/325°F, gas mark 3, for 3½ hours. Check the liquid level after a couple of hours and add more of the marinade and vegetables if a lot of liquid has evaporated.

When the meat is cooked, lift it out of the casserole, transfer it to a carving dish and keep it warm. Pour the pan juices and any remaining marinade into a saucepan and bring to the boil. Simmer for a few minutes while you prepare the ginger *beurre manié* by mixing together the flour, softened butter and ground ginger. Drop bit by bit into the saucepan, stir and cook for a further 10 minutes. Slice the meat, and strain the sauce over it, or into a sauceboat to hand separately. As a final touch, the meat can be flamed in a spoonful of heated Calvados.

PUCHERO

Beef and more beef, as well as sweet potatoes, corn and
pumpkin, go into this Argentinian dish. It makes a
marvellous big stew for a cold autumn day. If you're
making a pumpkin lantern for Hallowe'en, this is a perfect
way of using up the pumpkin flesh.

SERVES 8-10

2 lb/900 g beef brisket
1½ lb/680 g rolled beef rib
½ lb/230 g Toulouse or other
*   well seasoned sausage (cut*
*   into 1 in/2.5 cm pieces)*
¼ lb/110 g salt pork or bacon,
*   diced*
1 celery stalk, trimmed
1 leek, trimmed
salt
pepper
1 bay leaf
2 parsley stalks

¾ lb/340 g chickpeas, soaked
*   and parboiled*
water to cover
4 carrots, peeled and sliced
2 or 3 sweet potatoes, peeled and
*   diced*
1 lb/455 g pumpkin, peeled and
*   diced*
1 onion, peeled and chopped
3 corn cobs, each cut across into
*   4 chunks*
chopped fresh parsley

*P*UT the meats, celery and leek, salt,
pepper, bay leaf, parsley, chickpeas
and enough water to cover in a large
saucepan or casserole. Bring to the boil,
skim off any foam, cover and simmer
until the meat is cooked.

Add the vegetables, except for the
corn, and cook for a further 20 minutes
or so, then add the corn cobs and cook
for 5-10 minutes more.

Scatter with chopped parsley and
serve.

TORTELLINI IN BRODO

I learnt how to make this in the heart of the Modenese countryside, at the home of our friends the Lancellottis, who have a small hotel and restaurant and great big generous hearts. Their food is the best I have tasted anywhere, surrounded by all the good things which go into the *tortellini*: milk for the Parmigiana Reggiano cheese, which leaves whey as a by-product to feed the pigs, which in turn become Parma ham, *pancetta* and *mortadella*.

Angelo Lancellotti showed me how to make the filling and emphasised two points. Lightly brown the meats first and drain off the fat, which makes for both a lighter filling and a more developed flavour, and chop the meat by hand rather than using the food processor or mincer. The filling should have some texture. Angelo also likes to brown the meat in the neutral grapeseed oil rather than olive oil.

Mamma Lancellotti showed me how to make the pasta: 1 egg to *un etto* (100 g/3½ oz) of flour, which is not semolina but a mixture of 0 and 00 Italian flour. I use a mixture of plain flour and strong plain flour. Mama was not impressed when I said I made pasta dough in the food processor. In her kitchen it is mixed by hand on a board, kneaded until smooth, golden and elastic and rolled out to the thickness of a 20p piece.

The excellent recipe for broth can also be used for other soup recipes, and the chicken and beef in a simple *bollito misto*. Angelo specifies a real chicken.

A good 1 lb/455 g filling will make 2¼ lb/1 kg *tortellini*. An average serving of these in broth is about 2½ oz/70 g.

MAKES JUST OVER 1 LB/455 G STUFFED PASTA;
SERVES 6-7

For the filling:
4 oz/110 g Parma ham, with about ¼ in/0.5 cm fat around it
4 oz/110 g pork loin or fillet
3½ oz/100 g mortadella
1 tbsp grapeseed oil
1 egg
½ tsp salt
½ nutmeg, freshly grated

5 oz/140 g freshly grated Parmesan cheese
2 oz/60 g fine fresh soft breadcrumbs
For the pasta:
generous 10 oz/300 g flour
3 size-3 eggs
For the broth:
1 chicken
2 lb/900 g beef on the bone, such as a rib

10 pt/approx 6 l water
a little salt (unless you intend to use some of the broth for a reduced meat sauce)
fresh chervil
2-3 in/5-7.5 cm piece of celery stalk
1 small onion, peeled and halved
1 clove of garlic

*C*UT the meats into 1 in/2.5 cm dice and brown lightly in the grapeseed oil, cooking for about 8-10 minutes. Drain the meat and put it on a chopping board. Chop the meat finely, then mix in the egg, salt, nutmeg and Parmesan and finally the breadcrumbs. Mix by hand, knead and work for 5 minutes, until the mixture is thoroughly bound together, adding more breadcrumbs if the mixture is too soft. Put the meat in a bowl, cover and keep until required. Use the filling the same day.

Make the pasta. Pile the flour on to a work surface, make a well in the centre and slide in the whole eggs. Working with your fingertips, draw flour from the edges to the centre and gradually blend together by hand until the dough is formed. Sprinkle with more flour if the mixture is sticky, which it may well be if you are working in a humid atmosphere, and knead for 5-10 minutes until the dough is smooth and elastic. Cover and let it rest for 15 minutes at room temperature.

Roll out on a floured work surface to the thickness of a 20p piece, stretching and rolling the dough over the rolling pin. A long narrow pin, or *matarella* is used in Italy.

With a fluted cutting wheel, cut out squares of dough. Place a small pea-sized ball of filling in the centre. Fold one corner to the opposite and pinch the two edges of the resulting triangle together really hard to seal them. Bend the central point of the triangle up and over drawing the other two points together round the top of the same finger and pinch together to seal. Then put on a cloth until you have made all the *tortellini*. Leave covered until you are ready to cook them.

Make the broth. Put all the ingredients in a large saucepan, bring just to the boil, skim off the foam and simmer for 2-2½ hours, skimming fairly frequently. If you want a really well flavoured meat, and can make do with a lesser broth, put the meat into the water after it has boiled.

Remove the meat and strain the broth into a clean saucepan. Bring to the boil and put in the freshly made *tortellini*. Simmer for 2-3 minutes, then ladle into a heated soup tureen.

The pasta will continue cooking in the hot broth and will be just right by the time you serve it.

AJIACO SANTAFEREÑO

Santa Fe was the old Spanish colonial name for
Colombia's capital, Bogota, and it was there that we had
our first taste of this ambrosial stew of chickens, corn and,
cleverly, three kinds of potatoes – one to thicken, one to
give bulk and one to provide flavour and texture.
Originally an Indian dish cooked in a pot over a fire,
containing wild turkey, corn and roots, this has developed
into the sort of dish that sophisticated Bogotanos love to
serve to their friends and family at weekends and on
special occasions. Indeed, Saturday's *El Tiempo* advertises
delivery of *ajiaco* to your home by special companies:
Ajiaco Sabanero bikes it to you, Ajiaco Casero accepts
credit cards and Don Ajiaco packs it hygenically.
A small turkey cooked this way is also very good
indeed.

SERVES 8

4-5 lb/1.8-2.3 kg chicken
2 large onions, peeled and
quartered
a handful of coriander sprigs
5 pt/2.85 l water
1½ lb/680 g soft cooking
potatoes, peeled and thickly
sliced

1½ lb/680 g firm potatoes, peeled
and sliced
1 lb/455 g small waxy salad
potatoes, scrubbed and halved
(or left whole if small)
bunch of watercress, leaves only
3 or 4 corn cobs
chilli powder to taste
salt to taste

R INSE and dry the chicken and remove any cavity fat. Put it in a large
saucepan with the onion, coriander
stalks and water. Add more water if
necessary to cover the chicken. Bring to
the boil, remove any scum from the surface, cover and simmer gently for 15
minutes. Add the soft-cooking potatoes
and cook for a further 25-30 minutes. Remove the coriander and onion and discard. Take out the chicken and put to one
side.

Put in the rest of the potatoes and cook
for 15-20 minutes until the first batch is
quite soft enough for you to break up
with a fork and the other two kinds of

potato are still firm but cooked. Meanwhile remove the meat from the chicken carcase. Add the chilli powder and watercress to the pan with the corn cobs, each cut into three or four pieces, and bring to the boil. Put in the chicken meat and simmer for about 5 minutes until the corn is tender.

Ladle into deep soup bowls and serve very hot.

The traditional accompaniments for *ajiaco*, served in separate bowls for each to help themself, are: thick yogurt or cream, capers, chopped parsley and *aji*, a hot sauce of finely chopped spring onion or leek, tomato, fresh chillis and fresh coriander leaves mixed with lime juice or vinegar. Each person is also served half an avocado, peeled and sliced on to a side plate.

FESTIVE BORTSCH AND PIROSHKIS

A robust soup that I like to make at Christmas or New Year, when I have lots of turkey stock.

SERVES 6-8

1 tbsp olive oil or turkey fat
1 large onion, peeled and thinly sliced
1 carrot, peeled and thinly sliced
1 celery stalk, trimmed and thinly sliced
1 leek, trimmed and thinly sliced
1 lb/455 g fresh beetroot, peeled and diced
1/4 lb/110 g shredded white cabbage
1 lb/455 g tomatoes or 1 large tin peeled plum tomatoes, weight approx 14 oz/400 g, roughly chopped

3 cloves of garlic
1/2 tsp dill seeds or fresh dill
3 pt/1.7 l turkey stock (see p. 344)
2 tbsp wine vinegar
6 oz/170 g cooked turkey meat, off the bone
6 oz/170 g puff, flaky or shortcrust pastry (see p. 348)
milk or melted butter to glaze the pastry
To serve:
soured cream (optional)

ELT the fat in a large saucepan and stir in the first four vegetables. Cook until light brown. Add the beetroot, cabbage, tomatoes, crushed garlic and dill. Pour in the stock and vinegar, bring to the boil and simmer gently for 40 minutes, or until the vegetables are soft.

Scoop out a few of the vegetables and process with the cooked meat to moisten and flavour it. Season if necessary.

Roll out the pastry and cut into rounds or squares. Place a teaspoon of the meat mixture in the centre. Moisten the edges of the pastry, fold over and seal. Brush with milk or melted butter, place on a baking sheet and bake in a hot oven for 10-12 minutes. Hand piping hot with the soup, which you can either serve as it is, vegetables and all, or strain and serve as a clear soup. Either way, a spoonful of soured cream is quite a nice addition.

Strained and allowed to go cold, with the fat removed, this can also be served chilled, cooled down by an ice cube or two.

A FAIRLY PLAIN PAELLA

According to Tinuca Lasala, a Spanish cookery teacher I met in Madrid, an authentic Valencian *paella* is not a multi-coloured mixture of fish, shellfish, chicken and sausage, decorated with strips of pimiento to look like the Spanish flag. It is a rather plain dish, with a main ingredient of rabbit or chicken, to which in season might be added a handful of snails. For this recipe I use chicken and rabbit. You could use one or the other. It is important to use a wide shallow pan so that all the ingredients come into equal contact with the heat.

SERVES 6-8

¼ pt/140 ml extra virgin olive oil
pinch of salt
2 lb/900 g chicken breasts and thighs, each chopped into two or three
1 lb/455 g rabbit joints (from the back and legs)

½ lb/230 g fresh green beans, blanched
¼ lb/110 g ripe fresh tomatoes, peeled, seeded and chopped (or the equivalent in canned tomatoes)
2 cloves of garlic, peeled and finely chopped

½ tsp mild paprika
2 pt/1.15 l water
1 lb/455 g cooked or canned lima beans or flageolets
good pinch of powdered saffron
1 lb/455 g Valencia or Arborio rice

321

*H*EAT the olive oil in a large sauté or paella pan, put in a pinch of salt and the pieces of meat. Cook over a steady heat until the meat is golden brown. Then add the green beans, tomatoes and garlic. Cook for a few minutes more then stir in the paprika, water, lima beans and saffron. Bring to the boil and allow the pan to simmer for about 40 minutes.

Raise the heat, stir in the rice and cook for 10 minutes. Lower the heat and cook until the rice is tender, about 20-25 minutes in all. Remove from the heat, cover loosely and let the *paella* stand in a warm place for 10 minutes before serving.

COUSCOUS ROYALE

In the same way that Indian restaurants are now part of British tradition for eating out, so are North African restaurants in France. *Couscous royale* is one of our favourite things to order at an outdoor table in Paris in the summer.
This is a perfect summer dinner party meal, for the meat can be cooked on the barbecue. On the other hand, the robust and spicy vegetable stew which accompanies the meat makes it entirely suitable as a winter dish too.

SERVES 6-8

4 chicken joints
1 lb/455 g boned shoulder or
*   fillet of lamb*
olive oil, lemon juice and fresh
*   coriander leaves (optional)*
1 lb/455 g couscous
4 spicy sausages
For the vegetable stew:
2 tbsp olive oil
2 onions, peeled
½ tsp cardamom seeds

1 tsp crushed coriander seeds
1 tsp cumin seeds
2 carrots, peeled
4 small turnips, peeled
½ lb/230 g chickpeas, soaked
*   and cooked or from a tin*
1 pt/570 ml stock (see
*   p. 344)*
1 lb/455 g courgettes
celery, leeks, green peppers
*   (some or all of these in a*
*   small quantity)*

1 lb/455 g fresh tomatoes, or
*   1 large can (approx*
*   14 oz//400 g)*
1 tsp hot paprika or cayenne
*   or ½ tsp harissa*
salt and pepper to taste
fresh coriander leaves (if
*   available)*
To serve:
harissa or other hot pepper
*   sauce*

322

*F*IRST prepare the vegetable stew. Have all your vegetables peeled or trimmed and chopped or sliced. Heat the oil in a heavy-bottomed pan that will cook slowly on top of the stove and is of the right size to hold a steamer basket in which you can cook the *couscous*. When the oil is hot, put in the onions and spices and stir until the onion begins to change colour, but do not let it burn. Add the carrots and turnips, then the chickpeas. Add half the stock. Bring to the boil and add the courgettes, other vegetables and tomatoes. Cook the vegetables for about 45 minutes or until tender.

Season to taste and add the roughly chopped coriander leaves if you have them.

While this is cooking, you can prepare the meat and the *couscous*. Season the meats, letting them marinate for a while in olive oil, lemon juice and coriander if you like. Cut the lamb into chunks and thread them on to four skewers.

Empty the *couscous* into a dish and moisten with a few tablespoons of lukewarm water. Allow to swell for 10 minutes. Break up any lumps gently with your fingers. Moisten once more and allow to stand for a further 10 minutes. Line a steamer or a meatal colander with a damp cloth, pour in the couscous and set the steamer over the pot of vegetables that you already have simmering away gently on the stove. When the steam has penetrated the *couscous* and it feels hot to your fingers, it is done. Empty it on to a warm platter and toss in oil or butter.

While the *couscous* is gently steaming, this is the time to cook the meats. Heat the grill. Place the chicken and the sausages on the grill rack and cook under a high heat, turning it down after a few minutes. Put the lamb skewers on last as they will not take as long to cook. The length of time for grilling all these will depend on the thickness of the sausages and the chicken joints, and whether you grill breasts or thighs etc; the latter require longer cooking time.

When done, serve the meats on a separate flat dish or tray. Each guest helps him or herself to some *couscous*, some meat and some vegetable stew, eating them with a little hot sauce served separately. You can also serve warm pitta bread with this.

Instead of three different meats, you could, if you wanted, serve only grilled chicken or lamb kebabs, or meatballs, or spicy sausages.

SATAY

Of Indonesian origin, this is a favourite dish in oriental restaurants. It is not difficult to make at home and makes a very good first course at an informal dinner. *Satays* can be grilled or barbecued and thus are suitable for all seasons. They can also be served as finger-food at a buffet or drinks party.
Use lamb, beef, chicken or a mixture of all three, as suggested here.
The long (about 8 in/20.5 cm) thin bamboo skewers are available in most oriental food shops and should be soaked in water for 30 minutes before using to ensure that they will not burn in the direct heat.

MAKES 40 SKEWERS

½ lb/230 g lean lamb fillet
½ lb/230 g lean beef chuck,
    flank or skirt
2 chicken breasts, off the bone
For the marinade:
3 fl oz/85 ml coconut milk
    (see p. 227)
1 tbsp dark muscovado sugar
1 tbsp medium curry powder
1 tsp ground turmeric

1 tsp anchovy paste or essence
pinch of ground cinnamon
For the satay sauce:
2 tbsp groundnut oil
1 mild onion or 3 shallots,
    peeled and finely chopped
2 cloves of garlic, peeled and
    crushed
1 in/2.5 cm piece of lemon
    grass, finely chopped, or
    1 tsp grated lemon zest

1 tsp curry paste
3 oz/85 g crunchy peanut
    butter
2 tsp anchovy paste or essence
1 tbsp dark muscovado sugar
1 tbsp lime juice
4 fl oz/115 ml coconut milk
finely chopped fresh chilli to
    taste
salt to taste

*T*o enable the meat to be thinly sliced, partially freeze it first, then prepare slices that are about 4-5 in/10-12.5 cm long and 1 in/2.5 cm wide. Thread the meat on to the damp skewers and place in a dish. Mix the marinade ingredients, pour over the meat and leave for an hour.

To make the *satay* sauce, heat the oil in a small frying pan and lightly fry the onion, garlic, lemon grass and curry for 3 or 4 minutes without browning. Add the remaining ingredients and simmer for 10-15 minutes to thoroughly blend the flavours and thicken the sauce.

Have the grill or barbecue very hot and grill the skewered meat for a minute or two on each side.

Serve hot with the *satay* sauce.

POT-AU-FEU

Like the Italian *bollito misto* and the Iberian *cocido*, the beauty of this classic French dish lies in the variety of meats and vegetables used and, above all, in their quality.

It is the sort of order the butchers love to get.

But this is not a dish for a foursome. Treat it rather as a very special occasion dish, say Christmas lunch for eight or ten, or dinner on New Year's Eve. The ingredients can be varied since there is no single version of *pot-au-feu*. It usually has two or three cuts of beef (left in one piece) and perhaps some veal. I like to put in a pig's trotter for the richness it gives to the stock. In Albi, where I lived for a year, they use goose fat as well as adding white beans and cabbage. A lighter version can be made in the spring and summer, not with root vegetables but with green vegetables such as courgettes, small squash, green beans, peas and broad beans as well as tomatoes. The traditional carrots, onions, celery and leeks should still be used for the stock, however.

Finally, as will be obvious from the foregoing, a *very* large cooking pot - one that holds about 25 pt/15 l for a *pot-au-feu* such as this version – is required.

SERVES 8-10

2 lb/900 g shin of beef
2 lb/900 g rolled short rib of beef
2 lb/900 g oxtail, cut into 6-8 pieces
1 pig's trotter, split down the middle
2 lb/900 g shin of veal, sawn into pieces as for osso buco
For the broth:
6 pt/3.45 l water
3 small onions, peeled
4 cloves, stuck into one of the onions

2-3 cloves of garlic, unpeeled
1 celery stalk, trimmed
handful of parsley stalks
1 leek, trimmed, split lengthways and rinsed
2 carrots, split lengthways
1 tbsp sea-salt
2 tsp peppercorns
2 bay leaves
For the vegetables:
1½ lb/680 g new potatoes
6 sun-dried tomato halves

4 carrots, split in two (or 8 small ones)
8 small purple and white turnips (navets)
8 baby artichokes, trimmed
8 baby leeks, trimmed
½ lb/230 g green beans
4 courgettes
¼ lb/110 g mangetouts, shelled peas or runner beans
¼ lb/110 g asparagus tips

*B*RING the water to the boil and put in the various pieces of beef and the pig's trotter. When the water comes back to the boil, remove the scum. Put all the flavouring ingredients for the broth in with the meat, partially cover and turn down to the merest simmer. Cook gently for about 3 hours. After 1½ hours add the veal, bring back to the boil, skim and return to a simmer.

Meanwhile, prepare the vegetables. Use a mixture of the following, as available. The potatoes are cooked separately, either in water or in some of the broth, about 20 minutes before dishing up. About 20-30 minutes before the end of cooking time, add the dried tomatoes, carrots, turnips and artichokes to the pot. Ten minutes later add the leeks, beans and courgettes, and then, five minutes before you remove the pot from the heat, add the mangetouts and asparagus.

Remove the freshly cooked vegetables from the pot and transfer them to a large shallow oval serving dish, keeping each vegetable separate if possible. Don't forget the potatoes. Carefully remove the meat and arrange it in the centre of the dish.

Remove and discard the large *bouquet garni* of vegetables and the bay leaves. Skim any grease from the surface of the broth and pour it through a very fine sieve into a jug. Ladle some of it over the *pot-au-feu* before serving. The rest will make an excellent base for soup, but will be less successful for a reduced sauce because it already contains salt.

Serve the *pot-au-feu* with different kinds of mustard, gherkins, dill pickles and spiced pickled fruit, a bowl of coarse salt, home-made tomato sauce, and a jug of vinaigrette or a bottle of extra virgin olive oil.

BAECKENOFFA

This is a marvellous party dish: simple preparation a few hours in advance, and it looks after itself in a slow oven. Literally, its name means baker's oven casserole. Its origins are entirely practical. Monday was traditionally wash-day in Alsace and no-one had time to cook. On Sunday evening various meats were packed into a pot with potatoes and onions, a bottle of local wine poured over the top and the casserole sealed with flour and water luting paste. It was baked next day in the baker's oven after he had done the morning baking and it was ready by lunchtime. This recipe is based on a marvellous version we ate at the Caveau d'Eguisheim with Marc Beyer, head of Léon Beyer, one of the Grandes Maisons d'Alsace, growers of the best wine of the region.

SERVES 6-8

1 lb/455 g boneless shoulder of pork
1 lb/455 g boneless shoulder of lamb
1 lb/455 g blade steak or boneless shin of beef
1 chopped pig's trotter (optional)

1 bay leaf
12 black peppercorns
pinch of salt
1 tbsp chopped parsley
1 bottle (75 cl) Alsace Riesling or Sylvaner
1 oz/30 g butter or lard

1 lb/455 g onions, peeled and sliced
2 leeks, trimmed and sliced
2 lb/900 g potatoes, peeled and sliced
flour and water paste (for sealing the casserole)

TRIM any external fat and gristle from the meat and put it in a large bowl. Add the pig's trotter, seasonings and herbs, and pour on the wine. Cover and marinate overnight.

Next day peel and slice the vegetables and grease a large, lidded casserole.

Remove the meat from the marinade. Place a layer of onions and leeks on the bottom of the casserole, then a layer of potatoes followed by a layer of meat. Repeat the process and top with a final layer of potatoes. Pour on the marinade. Cover with the lid and seal the join with a firm paste of flour and water mixed to the right consistency.

Bake in the centre of a moderate oven, 180°C/350°F, gas mark 4 for 4 hours.

Remove from the oven, break the seal at the table and serve from the pot.

CASSOULET

Lamb, mutton, pork, sausage, duck and goose all have a
role to play in *cassoulet*. Not all in the same one of course.
It depends on whether you are in Toulouse, Carcassonne,
Castelnaudary or one of the small villages of the Bas
Languedoc. With so many regional variations, I am sure
no-one will be offended by my version, which I like to
cook in a clay pot. It's a particularly good dish to know
about if you also like to serve duck breasts, since this uses
up the legs and the carcase for stock. Soissons beans are
the ones traditionally used, but you can substitute other
dried white beans such as haricots or *cannelini* beans.

SERVES 8-10

4 duck legs
8 best end of lamb chops
1 lb/455 g Toulouse sausage
2 onions, peeled and sliced
2 celery stalks, trimmed and
    sliced
garlic cloves to taste, peeled and
    sliced
1½ lb/680 g haricot or Soissons
    beans, dry weight, soaked for
    several hours or overnight

salt
pepper
large can of plum tomatoes (about
    14 oz/400 g)
2 bay leaves
1½ pt/850 ml duck stock (see
    p. 344)
4 oz/110 g soft fresh breadcrumbs

Soak the clay pot in cold water for 15
muinutes. Trim any excess fat from
the duck and lamb. Cut the duck legs in
half and the sausage into 2 in/5 cm
lengths. Layer the beans, meat and
vegetables into the clay pot, lightly seasoning each layer. Rub the tomatoes
through a sieve into the pot, put in the
bay leaves and pour on the stock.

Cover the *cassoulet* and cook for 2½
hours at 160°C/325°F, gas mark 3, remove from the oven and stir. Sprinkle
the breadcrumbs on top and return the
cassoulet to the oven at a somewhat
higher temperature, 200°C/400°F, gas
mark 6, until the topping is crisp and
golden brown. Serve immediately, from
the pot.

Traditionally three crusts of breadcrumbs are allowed to form on top, the
first two being stirred back into the *cassoulet*.

COZIDO A PORTUGUESA

This is based on the Estremadura version described by
Maria de Lourdes Modesto, but similar meat and vegetable
stews are found all over Portugal. Use spring greens in
place of the long-legged *couve tronchuda* or *galega*
Portuguese cabbage. White pudding, the rather bland
sausage found here, is a better substitute for *farinheira*, a
bread sausage bound and flavoured with smoked bacon
fat, than the altogether too meaty French *boudin blanc*.
Pigs' ears and tails also find their way into the authentic
version.

SERVES 8

2 lb/900 g flank, blade or
   shin of beef
2 pig's trotters, split down the
   middle and chopped in two
   or three pieces
1/2 lb/230 g bacon, in a piece
1/2-3/4 lb/230-340 g black
   pudding
1/2-3/4 lb/230-340 g white
   pudding

1/2 lb/230 g chourico, or other
   spicy sausage
4 carrots, peeled and halved
2 small turnips, peeled and
   halved
1 lb/455 g spring greens,
   washed and roughly
   shredded
1 lb/455 g kale, washed and
   roughly shredded

1 lb/455 g potatoes, peeled
   and halved
1/2 lb/230 g butter beans,
   soaked and parboiled
1 lb/455 g rice
To serve:
1/2 lb/230 g crusty diced
   bread
sprigs of fresh mint
salt and pepper

*P*UT the beef, trotters and bacon in a large pan and cover them with water. Cover and simmer until almost cooked. Prick the sausages all over with a fork to stop them bursting and add them to the meat. Continue cooking until both the meat and sausages are done. Remove from the heat and keep the meat warm. Ladle out enough broth to cook the rice, which will take approximately twice its volume of liquid.

While the meat is cooking, prepare and cook the vegetables. Put the carrots and turnips on to cook first in a saucepan of water, adding the greens, kale and potatoes to them. Continue cooking the butter beans until they are tender. Drain and mix them with a little broth. Cook the rice.

To assemble the dish, put the bread in a large heated tureen. Scatter fresh mint over it and pour the broth over it. Pile the rice on to a serving dish. Garnish with slices of sausages. Cut up the meat and arrange it around the rice with heaps of the cooked vegetables.

PÂTÉ DE PÂQUES AU BIQUION

The Berry, a land-locked central province of France, is famous for its tender young lamb and its marvellous goat's cheeses, such as the Valençay and Chavignol, not to mention the crisp flowering-currant fresh wine of Sancerre. At Easter time, it also boasts this traditional pie containing pork, veal and kid goat. The puff pastry is made not only with butter but also a well-drained and not too young, say four or five days, goat's cheese. I have replaced the veal with lamb, which seems particularly appropriate for Easter. Although usually served hot, this also makes an excellent cold picnic pie. Individual pies can be made instead of a large one.

SERVES 4-6

For the pastry:
2½ oz/70 g goat's cheese (see above)
4 oz/110 g butter
10 oz/280 g flour
For the filling:
½ lb/230 g boneless hand or neck of pork
½ lb/230 g boneless shoulder or leg of kid goat

½ lb/230 g boneless shoulder of lamb
1 oz/30 g butter
1 small onion, peeled and finely chopped
2 tbsp finely chopped parsley
6 eggs
salt
pepper
freshly grated nutmeg

CRUMBLE the goat's cheese and mix it with the butter. Chill it again before making a puff pastry with the flour and butter/cheese mixture, giving it six turns in all. If you are using commercial puff pastry, roll it out, then dot with a mixture of butter and cheese, fold the pastry in three, roll it, turn, and repeat with more butter and cheese, using 1 oz/30 g butter and 1 oz/30 g goat's cheese. This will not only enrich what can sometimes be rather dull pastry, but will also impart the goat's cheese flavour.

Dice the meat very small and fry it in butter for 15-20 minutes. Mix in the onion, parsley and a lightly beaten egg yolk. Season lightly with the nutmeg, salt and pepper. Allow the mixture to cool. Hardboil four of the eggs and shell them.

Heat the oven to 200°C/400°F, gas mark 6. Roll out two circles of pastry, one for the base, slightly thicker than the other and about 10 in/25.5 cm in diameter. Put it on an oiled baking sheet. Pile the filling on to the base, leaving about 1 in/2.5 cm round the edges. Cut the eggs in half lengthways and arrange them, cut side down petal fashion on top of the meat, chopping any that won't fit and sprinkling amongst the meat. Beat the remaining egg with a little milk or water and brush it round the edge of the pie. Lay the second round of pastry on top, and seal it with tines of a fork. Knock up the edges. Brush the pie with beaten egg and make a slit or two in the middle for the steam to escape. Bake for 15-20 minutes, then for a further 20 minutes at 170°C/325°F, gas mark 3.

CHRISTMAS PIE

Chestnuts and cranberries turn this into a splendid dish to serve over Christmas and the New Year or for a special winter dinner. The sharp, fruity flavour of the cranberries marries well with the mild earthy flavour and velvety texture of the chestnuts. You can make the pie with one single meat, such as beef or pork, or use a mixture, as I have here. The meat can be casseroled the day before required and then the final assembly and cooking takes about three-quarters of an hour or so.

SERVES 6-8

¾ lb/340 g boneless shoulder of pork
¾ lb/340 g boneless shoulder of venison
1 lb/455 g braising beef (such as skirt, blade or chuck)
2 oz/60 g flour
1 tsp salt
½ tsp freshly ground black pepper
pinch of ground mace
2 tbsp olive oil

12 pickling or button onions, peeled
3 or 4 cloves of garlic, peeled and crushed
½ pt/280 ml dry red wine or brown ale
½ pt/280 ml beef stock (see p. 344)
1 bay leaf
3 or 4 parsley stalks
a sprig of fresh thyme

¾ lb/340 g fresh chestnuts, peeled
6 oz/170 g fresh or frozen cranberries
6 oz/170 g button mushrooms, wiped
1 oz/30 g butter
½ lb/230 g puff or flaky pastry (see p. 347)
To glaze:
egg yolk beaten in a little milk

*T*RIM the meat of any fat and gristle and cut it into 1½ in/4 cm cubes. Toss the meat in the flour seasoned with the salt, pepper and mace, and brown the pieces in the olive oil. Transfer the meat to a casserole. Fry the onions until golden brown and put them and the garlic with the meat.

Deglaze the frying pan with the wine, add the stock and bring to the boil. Pour over the meat and tuck in the herbs. Cover and simmer for 45 minutes to one hour. The dish can be cooked to this point in advance.

Put the chestnuts in one saucepan and the cranberries in another. Just cover both with water, simmer the chestnuts for 20 minutes and the cranberries for 5 minutes. Drain them and mix with the meat. Quicky fry the mushrooms in butter and mix with the meat. Heat the oven to 200°C/400°F, gas mark 6.

Transfer the mixture to an overproof pie dish.

Roll out the pastry and cover the meat, pressing the pastry at the edges to seal the pie. Lop off any overhanging pastry and use to make pastry leaves, flowers or other suitable decorations for the lid. Make a steam hole in the top and brush with the beaten egg glaze.

Bake for 20 minutes, then turn down to 180°C/350°F, gas mark 4 for 10-15 minutes. Serve hot.

GROUSE AND WILD BOAR PIE

There is something quite mediaeval in this magnificent pie. I learned how to make it in the Miller's kitchen in North Wales when I was on a cook's tour of Britain for the *Sunday Times*; writing about how people entertain in different parts of the country. David Miller had a herd of wild boar and, being an opera fan, had named them all after Wagnerian characters. This is a pie for a feast, serves 20 (and there'll still be leftovers).

332

2 grouse
½ lb/230 g wild boar loin,
  cut into strips
1 lb/455 g wild boar breast or
  shoulder (including fat)
1 lb/455 g chicken livers
3 lb/1.35 kg pork, with some
  fat (belly of pork is ideal)
2 cloves of garlic
salt and pepper
1 tbsp green peppercorns
1 tbsp pistachios (optional)
⅛ pt/70 ml Amontillado
  sherry

1 egg
3 lb/1.35 kg shortcrust pastry
  (see p. 348) or hot-water
  crust pastry (see p. 141)
For the marinade:
4 tbsp extra virgin olive oil
½ bottle of good red wine
1 tbsp juniper berries, crushed
1 tbsp fresh rosemary
salt
pepper
pinch of mace

For the stock:
grouse carcases, plus any
  other bones and game
  trimmings available
pork skin or pig's trotter
1 celery stalk
1 leek, trimmed
2 or 3 slices of peeled fresh
  ginger
watercress or parsley stalks
2 ripe tomatoes
2 pt/1.15 l water

*F*IRST mix the ingredients for the marinade. Then cut the breasts off the grouse and divide each into four strips. Add the boar loin and grouse to the marinade and leave overnight. In the meantime, make the stock. Put all the ingredients into a large saucepan, bring to the boil, skim and simmer gently for a couple of hours. Strain and put to one side.

If you are using shortcrust pastry, make it about an hour or so before making the filling and chill it, covered, until required. If, on the other hand, you are using hot-water crust pastry, the rest of the ingredients should be to hand, ready to assemble the pie before you start making the pastry, which must be used while still warm.

Heat the oven to 220°C/425°F, gas mark 7. Mince the wild boar breast or shoulder with the chicken livers, pork, garlic, seasoning, peppercorns and pistachios. Add the sherry and egg. Mix thoroughly. Drain the marinated meat well. Line a large 5-6 lb (2.7-3.6 kg) loaf tin mould or terrine with the pastry, rolled out to no more than ¼ in/0.5 cm and preferably thinner, but take care to avoid breaks. Spoon in and flatten alternate layers of mince and meat, finishing with a layer of mince. Pour in a little of the strained stock and top with a pastry crust, sealing it well. Make a hole in the centre and insert a paper roll to keep it open. Brush with beaten egg.

Bake for 45 minutes, then for a further 45 minutes at 180°C/350°F, gas mark 4. Remove from the oven and let it cool in the tin. Pour a little more stock through the hole, then let it set in the refrigerator overnight. It is important to bring the pie to room temperature before serving it. This is ideal for a buffet, or serve the pie as a starter with home-made chutney, pickled onions, fruit jelly and mustard.

Pigeon and Pork Pie: Use pigeons instead of grouse and replace the wild boar with 1½ lb/680 g pork tenderloin marinated for 3-4 days.

STEAK, KIDNEY AND OYSTER PUDDING

Just once in a while a steamed suet pudding is one of the
great all time treats. So rarely is it served now that your
guests will quite overcome their scruples about suet and
calories. In fact, properly made, suet dough can be very
light and airy, and not at all stodgy. For the quantities
below, use a 3 pt/approx 1.75 l pudding basin.

SERVES 6-8

For the filling:
12 oysters
2 lb/900 g chuck or blade
　steak
1/2 lb/230 g lamb's or calf's
　kidneys
12 pickling or button onions,
　peeled
1/4 lb/110 g button
　mushrooms, wiped clean

4 tbsp olive oil
1 oz/30 g plain flour
1/4 tsp salt
1/2 tsp freshly ground black
　pepper
1/4 tsp powdered mace
1 tbsp Worcester sauce
1/2 tsp Angostura bitters
7 fl oz/200 ml beef stock (see
　p. 344)

1 tbsp fresh chopped chives
　and parsley
For the suet crust:
1/2 lb/230 g self-raising flour
1 tsp baking powder
1/4 lb/110 g shredded suet
up to 3 1/2 fl oz/100 ml chilled
　water

*P*REPARE the filling first. Shuck the
oysters and put them into a sieve
over a bowl to collect all the liquid. Trim
off and discard the fat from the meat and
kidneys, and cut them into 1 in/2.5 cm
cubes. Fry the onions and mushrooms all
over until golden brown in half the olive
oil and remove them from the pan.

Put the flour, salt, pepper and mace in
a paper bag and shake the meat in it to
coat the pieces, a handful at a time. Fry
the meat, in batches, in the remaining oil
until nicely browned then add the sauces
and stock, scraping up any residues. Put
the onions with the meat, cover and cook
gently for 45 minutes. Add the mush-

rooms and oyster liquor and cook for
5-10 minutes more.

Remove from the heat and cool the
stew while you prepare the pastry. Sift
the flour and baking powder into a bowl
and fold in the suet with your hands.
With a knife stir in just enough water to
make a soft, pliable but not wet dough.
Quickly and lightly knead the dough on
a floured work surface. Roll out to a
12-14 in/30.5-35.5 cm diameter and cut
out a quarter to use for the lid. Grease the
pudding basin and lift the larger piece of
dough into it, shaping it to fill the basin,
pressing it into the base and around the
sides. Brush the top edge with water.

Spoon in the filling, arrange the oysters on top and scatter herbs over it. Pour in about 7-8 fl oz/200-230 ml of the cooking liquid from the meat. Roll out a lid from the remaining dough to fit the top of the basin and lay it over the filling. Pinch the edges together to seal it. Cover with a piece of greased greaseproof paper, pleated down the middle to allow for the pudding to rise, and cover with a thick piece of foil or tie a pudding cloth over it.

Place on a steamer rack in a saucepan and pour in enough boiling water to come to a quarter of the way up the basin. Cover and steam for 2 hours, adding more boiling water if there is a danger of the pan drying out. Serve from the pudding basin, which is traditionally wrapped in a folded clean white napkin.

BEEF AND PIGEON COBBLER

The first winter in our new flat, this became one of my favourite dishes to cook for friends. Not yet familiar with my kitchen, I wanted food that I could serve from its cooking pot rather than arrange on plates. A rich, meaty stew topped with a circle of golden, herby scones, it looked rustic and appetising, and the deep subtle flavours provided a perfect partner to a 1964 Château Latour that we served for some friends' 25th Wedding anniversary.

SERVES 8

3 oven-ready wood pigeons
3½ lb/1.6 kg chuck or blade
    beef steak in a piece
2 oz/60 g seasoned flour
2-3 tbsp olive oil
2 carrots, peeled and sliced
2 celery stalks, trimmed and
    sliced
1 onion, peeled and sliced
¾ pt/430 ml Guinness
freshly ground black pepper

pinch of powdered mace
sprig of thyme
1 pt/570 ml beef or game
    stock (see p. 344)
½ lb/230 g button or cup
    mushrooms, wiped clean
    (or ceps if you have them)
salt

For the scone topping:
¾ lb/340 g plain flour
6 tsp baking powder
pinch of salt
1 tsp dried rubbed thyme
3 oz/85 g butter
plain yoghurt or buttermilk to
    mix

REMOVE the breasts from the pigeons and cut each into three or four pieces. Chop the carcases, brown them in a heavy saucepan, cover with water and simmer gently to make stock. Trim the meat of any visible fat and gristle and cut into 1½ in/4 cm cubes. Toss them in the seasoned flour and brown them, a batch at a time, in the olive oil. Transfer to a casserole and put the sliced celery and carrots with the meat.

Fry the onion in the same pan as the meat until just brown. Pour on the Guinness and deglaze the pan, scraping up any residues stuck to the bottom and allowing the liquid to reduce somewhat. Add pepper, mace and thyme to the casserole and pour on the Guinness and onion. Cover and simmer, or cook in the bottom half of a low oven (150°C/300°F, gas mark 2) for 3 hours or so. Top up with stock from time to time.

The meat can be prepared to this point the day before required. Transfer it to a fairly deep ovenproof dish. If you are using ceps, soak them for 30 minutes in warm water. Halve the mushrooms and put them with the cooking liquid, together with the rest of the stock. Simmer for 10 minutes, reducing the juices to about ¾ pt/430 ml rich gravy. Pour half of it on the meat.

The scone topping should be made just before required. Heat the oven to 200°C/400°F, gas mark 6. Sift the dry ingredients together. Cut in the butter and rub in lightly. Mix in enough liquid to form a soft dough. Knead lightly on a floured worktop, then roll out the dough to about ¾ in/2 cm thick and cut it into 2 in/5 cm rounds with a pastry cutter.

Arrange the scones on top around the edge of the dish in an overlapping circle and bake in the top half of the oven for 15-20 minutes. Remove from the oven and pour the rest of the hot gravy into the middle. Serve steaming hot.

PASTICCIO DI MACCHERONI

I have had wonderful pasta pies served to me in parts of
northern Italy, particularly in Bologna, and a most
memorable one in Fini, the famous Modena establishment.
These are rich, sweet and savoury dishes that have
probably changed very little since the days of the Medicis.
The first version I ever ate, however, was in Lancashire,
cooked by Arabella Lennox-Boyd, a gifted landscape
gardener and talented cook who featured in a series I
wrote for the *Sunday Times* about amateur cooks in Britain.
Arabella is Neapolitan by birth.
Here is the dish I watched her make, and then
reproduced at home with great success. Much of it – the
stock, sauces, meatballs and pastry – can be prepared in
advance. It is an unusual recipe, combining sweet pastry
and custard with savoury meatballs and tomato sauce.

SERVES 8

For the sweet pastry:
1/2 lb/230 g plain flour
pinch of salt
2 oz/60 g caster sugar
1/4 lb/110 g butter, diced
4 egg yolks
egg and milk glaze
For the rich tomato sauce:
2 onions, peeled and chopped
2 cloves of garlic, peeled and
   chopped
4 tbsp olive oil
2 large cans plum tomatoes
   (about 14 oz/400 g)
1 tsp chopped fresh oregano or
   marjoram
2 bay leaves

1 tube tomato purée, weighing
   6 oz/140 g
about 1/2 pt/280 ml beef stock
   (see p. 344)
salt
pepper
For the meatballs:
6 oz/170 g minced veal
6 oz/170 g spicy sausage
   meat or minced pork
1 egg
1 oz/30 g finely grated
   Parmesan cheese
salt
pepper
olive oil to fry

For the custard sauce:
3/4 pt/430 ml full cream milk
2 tbsp sugar
2 eggs
For the filling:
1 1/2 lb/680 g dry pasta
   (buccatini or maccheroni)
olive oil to toss pasta
tomato sauce (as above)
meatballs (as above)
1/4 lb/110 g lightly cooked
   peas
6 oz/170 g mozzarella cheese,
   diced
seasoning
custard sauce (as above)

337

*T*o make the pastry mix the dry ingredients together, make a well in the centre and put in the egg yolks and butter. Gradually mix in with your fingertips and gather together into a ball, trying not to handle it too much. You *can* use a food processor; I do. Chill the pastry for an hour.

To make the tomato sauce, fry the onions and garlic in half the olive oil until soft and translucent then add the tomatoes, herbs and bay leaves. Simmer partially covered for several hours – four or five is not too long. Meanwhile squeeze the tomato purée into a saucepan and add the rest of the olive oil. Cook until dry and almost black, but do not let it burn. Stir in the beef stock. Sieve the cooked tomatoes into the pan and cook together, reducing or adding more stock if necessary, to make about 1 pt/580 ml tomato sauce. Season to taste.

To make the meatballs, simply mix all the ingredients together and, with wet hands, roll into ½ in/1 cm balls. Fry in olive oil for 8-10 minutes. Drain and put to one side.

The custard sauce is made in the usual way by bringing the milk to the boil, stirring in the sugar and pouring it over the lightly beaten eggs. Strain in back into the saucepan and stir over the lowest heat until it begins to thicken slightly. Cover and put to one side.

To finally put the dish together, cook the pasta in plenty of boiling, salted water until barely done. Drain and toss in olive oil. Cut into 2 in/5 cm lengths if using long thick pasta such as *buccatini*. The pasta can also be prepared in advance to this stage.

Roll out the pastry carefully, bearing in mind that it is very fragile. Line a buttered and floured deep cake tin with a removable base, leaving enough pastry to make a lid.

Heat the oven to 190°C/375°F, gas mark 5. In a large bowl mix the tomato sauce, meatballs, pasta, peas, mozzarella and seasoning and spoon the mixture into the pie, moulding it to a shallow dome shape in the centre. Pour the custard sauce over it and cover with a pastry lid, decorating it as you wish. Brush with an egg and milk glaze and bake for 45 minutes or so. Allow to rest for 10 minutes before easing it out of the tin and transferring it to a warm serving plate.

TIMPANA

This traditional Maltese pasta pie, related to the Greek *pastitsio* and the Napolitan *pasticcio*, is a way of making a little meat go a long way and is a Sunday lunch favourite.

Although gas and electric cookers are now common in many kitchens in Malta and its small sister island Gozo, it is not uncommon to see women carrying containers covered with snowy white cloths walking through the villages early in the morning. They are on their way to the bakery, where, after the morning bread is done, the *timpana* will be put into the log-fired stone ovens using a long wooden paddle to be done in time for lunch. In Malta it is often served as a starter with a rabbit stew to follow. Equally, it makes a good main course served with salad.

SERVES 8-10

1 onion, peeled and chopped
1 tbsp olive oil
3 tbsp tomato purée
¼ pt/140 ml water
1 tbsp sugar
½ lb/230 g chicken livers
½ lb/230 g bacon

½ lb/230 g minced beef
½ lb/230 g minced pork
1 lb/455 g dry weight
   macaroni or buccatini
4 eggs
4 tbsp single cream
3 oz/85 g grated cheese, such
   as Parmesan or Pecorino

6 oz/170 g ricotta cheese
2 hard-boiled eggs, shelled
   and chopped
salt
pepper
1 lb/455 g puff or flaky
   pastry (see p. 347)

FRY the onion in the olive oil until soft. Add the tomato purée, water and sugar. Bring to the boil and simmer until the sauce has thickened slightly. Clean and chop the chicken livers, and chop the bacon. Stir the meats into the sauce and simmer for 15-20 minutes.

Meanwhile, cook the pasta as instructed but for 2-3 minutes less than stated on the packet. Strain and mix with the meat sauce.

In a bowl, beat the eggs and cream and mix in the cheeses and chopped boiled eggs. Season lightly.

Heat oven to 190°C/375°F, gas mark 5.

Roll out the pastry and line a greased ovenproof dish with it, leaving enough pastry for the lid. Mix the egg sauce with the meat sauce and spoon into the pastry case. Cover with the remaining pastry, decorate if you wish, pierce the top and bake for 35-40 minutes.

339

TAMALES

I was taken round the staff canteen at the Carullo supermarket headquarters in Bogota after I'd been allowed to taste all manner of exotic fruits. The cooks were preparing *tamales* for the next shift and I'd love to have stayed to eat with them.

This is a good dish to do for a party; if possible, try to get one or two helpers. Ideally the *tamales* should be wrapped in banana leaves or cornhusks. Foil or greaseproof paper will do.

SERVES 8-10

1 lb/455 g corn meal
  (polenta)
4 tbsp flour
1 tsp salt
2 tbsp olive oil
2 tbsp wine vinegar
1/2 tsp cumin seeds
chicken or beef stock to mix
  (see p. 344)
1 lb/455 g raw chicken, off
  the bone

1 lb/455 g pork spare rib
  chops
1 lb/455 g lean pork
1/2 lb/230 g belly of pork,
  rind removed
1/2 lb/230 g chipolata
  sausages
1 1/2 lb/680 g onions, peeled
  and chopped

1 lb/455 g tomatoes, peeled,
  seeded and chopped
up to 1/2 pt/280 ml stock
  mixed with wine or water
12 olives, stoned and chopped
2 oz/50 g capers
3 oz/85 g seedless raisins
3/4 lb/340 g cooked or canned
  haricot or cannellini or
  other white beans

SIFT the *polenta*, flour and salt together. Mix in the olive oil, vinegar, cumin seeds and enough stock to make a smooth paste that is firm enough to handle.

Dice the chicken, pork and sausages into small bite-size pieces. Cook in a heavy saucepan with a little of the onion and tomato for about 30 minutes. In a separate pan cook the remaining onion and tomato until soft.

Cut greaseproof paper into 8×8 in/ 30.5×20.5 cm squares. Spoon 3-4 tbsp of the corn meal paste into the centre and flatten it to about 1/2 in/1 cm. On top pile a little meat, some of the tomato and onion mixture and some olives, capers, raisins and beans. Top with some more paste and smooth top and bottom together to seal the filling inside. Carefully wrap the greaseproof paper around the *tamale* so that it is watertight. Wrap each parcel in the same way, tying if necessary. Steam for 2 hours.

The *tamales* can be served with hot sauce if you like, eaten in the fingers, when cooled a little, or with knife and fork.

You can make the same ingredients into a *Tamale Pudding or Pie* by lining a pudding basin or pie dish with part of the corn mush, packing in the filling, then covering with the rest of the corn mush. If steaming, cover with pleated foil, or brush with melted butter and bake.

MEAT LOAF

This homely dish is perfect for feeding a large crowd on a cold autumn or winter day after vigorous outdoor activity. When my mother-in-law serves it to us in Pittsburgh we eat it with mashed potatoes, bread and butter pickles and Rolling Rock or Iron City beer. Many meat loaf recipes suggest minced beef, but a mixture of minced beef and pork gives a better texture. You can also add minced veal. This version is based on my mother-in-law's recipe.

SERVES 6-8

1 onion, peeled and chopped
1 tbsp olive oil
1 lb/455 g minced lean beef
½ lb/230 g minced belly of pork
½ lb/230 g minced lean pork
½ lb/230 g minced veal

¼ lb/110 g cooked rice
1 tbsp chopped fresh thyme or marjoram or
1 tsp dried herbs
1 egg yolk

1 tbsp strong meat stock (see p. 344)
1 tbsp brandy
¼ tsp powdered mace
salt
pepper

*F*RY the onion in the olive oil until soft and turning brown. Heat the oven to 170°C/325°F, gas mark 3. Mix all the rest of the ingredients and fry a teaspoon just to check that the seasoning is right. You might want to add more herbs and spices. Pack into a wetted loaf tin or ter-rine and bake for about 1½ hours. Cover the top with foil to stop it drying out.

Gently pour off the liquid which accumulates and use as gravy. Allow the meat loaf to rest in its tin for 10-15 minutes before turning it out and slicing it ready to serve.

PIGS IN BLANKETS

Golubtsi is the real name for this warming winter dish,
another of my mother-in-law's specialities. It uses the
same mixture as the meat loaf, but instead of being packed
into a loaf tin, it is used as a stuffing for cabbage leaves,
which are then baked in a sauce of stock and tomatoes.
She tells me they freeze well, so perhaps it is worth
making them in the quantities given for the meat loaf. If
you do not have stock, you can cook the pigs in blankets
in cider or beer.

SERVES 8-10

uncooked meat loaf mixture (see
  p. 341)
2 dozen large, sound, white
  winter cabbage leaves
large can of plum tomatoes
  (about 14 oz/400 g)
1 pt/570 ml stock (see p. 344)
2 bay leaves
salt and pepper

*P*REPARE the uncooked meat mixture,
as above.

Blanch the cabbage leaves in boiling
salted water for 2 minutes and refresh
them under cold water. Cut out the thick
central rib to about half way into the leaf.
Put a cabbage leaf on the work surface,
slightly overlapping the cut part so there
is no divide. Place a couple of tablespoons of the mixture in the centre and
roll into a neat parcel, folding in the
sides as you roll. If you pack the rolls
closely into a large greased ovenproof
dish, they will not need tying round with
cotton.

Rub the tomatoes through a sieve over
the cabbage rolls. Pour on the stock and
tuck in the bay leaves. Season lightly.
Cover with foil and bake for 1½-2 hours
at 170°C/325°F, gas mark 3.

Stocks, Sauces, Stuffings and Other
Accompaniments

Stock-making

*A*FTER YEARS OF FILLING MY STOCKPOT with carrots, onions, celery, leeks and other vegetables to give the stock flavour, I learnt the error of my ways. Two cooks of my acquaintance for whom I have great respect, Angelo Lancellotti in Modena and Bruce Cost in San Francisco – the one cooking in traditional Italian style, the other following the principles of Chinese cooking – both demonstrated to me that in doing this the flavours of the meat are absorbed by the root vegetables while the vegetables' release of flavour is but a poor exchange. Now I use minimal and non-absorbent flavourings in whatever stock I make.

Another bonus has resulted from this. The carrots and other starchy vegetables used to make the stock cloudy while these days it is much clearer.

Caramelising the onion is the secret to dark stock's rich brown colour. For light stocks such as chicken, lamb and pork, follow the same method but without caramelising the onion. Whilst you can make the stock just from bones, it has a much better flavour if you include some meat as well. It is quite possible to freeze chicken carcases and make stock when you have accumulated several. Poaching chicken (see p. 206) gives a good starting broth.

If you make the stock without salt, it can be used as a base for reduced sauces as well as for soups or in casseroles. The best way to store it is to freeze it in ice cube trays after initial cooling, or to freeze it in empty cottage cheese cartons, then store the tubes or tubs in the freezer.

BEEF STOCK

5-6 lb/2.3-2.7 kg beef bones
1 lb/455 g shin beef, in a
  piece
1 onion, with the skin left on

10 pt/about 6 l cold water
1 celery stalk, including leaves
2 slices peeled fresh ginger

6 parsley stalks
2 bay leaves
sprig of fresh thyme

*C*UT the onion in half, place it on a baking sheet and bake in a very hot oven until the sugar caramelises and the skin turns dark brown.

Meanwhile put the bones, meat and water in a stock pot. Bring to the boil, reduce the heat and simmer. Skim the foam off the surface as it accumulates. Add the rest of the ingredients, including the onion. Simmer for 6 hours, skimming from time to time.

Let the stock cool, then strain it. Refrigerate until cold and scrape off all the fat. Freeze as appropriate.

PAN SAUCES

I'M not really sure how else to describe the sauces that are made with the cooking juices left over from pan frying chicken breasts, noisettes of venison or all those small, neat pieces of protein that are the perfect dinner party standby.

The method goes like this. After you have fried the meat in the minimum of oil or butter and it is cooked to your liking, transfer it to a warm plate and cover. Splash into the frying pan a small glass (about ⅙ pt/100 ml) of wine, ideally of a similar kind to that which you will serve with the meal. Over a high heat reduce the wine, at the same time scraping up any cooking residues stuck to the pan, thus deglazing it. This may in itself be enough to give you a small amount of well flavoured gravy or sauce to serve with the meat, adding to it any juices that have drained out of the meat while it is keeping warm. At this point you can also add some stock and reduce it to the desired flavour or consistency. You can thicken it with *beurre manié* (opposite) or, into the reduced sauce you can add cream as an enrichment, which you stir and swirl into the sauce one at a time with a deft wrist movement, causing the fat and liquid to emulsify into a silky sauce.

It should be noted that these are rich sauces, and that the fat in them can mask the flavour of a good piece of meat. I usually prefer just to serve the meat with its cooking juices and the deglazed pan juices, hardly reduced at all.

BEURRE MANIÉ

*T*HIS mixture of softened butter and flour is useful to know about for thickening stews and sauces. It will give a little more body to a thin sauce, so that this will slightly coat meat, for example, without thickening to a gluey texture.

One tablespoon of flour is plenty for thickening a casserole for 6-8 people. Take slightly less than the same volume of softened butter and mix the two together. Add it about 10-15 minutes before cooking time is up, which gives sufficient time for the flour to cook. The taste of raw flour in a sauce is very noticeable and very disagreeable. This can be made in larger quantities, chilled, rolled into small balls and stored until required. The smallest amount can be used to make a pan sauce more substantial if you do not want to 'mount' it with butter or thicken it with cream.

TO STABILISE YOGHURT FOR USE IN COOKING

*Y*OGHURT can replace cream in sauces and casseroles (and soups) if it is stabilised first. For 1 pt/580 ml plain yoghurt, blend 1 teaspoon cornflour with 1 tablespoon water. Mix into the yoghurt, pour into a pan and simmer for 10 minutes. Cool and refrigerate. The yoghurt will not now curdle when boiled.

BASIC BREAD DOUGH

MAKES A LOAF APPROXIMATELY 2 LB/1 KG

1 pt/570 ml hand-hot water
pinch of sugar
1 tbsp dried yeast

1¾ lb/800 g strong white
* unbleached flour*
2 tsp sea-salt

Put half the water and sugar in a bowl and sprinkle on the yeast. Let it work for 10-15 minutes until a foamy sponge of live yeast has formed on top.

Sift the flour and salt into a large bowl and make a well in the centre. Pour in the yeast liquid and mix well, gradually adding the rest of the water and mixing to a dough. Transfer to a lightly floured work top and knead for 10-15 minutes until the dough is elastic. Place in a bowl and cover with a clean damp tea-towel or put the bowl in a large polythene bag. Let the dough rise for an hour or so until doubled in size.

Scoop out on to the work-top once more, pummel out the air and knead until smooth again. Shape the dough into a loaf and place it in a floured tin or on a baking sheet. Cover once more and let it rise to prove a second time, for about 30-40 minutes.

Bake in a preheated oven at 220°C/425°F, gas mark 7 for 10 minutes, then reduce the heat to 180°C/350°F, gas mark 4 for a further 25-30 minutes. When it is cooked the loaf will sound hollow when tapped on the bottom. Place on a wire rack and cool completely before slicing.

BASIC PASTA
(and some observations)

Pasta dough can be mixed by hand or in a food processor and can be rolled out by hand or by a wringer-like machine through a pair of heavy steel rollers. The latter gives the pasta a

smoother more slippery texture of which an Italian mamma would disapprove. I describe on p. 317 how Mamma Lancellotti taught me to make pasta dough. It is a satisfying occupation, but should not be attempted in a hurry. Avoid too, if possible, making it on a humid day, as the mixture stays too soft to handle.

It is worth making pasta at home, particularly because then you can devise your own fillings for it. I also make it when I want to cut shapes, such as *pappardelle*, which are rarely available commercially. However, if I am making a meat sauce to serve with *spaghetti* I will always use an Italian durum wheat dried pasta. There are excellent Italian brands widely available, such as Agnesi and De Cecco, and much of what passes for fresh pasta is heavy, dull and unpleasant.

To make pasta at home allow a good 3 oz/100 g flour for each size-3 egg. This is enough for one generous portion as a main course. Use a mixture of strong plain flour and plain flour, or just strong flour, which has a higher protein content and is a little firmer to handle.

If you are making pasta in a food processor, simply put in the eggs and flour and process until loosely bound together. Knead by hand until smooth on a floured work surface, let it rest, covered, for 15 minutes, and roll out to the thickness of a 20p piece. The resting period is important to let the dough relax and become elastic again.

To make the dough by hand, pile the flour on to a work surface, make a well in the centre and slide in the whole eggs. Draw the flour from the edges to the centre, covering the eggs, and, working with your fingertips, gradually mix in the flour and eggs until thoroughly amalgamated. Knead the dough for 10-15 minutes, until it is smooth and satiny.

SHORTCRUST PASTRY

To line an 8-9 in/23 cm pie plate or cover a
10 in/25.5 cm one

½ lb/230 g plain flour
1 scant tsp salt

¼ lb/110 g chilled butter
approx 6 tbsp chilled water

Sift the flour and salt together in a bowl. Cut in the butter and then, with the fingertips, rub the mixture lightly together until it resembles fine breadcrumbs. Mix in enough water with a palette knife to bind the dough together. Work it into a ball. Chill it for 30 minutes if you have warm hands or are working in a warm room. Flour a worktop and roll the pastry out with a rolling pin.

Richer pastry can be made using 6 oz/ 170 g butter and slightly less water, and an even richer one with the addition of an egg yolk and even less water.

FLAKY PASTRY

½ lb/230 g plain flour
1 scant tsp salt

6 oz/170 g butter
approx 4 tbsp water

MAKE the dough as described in the previous recipe, using half the butter.

Roll the dough, after it has been chilled, into a rectangle, with the short sides top and bottom. Dot half the remaining butter over the bottom two-thirds of the dough. Fold the top third down and the bottom third over it. Press it to seal the sides. Give it a quarter-turn and roll it out again into the same shape rectangle as you started with. Fold into three as before, give it another 90° turn and roll out into a rectangle. Dot with the rest of the butter, fold the dough as before, give it a turn, roll it and continue giving it two more turns.

After all that handling, chill the block of dough for 30 minutes before finally rolling it out for use.

RISOTTO

2 shallots, peeled and finely
    chopped
2 oz/60 g butter
12 oz/340 g arborio rice

2-2½ pt/1.15-1.45 l chicken
    or veal stock

salt
pepper
2 oz/60 g freshly grated
    Parmesan cheese

GENTLY fry the shallots in half the butter until transparent, then stir in the rice until it is well coated. Bring the stock to the boil and pour on ¼ pt/140 ml, stirring until it has been absorbed. Add the the same quantity again and continue stirring. Proceed in this way until most of the stock has been used and the rice is becoming tender. Season after about 20 minutes. You may not need all the stock by the time the rice has reached the consistency you like. I prefer my risotto really quite creamy, while others aim for a slight bite in the centre of the grain. Stir in the remaining butter and sprinkle on the cheese. Serve immediately.

BUTTERED RICE

A useful accompaniment to casseroles because it is cooked
in the oven too. Measure the rice and liquid by volume.

1 oz/30 g butter
2 breakfast cups of rice

4 breakfast cups of water
½ tsp salt

MELT the butter in a heavy casserole
and stir in the rice until each grain is
covered. Add the water and salt. Bring the
pan to the boil. Cover and put in the bottom of the oven. Bake for 35-40 minutes.

The rice is also very good cooked in
olive oil instead of butter. Various spices
can be added, such as saffron, cloves, cardamoms, a cinnamon stick, juniper berries, lemon grass, star anise, bay leaves,
depending on the dish the rice is to accompany.

WILD RICE

Extremely absorbent, wild rice is, despite its cost, really
rather economical. For a serving, 1 oz/30 g is quite
sufficient. You do need to experiment with it a little to
cook it to your taste. Sometimes it is served before the
grains have burst and that is too hard for me. I like it soft
and fluffy – even then it retains plenty of 'chew' to it. Wild
rice takes even longer than brown rice to cook, anything
up to an hour.

SERVES 8

½ lb/230 g wild rice
water
½ tsp salt

349

OUR the weighed rice into a measuring jug and then into a saucepan. Measure out three times its volume in water and add this, together with the salt. Have another measure of water ready to add as necessary. Bring the rice and water to the boil, add the salt, cover with a tight-fitting lid and simmer on the lowest possible heat until the rice is done to your taste.

COCONUT RICE

A traditional accompaniment to rice and fish dishes on the Caribbean coast of Colombia, coconut rice is also extremely good with south east Asian dishes and Sri Lankan curries, since both of these use coconut. Desiccated coconut can be used in place of fresh.

SERVES 6-8

¼ lb/110 g grated coconut
¾ lb/340 g basmati or
Patna rice

pinch of salt
2 in/5 cm cinnamon stick

½ pt/280 ml coconut milk
(see p. 227) and water,
mixed together to make
twice the volume of the rice

SE a very heavy saucepan with a tight-fitting lid. Heat it slowly and sprinkle the coconut in it. Stir it as it gently toasts. Do not let it burn, only brown delicately. Stir in the rice, add the salt, cinnamon and liquid. Bring to the boil, cover with the lid, turn down to the merest simmer and cook for 20 minutes, or bake in the middle of a pre-heated oven at 180°C/350°F, gas mark 4, without stirring. When ready to serve, fork it through to separate the grains.

POLENTA

HIS is a marvellous accompaniment for any richly flavoured dish that has a dark winy sauce. You can buy quick-cook *polenta* or the regular type. In either case, it is a good idea to follow the directions on the packet.

It is important to have a large enough pan, plenty of boiling water and a strong, steady wrist. The *polenta* packet should be open and near at hand. Once the water is boiling, stir it vigorously so that it swirls round in its own momentum. Pour in the polenta in a steady stream, with one hand, and stir continuously with the other. It is crucial to stir vigorously at this stage to avoid lumps. Once the *polenta* is s smooth and bubbling away, then you can season it. Take care when stirring it, as the *polenta* can spit and stick to your skin, and boiling *polenta* burns.

Serve the *polenta* as a soft mush or pour it into an oiled tin, let it set, then slice and grill or fry it.

SKIRLIE

SERVES 4

2 oz/60 g dripping or oil
1 onion, peeled and finely
    chopped

¼ lb/110 g medium or coarse
    oatmeal

HEAT the oil in a frying pan and in it fry the onion until soft and translucent. Stir in the oatmeal, which will spit and 'skirl' to begin with in the hot fat, but it will soon absorb the fat. Cook on a low heat for about 5 minutes. The mixture will resemble crumbs, and is indeed very like the fried breadcrumbs traditionally served with game. If using the mixture as a stuffing, bind it if you like with 2-3 tablespoons water.

DUMPLINGS

SERVES 4

½ lb/230 g self raising flour
¼ lb/11 g shredded suet

1 tbsp chopped fresh herbs
    (optional)

salt
iced water

351

Put the dry ingredients in a bowl and stir together. Mix in enough water to form a soft dough. Roll out into a rope about an inch or so in diameter and cut off one inch pieces.

Drop the dumplings into soup or stew and cook for the last 20 minutes before serving. Alternatively drop them into boiling water and poach until they rise to the surface. Drain and serve.

MASHED POTATOES

SERVES 4-6

2 lb/900 g maincrop potatoes, peeled
⅛ pt/70 ml warmed milk

⅛ pt/70 ml olive oil or meat stock (see p. 344)
salt
pepper

Put the potatoes in a large pan of cold water. Bring to the boil, cover and simmer until the potatoes give no resistance when pierced with the vegetable knife. Drain and return them to the pan.

Mash roughly and then pour in the milk. Mash until smooth, gradually adding the olive oil or stock. Add salt and pepper to taste. More butter or olive oil can be stirred in if you wish.

GRATIN OF POTATOES

This is one of my favourite accompaniments to rather plain meat dishes, such as roasts or pot roasts. It is also excellent with grilled meat, but I would only cook it if I had the oven on for something else.
Use waxy rather than floury potatoes; Wilja, Maris Peer and Spunta, not King Edward's or Maris Piper. New potatoes such as La Ratte can also be used and Pink Fir Apple potatoes, if you can get them, are probably the best of all.

½ lb/230 g potatoes per person
2-4 tbsp butter

PEEL and slice the potatoes quite thinly. Butter an overproof dish and layer the potatoes, lightly seasoning each layer and dotting with melted butter. Cover with foil or greaseproof paper and bake in the oven, at about 180°C/350°F, gas mark 4 for an hour or so. The butter and steam together will provide enough moisture for the potatoes to cook but there are other variations on this recipe. Stock, milk or cream can be poured in before you bake it, and grated cheese sprinkled on top for the last 10 minutes or so.

GAME CHIPS

REALLY the same thing as potato crisps, these are even nicer when done with other root vegetables, such as celeriac and parsnip. You will be surprised at how good carrot crisps are. Here is the version using potatoes.

Peel and rinse old potatoes. Cut into the thinnest rounds and soak in cold water for 20 minutes. Dry thoroughly.

Using a wok or deep saucepan, pour in sunflower or groundnut oil to a depth of 3-4 in/7.5-10 cm and heat it to about 190°C/385°F. Fry the chips – not too many at a time – for about 3 minutes, until golden brown and crisp. Drain on kitchen towels and serve immediately.

BREAD SAUCE

A traditional accompaniment to roast chicken and game
birds, this is much nicer than it sounds. Its origins
probably are in the Middle Ages, when soft breadcrumbs
were used as a thickening agent.

MAKES 1 PT/580 ML

1 small onion	*1 pt/570 ml full-cream milk*	*1 oz/30 g butter*
6 cloves	*¼ lb/110 g fresh soft white*	*salt and pepper*
1 bay leaf	*breadcrumbs*	*pinch of freshly grated nutmeg*

S TICK the onion with cloves and put it
and the bay leaf in a saucepan with
the milk. Bring to the boil, remove from
the heat, cover and infuse for 20-30
minutes.

Stir in the breadcrumbs and butter and
cook gently for 15 minutes. Remove the
onion and the bay leaf and season to
taste. I quite like a pinch of nutmeg in
this too.

FRIED BREADCRUMBS

A traditional English accompaniment to roast game birds,
fried breadcrumbs can also be served with roast chicken.

SERVES 4-6

1 oz/30 g unsalted butter
¼ lb/110 g fresh soft white
breadcrumbs

M ELT the butter over a moderate
heat. Stir in the breadcrumbs and

fry, stirring frequently, to a uniform
golden-brown crispness.

POULTRY STUFFING

I'm not at all keen on chestnut or sausage stuffing, but it's hard to beat this rather plain bread stuffing. I might sometimes dress this up with some chopped chicken liver, dried apricots or almonds. It is best made with day-old bread that has been left out to dry.

MAKES 6-8 SERVINGS

10 slices bread
¼ pt/140 ml milk
1 onion, peeled and finely chopped
2 celery stalks, finely chopped
2 cloves
1 tbsp finely chopped fresh parsley

1-2 tsp finely chopped fresh tarragon, chervil, thyme, chives or other herbs, depending on taste and availability
salt
pepper
2 tbsp lightly beaten egg

*T*EAR the bread into tiny pieces. Put the milk, onion, celery and cloves in a saucepan and simmer for 8-10 minutes. Strain, keeping the milk and vegetables separate. Discard the cloves.

Mix the bread, herbs and vegetables and season lightly. Stir in the egg and enough milk to bind together. Use for stuffing the neck end of a turkey or small birds only (see p. 33), or bake in an ovenproof dish.

ROOT PURÉE

Even swedes benefit from this treatment and make a most acceptable accompaniment to roast and braised dishes. My favourite combination is potatoes and celeriac, but be inventive with parsnips, kohlrabi, carrots and turnips, plus varying spices and herbs. A few, or a lot, of garlic cloves boiled with the roots certainly helps. Left-overs can be used to thicken game broth.

1 large head of celeriac
½ lb/230 g old potatoes
6 cloves of garlic (optional)
salt

*P*EEL the celeriac, cut into chunks, and drop into a pan of slightly acidulated water. Peel and cut the potatoes. Add them and the peeled garlic cloves to the pan. Drain and put in fresh water and a little salt. Bring to the boil and simmer until the vegetables are tender. Drain and mash with a potato masher. The mixture can be enriched with milk, cream, butter or olive oil. Some grated nutmeg and freshly ground black pepper provide sufficient seasoning, although ground cardamom seeds make a good alternative.

GRAIN MUSTARD SAUCE

Based on *sauce meldoise*, which uses *moutarde de Meaux*, this is a simple, agreeable sauce to serve with grilled steaks, roasts and even poached beef. It will keep for a few days in the refrigerator but takes so little time to make from scratch (barely 10 minutes) that it is hardly worth storing.

SERVES 6

2 tbsp grain mustard
½ pt/280 ml crème fraîche or
soured cream
½ tsp potato flour or cornflour

*M*IX the mustard and cream in a small saucepan and bring it slowly to the boil. Slake the flour with a little water and stir it into the mixture in the saucepan. Let it come back to the boil briefly then serve in a heated sauceboat.

CHUTNEY AND PICKLES

HOME-MADE chutney is very good with slices of cold left-over roast. It is easy to make, is excellent for presents and can be made of almost any fruit or vegetable, from the windfall apple to the mango. So it is also a good way of using up gluts and making the most of fruit that fails to ripen at the end of the season.

Pickles are not the same thing at all. Here the vegetable is blanched and put in a jar with spiced vinegar, so that the end result is crunchy and light rather than thick and jammy. A variety of pickles can be made throughout the season: small cucumbers, samphire, wild mushrooms, patty pan squashes, courgettes and, of course, all the baby vegetables. These are most attractive when bottled together. I use the same method for pickling peaches and pears, but usually give the fruit a little longer than a mere blanching and make the liquid into more of a syrup.

For both pickles and chutneys much boiling of vinegar is involved. The smell will get in your hair, in your clothes and all over the house. Try to choose a day when you can all the windows open.

PLUM CHUTNEY

This is a mild fruity chutney. If plums are in short supply,
use half apples, half plums.

2-3 lb/900 g-1.35 kg plums
1 lb /455 g sugar
1 oz/30 g salt
½ oz/15 g dry ginger or 1 heaped tbsp freshly grated ginger

1 tbsp ground cinnamon
1 tbsp allspice

4 cloves
seeds of 6 cardamom pods
1 tbsp mustard seed, lightly crushed
1 pt/570 ml strong wine vinegar or distilled vinegar

STONE and quarter the plums. Put the rest of the ingredients in a saucepan, bring to the boil and add the plums. Simmer until the plums are tender and continue simmering until the mixture begins to thicken, which will take about 45 minutes. Put in hot clean jam jars, cover and label.

357

PICKLED BABY VEGETABLES

2 lb/900 g mixed whole baby
    vegetables
For the spiced vinegar:
1½ pt/850 ml strong wine
    vinegar or distilled vinegar

¾ lb/340 g sugar
2 in/5 cm cinnamon stick
6 cloves

6 cardamom pods, crushed
6 allspice berries
12 peppercorns
1 in/2.5 cm piece of fresh
    ginger, peeled and sliced

*B*RING all the ingredients for the spiced vinegar to the boil, simmer for five minutes, then remove from the heat and allow to cool.

Drop the vegetables into lightly salted boiling water. Bring back to the boil for 30 seconds, then drain and rinse under cold water.

Pack the vegetables into preserving jars, pour on the cold vinegar, seal and leave for fortnight before using.

The pickling spices can be varied to your taste. I prefer sweet fragrant pickles. Others might prefer hot aromatic ones, in which case a dried chilli or two might be added, together with cumin and coriander seeds. Crushed mustard seeds, dill seed and turmeric are also favourite ingredients for flavouring and colouring pickles.

FRESH HERB SAMBOLS

*D*URING my travels in Sri Lanka I came across an idea which adapts readily to the Western table, especially with roast meats, grills and barbecues. Sambols are relishes or accompaniments and are made at the last minute in order to keep their fresh colour and flavour.

Green chillis, grated coconut, lime juice, salt and a pinch of sugar are usually the common ingredients, but then a variety of herbs, spices and green leaves can be added: mint, watercress, young spinach, basil, sorrel, rocket, salad burnet or purslane would all be good.

MINT SAMBOL

I have firmly adopted this mint sambol in preference to mint sauce with roast lamb. The simplest version has no chillis.

SERVES 4

1 tbsp finely chopped onion
3 cloves of garlic, peeled and
   crushed
2 tbsp grated coconut (lightly
   moistened dessicated coconut
   can be used)

8 black peppercorns
1 tsp sea-salt
2 oz/60 g mint leaves, washed
   and dried
lime juice

L IGHTLY roast the onion, garlic and coconut in a dry frying pan until the coconut begins to turn colour.

Grind the peppercorns, salt and mint in a mortar or food processor. Add the roasted ingre dients and enough lime juice to work into a paste.

Another version adds sugar and green chillis to the mixture.

PRESERVED LEMONS

Lovely with spicy food such as couscous and curries, a small piece of preserved lemon, finely chopped, will also add a depth of flavour to a chicken casserole, or indeed to the basic poultry stuffing recipe on p. 355. The method is from Claudia Roden. I have found it a particularly useful way of dealing with lemons left in the fruit bowl just before going away on a long trip. I slice the lemons, freeze them and deal with them on my return. Freezing and thawing softens them.

6-8 lemons
4 tbsp sea-salt
6 cardamom pods

6 cloves
2-3 in/5-7.5 cm cinnamon stick
sunflower oil

SCRUB the lemons well unless you know they are unsprayed organic lemons. Slice or cut into wedges and layer in a sieve, sprinkled with salt. Let them drain for 24 hours or so.

Pack the lemons into the jar. Crush the cardamom pods and tuck these in the jar with the rest of the spices. Cover with oil, seal and leave for 3-4 weeks before using.

SPICED SHALLOT AND KUMQUAT PRESERVE

MAKES ABOUT 2 LB/900 G

³/4 lb/340 g kumquats
1¹/2 lb/680 g shallots or mild
    onions, peeled and chopped
1 oz/30 g butter
2 tbsp sunflower oil

6 allspice berries
2 cloves
1 cinnamon stick, about 2
    in/5 cm long

6 juniper berries, crushed
2 lb/900 g Demerara sugar
1 pt/570 ml distilled malt
    vinegar

QUARTER the kumquats, remove the pips and put them in a saucepan just covered with water. Simmer gently until the skin is tender.

Meanwhile, in a large shallow pan such as a *sauteuse*, sweat the onions in the butter and oil until transparent and soft, then let them gradually caramelise – but do not let them burn. Add the kumquats and their cooking liquid to the onions together with the spices, which should be wrapped in a piece of muslin for easy retrieval. (If you do not have muslin, use a piece of coffee filter paper and staple the little parcel closed.)

Stir in the sugar and vinegar. Heat gently until the sugar has dissolved and then boil rapidly until the mixture thickens. Pot in clean, dry, warm jam jars, cover with wax discs and seal. Label clearly with the contents. This will keep like a chutney.

Fruit Jellies

I LIKE to extend the repertoire of these classic accompaniments to roast meats beyond cranberry jelly with turkey and redcurrant jelly with lamb. I use apples, pears, quinces, rosehips, crabapples, elderberries and all the soft fruit including blueberries, blackberries and cranberries. Sometimes I use them in combinations as I find them in the fruit bowl, and add spices to liven them up. A clear pink apple and pear jelly in which cardamoms and a cinnamon stick have been infused is very good with roast chicken. And using apple, quince or gooseberry as a base, since these have the set-inducing pectin, I make herb and tea-flavoured jellies too.

The same principle is followed throughout. First the fruit is cooked in water until soft, sometimes with a flavouring such as a herb or spice, as with gooseberry and elderflower jelly for example. Next the fruit pulp is allowed to strain through a jelly bag or muslin. This is the important stage. It must not be hurried by squeezing as this will cause the liquid to become cloudy. Finally the clear liquid is cooked with any spices or herbs and, usually, an equal volume of sugar until setting point is reached and the mixture potted in small clean jars which have been preheated in the oven. This prevents the glass from cracking when the hot syrup is poured into it.

MINT AND ELDERBERRY JELLY

MAKES ABOUT 5 LB/2.3 KG

1 lb/455 g cooking apples
3 lb/1.35 kg elderberries
(prepared weight)

2 oz/60 g fresh mint
3 pt/1.7 l water
sugar

C HOP the apples – peel, core and all – and put them in a large saucepan, together with the elderberries, stripped from their stalks, half the mint and the water. Cook until the fruit is tender, mashing to extract as much juice and flavour as possible. Suspend a jelly bag or large scalded muslin cloth over a bowl and ladle in the fruit pulp. Let it drip through overnight.

Measure out the juice and put it in a saucepan. Measure an equal volume of sugar, allowing 1 lb/455 g to 1 pt/570 ml juice. Add the rest of the mint. Cook gently until the sugar has dissolved, then bring to a rapid boil until setting point is reached.

Pour into the prepared jars, cover with wax discs and cellophane covers, label with date and contents.

Flavoured Oils and Vinegars

It is very easy to make up a whole range of oils and vinegars variously flavoured with herbs, spices, fruit and even flowers, for use in salad dressings, marinades and for cooking.

Barbecue Oil

*I*NFUSE a few cracked olives, bruised garlic cloves, sprigs of rosemary, bay leaves and thyme in a bottle of extra virgin olive oil for a few days, and use to marinate meat for the barbecue as well as brushing on the meat as it grills. Do not keep it for more than the very few weeks of the barbecue season as the garlic will turn it rancid. (Alternatively, leave out the garlic.)

Chilli Oil

*E*XCELLENT for adding a touch of heat, for example when frying meat or vegetables in preparation for a curry. Push two or three dried chillis into a bottle of olive or sunflower oil. The oil will get hotter and hotter with age.

Spiced Oil

*R*EPLACE the chillis with crushed cardamoms, a small cinnamon stick, some cloves and coriander seeds to make an oil for using in marinades. This will keep as long as the oil keeps.

Spiced Vinegar

*M*AKE in exactly the same way as the spiced oil. You can make hot spiced vinegar using chillies and mustard seed; aromatic spiced vinegar using ginger, coriander, cumin seeds and cardamom; and mild spiced vinegar with cloves, cinnamon, cardamom and allspice.

Herb Vinegar

*M*AKE sure the herbs are clean and dry. Pick on a warm, sunny day if possible once the dew has dried. Push the sprigs of herbs into a bottle of white wine vinegar and recork. Stand it on a windowsill for a week or two; the light helps to extract the essential oils from the herbs.

These will fade and can be replaced with fresh herbs before you put the vinegar back in the cupboard. Rosemary, tarragon and thyme are good flavouring herbs, used separately of course.

FLOWER VINEGARS

*T*HESE are most effective and can be made in exactly the same way as herb vinegar. Lavender, scented rose petals and clove carnations have the best scent and flavour to use in this way. Try deglazing calf's liver with a splash of lavender vinegar.

FRUIT VINEGAR

*R*ASPBERRY vinegar was a favourite with the Victorians and is very easy to make today. Blackcurrants, redcurrants, blueberries and strawberries can be used in the same way. These vinegars are particularly nice in marinades for game, pork and poultry, and are excellent for deglazing a frying pan or roasting tin.

Put a pound of sound ripe fruit in a bowl. Crush with a fork or spoon and pour on a pint of white wine vinegar. This will allow the true colour of the fruit to become the colour of the vinegar. Cover and leave it to stand for three or four days, stirring occasionally. Strain into a saucepan, boil for ten minutes and pour into sterilised bottles. Seal and label.

MELON AND AVOCADO SALSA

Here is a *salsa* for immediate use. The second, which I learned in California, is best left for a day or two to mature.

MAKES 6-8 SERVINGS

½ lb/230 g melon, diced small
juice of 1 lime
juice of ½ orange
1 ripe avocado, peeled and diced small

3 or 4 spring onions or baby leeks, trimmed and finely sliced

1 clove of garlic, peeled and crushed
2 tsp sugar
salt
pepper

*M*IX all the ingredients together, cover and allow to stand for at least 30 minutes to allow the flavours to develop.

363

PICKLED PAWPAW SALSA

MAKES 6-8 SERVINGS

1 large ripe pawpaw
3 oz/85 g seedless raisins
3 oz/85 g green pepper, seeded
   and diced
3 oz/85 g spring onions,
   trimmed and finely sliced
6 tbsp sugar

⅛ pt/70 ml white wine vinegar
1 clove of garlic, peeled and
   crushed
1 tsp freshly grated ginger
salt
pepper

*M*IX all the ingredients together. Cover and refrigerate for up to a week. Mango or pineapple salsa can be made in the same way.

SALSA ROSSA

This recipe is based on the description given to Edith Templeton and is remarkably like the recipe I was given in Reggio. The carrots are important.

1 shallot, peeled and finely
   chopped
1 tbsp olive oil
4 ripe tomatoes, peeled, seeded
   and chopped
2 carrots, peeled and finely
   chopped

½ oz/15 g butter
1 red pepper, charred, peeled,
   seeded and finely chopped
pinch of chilli powder (or more, to
   taste)
seasoning

*F*RY the shallot in the olive oil until transparent. Add the tomatoes, carrots and butter and simmer for 20 minutes or so. Add the pepper and chilli and cook for a further 10 minutes or until all the vegetables are tender and amalgamated into a thick sauce. Add seasoning to taste.

SALSA VERDE

I like to use a pestle and mortar for this one.

*1 clove of garlic, peeled and
 chopped
pinch of salt
2 tbsp finely chopped parsley
1-2 tbsp chopped capers*

*5 or 6 anchovy fillets, chopped
1 scant tsp Dijon mustard
a few drops of wine vinegar
⅛ pt/70 ml extra virgin olive oil*

P
UT the garlic and salt in the mortar and crush to a paste. Blend in the parsley, capers and anchovies, then add the mustard and wine vinegar. Blend well. Add the olive oil, sparingly at first, as if you were making mayonnaise, and mix well to incorporate it into the sauce. Continue until all the oil is used up.

OTHER INGREDIENTS IN MEAT COOKERY

*H*ERE MY MESSAGE IS SIMPLE. Do not spoil the flavour of a dish prepared with the very best meat by using inferior ingredients. It hardly seems worthwhile to spend time and effort hunting out organic free-range meat and then using eggs from intensively reared chickens, zest from lemons sprayed with chemicals and inferior, anonymous vegetable oil. Buy the best you can afford.

If you are eating meat much less frequently and on other days eating fish, vegetables, pasta and pulses, the rest of your cooking, too, will be enhanced by using high quality oils, fresh herbs and spices, unpasteurised cheeses, organic or home-grown fruit and vegetables, the very best bread you can buy or make and truly free-range eggs.

I am also particular about the spices and ingredients I keep in my store cupboard, or, as Tom calls it, hoarder's corner. This is where I squirrel away the unusual or exotic things I bring back from visits abroad: newly dried vanilla pods and foot-long cinnamon sticks from Sri Lanka; coconut vinegar from the Philippines and black rice and spices for 'pork ribs tea' from Singapore; blue corn meal, dried cranberries and garlic jelly from America; cans of *confit* and *cassoulet* from France; dried tomatoes, dried *porcini* and *mostarda di Cremona* from Italy; quince paste and olive oil from Portugal; more olive oil from Spain, from Greece, from Provence – and bags of sea-salt from the salt pans of Xwejni in Gozo, where you can still go and gather it by the handful. These ingredients are not for the sake of being fashionable, although I must confess to still having a small hoard of pink peppercorns, but because I enjoy recreating at home the flavours of a visit to a distant place. For me the smells that emanate from my kitchen when I'm cooking evoke images as powerful as any photograph, video or recording. And more than that, the ingredients are useful in all kinds of cooking. I use the coconut vinegar, for example, not only to impart an authentic flavour to Filipino dishes, but also in a salad dressing occasionally, or in a barbecue sauce.

But back to the shelves. First, a look at the staples.

Because I make my own bread, I use a lot of flour. I choose organic strong white flour, which I sometimes mix with wholemeal flour. The same flour is good for pasta and hot-water crust pastry, and can also be used for scones, pizzas, cobbler toppings and crumbles. Sauces can be thickened with it and meat dredged in it before frying. Corn-flour and potato flour also act as thickeners and are much lighter than wheat flour. They can also be used if you are cooking for someone on a gluten-free diet. Blue cornmeal, *masa harina* (yellow cornmeal) for tortillas, cornbread and polenta take up shelf-space usefully, I feel. Occasionally I buy chestnut flour in the autumn from one of the good Italian delis and use this in baking, but also to add body to game casseroles.

The rice jars contain wild rice, which is a marvellous accompaniment to game and poultry dishes; *arborio* or *vialone* for risottos; *basmati* rice for steaming or baking to serve with Indian and south east Asian curries, or with roast chicken or chicken casserole, and Thai fragrant rice to accompany oriental dishes. This rice has a slightly more glutinous quality than basmati and thus holds perfectly on a pair of chopsticks.

I keep to hand two kinds of dried pasta; one which is long and thin, such as *spaghetti, spaghettini* and *bucatini* for thin sauces; and one which is short, such as *penne rigati* and *fusilli* to hold thick chunky sauces better.

Dried beans, peas and lentils of all shapes and sizes are indispensable both for rib-sticking winter casseroles and soups such as *chilli con carne, cassoulet* and baked beans, and for serving cold in salads. Some, too, I like to serve as accompaniments: red lentils as *dhal* to go with curry, the small bluey green *lentilles du Puys* which are lovely with pork and chicken dishes, and white beans for pig's trotters and tripe.

Unrefined sugar comes in various textures and even flavours and I use most of them: demerara, light and dark muscovado and molasses. Maple syrup and honey can also be used in place of sugar in marinades, sauces and dressings. Either will alter the flavour, but agreeably so. In palm growing countries, palm sugar is used. It is known as *panela* in South America, and *jaggery* in the Indian subcontinent and Southeast Asia. It has a dark fruity flavour and is well worth buying if you come across it.

If I use salt in my cooking, I use sea-salt. To me it has real flavour and I find it is pos-sible to use less of it and get the same effect as with standard salt. I like the flaky Maldon as a table salt and then coarse sea-salt for kitchen use.

Vinegars and oils should be stored in the dark. Oils should not be kept too long, as they can turn rancid. This is an area in which I do indulge myself. A new olive oil or nut oil is quite irresistible to me and I try them all. My main standbys, however, are extra virgin olive oil for most cooking, and for marinades and salad dressings; hazelnut oil and walnut oil for marinades, dressings and to add at the last minute to sauces; toasted sasame oil for oriental dishes; grapeseed or sunflower oil if I require a neutral oil for cooking or mixing. For example, in making a mayonnaise I will use one of these oils for the bulk, and then add for flavour extra virgin olive oil, or occasionally one of the nut oils. Look for labels that state cold-pressed or first pressing. This will indicate that the oil has been extracted only by mechanical and not chemical processes. Most of the vegetable oils, both those extracted from named sources such as rape seed, soya and sunflower seeds and those simply labelled vegetable oil, will have undergone intensive processing involving petroleum based solvents, high temperatures and caustic soda. Some of the oils, such as toasted sesame oil, are not suitable for cooking because they have a low smoke point and burn easily, which causes them to degrade and give off toxins. This happens, too, when cooking oil reaches smoke point. The oil should be thrown away if that happens.

Like oils, vinegars can be used to give authentic flavour to certain dishes but I believe that it is quite in order to use a sherry vinegar in an oriental dish or a rice vinegar in a western dish. It is all a question of taste and balance. I particularly like the flavour of sherry vinegar and tend to use it more than anything else. My balsamic vinegar is given to me by my friends near Modena who, following the practice of the region, make their own in the attic using the traditional methods. It is a rich, thick precious liquid which I use occasionally as a seasoning on a cooked dish. The balsamic vinegars available commercially are not as thick, nor as old, but have almost the same flavour since they are made from the same grapes, cooked and then acetified in the same way. Only the aging process is lacking. These vinegars are excellent for deglazing the pan after cooking fillet steak or calf's liver. Cider vinegar is also a good all-purpose vinegar with a pleasant flavour.

Apart from home-made jellies, jams and chutneys, the preserves shelf might contain capers, olives in oil, dried fruits in wine and sun-dried tomatoes. We pick our capers in Gozo in the spring and early summer, and store them dry in coarse salt, in a pickling solution or in olive oil. They need rinsing before use. My father's prolific tomato plants are the source of my sun-dried tomatoes. I am very lucky in this because they are expensive to buy. Once dry, they take up little space and are extremely concentrated. I keep mine tightly packed in a kilo preserving jar, moistened with olive oil and interspersed with a few bay leaves. Half a dozen halves add as much flavour as a whole can of tomatoes.

But I also keep purée and cans of plum tomatoes for use in casseroles and sauces. These are much less expensive than the dried. The same cannot be said, sadly, for dried and bottled or canned mushrooms. I refer here only to wild mushrooms: cepes, *chanterelles* and *morels*. (There is no reason at all to give shelf-space to canned or dried cultivated mushrooms as these are so readily available.) Dried ceps (*porcini*) are worth buying in Italy. Just one or two tablespoons, finely chopped, will add an enormous amount of flavour, quite out of proportion to the amount used, to a sauce or a casserole. A jar of *morels*, a little white wine, some tarragon and cream will change a simple chicken casserole into a feast of a dish.

Angostura bitters, Worcestershire sauce, walnut ketchup, anchovy essence and Tabasco are all useful store cupboard items to add piquant touches and extra dimensions of flavour to all manner of sauces, dressings and marinades. Jars of dry grated horseradish can be used as the foundation of your own horseradish sauces. Mustards, too, are indispensable. I usually buy kilo jars of Dijon mustard in France and also keep mustard flour and mustard seeds with my spices. A coarse-grained mustard – for

368

example, the French Moutarde de Meaux or one of the English brands made in increasing numbers by high quality cottage industry food producers – is useful. *Mostarda di Cremona* or glazed whole fruit or chunks in a thick mustardy clear syrup, is an unusual ingredient with a remarkable bitter-sweet taste experience, best of all served with plain boiled meats. It is available in good delicatessens and of course in Italy where, depending on the region, you might also find another fruit and mustard speciality, the *mostarda di Venezia*, a purée of quince flavoured with white mustard.

Bite is also added to meat dishes with the introduction of peppers and chillies. I have mentioned Tabasco sauce but there is also the north African *harissa*, a thick, red hot purée usually sold in small highly decorative cans. If I do not have one in stock when I want to serve *couscous*, I make up a version using tomato purée, cayenne and a little oil. For those who like hot food, dried whole red chillis, or chilli flakes can be kept in a jar. In the same family as the chilli is the paprika, both mild and hot, used in powder form in Spain where it is called *pimentón*, and in Austro-Hungarian cookery. Peppercorns come in a number of versions, most of which I like to keep in stock. Black peppercorns I buy in fairly large quantities; they are less expensive that way and I seem to use a great deal of them. White peppercorns are useful too, particularly if you want to add the pepper flavour but not the black specks to a white dish. Green peppercorns, dried or in brine, also have their uses, as do pink peppercorns. I sometimes put a mixture of these four (dried) in the pepper mill to use at the table and in cooking. The Szechuan peppercorn is not of the same family as the vine pepper and, despite its name, is not even a pepper but the dried berry and husk of a type of ash tree. It is a pungent spice, fragrant rather than hot and with a curiously mouth-numbing quality should you bite on it. I use it in oriental cookery.

With all spices it is preferable to buy the whole rather than ground spice, in small quantities so that it does not have the chance to get stale, and to grind it when you need it. For this I use a pestle and mortar or, if I'm feeling lazy, a very carefully brushed out coffee grinder, which I then carefully clean again after use. A separate grinder specifically for spices is what the well-organised kitchen will have.

My store cupboard also contains nuts and dried fruit that I buy from a local health food shop with a fairly rapid turnover. Rancid nuts are incredibly nasty and will ruin a dish if used by mistake. This is also where I get desiccated coconut for making coconut milk (p.227). I have also used spray-dried coconut milk, which is now available. It has been processed more than desiccated coconut however.

I do not use cooking wine or cooking sherry. It is a false economy. Whatever you cook with in the way of wine and spirits should be of the same quality as you would drink. Thin sharp wine will produce a thin sharp sauce.

My refrigerator, a small one, does not reveal very much. I use full-cream and semi-skimmed milk in my cooking, and occasionally skimmed milk. Given their very differing fat contents (about 3.5%, 1.8% and 0.1-0.3% respectively), it is a matter of personal preference which you use. I tend to use full-cream milk in the pasta sauce on p.85, for the point is to enrich it. For pancake batters I might well use skimmed or semi-skimmed. The use of cream in sauces, too, is a matter of preference. I like the light acidity of *crème fraîche* and something of the same effect can be obtained using yoghurt in a sauce, although it needs to be stabilised first (see p. 345).

I like to use unpasteurised butter when I can get it, and unsalted, although I use it less frequently and in smaller quantities than some would. And I do like to use butter rather than margarine. All margarines and yellow fats, with the exception of butter, are highly processed. The hard fats, including lard, vegetable lard and margarine are hydrogenated, which means that the fat contains saturated fat. The soft margarines are only partially hydrogenated. If made from soya oil or sunflower oil, the soft margarines can be high in mono or polyunsaturates.

In choosing fresh ingredients – fruit, vegetables, herbs – I buy as often as possible as one way of making sure that I get really fresh food. My ideal is to be able to buy good quality organic, unsprayed, clean food all the time, and I try to get as close to this as possible. So if an ingredient for one of my recipes does not look fresh, I either leave it out or choose a substitute. Rather than use stale onions, use fresh shallots or the white part of leeks. If lemons are past their best, use limes or even a dash of fruit vinegar to sharpen a sauce. Try to buy untreated lemons and oranges if you wish to use the zest. If you cannot get celeriac in good condition, use the heart of a crisp, firm head of celery.

Vine-ripened tomatoes, sweet and bursting with flavour, are the ideal to aim for. Usually we have to put up with something much inferior. I find buying a tomato with flavour very much a hit and miss affair and during the winter months I rarely buy tomatoes and turn instead to my store cupboard. The huge beef tomatoes for slicing never seem to me to be worthwhile. Now the supermarkets have realised that taste is important and strains are being bred for this rather than for uniform size and ripening. Late in the summer we are sometimes lucky enough to see a few consignments of plum tomatoes from France and Italy in the shops and these are very good. Best of all, though, are home-grown tomatoes.

Good potatoes, too, are not always easy to find, although we are now seeing more and more named varieties rather than just 'reds' and 'whites'. It is important to choose the right type for a dish: floury for baking and mashing, firm and waxy for salads and gratins. Maincrop or 'old' potatoes are the large ones, available throughout the year. 'New' potatoes are the first of the crop, sometimes known as 'first earlies', and the later ones as 'second earlies'.

I use cabbage a good deal in my cooking. It is an inexpensive vegetable and because it's a native it does not have to suffer long-distance travel and is usually quite fresh. Fortunately it has a long season, too, if you make full use of its many varieties. I use red cabbage cooked slowly with spices, apple, sugar and red wine as an accompaniment to game dishes, the crisp Chinese leaves in stir-frys and salads, and similarly the crinkly Savoy cabbage. The heavy winter white cabbage is also very versatile and cooks well with spices such as juniper berries, dill seeds or cloves.

Fruit – including tropical – also plays a part in my cooking, mostly for the sharp flavour it adds. Pomegranates, passion fruit and calamansi all play this role. Obviously I can only buy them when available, and if not I will make do with something else. Ordinary lemon or lime will substitute quite well for the tiny fragrant calamansi.

Rather than use dried herbs, which I find on the whole have the colour, smell and appearance of hay (but not as much flavour!) I prefer to use fresh herbs or do without. This is particularly true of the tender herbs such as basil, chervil, chives, coriander, tarragon and even marjoram and oregano. The tougher oily herbs like rosemary and thyme can be dried and used in judicious amounts, and bay leaves are a good standby.

But my recipes are not intended to be chemical formulae. Please do not let the unavailability of a particular ingredient deter you from trying a recipe. Improvise and let it be the spur to your imagination, leading to new discoveries. That way the recipes will become your own.

Nutritional Content of Raw Meat

There is considerable difference between the leanest, trimmed meat and meat which has a certain percentage of fat.

	CALORIES PER 100 G		FAT IN G PER 100 G
Beef	lean	123	4.6
	sirloin	272	22.8
	72% lean, 28% fat		
Lamb	lean	162	8.8
	leg	240	18.7
	80% lean, 20% fat		
Pork	lean	147	7.1*
	leg	269	22.5
	73% lean, 27% fat		
Chicken	meat only	121	4.3
	meat and skin	230	17.7
Offal	pig's liver	154	2.7
	lamb's kidney	90	2.7

The original figure is based on McCance and Widdowson's The Composition of Foods *(1978). New calculations (MAFF/MLC 1990) indicate that the value is closer to 4 g fat per 100 g for the slinky slender porker now being reared.*

COMPARATIVE TABLE OF PROTEINS IN SOME COMMON FOODS

GRAMS PER 100 GRAMS *(approximate)*

Soya Beans	35 g
Beef	30 g
Cheddar Cheese	25 g
Peanuts	24 g
Herrings	22 g
Haricot Beans	21 g
Durum Wheat Pasta	12-16 g
Eggs	12 g
White Bread	8 g
White Rice	6 g
Milk	3 g

In addition to its high protein content, which is also of high quality since it contains all the essential amino acids, meat is a rich source of iron, zinc and other minerals, and some of the important B vitamins such as niacin, riboflavin and thiamin which are so important to the metabolism of other foodstuffs.

Bibliography

THIS is a list of books and other publications which have been particularly helpful to me during the course of writing this book.

Esther Aresty, *The Delectable Past*, George Allen & Unwin, 1964

Frances Bissell, *Sainsbury's Book of Food*, Webster Books/Sainsbury's, 1989

Frances Bissell, *The Pleasures of Cookery*, Chatto & Windus, 1986

Frances Bissell, 'Lamb for all Seasons', in *À la carte*, October 1987

Brillat-Savarin, *La Physiologie du Goût*, transl. Anne Drayton, Penguin, 1970

Business Forecasts in the UK Food Market to 1996, Charterhouse 1991

Chez Panisse, 'Chalk Farm Cheviot Lamb', unpublished report, November 1989

Colin Clair, *Kitchen and Table*, Abelard-Schuman, 1964

The Compleat Cook, 1655, Prospect Books reprint, 1984

Nicola Cox, 'A lamb by any other name', in *À la carte*, April 1988

Elizabeth David, *Mediterranean Food*, John Murray, 1950

John Edwards (translator and adaptor), *The Roman Cookery of Apicius*, Rider & Co., 1984

Feeding You the Facts, Vegetarian Society, May 1991

Patience Gray, *Honey from a Weed*, Prospect Books, 1986

Nancy Harmon Jenkins (ed.), *The Journal of Gastronomy*, Vol. 5, no 2, American Institute of Food & Wine, summer/autumn 1989

Madge Hart, *Eating and Drinking*, Sampson Low, Menston & Co Ltd.

Dorothy Hartley, *Food in England*, Macdonald & Co., 1954

Marcella Hazan, *The Classic Italian Cookbook*, Papermac, 1981

Tom Jaine, *Cooking in the Country*, Chatto & Windus, 1986

Ninette Lyon and Peggy Benton, *Meat at Any Price*, Faber & Faber, 1963

Maria de Lourdes Modesto, *Cozinha Tradicional Portugues*, Verbo, 1982

Giles MacDonagh, *A Palate in Revolution*, Robin Clark, 1987

Carlo Natall, *Abbruzzi e Molise in Bocca*, II Vespro, 1980

H.D. Renner, *The Origin of Food Habits*, Faber & Faber, 1944

Teresita Roman de Zurek, *Cartagena de Indias en la Olla*, published by the author, 1974

L. Saulnier, *Le Repertoire de la Cuisine*, transl. E. Brunet, Jaeggi & Sons Ltd, 1980

Reay Tannahill, *Food in History*, Penguin, 1988

C. Anne Wilson, *Food and Drink in Britain*, Penguin, 1984

Veterinary Record, 12 May 1990

Margaret Visser, *Much Depends on Dinner*, Penguin, 1989

Alan Watts, *Does it Matter?* Pantheon, 1968

Index